ללינור ומוריס היקרים
מקווים להנאתכם שנה
טובה וכאן בארץ ישראל
לתמיד!

שלכם
ירון ותמי הראל
ירושלים, חשון תשס״ג

INTRIGUE AND REVOLUTION

THE LITTMAN LIBRARY OF
JEWISH CIVILIZATION

Dedicated to the memory of

LOUIS THOMAS SIDNEY LITTMAN

who founded the Littman Library for the love of God
and as an act of charity in memory of his father

JOSEPH AARON LITTMAN

and to the memory of

ROBERT JOSEPH LITTMAN

who continued what his father Louis had begun

יהא זכרם ברוך

'Get wisdom, get understanding:
Forsake her not and she shall preserve thee'

PROV. 4: 5

The Littman Library of Jewish Civilization is a registered UK charity
Registered charity no. 1000784

INTRIGUE AND REVOLUTION

Chief Rabbis in Aleppo, Baghdad, and Damascus 1744–1914

❖

YARON HAREL

TRANSLATED BY
YEHONATAN CHIPMAN

Oxford · Portland, Oregon
The Littman Library of Jewish Civilization
2015

The Littman Library of Jewish Civilization

Chief Executive Officer: Ludo Craddock
Managing Editor: Connie Webber

PO Box 645, Oxford OX2 0UJ, UK
www.littman.co.uk

Published in the United States and Canada by
The Littman Library of Jewish Civilization
c/o ISBS, 920 NE 58th Avenue, Suite 300
Portland, Oregon 97213-3786

Published in Hebrew as Bein takhakhim lemahapekhah: minui rabanim rashiyim vehadaḥatam bakehilot bagdad, demesek, veḥaleb, 1744–1914

A catalogue record for this book is available from the British Library

Library of Congress Cataloging-in-Publication Data

Harel, Yaron.
[Ben tekhakhim le-mahpekhah. English]
Intrigue and revolution : chief rabbis in Aleppo, Baghdad, and Damascus, 1744–1914 / Yaron Harel ; translated by Yehonatan Chipman.
pages cm
Includes bibliographical references and index.
1. Chief Rabbinate—Syria—Aleppo—History.
2. Chief Rabbinate—Syria—Damascus—History.
3. Chief Rabbinate—Iraq—Baghdad—History.
4. Rabbis—Syria—Aleppo—Office—History.
5. Rabbis—Syria—Damascus—Office—History.
6. Rabbis—Iraq—Baghdad—Office—History I. Title.
BM750.H36 2015 296.6'1095691–dc23 2014036056

ISBN 978–1–904113–87–4

Publishing co-ordinator: Janet Moth
Copy-editing: Gillian Somerscales
Indexing: Bonnie Blackburn
Production, design, and typesetting by Pete Russell, Faringdon, Oxon.
Printed in Great Britain on acid-free paper by
TJ International Ltd., Padstow, Cornwall

In memory of

FLOWER IONE ELIAS
(1913–2008)

an author and lover of books whose ancestors hailed from Aleppo and Baghdad

❖

This book was translated from the Hebrew thanks to a generous contribution from

MR JOE DWEK CBE

of Manchester, through the Aleppo Jewish Heritage Center (Halab) in Israel

Preface and Acknowledgements

THROUGHOUT most of the Jewish world, the modern period has been marked by political power struggles involving rabbis and Torah scholars. In the Middle East, this process of politicization began around the middle of the eighteenth century as European influences began to penetrate the region, and was exacerbated by the Ottoman imperial creation of the position of *ḥakham bashi*. One of the facts that strikes the student of this period is that very few of those rabbis elected to the office of *ḥakham bashi* either completed their term of office or avoided embroilment in acrimonious conflicts. This book explores the turbulence and controversy so characteristic of Syrian and Iraqi Jewry at this time by building up a detailed picture of the communities in which rabbis were active and scrutinizing the political, social, and economic developments that took place within them.

My interest in this subject began almost twenty-five years ago when, while perusing some musty old documents in the archive of Rabbi Jacob Saul Elyashar, I became aware for the first time of the controversy surrounding the removal from office of the *ḥakham bashi* Rabbi Abraham Ezra Dweck Hakohen of Aleppo. Over the course of time, I discovered, one after another, similar episodes involving other rabbis. As I gathered the facts and assembled an increasingly clear picture, I realized that these incidents were not exceptional but on the contrary almost routine. My curiosity as a historian was ignited, along with the desire to uncover the truth and present it without decoration or prettification. Admittedly, revealing the involvement of Torah scholars—including sages of considerable stature—in disputes of this type entails an element of iconoclasm. Indeed, the picture that emerges from these affairs is at times diametrically opposed to the accepted image of rabbinic scholars in the Middle East, the patterns of behaviour expected of them, and the status accorded to them. Nevertheless, it seems to me that to present the full picture is to illuminate the humanity of these rabbis, in the spirit of the old rabbinic aphorism, 'The early ones were like human beings.'[1] This approach enables us to scrutinize the personalities of these scholars in all their complexity and to become acquainted with their strengths and sublime qualities, as well as their all-too-human weaknesses and ambitions.

This approach is diametrically opposed to the widely held and traditional religious position according to which Torah scholars are invariably pious and

[1] BT *Shab.* 112*b*.

unblemished figures, and anything suggesting the contrary should be ignored, on the principle that 'the honour of God lies in the hiding of the thing'.[2] This may be why, as a rule, the collective communal memory did not acknowledge and retain these incidents, for to do so would have blemished the image of the rabbinic scholars; and why, on the contrary, there was an overt or covert conspiracy of repression, silencing, and forgetting that consigned to oblivion the squabbles, claims, and counter-claims in which these rabbis were involved. It is clear that neither the personal nor the collective memory is necessarily historical; the challenge of the historian is, among other things, to uncover those elements that were concealed and, even more importantly, to examine the extant evidence and to ask why these specific records survived and whether they represent a true or a distorted picture of historical reality.

Through scrutiny of the incidents analysed in this book, the reader will become familiar with the new moods, goals, and wishes of the Jewish public in the Ottoman empire, and particularly of those who occupied the office of *ḥakham bashi* in the communities discussed here. Such familiarity is necessary in order to arrive at a broader understanding of the reality of the past, a reality whose echoes may still be heard in the present.

*

This book was initially published in Hebrew in 2007 by the Ben-Zvi Institute in Jerusalem. It enjoyed excellent reviews and was awarded the Shazar Prize of the Israel Historical Society for 2009.

I wish to express my thanks to the many good people who assisted me during the long years of writing.

Among the colleagues and friends who contributed their knowledge and made illuminating comments were Professor Nahem Ilan, Professor Shlomo Deshen, Professor Zvi Zohar, Professor Leah Makovetsky, Professor Noam Stillman, Professor Yaron Tsur, Professor Shimon Schwarzfuchs, Dr Yaron Serry, and Dr Zvi Yehudah.

My friends and colleagues in the Department of Jewish History at Bar-Ilan University contributed greatly to the pleasant and amicable atmosphere in which I worked on this project. My work was enriched by my students' questions and pertinent comments during (at times tumultuous) discussions in the classroom.

Special thanks are due to the dedicated staffs of the libraries and archives which I visited during the course of writing this book: the National Library

[2] Prov. 25: 2.

of Israel, the Central Archive of the Jewish People, the Library of Yad Ben-Zvi, and the Bar-Ilan University Library. I also received invaluable help from the staff of the National Archives in Kew, the archives of the French Foreign Ministry in Paris and Nantes, and the Austrian Royal Archives in Vienna, as well as from those at the archives of the Alliance Israélite Universelle in Paris, first and foremost from my good friend Jean-Claude Kuperminc. Special thanks go to Uri Ben-Mordechai, who made available to me the abundance of documentation in his possession concerning his great-grandfather, Rabbi Hezekiah Shabetai.

It is my pleasant duty to thank the Israel Academy of Sciences and Humanities for the generous grant they gave me to undertake the background research concerning the archives of the *ḥakham bashi* in Istanbul. I am also grateful to Professor Haggai Ben-Shammai, to Professor Menahem Ben-Sasson, and to Professor Aaron Maman, former heads of the Ben-Zvi Institute, who made it possible for me to conduct my research within the framework of the Oriens Judaicus project. Without this basic research, this book could not have been written.

I wish to thank from the depth of my heart all those who have helped me in the production of the English edition of the book. Without the generous support of Mr Joe Dwek, who encouraged me over the course of many long years to publish my research and disseminate it in the English language, this edition would not have come about. There are no words to express my gratitude for his efforts in this matter. My blessings to the translator of this book, Rabbi Yehonatan Chipman, and to the excellent staff of the Littman Library of Jewish Civilization—first and foremost to Connie Webber, to Ludo Craddock, to Janet Moth, to Gillian Somerscales, and to Bonnie Blackburn, who did everything possible to bring about the successful completion of this edition.

Last but not least, to my wife and life companion Tammi and to our beloved children and grandchildren, who sweeten my days.

Givat Zeev Y.H.
August 2014

Contents

PART III
RABBIS OF THE REVOLUTION

Note on Transliteration and Conventions Used in the Text

Hebrew

The transliteration of Hebrew in this book reflects consideration of the type of book it is, its content, purpose, and readership. The system adopted therefore reflects a broad approach to transcription, rather than the narrower approaches found in the *Encyclopaedia Judaica* or other systems developed for text-based or linguistic studies. The aim has been to reflect the pronunciation prescribed for modern Hebrew, rather than the spelling or Hebrew word structure, and to do so using conventions that are generally familiar to the English-speaking reader.

In accordance with this approach, no attempt is made to indicate the distinctions between *alef* and *ayin*, *tet* and *taf*, *kaf* and *kuf*, *sin* and *samekh*, since these are not relevant to pronunciation; likewise, the *dagesh* is not indicated except where it affects pronunciation. Following the principle of using conventions familiar to the majority of readers, however, transcriptions that are well established have been retained even when they are not fully consistent with the transliteration system adopted. On similar grounds, the *tsadi* is rendered by 'tz' in such familiar words as barmitzvah. Likewise, the distinction between *ḥet* and *khaf* has been retained, using *ḥ* for the former and *kh* for the latter; the associated forms are generally familiar to readers, even if the distinction is not actually borne out in pronunciation, and for the same reason the final *heh* is indicated too. As in Hebrew, no capital letters are used, except that an initial capital has been retained in transliterating titles of published works (for example, *Shulḥan arukh*).

Since no distinction is made between *alef* and *ayin*, they are indicated by an apostrophe only in intervocalic positions where a failure to do so could lead an English-speaking reader to pronounce the vowel-cluster as a diphthong—as, for example, in *ha'ir*—or otherwise mispronounce the word.

The *sheva na* is indicated by an *e*—*perikat ol*, *reshut*—except, again, when established convention dictates otherwise.

The *yod* is represented by *i* when it occurs as a vowel (*bereshit*), by *y* when it occurs as a consonant (*yesodot*), and by *yi* when it occurs as both (*yisra'el*).

Names have generally been left in their familiar forms, even when this is inconsistent with the overall system.

Arabic

A simplified system has also been used for Arabic transliteration. *Hamza* and *'ayn* are indicated by ' and ' respectively (apart from initial *hamza*, which is omitted), but otherwise no special signs are used. Long vowels are not indicated, and there is no differentiation in print between soft and hard *t*, breathed and unbreathed *h*, *sin* and *sad*, *dal* and *dad*, or *zayn* and *za'*. The letter *tha'* is indicated by *th*, *dhal* by *dh*, *kha'* by *kh*, and *shin* by *sh*. The definite article is represented throughout as al-, with no attempt to indicate elision, either following a vowel or preceding a sun letter. *Ta' marbuta* is indicated by *a*, except in the construct (*idafa*), when it is represented as *at*. All Arabic words, apart from proper names standing alone, are italicized. When proper names occur within a transliterated phrase, they are italicized and written with the initial letter in lower case.

Arabic sources listed in the references are cited with their full transliterated Arabic title following the English translation of the title. In the notes, they are referred to by this English translation (sometimes shortened), followed by (Arab.).

List of Abbreviations

AAIU	Archives de l'Alliance Israélite Universelle, Paris
ACRI	Archive of the Chief Rabbinate, Istanbul
AECADN	Affaires Etrangères, Centre des Archives Diplomatiques de Nantes
AECCC	Archives du Ministère des Affaires Etrangères, Paris, Correspondance Consulaire et Commerciale
AECPC	Archives du Ministère des Affaires Etrangères, Paris, Correspondance Politique du Consul
AENS	Archives du Ministère des Affaires Etrangères, Paris, Nouvelle Série
BofD	Board of Deputies of British Jews
BZI	Ben-Zvi Institute, Jerusalem
CHBJ	Center for the Heritage of Babylonian Jewry, Jerusalem
CZA	Central Zionist Archive, Jerusalem
FO	Foreign Office Archives, National Archives, London
HHSTA	Österreichisches Staatsarchiv, Haus-, Hof-, und Staatsarchiv, Vienna
JC	*Jewish Chronicle*
JMA	Municipal Archives, Jerusalem
JNUL, DMA	Jewish National and University Library, Department of Manuscripts and Archives, Jerusalem

Introduction

> Rabban Gamaliel considered appointing Rabbi Eleazar Hisma and Rabbi Yohanan ben Gudgeda as heads [of the Sanhedrin]. He sent for them and they did not come; he sent for them again, and they came. He said to them: 'Do you think that I am giving you rulership? Rather, I am giving you slavery.'
>
> BT *Horayot* 10*a*

THIS BOOK is a story of dramas. Its central aim is to analyse the appointment and removal of chief rabbis in the communities of Aleppo, Baghdad, and Damascus, and the circumstances that led to these events, from the mid-eighteenth century up to the First World War. The initial inspiration came from an extraordinary phenomenon I noted—namely, that most of the chief rabbis in those communities, particularly during the second half of the nineteenth century, were at some point removed from their posts.

This period was one of profound change in the Middle East, affecting all aspects of life. People were constantly changing their manner of dress, adopting clothing of a new weave or a new cut; old institutions assumed new forms, and new institutions were created alongside them or in their place; new languages, new customs, and foreign literature pervaded the region; a dizzying range of concepts were either invented or insinuated their way into the local languages; trains and steamships shortened distances between places, while the telegraph heralded a revolution in communication. European domination of the world led to the adoption of new ideas, rendering obsolete or insufficient many of the old ways that had previously provided for all people's needs. The mechanisms of the Ottoman state, including its judiciary and military, underwent a comprehensive reorganization based upon the European model, while financial and commercial markets expanded rapidly in the wake of revolutionary innovations in industrial manufacture and in travel and transport by land and sea.

Although this book is primarily concerned with the history of the rabbinate, and its main characters are rabbis, the history of the rabbis and of the rabbinate cannot be considered in a vacuum. Accordingly, I shall also examine changes in social patterns and in individual consciousness between the end of the eighteenth century and the beginning of the twentieth. In other words, this study is concerned not only with the events that befell a particular group of people, but also with gaining an understanding of the society in which they lived, in all its variety, and of the interactions among its members. The social historian cannot separate the objects of research from their social environment.

This book is concerned, first and foremost, with Jewish urban society. The Jewish society that absorbed the above-mentioned changes—as much as, and perhaps more so than, the majority Muslim society that surrounded it—was no longer a purely traditional society. During the course of transition from the old, traditional world to the new, modern world, changes occurred in all aspects of Jewish life, encompassing education, lifestyle, and leisure patterns. Some groups and sectors of society gained new prominence, while others lost the status they had formerly enjoyed. New types of Jews appeared, such as the *maskil* or enlightened Jew, the westernizer, the military man, and the political activist, among others.

I shall observe the rabbis who are the focus of this study not only in the immediate context of their rabbinic activity, but in other contexts as well: in their personal relationships, in their aspirations, and in their writings, as well as through their public sermons, both written and oral. All these perspectives will deepen and enrich our understanding of the actors in this scene. At the same time, I shall attempt not only to examine the particular cases of specific individuals, but also to formulate certain generalizations concerning the function of the rabbi in the community. The subject is examined from the prosopographic angle as well: that is, did the rabbis discussed in this book have any particular characteristics as a group? Did the specific social institution within whose framework they worked—namely, the rabbinate—acquire new characteristics and nuances during the period in question? This study, then, will not confine itself to presenting incidents in the history of the rabbinate in Baghdad, Damascus, and Aleppo, but will attempt to propose a certain understanding (albeit not the only possible one) of the processes involved, based upon the incidents examined.

The unique characteristics of each of these rabbis—and of the office they occupied—are closely connected with the culture and society within which they lived and worked. In each chapter I will give due attention to this background, setting out the main developments in and around the city or region chiefly concerned during the period under discussion, and their significance for and impact upon the Jewish community and its institutions. It is important to note at this point that the phenomena discussed are not unique to the three communities that constitute the main focus of attention in this book.

In other communities, too—including those of Mosul, Beirut, Tiberias, Safed, İzmir, and Istanbul—chief rabbis were appointed and deposed for reasons to do with political and personal circumstances.[1] The decision to limit the discussion geographically to the three major cities of the Fertile Crescent derives primarily from the unique connections among these communities, which are germane to the main subject of the book. The communities discussed here obviously had connections to other communities as well; nevertheless, they also had unique connections with one another, deriving not only from the movement of commercial caravans and travellers among them, but also from the fact that several rabbis of considerable stature served in prominent positions in more than one of them. Thus, for example, Sadkah Houssin of Aleppo served in the rabbinate in Baghdad; Obadiah Halevi went from Damascus to Baghdad; Aaron Jacob Benjamin came from Baghdad to Damascus, where he served as chief rabbi; Raphael Kassin left Aleppo for Baghdad, served as *ḥakham bashi* there for a period, and subsequently returned to Aleppo, where he attempted to create an alternative to the existing traditional community. Further work will be required to arrive at a full picture of the status of rabbis in the Jewish communities of the Ottoman empire; I hope that the present study may encourage a critical examination of the institution of the rabbinate in other communities, and perhaps even a comparative study of the status of Christian and Muslim clergy in the Ottoman empire during the period under discussion.

The rabbi is usually perceived as a spiritual leader. However, in this study I will be examining rabbinic leadership specifically from the socio-political perspective, and so will not be analysing in depth the rabbis' spiritual writings or attainments.[2] There is a widely held conception that, throughout history, the rabbi was the ultimate Jewish leader and, in the absence of counterbalancing community institutions, had the final word in all matters. In fact, throughout the ages Jewish communities have been headed by two parallel forms of leadership, both enjoying legal authority. One was the civil or secular leadership, which usually derived its authority from the national or imperial government. Various legal institutions and bodies operated under the rubric of this leadership, including *mishpat hamelekh* (the biblical 'rule of the king'), the elders, the institution of the *nasi*, the exilarch, and the communal regulations (*takanot*). The other form of leadership was that of the

[1] Similar phenomena also occurred in other Jewish communities in totally different geographical and political milieus. On the struggles of rabbis over issues of rule and authority in Germany, for example, see Zimmer, *The Fiery Embers of the Scholars* (Heb.), 29–174.

[2] For work that does address this area, see the numerous studies of Zvi Zohar.

rabbinate, composed of sages and rabbinic bodies whose rulings and judgments were derived from Torah law.

Throughout Jewish history, 'Torah law' and 'the law of the rulers' have complemented one another.[3] Nevertheless, the rabbi heading a community has always been considered a spiritual influence, teacher, halakhic decisor, judge, and role model; and, as society was almost entirely based on religious principles and allegiances, the halakhic and ethical authority of the rabbi and his involvement in almost every aspect of life, from family life to matters of public importance, was generally accepted. The rabbi's instructions and halakhic rulings touched upon all areas of law, economics, politics, and relationships with the surrounding society. In effect, the rabbi supervised all the business of the community, and his agreement was the required seal of approval for the activities and decisions of its secular leaders, the *parnasim*. He held his position in most cases by virtue of either election, by all or part of the community, or inheritance. For Jews within the Ottoman empire, the right to appoint their rabbis was part of the autonomy they enjoyed, an aspect of the community's life with which the imperial authorities were not involved.[4] Those authorities' recognition of the chief rabbi, once appointed, as head of the community was not based upon any law, but derived from considerations of convenience, the imperial administration preferring to deal with the Jewish community as a body with a single leadership rather than having to relate to various secondary groups with different leaders.

In any event, a Torah scholar of stature had no need for official recognition in order to wield spiritual authority. The voluntary recognition of his halakhic and ethical authority by members of the community gave him great influence over both the life of society and that of the individual. Such authority as he derived from recognition by the government was still marginal and incidental. Over the period under discussion, the strengthening of the chief rabbi's position led to friction with various elements in the community whose authority was limited by the rabbinate and who became secondary to him. These included, primarily, members of the secular leadership of the community or its political arm—i.e. the *nesi'im*, the *gevirim*, and the *parnasim*.[5] Moreover, the concentration of what others considered excessive power in the hands of the rabbi who headed the community, and the steps taken by the

[3] See in detail Stern, *State, Law, and Halakhah*, i (Heb.); see also Walzer et al. (eds.), *The Jewish Political Tradition*, i, esp. 379–429.

[4] See e.g. Benayahu, *Preacher of Torah* (Heb.), 19–20; Hacker, 'Community Organization' (Heb.), 288 and references therein.

[5] The same observation applies to any traditional Jewish society, including those outside the Middle East. See e.g. Katz, *Tradition and Crisis* (Heb.), 107–11.

chief rabbi that impinged on the status of other Torah scholars, at times led to fissures in the unity of the scholarly class and to its taking a stand against the senior elected figure from among its number.

As the status of the chief rabbi grew, so did the community's expectations of him. It became an accepted principle that he was responsible for what occurred in the community and for its conducting itself on a firm ethical basis, and as a result struggles began to develop within the communities, focused upon the issue of the authority of the chief rabbi. These struggles did not usually lead to revolution or change but, on the contrary, were intended to prevent it. During the second half of the eighteenth century they were the exception rather than the rule, the first harbingers of the power struggles that were to come in the following century as new social forces began to make themselves felt and modern outlooks began to penetrate these communities. At the same time, the Francos—Italian Jewish merchants of Spanish or Portuguese origin who settled in the port cities of the Middle East—helped shape the public's understanding of matters relating to rabbis and the institution of the rabbinate, notwithstanding their public declaration of detachment from the affairs of the communities. The first part of this book deals with two struggles of this type, and is entitled 'Harbingers of Upheaval'. The disputes depicted here date from the second half of the eighteenth century and are presented in chronological order. The first chapter deals with the struggle between the *nasi* of the community of Baghdad—a figure of the old order who joined with the local Torah scholars in order to create a united front—and Rabbi Sadkah Houssin, who was sent from Aleppo to serve as rabbi of the Baghdad community, where he attempted to extend his authority at the expense of the *nasi* and the other Torah scholars. The second chapter deals with a bitter conflict within the Aleppo community that ostensibly revolved around the issue of inheritance of rabbinic office but was actually about the authority of the chief rabbi. This conflict was the first to involve political issues relating to the subjugation of foreign subjects to community regulations and the involvement of representatives of European powers in the internal affairs of the communities. Max Weber distinguishes three types of authoritative leader, which he defines as archetypes of authority: traditional authority, based upon continuity of a sanctified tradition, in which leadership is justified through origin or status; rational-legal authority, deriving from legal or institutional authority; and charismatic authority, in which the leader exerts influence by the force of his personality alone. This last type of authority derives from the belief that the leader has special powers and that disobedience to him is likely to bring about immediate divine punishment.[6] Two

[6] Weber, *Charisma and Institution Building*, 28–9. The literature on this subject is extensive

of Weber's three archetypes, the traditional and the charismatic, thus derive their authority from the core beliefs of the society. This typology is highly significant in the present context, as this book is mainly concerned with the rabbi as a political leader.

The creation in 1835 by the Ottoman authorities of the institution of *ḥakham bashi* transformed the chief rabbi from the senior religious figure within Jewish society into its senior government official. With this change the long arm of the government began to reach into Jewish communal affairs, and as a result Jewish autonomy gradually weakened.[7] In the past the rulers had recognized the chief rabbi only de facto and not de jure; hence the attitude towards the holder of this office was primarily a matter of concern for the community rather than for the government. But from this point on, his relationship with the rulers became the most important aspect of his position.[8] This tendency was strengthened throughout the period of the Ottoman reforms (1839–76), during which security, protection, and equality before the law were promised to members of all religions.[9]

As the office of *ḥakham bashi* was an explicitly secular and political one rather than a religious one, those chosen to occupy it were not usually the greatest Torah sages, but those individuals considered to have the best political talents. In other words, talmudic erudition, which had always been a *sine qua non* for election as chief rabbi of a community, was not a necessary qualification for the office of *ḥakham bashi*, which was explicitly conceived as a role of public administration rather than of spiritual, scholarly, and ethical authority. The political function of the *ḥakham bashi* was thus similar to that formerly exercised by the *resh galuta* (head of the diaspora), the *nasi*, or the *nagid*. Hence, for example, the *ḥakham bashi* in Istanbul was referred to in terms of kingship: 'the king who sits upon his throne' or 'the king of the Jews'.[10] Nevertheless, the *ḥakham bashi* was always a religious figure, because in the Ottoman system each community, Jewish, Muslim, or Christian, was headed by a religious leader. However, while the *ḥakham bashi* was often referred to as the 'chief rabbi', he was not given the title *rosh harabanim* ('the

and still expanding. See e.g. Arieli, 'The Role of the Leadership Personality'; Malkin and Tsahor, *Leader and Leadership* (Heb.).

7 See Levy, 'The Founding of the Institution of the *Ḥakham Bashi*' (Heb.), and Ch. 3 below.

8 On the religious leadership's relationship with the community, see Katz, 'On the History of the Rabbinate' (Heb.); Friedman, 'Basic Problems' (Heb.), 135–7.

9 On the reform decrees and the struggle for their implementation, see Davison, *Reform in the Ottoman Empire*; Lewis, *The Emergence of Modern Turkey*, 122–47, 437–40; Maoz, 'Transformations in the Status of the Jews' (Heb.).

10 On the use of similar titles for the *rishon letsiyon* in Jerusalem, the chief rabbi, see Zohar, *The Luminous Face of the East* (Heb.), 223–5.

head of the rabbis'), or *rosh haruḥani'im* ('the head of the spiritual ones'), both of these titles generally being reserved for the head of the community's religious court. This indicates that the office of *ḥakham bashi* did not in fact fully combine the two functions of secular and rabbinic leadership.[11] Moreover, at least officially, the *ḥakham bashi*'s authority was limited to those matters that pertained to the proper administration of the community according to the directives of the imperial authorities.

A clear and official separation between the two kinds of leadership was made in the Jewish millet decree promulgated in 1864 (and entering into force the following year). This decree gave explicit expression to the growing involvement of the Sublime Porte in the organization of the Jewish community or 'millet'. It laid down specific rules for the election of the *ḥakham bashi* and defined who was eligible to hold the office, his functions, his obligations, and his areas of authority. It further provided for the creation of new official communal institutions: in each community, a general assembly of eighty members was established, from among whom seven rabbinic sages were chosen to serve on the spiritual committee, and nine public figures to serve on the lay steering committee. For the election of the *ḥakham bashi* of Istanbul, who was considered the head of the entire Jewish millet in the eyes of the authorities, another forty representatives of Jewish communities from various districts throughout the empire were added to the city's general assembly.[12]

This decree created a problem in separating the secular prerogatives of the *ḥakham bashi* from the religious prerogatives of the community's spiritual head. Over the course of the many generations prior to the promulgation of this decree, during which rabbis served as the leaders of the communities, the boundaries between the secular and sacred realms, the political and the religious, were often blurred. After 1835, learned rabbis who served in the office of *ḥakham bashi*, with formal endorsement by the Ottoman authorities, were considered relatively high-level government officials. Their responsibilities were more onerous than those of the community leaders of former times, and there was tension between their functions as representatives of the community to the authorities and as representatives of the authorities to the community. As we shall see below, there was also a certain tension between them and those who served as spiritual heads of the community.

Within Weber's typology, the *ḥakham bashi* would be most appropriately described as conforming to the rational-legal model. True, the *ḥakham bashi*

[11] For a summary of the approach which sees the *ḥakham bashi* as uniting these two functions, see Tobi, 'Organization of Jewish Communities' (Heb.), 199–200.

[12] See Davison, *Reform in the Ottoman Empire*, 129–31; also Ch. 6 below.

was a traditional figure, a Torah scholar, but his authority did not primarily derive from tradition. Nevertheless, by virtue of this status as a traditional figure, it appears that those who held this position used the new decree to bolster their authority only when they felt the power of their own personalities insufficient to ensure the support of the community. The *ḥakham bashi* thus represented a new type of Jewish religious leader in the Ottoman empire —one whose formal authority, at least, derived primarily from the secular ruler, that is, from outside Jewish society. As we shall see, many of the rabbis discussed in this study were not particularly beloved by their communities —and at times matters were far worse than that.

In the light of all these observations, the question arises whether, by the very fact of his endorsement by the authorities, the *ḥakham bashi* became a *rav mita'am*—a puppet of the government. In fact this loaded term, borrowed from the east European rabbinate, is not really suitable to the cases discussed in this book.[13] While the *ḥakham bashi*'s appointment did have to be officially approved by the government authorities, the rabbi chosen thereby did not need to demonstrate any level of general education or mastery of the vernacular. Moreover, even if the authorities expected the *ḥakham bashi* to implement the principles promulgated by the rulers within the Jewish community, they never, with the exception of one case to be discussed in this book, chose a specific individual for this office. Rather, the proposal of a candidate was left in the hands of the Jewish community; the rulers contented themselves with ratifying the appointment, after ascertaining that the rabbi chosen was in reality capable of leading the Jewish community while fully implementing Ottoman law.

It follows that the more germane question is whether the office of *ḥakham bashi* in fact belongs to the history of the rabbinate or more properly to that of secular Jewish communal leadership. The basic assumption of this study is that in the events described here we are dealing primarily with the history of the rabbinate as an institution of rulership rather than as one of halakhic rulings and instructions. What we are looking at here in effect is the breakthrough of the rabbinic elite into a realm that had hitherto belonged to the hereditary or moneyed elites within the community. For the first time, an explicitly religious figure was incorporated within the system of the Ottoman administration on a relatively high rung of the bureaucratic ladder. It is nevertheless worth remembering that, during the first years following the creation of the office of *ḥakham bashi*, no new type of rabbi had been created;

[13] See Shohet, *The Institution of the 'Official' Rabbinate* (Heb.).

rather, a rabbi of the traditional type was generally called upon to fulfil this new function. New types of rabbis developed only at a later stage.

At times, the creation of the new office and the changed situation it brought into being caused confusion and friction between the *ḥakham bashi* and elements of Jewish society—sometimes between him and the community as a whole. As the leader serving in this secular office was nevertheless a religious figure, there was widespread confusion regarding his place in the hierarchy of social relationships. At times this ambiguity was felt by the *ḥakham bashi* himself, who on more than one occasion sought to extend his authority into the spiritual and ethical realms. Thus the office of *ḥakham bashi* was surrounded by struggles, passions, friction, and revolts, which in turn called into question the status of those who held this office. It was easier for the public to oppose these rabbis who, although deemed to belong to the class of sages, were lacking in any spiritual authority. In other words, it was easier to undermine the status of a *ḥakham bashi* whose authority derived exclusively from his office and his appointment rather than from his personal qualities as a spiritual figure. These rabbis were government officials, and attitudes towards them reflected this fact.

The new office and its responsibilities led to a change in the function of the rabbi. Expectations of the office holder focused upon his capacity to fix problems of practical social policy rather than to provide ethical guidance. On this point the typology applied by Eliezer Don-Yehiya is useful. In attempting to distinguish between the type of the religious leader and that of the political leader, he suggested three attributes as vehicles for examining different types of religious leadership: talents, resources, and functions.[14] We have already noted that such qualities as talmudic erudition, expertise in Torah, and ethical or even mystical power were not demanded of a candidate for the office of *ḥakham bashi*. Instead, other specific qualities and talents, such as organizational and executive skill, the ability to make decisions, and the ability to conduct negotiations with the rulers, were the decisive factors in his selection by the community. The *ḥakham bashi* derived his authority primarily from the rulers: it was they who gave him backing and, when necessary, made available to him policing powers and various means of law enforcement, such as imprisonment and exile.

The *ḥakham bashi* did not usually bear responsibility for such traditional rabbinic functions as issuing rulings on halakhic matters, judging legal cases, delivering sermons, and providing ethical guidance. Rather, he was expected

[14] On the distinction between two kinds of leadership in Jewish society throughout history, see Don-Yehiya, 'Religious Leadership and Political Leadership' (Heb.).

to focus upon the everyday life of the community, relations among its members, and relations between the community and the government or the surrounding society; not on those between man and God. One of the main expectations imposed upon those who held this office was that they would act equitably in the matter of tax collection. If the *ḥakham bashi* did not fulfil this expectation, he was accused of failure, and at times even of corruption—accusations that in turn fuelled demands for his deposition. By contrast, we do not find any such challenge to the authority of the rabbi who headed the religious court. This figure, who usually served alongside the *ḥakham bashi*, was perceived as the highest halakhic, spiritual, and ethical authority of the community. Hence attitudes towards him continued to be determined by the respect traditionally accorded by the Jewish public to its spiritual shepherds.[15]

The Jewish millet decree was intended to create a balance of power in the community among the three points of the triangle formed by the *ḥakham bashi*, the lay leaders (the *gevirim* and *parnasim*), and the Torah scholars. However, the removal of the *ḥakham bashi* from the area of spiritual leadership and the restriction of his authority to the political realm led to tension both between the *ḥakham bashi* and the Torah scholars, and between himself and the lay leadership. Likewise, as noted above, the 'separation of powers'—that is, of those concerning matters of society, leadership, and rulership from those concerning the spiritual aspects of the community—combined with the placing of responsibility for secular matters in the hands of a religious figure rather than in those of an individual from outside the circle of rabbinic sages, created confusion among the public at large, and on occasion even in the office holder himself, with regard to the function and authority of the *ḥakham bashi*. It is worth remembering that in the past, when the *parnasim* fulfilled many of the functions that were now imposed upon the *ḥakham bashi*, their job had been easier, as they acted within the framework of the general political and economic system and knew its rules, its laws, and the way in which it was run. This was not the case for the *ḥakham bashi*, who came from the world of Torah and prior to his appointment had not been connected to any extra-communal framework. As a result, the *ḥakham bashi* was often dependent upon the connections of the *gevirim* with the government bureaucracy—a dependence the *gevirim* were keen to strengthen—and in consequence vulnerable to their criticism.

Another source of conflict arising from the creation of this new office by the Ottoman authorities was the potential for head-on confrontation

[15] As described by Rabbi Aaron Azriel, the whole matter of dismissal from office was customary only 'with regard to treasurers, but not for sages who are teachers of halakhah and fear of God; Heaven forbid such a thing should happen among Jews' (Azriel, *Kapei aharon*, ii. 38*b*).

between the 'traditional charismatic leader' and the 'legal leader' of the community. On more than one occasion, the *ḥakham bashi* attempted to encroach upon the authority of the head of the rabbinic court and to replace him, or at the very least to sit within the tribunal of the *beit din*. Controversies also ensued over the question of who would preach in the synagogue on those special sabbaths of the year on which the delivery of a major sermon was considered the prerogative of the chief rabbi.[16] At times, this situation led to a split within the circle of the rabbinic sages from which the *ḥakham bashi* emerged and of which he was a significant member. Attempts by the *ḥakham bashi* to assume control over religious matters often led to controversy and to calls for his removal. Few rabbis in the Ottoman empire served both as *ḥakham bashi* and as head of the rabbinic court, and the attempt to fill both these positions simultaneously generally led to a failure in one or other of them.[17] In such cases, for example in Jerusalem and İzmir, public criticism of the political behaviour of the *ḥakham bashi* often outweighed the feelings of respect felt towards him by virtue of his spiritual and ethical authority as a rabbi and Torah scholar. The result was frequently a campaign against him that on more than one occasion led to his dismissal.

Part II of the book is entitled 'Rabbis of the Reform'; its five chapters deal with the appointment and dismissal of rabbis during the period of the Ottoman reforms, up until the final decade of the nineteenth century. The term 'reform' has a double meaning here, referring on the one hand to the Ottoman reforms and on the other to attempts within the Jewish community to bring about changes in the communal institutions and in the way in which they were run—occasionally to the extent of creating an alternative community, as in the case of Rabbi Raphael Kassin, who attempted to establish a reformist community in Aleppo. Chapter 3 describes and analyses the upheaval created by Kassin both in his community of origin, Aleppo, and in Baghdad. Chapter 4 examines the chaos that ensued in the Baghdad community for more than a decade in the wake of the struggle between the supporters of Rabbi Samoha and those of Rabbi Dangoor. Chapter 5 returns to the community of Aleppo and describes the transformations that took place

16 There were four such sabbaths during the course of the year: Shabat Hagadol before Passover, Shabat Kalah before Shavuot, Shabat Teshuvah before Yom Kippur, and Shabat Zakhor prior to Purim. On these sermons as among the functions unique to the sage of the community, which no other Torah scholar was allowed to perform, see Benayahu, *Preacher of Torah* (Heb.), 41–7.

17 See what Rabbi Hayim Palagi wrote of his own experience in this respect: Palagi, *Tsava'ah meḥayim*, 30–1; and cf. the attempts in various communities in Poland to unite the political and spiritual aspects of the rabbinate in the hands of one rabbi, as described in Bacon, 'The New Jewish Politics', 449–50.

there during the final decade of the nineteenth century and the controversy over the removal of Rabbi Abraham Dweck Hakohen from his office as *ḥakham bashi*. Chapter 6 concerns Rabbi Yitshak Abulafia's struggle against the extended family of Rabbi Shalom Moses Hai Gagin of Jerusalem and the *gevir* Shemaiah Angel of Damascus. Chapter 7 continues the story of Yitshak Abulafia, describing the events that led to his removal not long after he finally overcame the obstacles to his appointment to the office of *ḥakham bashi*.

The third part of the book, entitled 'Rabbis of the Revolution', deals with the appointment and removal of rabbis after the revolution of the Young Turks in 1908. Chapter 8 portrays the unrest within the Damascus community during the period after the revolution, leading to the removal of Rabbi Solomon Eli'ezer Alfandari following years of struggle and hostility between himself and the majority of the community. Chapter 9 concerns the appointment of Jacob Danon as chief rabbi of Damascus and his response to the new situation that confronted him in the community in the wake of the revolution. Chapter 10 concerns the attempts of the Francos in Aleppo to reassert their separateness from the community in order to exert pressure for the removal of Rabbi Hezekiah Shabetai from his position as *ḥakham bashi*. In this connection it is worth drawing attention to the fact that the European (or perhaps more accurately the pseudo-European) sector of Jewish society, which exercised such a great influence upon events in the Aleppo community, did not play a role in Damascus or Baghdad during the period in question. Chapter 11 deals with the appointment of Rabbi David Pappo as *ḥakham bashi* in Baghdad, and his removal by the Ottoman rulers after coming under suspicion of involvement in seditious political activity.

It should be noted that the division of the book into three parts, dealing with three chronological periods, is based upon my own retrospective perception as a historian. One may reasonably assume that the people involved in the events described had only fragmentary awareness of the revolutionary significance of the transformations taking place at the time or of the transitions from one period to another. It is also worth emphasizing that the division I have proposed here is only one of the possible ways of structuring the topic.[18]

I have attempted in this book to address a number of questions concerning the office of the *ḥakham bashi* and those who occupied it. Why did these controversies and conflicts erupt specifically during the nineteenth century, and more particularly during its second half? For centuries rabbis had been

[18] Yaron Tsur, for example, uses the term 'rabbis of the Tanzimat' to refer to those rabbis who acted in conjunction with wealthy laymen close to reformist circles in the Ottoman administration: Tsur, *Introduction* (Heb.), 3.

appointed solely by their communities, and as a result had depended heavily upon wealthy individuals. Did the rabbis suddenly become more independent as a result of the new authority they gained by the government endorsement bestowed upon them under the Ottoman reforms and the Jewish millet decree? Was this the source of the increased friction we see among the communal leadership? And who emerged from these conflicts the stronger—the rabbis or the *gevirim*? Did the circle of Torah scholars unite in unanimous support of the chief rabbi? Was the unity of this social group self-evident? What motivated the Torah scholars to oppose or support the chief rabbi: attachment to halakhah? Financial considerations? Or perhaps power struggles and personal ambitions? And to what extent did these struggles influence their halakhic rulings?

The existing research literature on these questions, within the context of the communities of the Ottoman empire, was enriched some years ago by Avner Levi's study examining the factors underlying changes in the leadership of the Sephardi communities. However, this study dealt only with the communities of Istanbul, Salonica, and İzmir. Around the same time, Avigdor Levy wrote an article about the institution of the *ḥakham bashi* in the Ottoman empire covering its establishment and development between 1835 and 1865. Further valuable additions to the recent literature include studies by Zvi Zohar and Zvi Yehudah, among others, which have augmented the earlier studies by Abraham Ben-Ya'akov. Esther Benbassa's studies of the *ḥakham bashi* Hayim Nahum serve as a basis for understanding the connections between the central rabbinate in the Ottoman capital Istanbul and the provincial communities after the revolution of the Young Turks. Yaron Tsur is shortly to publish an important study about the wealthy Jewish laymen in the communities of the Ottoman empire, which will cover among other things their relations with the chief rabbis.[19]

Notwithstanding this abundance of studies, including those mentioned above and others written in recent years, we do not yet have a full historical understanding of Jewish life in Islamic lands. This book sets out to fill one gap in that understanding by undertaking a multidimensional examination of the leadership of three communities in particular, presenting a series of parallel narratives that display both some common elements and some distinctive features.

Six primary sources shed light upon the historical events described and analysed in this book, offering an impressive wealth of information to the

[19] For details of books and articles by the authors mentioned in this paragraph, see the bibliography.

researcher. The most important innovation in the research on which it is based lies in the extensive use of documents from the archives of the chief rabbinate of Istanbul. No study dealing with any one or more of the communities of the Ottoman empire can be complete without recourse to this archive.[20] Among its vast store of documents are letters from many different communities throughout the Middle East that shed light upon numerous incidents involving the appointment of rabbis and their removal from office, as well as upon the various personalities and other factors involved in these events. They include appeals from rabbis serving as *ḥakham bashi* in the various communities, and from their supporters, to the *ḥakham bashi* in Istanbul—in the earlier years covered here Rabbi Moses Halevi and later Rabbi Hayim Nahum—during the times when they were in danger of being removed from office. There are also letters to the same individuals from those seeking the rabbis' removal and from emissaries from Erets Yisra'el (Palestine) who were involved in the affairs of these communities at these times.

The second source, complementary to and no less important than the first, is the archive of the Alliance Israélite Universelle (AIU) in Paris. It is difficult to exaggerate the importance of this archive for the history of Middle Eastern Jewish communities: representatives of the Alliance were active in almost all the major communities in the region and wrote detailed reports about them, covering a wide range of topics including spiritual and cultural life, forms of leadership and self-government, relations with the government authorities, and the surrounding social environment. Moreover, while the documents in the archive of the Istanbul chief rabbinate reflect the communities' self-image and their own sense of their functioning, the AIU reports were written by outsiders, and so offer a very different perspective. On more than one occasion, their allegiance to the modernizing ideas of the Alliance led them to depict what they observed in sombre colours.[21]

The third source consists of the archives of the foreign ministries of the European powers, particularly those of Britain, France, and Austria. The extensive involvement of European consuls in defending the rights of minorities in the Ottoman empire, as well as those of citizens and wards of their own states, meant that substantial parts of their reports dealt with the situation of the Jewish communities where they were posted. These reports,

[20] On this archive and a description of the documents it contains, see Harel, 'The Importance of the Archive'.

[21] See Rodrigue, *Images of Sephardi and Eastern Jewries*; and cf. Dumont, 'Jewish Communities in Turkey', 210–16.

written from an external, non-Jewish perspective, present an interesting and original glimpse view of the Jewish communities and of those that head them.

The fourth major source used was the archive of the *rishon letsiyon*, the chief rabbi of Erets Yisra'el—in this period, Abraham Hayim Gagin and then Jacob Saul Elyashar. The rabbinic courts of the Jerusalem sages constituted, in the eyes of the Middle Eastern communities, 'the supreme court': that is, the highest possible spiritual and ethical authority. This being the case, not only the reports of emissaries from the Land of Israel but also many complaints and requests from the communities themselves were directed to the leading rabbis in Jerusalem—sometimes asking that the sages in Jerusalem exert their influence on the *ḥakham bashi* in Istanbul to persuade him to meet the correspondents' wishes. The documentation in these archives is priceless.

The fifth source consists of the Torah literature of various genres written by the sages of the communities with which this book is concerned. The responsa, and the ethical, halakhic, and homiletic literature written during the period under discussion, yield a great deal of information concerning both routine and unusual events in these communities. Some of this material was written by individuals directly involved in particular controversies, and in these instances the authors sometimes altered the names of individuals involved and even the purported location of events in order to present their discussion in ostensibly theoretical terms, arguing on a purely halakhic basis. However, by cross-checking these sources against information in others it has been possible to uncover the actuality disguised beneath this tendentious anonymity. In other cases, the principals in such events did not shy away from writing outspoken polemics in direct response to their rivals' accusations, revealing their own opinions, thoughts, and feelings without inhibition.

The sixth source used was the Hebrew press, which attached great importance to offering its readers descriptions and reports of the lives of the various communities. It should be emphasized that we are not speaking here specifically of those newspapers that flourished in the particular communities discussed in this study, but rather with the European Jewish press, and at a later period also that of the Jewish community in Erets Yisra'el. These periodicals were profoundly interested in what was happening in the communities of the Near East, and the various social conflicts they experienced are accordingly reflected in their pages—whether through reports from local people or through the comments of Jewish travellers who readily shared with their co-religionists in Christian Europe their observations and impressions of what they saw in those communities that lived under the protection of Islam.

Some of these sources reveal events that would otherwise be totally unknown; others offer a new perspective on familiar incidents or conflicts relating to the office of *ḥakham bashi*. In both ways they enable us to examine these events in depth and to come to a detailed understanding of both what happened and why, in the murky realm lying between intrigue and revolution, and between the rabbinate and politics.

PART I

HARBINGERS OF UPHEAVAL

CHAPTER ONE

Sadkah Houssin's Struggle for Control over the Baghdad Community

They wished to appoint Rabbi Akiva as *parnas*. He told them: 'I will go home.' They followed after him. They heard him saying: 'In order to be shamed, in order to be insulted.'

JT *Pe'ah* 8: 6

Connections Between Baghdad and Aleppo

The traveller Wolf (William) Schur, who visited the Jewish communities of the Middle East during the mid-1870s, noted that Aleppo and Baghdad were the only two of those communities where yeshivas were still presided over by serious talmudic scholars:

Only in Aram Zova [Aleppo] and in Baghdad, which is Babylon, are there still people who know how to swim in the sea of Talmud, to plunge to its depths and to extract its pearls. But in other places—in Syria, Kurdistan, and Arabia—there is no one who knows how to cast his net over that great sea. The paths of the earlier authorities [*posekim*] are also not paved before them, they follow only the path of the *Shulḥan arukh*.[1]

Is it a mere coincidence that advanced Torah study was evident in these two particular communities at the time Schur was writing? One hundred and thirty years earlier, Torah learning in Baghdad had been in a state of severe decline. Local tradition attributes this state of affairs to a cholera epidemic that ravaged the city during 1742–3, killing most of its scholars.[2] In fact, we know very little of the Baghdad community's history and its spiritual and material leadership prior to the outbreak of the epidemic, as Rabbi Ezra Reuben Dangoor, chief rabbi of Baghdad from 1923 to 1928, noted in his

[1] Schur, *Pictures from Life* (Heb.), 111. It is nevertheless worth mentioning that Schur did not visit Damascus on his travels and that there is certainly a great deal of exaggeration in his account. At the time Schur was writing, for example, Rabbi Yitshak Abulafia, who was considered one of the great *posekim* of the Near East during the second half of the 19th century, was living in Damascus.

[2] See Ben-Ya'akov, *Babylonian Jewry from the End of the Geonic Period* (Heb.), 99.

introduction to Rabbi Sadkah Houssin's *Tsedakah umishpat*:

There is no remnant left of the early days of the cities of Babylonia, mother of the Talmud, and we have hardly any record of the history of its rabbis and sages prior to the generation of the great rabbi, this author [Rabbi Sadkah Houssin]—neither traditions received from them, nor their writings, and even their burial places are unknown. Nor is there any remnant of things written in their own hand from which we might at least derive some notion of their lives and of their names. The reason for this is that, in addition to the harshness of the Exile, from time to time pestilence and plague raged in these cities, causing the inhabitants to leave homes filled with all good things, and flee for their lives from the destroyer. Every thirty years, almost, the plague came, bringing annihilation—may it not happen to us![3]

In those times, whenever an epidemic broke out many people left the city and went to live in the outlying areas. Some people went so far, in the wake of the destruction and death wrought by the disease, as to leave the region completely and migrate to other places, including Aleppo in Syria.[4] During the eighteenth century, the Aleppo community exerted significant influence on the communities of Baghdad and Basra, with colonies of Aleppo Jews in both cities who maintained familial and commercial connections with their city of origin. Among the immigrants from Aleppo to Baghdad and Basra were members of the social and economic elites who began to play a role in the material and spiritual leadership of the communities that absorbed them.[5]

Given this background, it should come as no surprise that the head of the Baghdad community, Moses ben Mordecai Shandukh, wrote to Rabbi Samuel Laniado, chief rabbi of Aleppo, asking him to send a rabbi of some stature to Baghdad to fill the vacuum the epidemic had left in the spiritual leadership of the community. It seems that the large number of deaths in the community had given rise to many problems relating to family law, such as procedures for divorce, and for levirate marriage and release therefrom (*yibum* and *halitsah*)—areas that demanded particular halakhic expertise.[6] The rabbi sent to Baghdad was one of the most promising figures of the younger generation of Aleppo sages, Rabbi Sadkah ben Sa'adiah Houssin. Baghdad tradition relates various legends and miraculous deeds surrounding Houssin's birth and childhood. One such claim is that the young scholar was

[3] 'Introduction by Rabbi Ezra Reuben Dangoor' (Heb.), in Houssin, *Tsedakah umishpat*. The little that is known to us is well summarized in Yehudah, 'Transformations' (Heb.), 9–17. See also Ben-Ya'akov, *Babylonian Jewry from the End of the Geonic Period* (Heb.), 93–9; id., *Rabbi Sasson* (Heb.), 15; and cf. Benayahu, *Books* (Heb.), 9–13.

[4] Ben-Ya'akov, *Babylonian Jewry from the End of the Geonic Period* (Heb.), 99.

[5] See Yehudah, 'Transformations' (Heb.), 18–19, and id., 'Connections' (Heb.).

[6] See Houssin, *Tsedakah umishpat*, 94*a*–*b*.

already preaching publicly in the Aleppo community at the age of 15.[7] According to another tradition, Rabbi Houssin did not arrive alone in Baghdad, but was accompanied by a group of some fifty families, including members of the Laniado, Twena, Levi, and Kamar families.[8] Whether or not this account is correct, it appears that when Rabbi Houssin arrived in Baghdad around 1744 he did find a substantial group of Aleppo Jews awaiting his arrival with even keener anticipation than the local people. They hoped that a rabbi from their own city would restore Baghdad to its former glory, establishing the type of leadership and discipline that had been customary in the Aleppo community. It seems plausible that these people organized themselves in a manner different from that characteristic of the local Baghdad community, in an attempt to maintain their unique character.

The Aleppo Model Comes to Baghdad

Rabbi Houssin laid the foundation for the renewal of Torah study in Baghdad. During the modern period, the Jewish scholarship of Baghdad originated in Aleppo: in practice, from the middle of the eighteenth century until the founding of the rabbinic seminary Midrash Abu Minashi in 1840, under the leadership of Rabbi Abdallah Somekh, Baghdad relied upon the spiritual resources of Aleppo. There is general agreement among both Baghdad Torah scholars and researchers into Iraqi Jewry that the flourishing of Torah study in this community during modern times began following Houssin's appointment as rabbi of the city. Various authors vie with one another in praising the rabbi's contribution to the community. For example, Abraham Ben-Ya'akov writes: 'In Baghdad [Rabbi Houssin] succeeded in bringing about a revolution in the spiritual situation. The study of Torah increased, and with it a new period began.'[9] Zvi Yehudah goes further, emphasizing the influence of the revitalized community on other regions: 'The appointment of a rabbi of stature to stand at the head of the spiritual leadership strengthened the spiritual institutions of the community, leading to the creation, in nineteenth-century Baghdad, of a Torah centre that would shed its light both upon neighbouring communities and upon the colonies of Iraqi Jews in the Far East.'[10] In his introduction to Rabbi Houssin's work mentioned above, Rabbi Ezra Reuben Dangoor wrote: 'And he restored the crown as in days of old; he taught Torah to the multitude, filling its borders with disciples and making

[7] BZI, MS 3750. [8] Ben-Ya'akov, *Babylonian Jewry in Recent Times* (Heb.), 88.

[9] Ibid.; Ben-Ya'akov, *Babylonian Jewry from the End of the Geonic Period* (Heb.), 118.

[10] Yehuda, 'Transformations' (Heb.), 21.

numerous edicts and regulations; and from that point on the [study of] Torah did not cease.'[11] A descendant and namesake of Rabbi Houssin argued also that, 'had he not come, the Torah would have been forgotten from Babylonia [Iraq], Heaven forbid, for before his coming . . . the saving remnant had been left without a rabbi or teacher to instruct them in the way of God, and he came and restored the crown as of old, and raised up numerous disciples'.[12]

Jacob Obermeier, a native of Vienna who was living in Baghdad in the mid-1870s and working as a French teacher in the home of the exiled Persian prince Abbas Mirza, emphasizes that, with Rabbi Houssin's arrival in Baghdad from Aleppo, a new era began in the history of this Jewish community:

For he did many great things in his community, and from him there began a new age for the Jews of Baghdad, for they too began to engage in the Torah, their heritage, and to understand the Talmud, which until then had been alien to them, and to purify their actions following the inspiration of the rabbis and of many of the emissaries from Erets Yisra'el that came here year after year.[13]

Rabbi Houssin introduced new regulations and altered long-standing habits that had been accepted in the Jewish community of Baghdad. For example, people had been accustomed to stroll about the streets and marketplaces of the city during the afternoons of festival days. The new rabbi was shocked to observe that this included the two days of Rosh Hashanah. Feeling that the public's frivolity was causing them to forget the sense of awe proper to the Day of Judgement, he introduced a rule that on both festival days, after kiddush and the midday meal, the people of the community were to gather in groups to read the book of Psalms and *Idra zuta* or *Idra rabah* (sections of the Zohar) until the time for the afternoon prayer. This custom was accepted in Baghdad, and even spread to the communities of Persia and India. Another edict attributed to Rabbi Houssin instructed pregnant and nursing women not to fast on public fast days, with the exception of Yom Kippur, owing to the oppressive heat in Baghdad that was likely to endanger their health.[14]

[11] 'Introduction by Rabbi Reuben Dangoor' (Heb.), in Houssin, *Tsedakah umishpat*.

[12] Ibid.; 'Introduction by Rabbi Sadkah Hai Moses Houssin' (Heb.), in Houssin, *Tsedakah umishpat*.

[13] *Hamagid*, 48 (15 Dec. 1875), 424. Obermeier mistakenly writes that fifty-two years earlier (i.e. in 1824) the Baghdad community first decided to bring Torah teachers from Damascus and Aleppo, the first of whom was Rabbi Sadkah Houssin.

[14] 'Introduction by Rabbi Sadkah Hai Moses Houssin' (Heb.), in Houssin, *Tsedakah umishpat*. For discussion of the penetration of customs from Aleppo and Yemen into Baghdad over the course of generations, see D. Sassoon, *Come Yemen* (Heb.), and D. S. Sassoon, *Journey to Babylonia* (Heb.), 193–4.

Up to the mid-nineteenth century, the Baghdad community was headed by a *nasi* ('president'), a 'secular' leader who was in no sense a Torah figure. The *nasi*'s appointment was closely connected to relations with the Ottoman governor. It was customary throughout the Ottoman empire for senior officials to be appointed and promoted on the basis of their ability to find some influential person—a close relative or other benefactor—to sponsor them. This phenomenon is referred to in the research literature by the Arabic term *intisab*, meaning 'patronage', and it created a network of functionaries who were personally loyal to a given individual and who used one another in order to attain various benefits. These networks included the very highest levels of the ruling group in Istanbul.[15] The phenomenon of *intisab* also characterized the patterns of leadership in Baghdad: the governor chose one of the distinguished members of the Jewish community, generally from among the hereditary and moneyed elites, to serve as his chief banker, known in Arabic as the *sarraf bashi*. It is hardly surprising that this banker—a member of the governor's inner circle, with connections even to the imperial administration through the extensive networks of senior officials and Jewish bankers who were close to the court of the sultan in Istanbul—was recognized as the head of the Jewish community and as its representative before the authorities. In according this recognition, the community was essentially assuming that as *nasi* the *sarraf bashi* would exploit his multifarious connections in order to act on their behalf.

This tradition of appointing a *nasi* goes back as far as the time of the *ge'onim* and the exilarch. Until the end of the seventeenth century, the community took care that the person appointed as *nasi* was one who could trace his lineage back to the royal Davidic house, but from the eighteenth century on this insistence upon the *nasi*'s pedigree ceased, and those appointed to the office were, as a rule, members of the economic elite.[16] On more than one occasion struggles broke out regarding this position of power, and those who competed for the office were not above mutual denunciation, bribing the authorities, or fomenting agitation within the community. These struggles tended to lower the standing of the *nasi* not only in the eyes of the community, but also in those of the governors, who appointed and deposed *nesi'im* on the basis of the bribes slipped into their pockets.[17]

There was no official position of chief rabbi for all the communities of the region. Each of the larger communities—and many of the smaller ones—was

15 On *intisab*, see Kushner, *I Was a Governor* (Heb.), 199–200; Tsur, *Introduction* (Heb.), 1.

16 See Ben-Ya'akov, *Babylonian Jewry in Recent Times* (Heb.), 109; id., *Rabbi Sasson* (Heb.), 25–9.

17 Ben-Ya'akov, *Babylonian Jewry from the End of the Geonic Period* (Heb.), 110.

accustomed to choosing or appointing its own chief rabbi or head of the religious court. Officially, the rabbi's authority applied only to members of his own community; hence, it is not known what the status of the chief rabbi was in Baghdad prior to the arrival of Rabbi Houssin, and whether his term of office and functions were understood in the same manner as in other Jewish communities. In Baghdad the chief rabbi headed the communal rabbinic court; however, his activity was generally overshadowed by the figure of the *nasi*.[18]

The fact that Rabbi Houssin came from Aleppo, a community with a totally different tradition of leadership, inevitably led to conflicts with the *nasi* of the Baghdad community. R. Houssin introduced various Aleppo customs to Baghdad and strengthened the ties with his own community of origin, leading the *nasi* to feel that his own status was under threat. One of the explicitly Aleppan customs introduced by Rabbi Houssin was his practice of sitting in the rabbinic court as a single judge, rather than at the head of a tribunal of three, as was customary. Up to the end of the eighteenth century it was entirely acceptable, indeed usual, in Aleppo for the chief rabbi to sit as a single judge; but in Baghdad it was seen as a revolutionary innovation.[19] Rabbi Houssin's somewhat high-handed manner in introducing his innovation extended to suggesting that what was good for Aleppo was good for his new community: 'And in all those places where we have seen and heard that they have a fixed judge, he judges by himself. And in the prominent Jewish city of Aram Zova [Aleppo], the rabbi judged alone and today his son also judges by himself.'[20]

During Rabbi Houssin's first ten years in office there was no public objection to this practice, either by the other Torah scholars or by the community leaders. The other scholars appear to have recognized his superiority as a Torah genius, indeed a prodigy, and the authority conferred by his having been sent by Rabbi Samuel Laniado—all the more so given the lack of scholars within Baghdad of sufficient stature to question his claim to supreme rabbinic leadership. As for the lay leaders of the community, the *nesi'im*, they too do not seem to have questioned Rabbi Houssin's practice of sitting in solitary judgement for that first decade, probably owing to the precariousness of the institution of the *nasi* during those years. At this time in Aleppo it was accepted that the community should be headed by the sole figure of the chief

18 Benayahu, *Books*, 6.

19 On the beginning of the questioning of this practice in Aleppo, see Ch. 2 below.

20 Houssin, *Tsedakah umishpat* (Heb.), 94*a*. The rabbis referred to are Rabbi Samuel Laniado and his son Raphael Solomon Laniado.

rabbi.[21] By contrast, in Baghdad the community was headed by the *nasi* rather than by one or more rabbis. Indeed, the *nasi* exercised almost absolute dominance in the community, by virtue of which he was able to appoint rabbinic judges and to remove them from office. This overriding authority stemmed primarily from his relationship with the local governor—that is, from the secular government, not necessarily from his own community.[22] Having said that, a close examination of the list of *nesi'im* who headed the Baghdad community during the first ten years of Rabbi Houssin's leadership discloses some interesting facts. For his first year in office, the *nasi* of the community was Moses ben Mordecai Shandukh. That same year, in the wake of malicious rumours against him, the local governor sentenced the *nasi* to death, a sentence that was commuted in exchange for payment of a large bribe; however, he did not live out the year and died shortly thereafter.[23] Following this his brother Ezekiel was appointed as *nasi* and *sarraf bashi*; but he too occupied these offices for only a few months.[24] His successor, Joseph Gahtan, likewise served only a brief period in office, as did *his* successor, David ben Mordecai Cohen.[25] This situation—in which there was both a lack of Torah scholars of high stature and an unstable secular leadership—was evidently exploited by Rabbi Houssin to extend his own authority into areas that had previously been within the remit of the *nasi*. In effect, the chief rabbi became the supreme authority within the community, and it seems likely that he sought to fashion the frameworks of leadership and rule in Baghdad according to the accepted model in his community of origin, Aleppo.

Another two years passed until, in 1745, Yitshak ben David ben Yeshua Gabbai was appointed *nasi* and *sarraf bashi*.[26] Although he was to remain in post for eighteen years, it seems reasonable to assume that at the outset, like his predecessors, he was not free to pit his own strength against the growing status of Rabbi Houssin, whose position as the leading figure in the community was further entrenched with each passing year. Throughout these years, Rabbi Houssin maintained close connections with his friends in rabbinic circles in Aleppo, who continued to be his primary reference group throughout his tenure in Baghdad.[27] In particular, he kept in touch with his friend

[21] See Harel, 'Controversy and Agreement' (Heb.), 130.

[22] Benjamin, *Travels of Israel* (Heb.), 45.

[23] See Ben-Ya'akov, *Babylonian Jewry from the End of the Geonic Period* (Heb.), 111; id., 'Rabbi Sasson' (Heb.), 25–9.

[24] Ben-Ya'akov, *Babylonian Jewry from the End of the Geonic Period* (Heb.), 111.

[25] Ibid. 112.

[26] Ibid.

[27] The only extant eulogy of Rabbi Houssin was published in Aleppo by Isaiah Attiah, *Bigdei yesha*, 154–8.

Rabbi Raphael Solomon Laniado, who until his last days continued to impose his authority on the community of Aleppo.[28] It is not impossible that the example and influence of Laniado lay behind Houssin's choice to exercise the functions of his office in a particularly unyielding and strong-minded fashion.

The Struggle for Rulership over the Community

The gradual recovery of the circle of rabbinic sages in Baghdad, combined with the renewed stability of the institution of *nasi* under the leadership of Yitshak Gabbai—a strong character with considerable leadership talents, whose firmness earned him the title 'Sheikh Yitshak Pasha'—prepared the ground for a movement to reverse the changes in community governance made by Rabbi Houssin. It would appear that the local Torah scholars began to complain about Houssin's sitting alone as judge, without inviting two other local sages to join him—a practice perceived as a sign of arrogance on the part of the newcomer from Aleppo. The Baghdadi rabbis gained the support of the new *nasi*, who had already been involved in a dispute with Rabbi Houssin on another matter. To him they were welcome allies in his struggle to restore the balance of authority in the community in his own favour and to regain those prerogatives which the incomer had abrogated to himself. The following is Rabbi Houssin's own account, though phrased in the third person, of the episode in which the conflict came to a head:

> Reuben had been the permanent judge in a certain city for more than ten years and all the people of the city had accepted him as rabbi and sole judge. The earlier *nesi'im* had brought him from Aram Zova, and in Aram Zova he had been a teacher of halakhah in Israel whose rulings illuminated the entire world, and his wisdom was known throughout the land, etc. But the present *nasi* quarrelled with him concerning a certain matter, and when gossips saw this—especially as they thought themselves wise in their own eyes and sought greatness for themselves—they told the *nasi* that this rabbi had at times made certain errors in judicial matters and that it was forbidden for him to sit as judge by himself. And the *nasi* did not tarry, but sent [a messenger] to inform this judge that from this day on he may not judge by himself and that two other judges must sit with him in judgment.[29]

It is clear that, after a lengthy period of relative impotence, the *nasi* sought to reassert his authority to determine the identity and number of

[28] See Ch. 2 below.

[29] Houssin, *Tsedakah umishpat*, 92*b*. According to the Baghdad tradition, articulated in the writings of Rabbi Joseph Hayim, the question under consideration here—which Rabbi Sadkah Houssin described without identifying the persons involved—concerns Rabbi Houssin himself. This appears to be corroborated by Hayim, *Rav pe'alim*, ii, 'Even ha'ezer', no. 33.

judges within the community. On one side of the scale there stood the *nasi* and the local Torah scholars; on the other side Rabbi Houssin, who evidently enjoyed the backing not only of the rabbis back in his home community of Aleppo, but also of the Aleppo Jews living in Baghdad, who maintained their identity as a distinct group apart from the local community. These Aleppo Jews in Baghdad dissociated themselves from the steps taken by the *nasi* in order to limit the authority of the venerated rabbi from their own city; thus, for the first time, the Baghdad community saw a fissure open up in the unity and solidarity of the learned class. The unprecedented phenomenon of Torah scholars taking sides with the *nasi* against the chief rabbi particularly pained Rabbi Houssin, whose opponents included some young rabbinic scholars who had previously been his own students and disciples. He placed the entire blame for this offence against him upon the Torah scholars of Baghdad, arguing that they had incited the *nasi* against him:

> But the judge did not accept this insult, for he knew that their intention was to anger him and to affront his honour. And they act as if their intention is for the sake of Heaven, but God knows whether their acts were not twisted and out of crookedness. And from the day he arrived here they learned a great deal from him, but even so they turned about and became his enemies, defaming him before the *nasi* and his household.[30]

It would appear that at this point the *nasi* wielded sufficient power to take unilateral action without fear of the government response; he may even have acted with the backing of the government authorities. In any event, he removed Rabbi Houssin from his judicial office, appointing in his place a new rabbinic court (*beit din*) composed of three local judges (*dayanim*).[31] He even forbade the Jews of Baghdad to take their cases before Rabbi Houssin, requiring them instead to have recourse only to the new *beit din* which he had set up.[32] With this step, the turn-about was completed. The imported rabbi had been removed from all positions of power and the *nasi* had recovered the authority he had enjoyed in the past to appoint the *dayanim* of the city. His self-confidence was so great that he felt able to ignore appeals from representatives of both the local Baghdad community and those who had come from Aleppo. There were two elements to these protests: anger both at the deposing of Rabbi Houssin and at the appointment to the rabbinic bench of Torah scholars who had not reached the customary age threshold of 40 years and who were not sufficiently learned.[33] The 'ignorance' of these new *dayanim* is described in harsh terms by Rabbi Houssin himself:

30 Houssin, *Tsedakah umishpat*, 92*b*; and cf. ibid. 93*b*.

31 Ibid. 92*b*.

32 Ibid.

33 Ibid.

> But those students who had not studied Torah sufficiently and had read neither the Rambam nor the 'four gates' [the *Shulḥan arukh*], nor ever seen the light in the books of the former and later *posekim*, but only studied a little bit of Talmud and Tosafot, reading it in the way children learn—how dare they presume to sit at the head, in place of someone greater than them in wisdom and in age . . . For even now, in our own day, these disciples have extinguished the lamp of Torah and increased disputation in Israel and despoiled the vineyard of the Lord of Hosts. May God punish the evildoer according to his evil, and may the soul of those who spread wicked stories depart their body. For [shall one say that] because the rabbi of the city forgot one or two things during the many years that he was fixed [as judge] in the city and he made an error in his rulings once or twice—and even that not a real error, but only because of the burden of leading the community that he carries on his shoulders . . . that he is not a great man? Is it better in God's eyes that they harm the honour due to the rabbi and defame him before the masses? And they sought to uproot his honour and increase their own honour. Now the honour of their rabbi remains as it was, and their own honour has turned to shame, and the Holy One, blessed be He, shall take retribution against them in the future.[34]

Rabbi Houssin saw with pain that his own students, who owed their knowledge of Torah to him, were turning against him. Filled with bitterness by their behaviour and that of the *nasi*, he decided to leave Baghdad.[35]

Back to the Old Order

We have no extant sources detailing the conclusion of the dispute between the *nasi* and the local rabbis, on the one hand, and the chief rabbi, on the other. In the end the two sides seem to have made their peace and Rabbi Houssin returned to resume his position, evidently after agreeing to forgo some of the prerogatives he had claimed and to sit with two other local rabbis as judges. Thus the old order was restored. The *nasi* recovered full rule over the community, to the extent of imposing his will upon the sages in general and upon the judges in particular, and the rabbis were pushed away from the political arena into their own realm of halakhah.

Over his thirty years of service in Baghdad, until his death from plague in 1773, Rabbi Sadkah Houssin succeeded in raising the community from a state of spiritual desolation to one of spiritual flourishing. From having itself been a satellite community dependent on Aleppo, the Baghdad community was transformed into a spiritual centre for many of the communities to the north and east—Kurdistan, Persia, and India.[36]

[34] Houssin, *Tsedakah umishpat*, 93*a*–*b*.

[35] Ibid. 95*a*.

[36] See Benayahu, 'Sources' (Heb.), 19. Rabbi Sadkah Houssin enjoyed great prestige among the sages of his generation, particularly those of Aleppo, and his reputation extended all the way

The *nasi* continued to exercise absolute dominance over the Baghdad community for another eighty years, until the arrival of another rabbi from Aleppo: Rabbi Raphael Kassin.

to Jerusalem. Rabbi Raphael ben Samuel Meyuhas, for example, wrote the following dedication upon sending Rabbi Houssin the third part of his book, *Peri adamah*: 'This is sent as a gift to the king, the man of glory, the complete sage, the excellent judge and the chief rabbi; who can relate the virtues of the Head of the Place and the Head of the Yeshiva, Rabbi Sadkah Houssin; may the shield of our forefathers be at his side. Signed by myself, the inhabitant of Jerusalem, the Holy City.' I wish to thank my colleague Hakham Ya'akov Zamir of the Babylonian Jewry Heritage for showing me this document. On Rabbi Sadkah Houssin's reputation among the sages of Aleppo, see Ben-Ya'akov, *Babylonian Jewry* (Heb.), 118 nn. 4–7. For another analysis of this affair, see Regev, 'Crisis of Leadership' (Heb.).

CHAPTER TWO

Raphael Solomon Laniado and the Struggle in Aleppo against the Inheritance of the Rabbinate

Rabbi Hama bar Hanina said: 'Why did Joseph die before his brethren? Because he acted in a lordly way.'

BT *Berakhot* 55*a*

Jewish Community Leadership within the Eighteenth-Century Ottoman Empire

During the second half of the eighteenth century, the population of Aleppo incorporated dozens of different religious, ethnic, and linguistic groupings. Alongside the Sunni Muslim majority, which numbered about 90,000 people, there were two large religious minorities—the Christians and the Jews—each of which was made up of several smaller sub-groups, all with their own particular characteristics. In all, there were about 20,000 Christians and 4,000 Jews. Until the end of the century, the legal arrangements governing relations among Muslims, Christians, and Jews were accepted by all sides, providing a framework within which non-Muslim minorities enjoyed well-defined rights and a status mutually agreed by each community and the imperial rulers. As the variegated Ottoman society was structured on a religious basis, it was run according to the law of the various religions. The communities defined themselves by religion and each was organized around its place of worship, headed by an imam, a priest, or a rabbi; thus, each religious community was subject to its own religious leadership.[1] Members of these minority groups, known as *dhimmi*, enjoyed considerable tolerance and broad autonomy in running their internal affairs. In exchange for paying the *jizya* tax, and accepting certain limitations reflecting the presumption of inferiority to Muslims, Jews and Christians were allowed to choose their own leader-

[1] See Lewis, *The Jews of Islam*, 125–6.

ship, to organize an independent system of tax collection, to maintain an independent system of religious courts, to run an independent school system, and to conduct their own communal lives with a bare minimum of outside interference.

The Ottoman authorities gave practical recognition and even a degree of support to the Jewish leadership. The leading figure of the Jewish community, the chief rabbi, fulfilled a dual role: on the one hand, he represented the community to the imperial authorities; on the other, he served as spokesman for those authorities to the community. Alongside him served a public lay leadership of seven *parnasim*, usually selected from the hereditary elites of pedigree and wealth. The loyalty of these lay leaders to the values of the community and their desire to advance its interests were among the basic assumptions of Jewish society. In practice, the rabbi and the *parnasim* depended upon one another to pursue their goals. The rabbi required the resources of the wealthy *parnasim*, while the latter required the halakhic and ethical seal of approval of the rabbi to support their actions.[2] Thus the authority of the community leadership, headed by the rabbi, stemmed in large part from its voluntary recognition by the members of the community, but also from its practical recognition by the imperial government, which gave it validity and powers of enforcement. For their part, the Ottoman rulers preferred dealing with groups rather than with individuals, and accordingly supported the respective leaderships of the various minority groups, hoping thereby to achieve stability and tranquillity throughout an empire filled with different religious and ethnic groupings.[3]

Inheritance of the Rabbinate: A Contested Custom

In the Jewish community of Aleppo, as in its counterparts in Europe, the stability of the leadership headed by the rabbi was a direct consequence of the identity that existed in the public mind between the community and its religion.[4] One expression of this stability was the custom of passing on the position of rabbi by inheritance. Since earliest times, it had been customary in Aleppo for the community leadership to be passed from father to son. When the exiles from Spain arrived in the city at the beginning of the sixteenth century, they found a long-established leadership enjoying extensive authority. The old local community, the *musta'ribun*, whose families had lived in Syria for many generations, had been led by successive members of the

[2] See Levi, 'Changes in the Leadership' (Heb.), 242.

[3] See Barnai, 'The Jews in the Ottoman Empire, 1650–1830' (Heb.), 83.

[4] See Katz, *Tradition and Crisis* (Heb.), 109.

Dayan family, which traced its lineage back to King David.[5] Alongside the *mustaʿribun* there existed the Sephardi community, so that in effect there were two parallel communal systems.[6] It was only at the very end of the seventeenth century that the spiritual and political leadership of the community was united in the hands of the Sephardi Laniado family, who adopted the local traditions of communal leadership, including the inheritance of rabbinic office.[7]

The first member of the Laniado family to serve in the Aleppo rabbinate was Rabbi Samuel Laniado, known as Ba'al Hakelim, who held office towards the end of the sixteenth century.[8] From his time on the position remained within the family, eventually passing in 1750 to Rabbi Raphael Solomon Laniado (Rashal). In 1787, after thirty-seven years of service to the community as chief rabbi, Rabbi Laniado attempted to appoint his only son, Ephraim, as his successor during his own lifetime.[9] His justifications for the appointment were objective and circumstantial: on the one hand, his own inability to continue to function in his office, owing to his advanced age and the great burden it placed upon him; on the other hand, the talents and qualifications of his son Ephraim, which made him eminently qualified for the task. As he put it:

> I, in my poverty and misfortune, have sighed and been exhausted by all my toil because of the pressure of the community. Many rise up against me day and night, without cease, and the hand of the princes and rulers has been in this desecration as well, the princes and judges of the land are a care to me, and suddenly old age and elderly appearance are seen in me . . . For many years I have guided my son [to take] my place, the perfect sage and outstanding judge, my beloved son Ephraim, may the All-Merciful guard him and protect him, that he may teach and judge, as he has attained the level of being able to rule as a rabbi, both in wisdom and in age, praise be to God, may He be blessed![10]

[5] The Dayan family tree is printed in Moshe Dayan, *Yashir mosheh*, in an introduction to the genealogy of the Davidic line (without page numbers). On the origins of the custom of inheriting the rabbinate in Europe and in the East, see Grossman, 'From Father to Son'. On the development of the custom, see Bornstein, 'Leadership' (Heb.), 146–50.

[6] See Harel, 'Controversy and Agreement' (Heb.), 119–33.

[7] The justifications given by members of the Laniado family for the custom of inheriting the rabbinate are identical to those given by the *mustaʿribun* and draw upon the words of the latter. See R. S. Laniado, *Kise shelomoh*, *6a–9a*.

[8] This nickname was derived from the names of his books, *Keli ḥemdah*, *Keli yakar*, and *Keli paz*. Rabbi Samuel Laniado died in 1605.

[9] Some include in Rabbi R. S. Laniado's length of service the years during which he served as a judge during his own father's lifetime, as well as those that followed the appointment of his son. According to this calculation, Rabbi R. S. Laniado served as rabbi for fifty-four years.

[10] R. S. Laniado, *Kise shelomoh*, *1a*, no. 1.

When people began to challenge his decision, Rabbi Raphael Solomon Laniado set down in writing both the appointment itself and the arguments of those opposed to it, which he analysed in accordance with halakhah. The opponents presented two arguments: the first challenged the very notion of granting the son priority in succession to his father's position; the second challenged Rabbi Ephraim Laniado's practice of sitting on the bench by himself, as sole judge. According to the latter argument, in order for judgment to be properly rendered in accordance with halakhah, two more rabbis should be added to the rabbinic leadership. The proponents of this argument expressed the hope that the community rabbi would continue to teach Torah, speak, preach, and exercise other rabbinic functions, but not sit as sole rabbinic judge with far-reaching authority. Rabbi Raphael Solomon Laniado inferred from this that the criticism was implicitly directed at himself as well, as he was also accustomed to sitting as sole judge.[11]

The opponents of Rabbi Ephraim Laniado's appointment were led by Rabbi Elijah Dweck Hakohen, of whom Rabbi Raphael Solomon Laniado spoke extremely harshly, to the extent of insulting and even cursing him.[12] The hostility between the two was exacerbated by the fact that Rabbi Dweck Hakohen had been among the leading opponents of Rabbi Laniado in the great controversy that had agitated the Aleppo community some years previously concerning the subjugation to (or immunity from) the community's laws and regulations of the Francos, the Italian Jews who had settled in Aleppo since the end of the seventeenth century.

The question arises whether the objections to Rabbi Ephraim Laniado's inheritance of the rabbinate, and indeed Rabbi Raphael Solomon Laniado's decision to appoint his son during his own lifetime, were in fact based on the reasons expressly advanced on each side, or whether both the appointment and the opposition to it were prompted by social, economic, and political factors that would in due course challenge the entire structure of leadership in the Aleppo community on the eve of the nineteenth century. In order to address this question, we must first turn to the Francos and their anomalous position in the Aleppo community.

The Francos and Their Influence upon the Community

Viewed from outside, the Jewish community of Aleppo seemed like a homogeneous unit with a single leadership. But in practice, the community was

[11] Ibid. 1*a–b*, no. 1.

[12] Rabbi Elijah Dweck Hakohen's main arguments are cited in Dweck Hakohen, *Birkat eliyahu*, 99*a*, no. 14; On Rabbi Elijah Dweck see in Laniado, *For the Sake of the Holy Ones* (Heb.), 16–17.

composed of two distinct groups, the Sephardim and the *musta'ribun*. True, during the time that had passed since the settlement of the Spanish exiles in Aleppo, many of the differences between the two groups had become obscured and they seemed to be moving towards complete unity. However, from the end of the seventeenth century onwards Sephardi Jewish merchants, primarily from Leghorn (modern-day Livorno) and Venice, began to settle in Aleppo. These were referred to by the local Jews as 'Signores Francos' or simply 'Francos'. While these Francos were separate from the community, they strengthened the identity of its Sephardi component and thereby retarded its process of homogenization.

Drawn by Aleppo's location at a key crossroads in the international trade between East and West, European traders and representatives of continental commercial houses had lived there for centuries. From the seventeenth century onwards in particular, European powers increased their economic penetration of Mediterranean trade, primarily through various Levantine companies.[13] Trade agreements (capitulations) concluded between the Ottoman empire and the European powers gave European merchants living in imperial territories special commercial and legal privileges: notably, they were not subject to Ottoman law, but rather to the consular representatives of their own country of origin. In Aleppo these merchants, who together numbered no more than a few dozen, included several Jews, and more arrived during the economic expansion of the first half of the eighteenth century.[14]

The European merchants, even those who had lived in Aleppo for many years, never saw themselves as 'Aleppans', but maintained their European identity. They continued to see the city as a temporary place of residence, for business purposes only, rather than as their permanent home. Many did not bother to learn Arabic, and only a small number brought their wives or members of their family to Aleppo or married local women. They even lived in a separate district of the city, rather than in the same neighbourhoods as the local people.[15] Similarly, the European Jewish merchants neither lived in the Jewish neighbourhood nor considered themselves part of the Jewish community so far as most aspects of their lives and their activities were concerned; rather, they viewed themselves as an adjunct to the European colony in the city. Exempt from the discriminatory Ottoman laws that applied to local Jews, they lived under the protection of the European powers—primarily

[13] On the place of Aleppo in trade with the West until the mid-18th century, see Masters, *The Origins of Western Economic Dominance in the Middle East*.

[14] On the capitulations and their influence upon the early settlement of European Jewish merchants in Aleppo, see Lutzky, 'The Francos in Aleppo' (Heb.); see also Rozen, 'Archives of the Chamber of Commerce of Marseilles' (Heb.).

[15] Marcus, *The Middle East*, 45–6.

France.[16] Nevertheless, by virtue of their religious identification with the local Jewish community, the Jewish merchants did not remain as separate as their non-Jewish counterparts. While they too initially saw their residence in Aleppo in temporary terms, over the course of time they began to take a more active part in the religious life of the local Jewish community, whose ways were not alien to them. They married local Jewish women, had children, and gradually became established as permanent residents.[17] In consequence of this combination of separation and integration, the Francos played the role of bearers of European culture among the Jews of the eastern Mediterranean. They dressed differently from the local Jews, the men were accustomed to shaving their beards, and, as we shall see below, their attitude with regard to the role and proper behaviour of women was different from that generally accepted in the Aleppo community.[18] Thus, during the course of the eighteenth century, there gradually began to emerge, alongside the local Jewish community, a small, wealthy Jewish elite with European social attitudes.

Given this community's identification with the European colony in Aleppo, a group with a high social status, rather than with the marginal Jewish community, one might have expected the Francos to have organized a separate communal framework to meet their needs as Jews. However, rather surprisingly—and enabled to do so precisely because of their free functioning within the broader social framework of Aleppo—they did not attempt this, but rather turned to the institutions of the local community to fulfil their religious needs, taking part in public worship with the other Jews of the city. Nor did the Francos restrict their participation in communal life to the purely spiritual; they drew on the extensive wealth generated by their commercial activities to give generous support to communal institutions of charity and self-help, to institutions of Torah study, and to the rabbinic scholars. Among other things, they served as treasurers of the *bikur ḥolim* (communal health funds) and *gemilut ḥasadim* (charitable society), and took care to import the 'four species' needed for observance of the Sukkot festival—all on their own initiative, without any compulsion.[19] Nevertheless, the Francos took care not to be subject to the regulations of the community or governed by its institutions.

[16] See Harel, 'The Status and Image of the Picciotto Family' (Heb.), 173.

[17] See R. S. Laniado, *Beit dino*, 501, 'Ḥoshen mishpat', no. 39; Y. Kassin, *Maḥaneh yehudah*, pt. 1, introduction, 1*b*.

[18] On the important role played by the Francos in modernization of the Jewish communities of the Ottoman empire, see Rodrigue, *French Jews*, 39–40.

[19] See Y. Kassin, *Maḥaneh yehudah*, 'Halakhot pesukot', 38*b*, no. 26. For a summary of the social status of the Francos in the community and their involvement in economic and charitable matters, see Lutzky, 'The Francos in Aleppo' (Heb.), 64–72.

This, then, was the first of the new elites that emerged in Aleppo during the eighteenth century. However, it did not grow from within, but rather arrived from outside, developing alongside the community. Given this origin, and its acceptance of the local framework of religious life, this elite did not constitute a threat to the community. Moreover, as a result of its success, the community itself grew and flourished. However, the growth of the Franco elite led in turn to the development of a new elite that did emerge from within the community, and one that wished to shake off the burden of its subordinate status.

One of the important benefits derived by the Aleppo Jewish community from the position of the Francos was the wide variety of opportunities for employment in their service opened up by their presence. To assist in their commercial activities, the European Jewish merchants employed armies of translators, officials, accountants, agents, storehouse managers, workers, and servants, most recruited from among the local people. These individuals helped the European merchants to cultivate the local markets and to become acquainted with the local culture. In selecting appropriate employees, the Francos quite naturally preferred the services of their local co-religionists. Many of those they appointed not only enjoyed a good income, but received special rights and privileges as a result of their status as employees of Europeans, who were exempt from Ottoman law. In consequence, acquiring work with the Francos was the ambition of many community members, both because of the good salaries the jobs carried and because of the special privileges and high social status that accompanied them.[20]

Moreover, the European consuls, seeking to increase both their influence in the city and their income, offered their protection to various of these functionaries, particularly translators, who thereby became exempt from Ottoman law.[21] This consular protection was sold for considerable sums of money, and those who purchased it were then listed fictitiously as employees of the consul. When the consul himself was a Jew—for example, when Raphael Picciotto was appointed in 1784 as chief of Austria's consular agents in Aleppo, and thereafter as consul of the state—this protection was extended to many of his co-religionists.[22]

[20] R. S. Laniado, *Beit dino*, 482–3, 'Ḥoshen mishpat', no. 35.

[21] The consuls employed many translators. Thus, for example, during the period in question the British consulate employed twelve translators: eleven Christians and one Jew. A similar number were employed by the Dutch consulate. For the number of translators in the different consulates, see Tawtal al-Yashu'i, *Historical Documents* (Arab.); al-Tunji, 'Social Interaction' (Arab.), 222–4; Cunningham, '"Dragomania"'.

[22] On the circumstances of Raphael Picciotto's appointment and the reactions it elicited, see Harel, 'The Status and Image of the of the Picciotto Family' (Heb.), 177–9; Schwarzfuchs, 'La

The local people, both Jews and Christians, who worked in the service of the consuls and the foreign merchants, sought to create for themselves an identity distinct from their original community, to receive recognition from the authorities of their separate organization, and thereby officially to free themselves from the twin financial and social burden of liability to the *jizya* tax and the inferior status of Ottoman subjects belonging to non-Muslim minorities. But the members of this new class wished to go further, seeking to make use of the foreign protection granted them to avoid paying internal taxes in their communities of origin; some went so far as to refuse to recognize the heads of these communities as their representatives.[23] This new elite, whose members may be categorized on the whole as *nouveaux riches*, constituted a significant threat to the strength and integrity of the community from which it had emerged and from which it now wished to separate itself. Among its number were several of the *parnasim* who had found in it a new reference group apart from the old community framework. These *parnasim*, and the other *nouveaux riches*, began to wonder in what way the Torah scholars were better qualified than themselves to determine community norms. They began to treat the instructions of the rabbis with contempt and showed no inclination to protect the old order.[24] In all this, they posed a grave threat to the status and authority of the head of the community, Rabbi Raphael Solomon Laniado.

The Controversy Regarding the Servants of the Francos

So long as the Francos were perceived as temporary residents in Aleppo, the leadership of the local community could ignore the issue of their exemption from the edicts of the community and its taxes—particularly in view of their generous contributions to community's institutions and their capacity, as European consuls, to protect it and its members in times of trouble. However, as they began to put down local roots, the question of their subjection to community regulations began to arise and to trouble the leadership. This problem might have been suppressed or resolved by means of a compromise acceptable to both sides, had it not been compounded by the separate but related question of whether the Francos' exemption from community taxes applied also to those local Jews who worked for them. Both controversies

"Nazione Ebrea"', 717–18; Le Calloc'h, 'La Dynastie consulaire', 139–42. See also HHSTA, Türkei, II, 129, De Testa au Comte de Colloredo, Pera de Consple, 25 July 1802.

[23] See Marcus, *The Middle East*, 46.

[24] R. S. Laniado, *She'elot uteshuvot*, 74, no. 5.

broke out one after the other during the early 1770s. The controversy regarding the Francos themselves continued for more than fifteen years.[25]

The Aleppo community was subject to very heavy taxation by the Ottoman authorities. These dues were not collected directly from the individuals within the community by the government; rather, they were imposed upon the community as a whole, which was granted the freedom to decide how the burden was to be divided among its members.[26] During the second half of the eighteenth century the difficulty of allocating liability was exacerbated by the reluctance of those working for the Francos to pay their fair share alongside the other members of the community. This issue was the subject of intensive halakhic discussion, occupying five separate chapters in the collection of Rabbi Raphael Solomon Laniado's responsa, *Beit dino shel shelomoh*.[27] It came to a head in the case of a storekeeper employed by the Francos, who claimed exemption from community taxes on the grounds that his employer held a special licence from the Austrian ambassador in Istanbul. Rabbi Laniado presented a series of arguments intended to refute such requests. His central argument was that the servants of the Francos had been counted among the members of the community since their employers had first arrived in Aleppo; if they did not now participate in paying the taxes, this would impose a heavier burden upon the other members of the community and cause financial loss to many people.[28] Moreover, in many cases those employed by the Francos had flourishing businesses of their own, which they wished to make even more profitable thanks to the special dispensations and privileges deriving from their close connections with the Francos. Indeed, it was often specifically the wealthier people who attempted to free themselves of the burden of communal taxes. The damage caused thereby was all the greater, as the result was an even heavier tax burden on the less well-off members of the community.[29] Rabbi Laniado also dropped strong hints that sev-

[25] On the basis of the extant sources, it is impossible to determine precisely when the controversy surrounding the tax exemption of the Francos' servants arose. As Rabbi Yitshak Berakhah discusses the subject, it clearly occurred prior to his death on 16 Adar II 5532 (21 March 1772). In any event, there is no doubt that the controversy involving the Francos' servants broke out before that concerning the Francos themselves, as during the former the Torah scholars in Aleppo still presented a consistent, united front.

[26] For examples of the kinds of taxes imposed upon the community by law or by the arbitrary decision of the governor, see R. S. Laniado, *Beit dino*, 497, 'Ḥoshen mishpat', no. 37; Y. Kassin et al., *Ro'ei yisra'el*, 19*b*–23*a*, nos. 5–6.

[27] R. S. Laniado, *Beit dino*, 459–501, 'Ḥoshen mishpat', nos. 34–48. See also Laniado's words as quoted in Y. Kassin et al., *Ro'ei yisra'el*, 20*a*, no. 5.

[28] R. S. Laniado, *Beit dino*, 493, 'Ḥoshen mishpat', no. 36.

[29] Ibid. 481, 'Ḥoshen mishpat', no. 34. See also Dweck Hakohen, *Birkat eliyahu*, 87*b*–88*a*, no. 2.

eral people who worked for the Francos enjoyed concessions and exemptions gained from the ambassadors by dishonest means, including giving false information about their origins.[30]

One indication that Rabbi Laniado's claim to exclusive rabbinic authority was beginning to be questioned by members of the community is the unprecedented action by the storekeeper in the example mentioned above in turning to three other senior rabbis from outside Aleppo for their opinions on this matter. These were Rabbi Raphael Meyuhas, one of the leading rabbis of Jerusalem; Rabbi Mordecai Ruvio of Hebron; and Rabbi Sadkah Houssin, the Aleppo sage who at the time was serving as rabbi in Baghdad. All three of them backed the plaintiff, ruling that the storekeeper was to be exempt from community taxes. Rabbi Laniado rejected the arguments of these rabbis one by one.[31] As for the rabbis of Aleppo, with the exception of Rabbi Yitshak Berakhah, who raised certain questions regarding Rabbi Laniado's ruling, they all publicly supported his position.[32] Although the storekeeper claimed that he had in his possession written halakhic rulings from other local sages who supported his claim to exemption from community taxes, he refused to show these to Rabbi Laniado. The rabbis of Aleppo, in supporting Rabbi Laniado, seem to have understood the underlying motivation for his ruling: namely, the wish to avoid undermining the collection of community taxes, which would in the final analysis be to their detriment as well. In response to Rabbi Laniado's ruling, the storekeeper refused to appear before his rabbinic court in Aleppo; nor did he respond to the demand that he pay the taxes deemed due by the committee responsible for such calculations. This defiance signalled a further fissure between the members of the Aleppo community and its leader and a further challenge to his authority. Nevertheless, Rabbi Laniado continued to enjoy strong support as chief rabbi among the majority of the community and among the Torah scholars, who indirectly benefited from his status. Rabbi Elijah Dweck Hakohen described the strength of Rabbi Laniado's position during the years preceding the outbreak of this controversy as follows:

The awe of our venerated teacher, the rabbi—may the Merciful protect and save him—is over all, great and small, because our master the king [Rabbi Laniado]—may the Rock protect him and give him life—is renowned in all of the countries, from Damascus to Babylon and in Basra and all its environs, every difficult matter is

[30] R. S. Laniado, *Beit dino*, 498, 'Ḥoshen mishpat', no. 37.

[31] See ibid. 481–99; also R. S. Laniado, *She'elot uteshuvot*, 1–42, nos. 1–2; 67–75, no. 5.

[32] See Dweck Hakohen, *Birkat eliyahu*, 101*b*, no. 16. On Rabbi Yitshak Berakhah, see Harel, *The Books of Aleppo* (Heb.), 398.

brought before him . . . And heaven and earth are my witness, that of all the sages and all the emissaries of Erets Yisra'el whom I have seen, there is none comparable to him in wisdom and in piety, and he judges a true judgment, for both rich and poor—everybody is equal before him in judgment. And my eyes have seen—and for well-known facts there is no need for proof—that three individuals from among the members of the holy community—may the Rock protect them and give them life—who were among the outstanding persons of the community, had written authorization from the government—may his excellency be exalted—that they are exempt from all [payments]. Yet nevertheless, as he saw that they are obligated in law to pay all kinds of taxes, when they declined to pay their dues together with the other members of the community, he placed a public ban upon them in the synagogue, and feared neither them nor those strengthening their hand, and he dedicated himself to carrying out the law of the Torah in truth. And, thank God, they again began to pay as was proper . . . And he did such things and their like many times . . . And to the contrary, the fear of our teacher, the rabbi was felt by the wealthy people and the *parnasim*, for it happens in our days that the wealthy people exalt the sages, and they stand up before even the smallest of the sages, and set him above themselves.[33]

Rabbi Laniado's insistence that all those who served the Francos were obliged to pay their share of the communal taxes was entirely in line with the stance of the Ottoman authorities. They too viewed askance the increasing numbers of those who had acquired consular protection and were therefore claiming exemption from taxes, as this detracted from their own income, and they too now sought to repeal these special privileges. Moreover, the traditional system of relations between Muslims and other minority groups, particularly Christians, was beginning to change. The increasing involvement of foreign consuls in internal matters of the empire, coupled with their attempts to help those who enjoyed their protection, was disturbing the delicate intercommunal balance and arousing suspicion, fear, and hostility towards the Christians among the Muslims.[34] The growing role of the foreign consuls, as we have seen, was also affecting the internal affairs of the Jewish community and undermining the authority of its head.[35] In brief, while this controversy, which arose within the community and threatened its institutions, did not significantly harm Laniado's status, it did open up the first cracks in the firm basis of his authority over the members of the community. Nevertheless, he could still count on the support of the rabbis and Torah scholars, who depended on his rulings for the preservation and protection of the framework of leadership and rule within the community—and thereby of their own

[33] Dweck Hakohen, *Birkat eliyahu*, 102*a*, no. 16.

[34] Marcus, *The Middle East*, 47.

[35] See Lutzky, 'The "Francos"' (Heb.), 59–60.

privileged position as its most learned members. This united front was completely shattered by the controversy involving the Francos themselves.

The Controversy over the Francos

The controversy began as a domestic quarrel involving one of the Francos, who wished to restrict the activities of his assertive, strong-minded, and independent wife, who was also of Franco descent. In an attempt to impose his wishes upon her, the husband asked Rabbi Laniado if the Francos (and therefore his own wife) were subject to the regulations governing the community. The latter answered that they were indeed obliged to fulfil all of the edicts and agreements of the community; hence their womenfolk were also subject to the customs governing the women of the community. The husband's appeal to Laniado angered the leaders of the Francos, who saw it as offering the chief rabbi a pretext for changing the established pragmatic policy towards the Francos and an opportunity to attempt to impose his authority upon them. The development of this affair was recounted as follows by Rabbi Yehudah Kassin, the leader of those who disagreed with Laniado's ruling:[36]

A certain person came to live here and took a wife from a good family, daughter of one of the important and great men of the Francos. And when he was in the synagogue, he heard of the agreement that the women ought not to go about, to stroll in the streets of the city, in the gardens and the orchards. And after a certain time his wife went out to stroll with her mother and her father's family . . . And that evening, when the man came home, he was told of his wife's going out, and he pretended not to know the custom of the Francos, and he asked his wife: 'Why did you do this, strolling about outside to the water spring, against the agreement of the rabbis of the city?' 'Yea,' she returned answer to him: 'Do you not know? Have you not heard? The Francos are not included in the agreements of the inhabitants of the people of the city, and all the women of the Francos go out in song and return in song, so why should I not be like one of them, to walk about in the streets of the city?' . . . And the man went and asked Rabbi Raphael Solomon Laniado—may the Merciful guard him and deliver him—if the thing was true . . . And his answer was that the rumour was not good, and that the practice of the women of the Francos to go about in the gardens is a mistaken custom, and that the Francos are also obligated to fulfil all of the agreements and edicts of the city, and no one exempts them.

[36] Rabbi Yehudah Kassin was ideologically opposed to Rabbi R. S. Laniado on many other matters as well as this one. Thus, for example, in response to incidents of sabbath desecration, Rabbi Laniado introduced a rule prohibiting walking to the grave of Ezra the Scribe in the village of Tadef, near Aleppo, on the sabbath. According to extant testimonies, Rabbi Kassin forced him to nullify this prohibition. See Antebi, *Ohel yesharim*, 135. On a dispute regarding the Musaf prayer, see Hayim Attiah, *Arshot haḥayim*, in Abadi, *Ma'ayan ganim*, 415, no. 6.

And the man brought his wife to the house of the rabbi, and he released her [from this practice], because it was an error . . . And when the woman's father heard of the incident, he was very wrathful, and this pure man gathered together the entire community of the Francos, and they sent delegates, and they called the son-in-law to the house of the *nasi* and they rebuked him in his presence, saying: Why did you do thus, to bring in something new, to involve yourself in the agreements and edicts of the city, which our fathers and our forebears never saw? And we are old, advanced in years, and we have never been accustomed to enter into any agreement, from the day we arrived in Aleppo until this day . . . And why did you hasten to seek out Rabbi Solomon Laniado? . . . You ought to have enquired of us regarding our custom . . . And now you have done foolishly, to arouse controversy between the Francos and Rabbi Laniado . . . for now it will be easy for him to impose his edicts . . . Because he has a different spirit, to behave in high-handed fashion with us, but we do not live according to his sayings, to introduce any new thing.[37]

This controversy erupted with full force in 1775 upon the publication of Laniado's book *Beit dino shel shelomoh*, which contained his ruling, in opposition to all the other sages of the city, requiring the Francos to accept community regulations. Some nine years later, Rabbi Kassin devoted part of his own book, *Maḥaneh yehudah*, to the subject, including in it both his own responsum and that of the other Aleppo sages opposed to this ruling of Rabbi Laniado concerning his authority in the community. For fifteen years, up to the end of the 1780s, controversy alternately flared up and died down, according to circumstances and the various parties' evaluation of the situation. Every time it resurfaced, Rabbi Laniado, with the encouragement of those close to him, particularly his son, attempted to impose his authority upon the Francos.[38]

The hard line taken by Rabbi Laniado on this issue was exacerbated by his earlier rulings that no Torah scholar apart from himself had the authority to judge disputes between people, and that no one was allowed to challenge or question his rulings, even if it appeared to the other rabbis that he had erred. Another complaint against Rabbi Laniado was that he forbade any rabbi apart from himself to write legal documents, thereby restricting their income and increasing his own.

[37] Y. Kassin, *Maḥaneh yehudah*, 'Introduction' (Heb.), 1*b*–2*a*. It should be noted that Aleppo was not the only place in which disputes occurred between the local communities and the Francos. On the failure of the attempt to establish a separate organization of the Francos in İzmir in 1869, see Rodrigue, *French Jews*, 53. On the split between the Grana, as the Francos were called in Tunisia, and the local community, see Tsur, 'France and the Jews of Tunisia' (Heb.), 10–13 and references there. On the attempt to force the Francos to accept the communal regulations of Salonica regarding the shaving of beards, see Irgas, *Divrei yosef*, 73*b*, 'Yoreh de'ah', no. 36.

[38] Y. Kassin, *Maḥaneh yehudah*, 'Introduction' (Heb.), 2*b*–3*a*.

The Francos presented their own arguments to the various rabbis of Aleppo, accompanied by a series of threats. If, they said, the other rabbis did not sign a document confirming their exemption from communal regulations, the Francos would divorce themselves completely from the Jewish community, setting up their own separate communal institutions, bringing in their own rabbis from Erets Yisra'el, and cutting off all their financial contributions to the community.[39] These were not threats to be lightly dismissed. The rabbis' dependence upon the generosity and support of the Francos was almost absolute. Cessation of their support would affect, first and foremost, their own incomes, but also the future of the teaching of Aleppo traditions.[40]

Among the justifications offered by the rabbis for exempting the Francos from the edicts of the community, three arguments stand out: first, that the Francos had enjoyed that exemption since their arrival in Aleppo, so that Rabbi Laniado was attempting to change the status quo; second, that when the rabbis initially decreed the various edicts and regulations, they specifically intended that they would not apply to the Francos; and third, that it was of paramount importance to avoid creating a split within the community. The rabbis were afraid that this controversy would drive the Francos to act on their threat to break away from the community completely and to cease all their contributions and activities on its behalf, as well as causing extensive loss to those members of the community whom they employed.[41]

Rabbi Laniado's counterarguments were concrete and to the point. He claimed that declaring the Francos subject to the communal regulations involved no innovation, and pointed out that his own father, Rabbi Samuel Laniado, had included the Francos among those who were subject to the community regulations.[42] In his view, the period during which the Francos might have been considered temporary residents had passed. Now they had married and built homes, and some had even been born in Aleppo, they were to be considered full members of the community, including with regard to communal regulations.[43] Nor did their exemption from taxes by virtue of being foreign subjects exempt them, as Jews who used the services of the

[39] It should be noted in this context that the Francos were accustomed to using various kinds of threats in even the most insignificant disputes. See Y. Kassin et al., *Ro'ei yisra'el*, 24*b*–25*b*, no. 9.

[40] Y. Kassin, *Maḥaneh yehudah*, 'Halakhot pesukot', 38*b*, no. 26. The Francos were in the habit of maintaining a kind of court or household rabbi who, in exchange for support, would study Torah regularly with the householder with whom he lived and serve as teacher for his sons. See Harel, *Syrian Jewry*, 37.

[41] An extensive summary of halakhic rulings concerning the dispute of the Francos, containing sixty-nine sections, is provided at the end of Kassin's *Maḥaneh yehudah*.

[42] R. S. Laniado, *Beit dino*, 501, no. 39.

[43] Ibid. 508–10, no. 39.

community, from its regulations.[44] According to Rabbi Laniado, controversy was more likely to break out in the future if the Francos were specifically exempted from the regulations, as other members of the community would feel that there was no equality before the law.[45] But his strongest argument related to the Francos' claim that the other rabbis of Aleppo, apart from himself, had not intended their regulations to apply to the Francos. Rabbi Laniado accused the sages of Aleppo as a group of pandering to the Francos because they were dependent upon them for their income—and thereby undermining his own leadership.[46] Moreover, he asserted that the decisions and intentions of the other rabbis were worthless if not pursued in concert with him, as he was the one, among all the Torah scholars, who had been chosen to head the community.[47] Here the seeds were sown of the controversy regarding the authority of the chief rabbi to sit in solitary judgment—the issue that would later serve as the basis for the opposition to Rabbi Ephraim Laniado's appointment as rabbi of the community during his father's lifetime.

In refuting Rabbi Raphael Solomon Laniado's halakhic arguments one by one, Rabbi Yehudah Kassin and the other sages of Aleppo were aware that he was attempting to extend his authority into areas which had not previously been under his jurisdiction, completely ignoring their opinions. They were afraid that, were they to support him, a great split would come about that could well lead to the collapse of the community in the wake of the Francos' withdrawal and the loss of all of the material benefits it had received from them. In consequence, all the Aleppo sages without exception, including Rabbi Raphael Solomon Laniado's own brother, Rabbi David Laniado, stood firmly against what they perceived as his desire for sole rule and concentration of authority in his own hands.[48] They were backed by the rabbis of Jerusalem and Damascus, who concurred in the ruling of the Aleppo sages.[49]

The results of the dispute and its outcome were immediately clear. The sweeping support for the Francos' position by all the Torah scholars of Aleppo barring the sole figure of Rabbi Laniado, on the one hand, and the Francos' unique status as foreign subjects, on the other hand, ensured the continuance of their exemption from communal regulations for many more years.[50]

[44] R. S. Laniado, *Beit dino*, 512, no. 39.

[45] Ibid. 518, no. 39; id., *She'elot uteshuvot*, 74, no. 5.

[46] R. S. Laniado, *Beit dino*, 513, no. 39; id., *She'elot uteshuvot*, 75, no. 5.

[47] R. S. Laniado, *Beit dino*, 519, no. 39; see also ibid. 521, 523, no. 39; cf. Y. Kassin et al., *Ro'ei yisra'el*, 22*b*, no. 5–6.

[48] Y. Kassin, *Maḥaneh yehudah*, 'Halakhot pesukot', 39*b*, no. 43.

[49] Ibid. 19*b*–31*a*.

[50] In practice, this situation persisted until the beginning of the 20th century. See Ch. 5 below.

Harbingers of Change

During the eighteenth century the population of Aleppo vacillated between conservatism and far-reaching changes in almost every area of life. The sense of change was greater in Jewish society than in Muslim society, owing to the Francos' presence. Within Aleppo's Jewish community, the emergence of new elites changed the balance of power, creating alongside the traditional leadership new foci of power not drawn from within the community, but based upon external political forces—namely, the capitulation agreements with European powers and the patronage offered by their consuls. To a great extent, then, the Jews' dependence upon the Ottoman rulers diminished in all matters relating to the framework of their community life. Moreover, the new economic possibilities created a new moneyed elite that sought to assert its position alongside the old hereditary and scholarly elite. Thus a new middle class began to come into existence, which over the following decades became dominant in the Aleppo community.

These harbingers of change in social structure were accompanied by corresponding signs of change in world-view. Up to this time, Jewish society had been based upon mutual responsibility and social cohesion; however, during the second half of the eighteenth century these principles began to lose some of their dominance as Aleppo Jews found both social and occupational opportunities beyond the local community opening up to them. New reference groups came into being, based not upon religious identity but upon political or economic status. This shift found expression, albeit only infrequently, in joint gatherings of Jews and non-Jews, and in their mutual participation in one another's family celebrations.[51] This by no means amounted to full Jewish involvement in society at large; however, it seems clear that meetings with non-Jews did have an effect in, and on, Jewish society. Generally speaking, Jews' social connections were not with the local Muslim community, but with members of the European Christian colony and, to some extent, also with local Christians. This new network of contacts was in itself a major, unexpected innovation, facilitating the penetration of modern European social perceptions into the Jewish community of Aleppo.

This process had a number of results. Among them was a weakening of the principle of non-equality, which had in the past been understood as a natural order of things within which extra rights and a preferential social status attached to nobility of pedigree. Specifically, the custom within Jewish society, influenced by the practice in the Muslim Middle East, whereby

[51] See e.g. Isaiah Attiah, *Bigdei yesha*, 31*a*.

spiritual leadership was passed on by inheritance, clashed with the social principles penetrating society from the West.[52] Conformity and blind obedience to the institutions of leadership were increasingly called into question. For some people, refusal to be judged by the local rabbinic court served as a means of protest against the established system and those who headed it, and as an expression of lack of trust in those institutions and leaders. Whereas in the past most individuals had perforce accepted their entire submission to the community's rules, as an element of choice appeared the tension between the needs and wishes of the individual and his obligations to the community became sharper. The Francos, in refusing to obey the authority of the chief rabbi of the community and observe his regulations, were registering their desire to limit the latter's authority to the narrow confines of the synagogue, so as not to disturb their own integration into non-Jewish society and adoption of its customs, along the lines customary in the European states from which they originally came. It is worth emphasizing that, notwithstanding this resistance to aspects of rabbinic authority, the Francos and their supporters made no attempt, in either argument or practice, to influence or restrict the rabbinate in any matter relating to its religious functions. The extant sources give not the slightest hint of any attempt to refashion the rabbinate along modern, west European lines.

Over the course of the eighteenth century a change took place in the status of the Torah scholars of Aleppo. Their dependence upon the community lessened and they found themselves relying almost entirely upon the largesse of the Francos. The support given by the rabbis to these benefactors may have derived from a combination of gratitude and the ambition to strengthen their own status, even if this involved defying the authority of their chief. It is well known that, throughout the Jewish diaspora, the stance taken by Torah scholars was frequently influenced by concern for their own status and personal interests.[53] As for the *parnasim*, the traditional lay leaders of the community, this group remained passive, even apathetic, choosing not to support Rabbi Raphael Solomon Laniado in his struggle—primarily owing to their own commercial involvement with the Francos. Significant elements of this group had already begun to involve themselves in the new socio-economic order and, in practice, had begun to look outside the community as well as within it for their social and professional contacts.

The *parnasim*'s withdrawal from community matters created a vacuum within the leadership that was rapidly filled by the Francos. Notwithstanding

[52] See Grossman, 'From Father to Son' (Heb.), 199–200.
[53] See e.g. Levi, 'Changes in the Leadership' (Heb.), 246 ff.

their separate status—possibly even because of it—they began to become increasingly involved in the internal affairs of the community, while remaining exempt from its edicts and regulations themselves. Thus, for example, during the years following the controversy described above, the community asked the Francos to take responsibility for estimating the sums of tax payable by individuals in the community—a function that had in the past been fulfilled by a committee of *parnasim* with which the Francos had no involvement.[54]

The change in the balance of power strengthened the new, 'secular' elements within the Jewish community at the expense of the older 'rabbinic' forces, posing a particular challenge to the absolute authority of the chief rabbi over the community institutions. The danger to the traditional communal frameworks was exacerbated by the possibility that the Francos might establish an alternative community. Rabbi Laniado's concerns were hence understandable. He was afraid that any sign of compromise on his part would accelerate the break-up of the community and, indirectly, lead to the loss of his own status within it. But he does not seem to have properly evaluated the power that the Francos had accumulated in the community, particularly among the rabbinic class which they supported. In attempting to impose his own authority upon the Francos, he was in fact attempting to restore the traditional balance of powers within the Aleppo Jewish community. After all, disputes and conflicts between rabbis and *parnasim*, some amounting to crises, had occurred in the past as well. According to the model familiar to Rabbi Laniado, these always concluded with a halakhic solution, and sometimes involved the use of administrative religious sanctions such as *nidui* and *ḥerem* (ban and excommunication); he sought to deal with this crisis too by traditional methods, believing that it could be resolved through halakhic solutions alone. Perhaps he thought that, were he to succeed in making the Francos submit, he could also suppress their local servants, who challenged the community structure from within. The absolute failure of this move, ending in Rabbi Laniado's defeat, led to a severe crisis of trust between himself and the other rabbis, and this crisis filtered down to other sectors of the community. For the first time, the community saw defeat inflicted on the absolute rabbinic leadership they had hitherto known, and Torah scholars in open confrontation with their chief member.

In essence, this crisis revolved around a failure of the rabbi's leadership. While he recognized the social ferment in his community, he failed in his evaluation of the new forces that had gained in relative power as the social,

[54] See JNUL, DMA, 8vo 196, 186 ff.

political, and economic system changed. As noted above, when Raphael Picciotto was appointed in 1784 to head the Austrian consular agency in Aleppo, a position which enabled him to expand the circle of those enjoying Austrian protection, the number of members of the Jewish community who sought to escape their obligations towards it grew even further. During that same year, shortly before his death, Rabbi Yehudah Kassin wrote the first part of his book on the dispute, *Maḥaneh yehudah*. About the same time, the sages of Aleppo published the sixty-nine 'binding decisions' concerning the Franco controversy.[55]

Winning the Battle but Losing the War

The pressure on Rabbi Laniado became progressively greater, until eventually he felt the lack of trust and co-operation to be unbearable. We can now fully understand the passage cited earlier, in which he complained that he was tired and that those who made it most difficult for him were 'the princes and judges of the land'. While his position was still too strong for him to be deposed, his worries now revolved around his son, Ephraim, who he hoped would perpetuate the Laniado dynasty's hold on the chief rabbinate, but who he feared would become the target of his opponents' revenge; hence he attempted to appoint the latter as a rabbinic judge during his own lifetime, ensuring the continuation of the dynasty. But again Rabbi Laniado misjudged the reaction to this unprecedented move on his part. A significant segment of the public, including the Torah scholars, headed by Rabbi Elijah Dweck Hakohen, saw it as another attempt by Rabbi Laniado to exert absolute authority over the community, completely disregarding the views of the other rabbis. It is reasonable to assume that Rabbi Ephraim Laniado, who supported his father's position in the controversy with the Francos and perhaps, as hinted above, even encouraged him to remain unyielding, was also unacceptable to them. The Francos, as a separate group within the community, took no part in electing a chief rabbi, and did not directly express their opinion on the matter; but they presumably made that opinion known to the sages and encouraged them to oppose this appointment. Rabbi Ephraim Laniado, a Torah scholar of considerable stature in his own right, was thus forced to act, even though he had been appointed by his father. He formulated a document obligating those who signed it to accept his rulings and to ask his permission whenever they wished another person to sit in judgment.

[55] It should be noted that the tractate *Maḥaneh yehudah* was not published at the time of the controversy, but only in 1803. We do not know why it was published at that particular juncture; perhaps questions connected to the status of the Francos resurfaced around that time. In any event, the publication was entirely funded by the Francos.

Many members of the community did sign this document; however, others questioned its validity.[56]

Rabbi Raphael Solomon Laniado supported his son and protected him, asserting the halakhic validity of his appointment, even though he was prepared to admit that there were other sages in the community who were more learned than him and of greater stature. Right up to his own death on 7 Tevet 5554 (1793), he stubbornly ignored the murmurings against his uncompromising insistence upon his own opinion; indeed, after the appointment of his son he became even more stubborn, perhaps because he felt the growing change in the society that refused to recognize his authority or to submit to him. It was difficult for Raphael Solomon Laniado to accept that he might be the last link in the dynastic chain, the last of his family to head the Aleppo community after an unbroken hereditary succession of so many generations. He was a product of the old, traditional value system. His office and status, like that of his son after him, depended upon this tradition; hence he was unable to accept, or even to engage in a meaningful way with, any challenge to its validity.[57]

Rabbi Laniado won the battle, but the Laniado dynasty was defeated in the war. True, after his death things calmed down: Ephraim Laniado continued to serve in the office until his own death twelve years later, on 28 Shevat 5565 (28 January 1805).[58] But as he had no children, after his death the sages of Aleppo were able to ignore the other members of the Laniado family and to choose as rabbi one of the other sages of the community, who enjoyed the status of first among equals. Thus ended not only the chain of Laniados at the head of the community, but also the practice of inheritance of the rabbinate in Aleppo. Not a single one of the rabbis who headed the Aleppo community in subsequent generations bequeathed his office to his son after him.

Long-Term Influences

This episode raises a number of questions. What repercussions, if any, did it have for the image of the rabbinate in Aleppo in the nineteenth century? Did the new winds which began to be felt in the community create a demand for a

56 On the wording of this document and the questioning of its validity, see R. S. Laniado, *Kise shelomoh*, 5*b*, no. 1; cf. Dweck Hakohen, *Birkat eliyahu*, 99*a*–101*a*, no. 14.

57 An explicit expression of Rabbi R. S. Laniado's conviction on this matter may be seen from his sermon, 'On One Who Bequeaths His Crown to His Son' (Heb.), which was published years prior to the controversy. See R. S. Laniado, *Hama'alot lishelomoh*, 170*a*–172*b*.

58 Even after the death of his father, tension persisted between Rabbi Ephraim and Rabbi Elijah Dweck Hakohen, and the former's statements about the latter are sharp and contemptuous. See e.g. E. Laniado, *Degel*, 'Ḥoshen mishpat', 42*b*, no. 5.

rabbi with different qualities or with more modern training? The answer to both questions is negative. At the beginning of the nineteenth century, the order of government and administration in the Ottoman empire had only begun to change under the influence of the European powers, and a modern approach to the status and authority of the chief rabbi had not yet taken shape. In practice, his spiritual authority was not diminished and he continued to be seen as the head of the community, both in the eyes of the community itself and in those of the Ottoman rulers. Substantial change in the status and functioning of the chief rabbi of Aleppo, and of his counterparts in other communities throughout the Ottoman empire, began to make itself felt only during the second half of the nineteenth century, after the expansion and consolidation of the middle and educated classes, and after the implementation of the Jewish millet decree, which was promulgated in 1864–5.[59]

Another important question is whether the incident discussed above represented a turning point, or at least a shift in direction, in the history of the Aleppo community in its transition from the old world to the new. It is worth examining this question in the broader framework of the city of Aleppo in general. During the eighteenth century, processes of change and modernization began to take place in many areas of the lives of the people of Aleppo, but in many cases their repercussions became clear only in the nineteenth century. Abraham Marcus has already stated decisively that, notwithstanding numerous changes, eighteenth-century Aleppo was still in the earliest stages of its transition to modernity and western influence.[60] This holds true for the Jews as well as for other groups; nevertheless, this community differed from the Muslim community in its absorption of European Jews who may be considered as carriers of their culture to the Middle East. That is, the new world and all its associated values penetrated the Jewish community directly and acted within it and from it. The coming of the Francos and their separation from the established community simultaneously influenced the culture and created a new situation, in which the identification of a community with its religion and culture, one of the express characteristics of communal rule over the centuries, began to weaken. Whereas in the past the community had been accepted as a unifying factor joining all its permanent residents in a cohesive whole, the Jews of Aleppo now began to perceive the outlines of a new world-view, one different from the old and well-known historical reality, in which one might simultaneously remain outside the community and yet act within and influence it. The Francos were Jewish, and yet they maintained a physical

[59] See Levi, 'Changes in the Leadership' (Heb.), and also the following chapters of the present work. On the Jewish millet decree, see Barnai, 'The Jews in the Ottoman Empire' (Heb.), 227–8.

[60] Marcus, *The Middle East*, 230.

separation from the community, living as they did outside the Jewish quarter, and their social point of reference was not specifically Jewish. All this represented a striking innovation in the eyes of Aleppo's Jews. In the dispute surrounding Rabbi Raphael Solomon Laniado described in this chapter, the Aleppo Jews were exposed to another new situation, in which the leaders of the community, both lay leaders and rabbis, acted in opposition to the officially appointed chief rabbi. The interdependence between the rabbinate and the *parnasim*, including the Francos, the new natural leadership, who initially opposed any kind of dependence upon any local rabbi, was breached. The presence in the community of Jews who reside outside the Jewish neighbourhood, who officially do not belong to it, and who question the status of the chief rabbi, are the explicit signs of change in the ways of the Jewish community and its functioning in the new world. Hence we may argue, with a degree of caution, that the entrance of the Aleppo community into the 'modern period', which began with the settlement of the Francos in Aleppo, took further strides around the time of the crisis relating to Ephraim Laniado's inheritance of his father's rabbinic office.[61] Nevertheless, the true fruits of this change, in the actual entry of the Aleppo community into the modern world, became apparent only much later, well into the nineteenth century, after a long period during which the Francos continued to carry the banner of progress, westernization, and modernization of the community, and during which change in the community occurred only slowly.[62] Unlike enlightened European Christian society, conservative Muslim society in the Middle East did not encourage such changes, either within its own communities or among the non-Muslim minorities who lived among them.

[61] Further research is also needed to examine whether and how this incident related to events in other communities in Syria. For example, during the same years in Damascus, while the Galante family held the leadership of the community, the practice of the son inheriting the rabbinate from his father ceased.

[62] For the Francos' influence upon, for example, the penetration of modern education into Aleppo, see Harel, *Syrian Jewry*, 83–91.

PART II

RABBIS OF THE REFORM

CHAPTER THREE

The Saga of Raphael Kassin: From *Ḥakham Bashi* in Baghdad to Reform Rabbi in Aleppo

When a communal leader lords it over the public, The Holy One—blessed be He—weeps on him every day.

BT *Ḥagigah* 8*b*

The Background and Youth of Raphael Kassin

According to family tradition, the first Kassins to come to Aleppo arrived in the wake of the expulsion from Spain. They and their descendants lived in the city continuously from that point on. Over the generations, many members of the family became prominent Torah scholars, some of them even serving as rabbinic judges in the community.[1] The greatest of these was Rabbi Yehudah Kassin who, towards the end of the eighteenth century, opposed the attempt by the chief rabbi of Aleppo, Rabbi Raphael Solomon Laniado, to impose upon those European Jews who had settled in Aleppo—the 'Francos'—the edicts and regulations of the established local community.[2] Yehudah Kassin's grandson, Raphael Kassin, was the only son of his father, Elijah Kassin, who also served as head of the rabbinic court in Aleppo. Rabbi Elijah Kassin was a wealthy man, who spoiled his son and gave him everything he needed so that the young man could devote himself entirely to study, without having to earn his own living. As Raphael Kassin himself testifies:

I was the young and only son of my father and lived in an '[ivory] tower' while I was growing up . . . He provided me with my daily bread to my full satisfaction, as well as raiment; altogether, he spared me naught—bed, table, chair, and lamp—to magnify and glorify Torah. And his proper intention was that I sit and increase in wisdom, and he graciously told me: I shall provide whatever you lack, even if there is the slightest doubt of what is needed for [studying] Torah . . . and I, in humility,

[1] See J. Kassin, *Peri ets hagan*, 122–4.
[2] See Ch. 2 above.

nodded my agreement . . . all those years [i.e. when his father was alive] I sat calm and contented in my house in my palace, sitting in wisdom, and I inclined my ears to my teachers and was diligent in my studies, and did not stir from within the tent.[3]

The studious young Raphael Kassin acquitted himself well, and acquired a reputation for having a sharp mind as well as expertise in Torah and Jewish law. By the time of his father's death in 1830, he had already written three books: *Ma'arekhet hashulḥan*, consisting of dialectic narratives (*pilpul*) and practical halakhah on Joseph Karo's *Shulḥan arukh*, 'Ḥoshen mishpat'; *Yein harekaḥ*, sermons on Torah; and *Leḥem hama'arekhet*, glosses and *pilpul* on Rabbi Shabetai ben Me'ir Hakohen's book *Tekafo kohen*.[4]

His father's death was a turning point in Raphael Kassin's life. The loss of his economic support, combined with his failure to gain appointment as head of the rabbinic court in his father's place, prompted him to leave Aleppo on a journey of wandering and seeking:

My pain was very great when the holy ark, the head of the rabbinic court . . . the rabbi, my master and father, was taken . . . My soul was hardly left in me . . . I was benumbed and depressed, and I became ill with consumption and fever . . . And from the time that my beloved one departed, I am in the midst of exile, tossed about like a man at unease . . . I am estranged from Aram Zova, the city of my birth.[5]

In the course of his wanderings, Raphael Kassin went to Persia. There he encountered, for the first time in his life, remote Jewish communities on the point of abandoning their religion, both because of their distance from the study of Torah and because of the pressures of the surrounding Muslim society. Raphael Kassin engaged in polemics with both Muslim and Christian scholars on issues of faith and religion in the presence of the Persian shah and, by his own testimony, won the argument.[6] At the end of his travels, Kassin turned westward once again, to Baghdad. His arrival there in 1846 marks the beginning of a new chapter in the history of Baghdad Jewry. Here he was appointed as the city's first *ḥakham bashi*, an appointment ratified by

[3] R. Kassin, *Derekh haḥayim*, author's introduction.

[4] There are contradictory data concerning the date of Raphael Kassin's birth. Ben-Ya'akov, relying upon the statement of the traveller Benjamin II, states that in 1848 Kassin was 30 years old, and rejects the statement of Rabbi Jacob Saul Kassin (*Peri ets hagan*, 129) that Rabbi Kassin was in fact 58 years old in that year (Ben-Ya'akov, *Babylonian Jewry from the End of the Geonic Period* (Heb.), 157 n. 9). While the testimony of Benjamin II, who was a contemporary of Rabbi Kassin, is more likely to be correct, he probably meant that at that time the rabbi was in his thirties. Otherwise it is difficult to understand how he managed to write the three books mentioned here at such an early age.

[5] R. Kassin, *Derekh haḥayim*, author's introduction.

[6] Ibid. On the background of the disputes that occurred in Persia during Kassin's stay there, see Harel, '"Likutei amarim"' (Heb.).

the Ottoman sultan.[7] This brought to an end the rule of the Baghdad community by the *nasi*; in its stead came a series of chief rabbis endorsed by the imperial authorities. Underlying this great change was the gradual implementation of the Ottoman reforms laid down in the Hatt-i şerif of Gülhane in 1839.

The Ottoman Reforms and Jewish Communal Organization

The inferior position occupied by the Jews in Ottoman society and the different status accorded them in Ottoman law, as well as their ethnic, religious, and cultural separation from the surrounding society, all contributed to their creation of a separate, autonomous social framework. Underlying the creation of this framework was the desire to protect the community and its members, and—as far as possible—to improve Jews' living conditions. As noted above, the Ottoman system of government permitted and even encouraged the various religious communities within its territories to organize their own internal institutions and to conduct themselves in accordance with their own laws in matters of religion and personal status. Given that communities at this time and in this region tended to identify themselves primarily by religious allegiance, the placing of a rabbi at the head of the Jewish community was consistent both with the Ottoman system of government and the inclinations of the Jewish public, who looked to their rabbis for guidance and instruction. The rabbi's expertise in halakhic literature—on which everyday Jewish life was based—made him a figure of authority.

The rabbi was not, however, the sole source of authority in the community. It is worth noting in this context that in a number of communities it was specifically one of the *parnasim* who in practice headed the community, and to whom even the rabbis were at times subject. Such was the case in Baghdad: until the middle of the nineteenth century the community was headed by the *nasi*, who was in no sense an authority on Torah. The rabbi, as head of the religious court, worked alongside the *nasi*, but was usually overshadowed by him.[8]

During the middle years of the nineteenth century the institutions of

[7] Details of this appointment were published by Ben-Ya'akov, *Babylonian Jewry from the End of the Geonic Period* (Heb.); id., *Babylonian Jewry in Recent Times* (Heb.). Ben-Ya'akov states that, in describing both this and other incidents, he also drew upon the diary of Rabbi Samuel Abraham Sadkah. In practice, as he himself admits, he never saw the complete, original diary, but only three collections of excerpts. While I of course made use of the words of Ben-Ya'akov, I also referred to BZI MS 3750, which is in turn also based in part upon the diary of Rabbi Samuel Abraham Sadkah.

[8] See Ch. 1 above.

Jewish communities throughout the empire underwent a process of reorganization and restructuring, prompted by similar processes of reform in Ottoman governance and aiming to bring the Jewish framework more into line with Ottoman institutions. Although this refashioning was largely conducted under the guidance and encouragement of the imperial authorities, it also represented an expression of social ferment and dissatisfaction with the old leadership arrangements.

As part of its mid-century reform of government and administration, the Ottoman regime re-examined its relations with the empire's non-Muslim minorities, with a view to achieving more effective rule by means of greater involvement in minority self-government. The outcome for the Jews was the creation by the Ottoman rulers of an administrative and representative position to be occupied by a senior Jewish official—the *ḥakham bashi*—whose function was to represent the Jewish community at state ceremonies, and to a certain degree also to serve as the point of contact between the imperial rulers and the Jewish public.[9] This innovation took the community's secular affairs out of the hands of its titular chief—in the case of Baghdad, the *nasi*. In practice, a separation came about, albeit unofficially, between the handling of the community's spiritual affairs and that of its practical, worldly concerns. The *ḥakham bashi* did not necessarily need to be a Torah scholar of stature; the priority was that he should be a rabbinic figure of proven political talents. His authority derived, first and foremost, from the ruling powers, and only thereafter from his selection and approval by the community.

A contemporary observer described the new office in the following terms:

A new thing has been introduced by His Majesty the King: that there should be a *ḥakham bashi* in all places of his rule. This matter is unrelated to the position of the rabbinic court judges, who are the crown of Torah, for the crown of Torah rests upon the greatest rabbi in the city . . . rather, this rule [i.e. that of the *ḥakham bashi*] is under the aegis of the king, [and is thus] the crown of kingship. And the proof of this is that in Kushta [Istanbul] which is the king's main capital city, we have an 'old father', the rabbi of the community—may the Merciful One guard and save him—but this royal seal is given to the one whom the public has elected to rule over them as an official of His Majesty the King. Thus, the prerogatives of this individual do not and will not touch upon those of the rabbinate, albeit it would have been fitting that the one who has merited the crown of Torah should also merit this crown of kingship, as mentioned. But since the King does not wish this, we return to the rule

[9] On the origins of the institution of the *ḥakham bashi* in Istanbul, see Levy, 'The Founding of the Institution of the *Ḥakham Bashi*' (Heb.).

that the 'the law of the land is the law' (*dina demalkhuta dina*). After all, this post is a gift that His Majesty the King gave to the one he prefers.[10]

This lucid account makes it clear beyond doubt that the initiative in creating the office of *ḥakham bashi* was taken by the governing authorities.[11] The creation of the new office threatened to render the office of *nasi* in Baghdad superfluous. At the time when Rabbi Raphael Kassin arrived in Baghdad, the campaign being waged by the wealthy *gevirim* of the community to abolish the office of *nasi* and to establish a board of seven of their own number to run the community in its place was at its height. The tension between the *nasi* and the other wealthy laymen would play a prominent role in the struggles that ensued around the functioning and position of Rabbi Kassin in Baghdad.

The Struggle to Create an Alternative to the *Nasi*

Throughout the 1840s the *nasi* in Baghdad was Joseph Moses David Benjamin, known as Abu Farkha. Alongside a significant number of reports by travellers and rabbinic emissaries which describe him in glowing terms, for example as a 'wise and wealthy and generous man',[12] or 'the tremendous *gevir*, the prince in Israel, the renowned righteous man, who executed the just commands of the Lord and His laws in Israel',[13] there are other accounts according to which he ruled the community in a high-handed manner. The main expression of the latter view appears in a letter by Rabbi Obadiah Abraham Halevi, head of the rabbinic court in Baghdad, to the *rishon letsiyon* in Jerusalem, Rabbi Abraham Hayim Gagin. Halevi was born in Damascus, but emigrated to Erets Yisra'el and settled in Jerusalem. In 1841 he was sent as an emissary to Baghdad, and there he was asked to replace Rabbi Elijah ben Yehoshua Obadiah as head of the rabbinic court.[14] It would appear that the *nasi*, Joseph Benjamin, chose him not only because he was a great Torah scholar, but also because he was 'extremely modest and humble',[15] and—as a foreign rabbi who lacked a local power base and was not involved in internal communal politics—would be entirely dependent upon the *nasi*, to whom he owed his office, his status, and his salary. It would seem that this appointment was imposed upon the sages of Baghdad, for there was an excellent candidate

[10] Y. Alfandari, *Porat yosef*, 'Ḥoshen mishpat', 69*a*, §2. See also Yadid Halevi, *A Ruling* (Heb.), 15–18, 35–7.

[11] For a discussion of this issue see Levy, 'The Founding of the Institution of the *Ḥakham Bashi*' (Heb.), 42–54.

[12] See e.g. Benjamin, *Travels of Israel*, 45.

[13] Schneour, *Zikhron yerushalayim*, 21*a*; cf. *Hamagid*, 49 (16 Dec. 1868), 387.

[14] On these two rabbis, see Ben-Ya'akov, *Babylonian Jewry from the End of the Geonic Period* (Heb.), 136–7, 157, 161–2.

[15] *Hamagid*, 2 (12 Jan. 1876), 13.

already available in the city: the outstanding Torah scholar Rabbi Abdallah Somekh, who was in his early thirties at this time and was already the well-regarded head of a well-established *beit midrash*.[16] However, while the sages could have appointed a chief rabbinic judge from among their own number, they did not have the authority to impose their choice upon the *nasi*.[17]

On more than one occasion the *nasi* ignored the rulings of the head of the rabbinic court whom he himself had appointed. So long as he had no backing from any other source, Rabbi Halevi was unable to assert his authority over the secular chief. Then, about three years after Halevi's appointment, a rift opened up between the head of the rabbinic court and the *nasi*. Rabbi Halevi ruled against one of the *nasi*'s associates in a financial dispute with some Jewish traders in Basra. Benjamin delivered his response to the judgment in the synagogue before the whole community. As he cursed and insulted Halevi for daring to deliver such a ruling, his son attacked the rabbi physically and began to beat him; the supporters of the *nasi* joined in the assault. The bleeding rabbi was saved only by the intervention of a rabbinic emissary from Hebron who happened to be present, and who came to his rescue together with a number of members of the community. No wonder, then, that Rabbi Halevi wrote that Joseph Benjamin ruled the community with an iron hand, and without restraint, by virtue of his great wealth and the verbal and physical violence he wielded against his opponents.[18]

This event marked a turning point in the governance of the Jews of Baghdad. The wealthy men of the community, who had evidently been unhappy with the *nasi*'s autocratic and authoritarian rule for some time, attempted to make use of the assault not only to remove him from office, but to abolish the position altogether and to set up an alternative system of collective leadership consisting of seven individuals selected from among the wealthy and prominent members of the community. Nevertheless, the *gevirim* did not complain about the *nasi* to the Ottoman authorities, possibly suspecting that the *nasi*'s business connections with the imperial rulers would tip the scales in his favour from the outset. Instead, they issued an appeal to the rabbis of Erets Yisra'el, headed by the *rishon letsiyon*, Rabbi Abraham Hayim Gagin, asking them to limit the authority of the *nasi* and require him to act in accordance

[16] On Rabbi Abdallah Somekh and his activities, see Ben-Ya'akov, *Biography of Rabbi Abdallah Somekh* (Heb.); cf. Zohar, 'The Attitude of Rav Abdallah Somekh' (Heb.).

[17] Ben-Ya'akov argues, probably out of respect for the sages of Baghdad, that they gave way on the point 'out of honour to Jerusalem': Ben-Ya'akov, *Babylonian Jewry from the End of the Geonic Period* (Heb.), 157 n. 7.

[18] JNUL, DMA, V-736/51, Ovadiah Halevi to Rabbi Aga'n, 10 Elul 5604; the letter appears in Ben-Ya'akov, *Babylonian Jewry in Recent Times* (Heb.), 174–8.

with the instructions of the rabbinic court. In order to emphasize the gravity of the issue, the question was presented to the rabbis of Jerusalem and Hebron first and foremost as an insult to the emissaries from Israel. After all, the *gevirim* argued, Rabbi Halevi had come to Baghdad in the first instance as a rabbinic emissary, and his subjection to verbal and physical abuse might well deter future emissaries from visiting the city, to the detriment of efforts to gather money for Erets Yisra'el.[19]

Even before the assault on Rabbi Halevi, the *gevirim* had attempted to establish a collective leadership to organize tax collection, charitable activities, and contributions to the emissaries, motivated by suspicion that the *nasi* and his circle were not contributing adequately to the communal coffers, thereby causing the burden to fall disproportionately upon other members of the community. However, the *nasi* contrived to foil their plans in various ways. Now, following the beating of Rabbi Halevi, the *gevirim* took up the campaign once more, turning to the *rishon letsiyon* in Jerusalem to ask for his support for a new communal leadership body, to be composed of seven *gevirim*.[20]

Yet again, it seems, the *gevirim*'s attempt to rein in the *nasi* failed, and Joseph Benjamin continued to run the community's affairs in an arbitrary and high-handed manner. Rabbi Halevi seems to have made his peace with the *nasi*, maybe willingly, maybe simply because he had little choice. In any event, the mood of the community continued to be turbulent and internal struggles continued. The status of the local Torah scholars, most of whom supported the *gevirim*, was at the lowest conceivable level. Nor was much respect paid to emissaries from Erets Yisra'el, who came to Baghdad every three years to solicit contributions. The emissary of the Sephardi community in Jerusalem was the only one invited to stay as a guest in the home of one of the wealthy members of the community and to eat at his table. The others—such as the representatives of the North African community, or those of the kabbalistic Yeshivat Bet-El—as well as poor people passing through Baghdad in the course of their wanderings and seeking food to keep themselves alive, were forced to live in the courtyard of the *beit midrash* of the *talmud torah* or as guests in one of the *khans* (inns) scattered throughout the city. The failure of the Jews of Baghdad to open their homes to these guests was justified by a contemporary in terms of their desire to protect their wives from the gaze of strange men.[21]

[19] Ben-Ya'akov, *Babylonian Jewry in Recent Times* (Heb.) 177–8. On the emissaries and the attitude towards them, see Ben-Ya'akov, 'Emissaries from Erets Yisra'el' (Heb.).

[20] Ben-Ya'akov, *Babylonian Jewry in Recent Times* (Heb.), 178.

[21] See JNUL, DMA, V-736/88, Nisim Farhi to Abraham Hayim Gagin, Baghdad, 5 Tevet

It was against this background that Raphael Kassin arrived in Baghdad on Rosh Hodesh, Iyar 5606 (1846).

Raphael Kassin's Involvement in the Baghdad Community's Internal Conflicts

Kassin did not receive a gracious welcome in Baghdad. According to extant accounts, neither the *nasi* nor any of his supporters, even though they already knew the rabbi from the period when he had stayed in the city on his way to Persia, offered him hospitality in their homes. Kassin was thus forced to rent a room in a *khan* owned by non-Jews. Some months later, in September 1846, he was invited by the wealthy householder Ezra Zilkha and his sons to stay in their home. During the cholera epidemic that broke out in the city that month the *gevir* died, and his sons, accompanied by Raphael Kassin, fled to one of the surrounding villages until the epidemic had passed. It would seem that it was during his stay in the Zilkha home that Rabbi Kassin, who was deeply hurt by the community leadership's attitude towards him, became aware of the severity of the community's internal struggles, and of the profound hostility that existed between the *gevirim* and the *nasi*. He was deeply pained by the *nasi*'s derogatory attitude towards both the local sages and the emissaries from Erets Yisra'el, and he urged Ezra Zilkha's sons and their supporters to oppose Benjamin—demanding in addition that he cease the practice of not offering hospitality to scholars.[22]

This was the beginning of Kassin's entanglement in the dispute between the wealthy laymen and sages of the community, on the one hand, and the *nasi* and his supporters, on the other. Evidently a charismatic figure and an impressive leader, he continued to act openly against the authority of the *nasi*, contesting particularly the latter's arrogation to himself of the right to act as he pleased, even in cases where he should have consulted the rabbinic authorities. Thus, for example, Rabbi Kassin ruled that the gates of the synagogue building, which the *nasi* had decreed was to be reassigned as a *talmud torah* for small children, were to be reopened.[23]

Finding this new and able figure in their midst, the wealthy laymen and their associates among the sages and scholars of the city now took to ignoring Rabbi Halevi, the head of the rabbinic court, who was in practice the puppet of the *nasi*, and addressing their halakhic questions instead to Rabbi Kassin.

5607; reproduced in Ben-Ya'akov, *Babylonian Jewry in Recent Times* (Heb.), 167–8. Cf. also the comments of Ya'akov Obermeier in *Hamagid*, 5 (2 Feb. 1876), 40.

22 Ben-Ya'akov, *Babylonian Jewry in Recent Times* (Heb.), 167; cf. BZI, MS 3750.

23 Ben-Ya'akov, *Babylonian Jewry in Recent Times* (Heb.), 167; cf. Y. Alfandari, *Porat yosef*, 65*a*.

Thus, in effect, the foreign rabbi became the leader of the rebellion against the *nasi*, who had in the past been able to suppress any spark of rebellion among the scholars, both the local rabbis and the emissaries from Erets Yisra'el. The fact that R. Kassin was not a native of the city exacerbated the hostility of the *nasi* and his supporters, who took to asking: 'What business has this foreigner among us'?[24]

The *nasi* and his supporters would have been unable to act against Rabbi Kassin had they not enjoyed the support of several of the most important rabbis and scholars of the city—who were not, it must be noted, above allowing pragmatic calculations to influence the positions they chose to take. This group of rabbis was led by Rabbi Elijah Hayim, son of Rabbi Moses Hayim and father of Rabbi Joseph Hayim, who years later came to be known as the Ben Ish Hai. Elijah Hayim was evidently less talented than his father, who over the course of many years had trained a number of local rabbinic scholars, conferring upon them some of his authority. When, in the last years of his life, he retired from his position as a rabbinic judge, he set up a court of three of his students, but did not include among them his son Elijah.[25] Elijah Hayim was primarily a preacher and active community worker, responsible for the distribution of alms and other welfare activities. Raphael Kassin had a modest opinion of his abilities, describing him as follows: 'The Hakham Elijah, son of our Teacher Moses Hayim of blessed memory, does not take the place of his ancestors in wisdom . . . and he has not even one of ten parts of wisdom in comparison to his own father.'[26]

The wealthy leaders of the community had for some time suspected Elijah Hayim of embezzling some of the charitable funds for which he was responsible. Judging the income of these funds to be far greater than the sums used by Hayim to assist the poor people of the community, they suspected that he had pocketed the difference. Some years before Rabbi Kassin's arrival in the community, the *gevirim* had demanded that Rabbi Hayim produce accounts for these funds, but he had refused to co-operate. Now they turned to Rabbi Kassin to support their demand, which would lend it halakhic force.[27] Moreover, as well as making repeated appeals to Rabbi Kassin to issue halakhic rulings concerning the internal matters of the community, those *gevirim* who were opposed to the *nasi* expressed their desire to appoint

24 Ben-Ya'akov, *Babylonian Jewry in Recent Times* (Heb.), 167.

25 See Ben-Ya'akov, *Babylonian Jewry from the End of the Geonic Period* (Heb.), 128; id., 'A New Source' (Heb.).

26 Y. Alfandari, *Porat yosef*, 65*a*.

27 On the suspicions about Elijah Hayim, see Y. Alfandari, *Porat yosef*; Ben-Ya'akov, 'A New Source' (Heb.), 161.

him as head of the rabbinic court in place of Rabbi Halevi. These moves represented a challenge to both Elijah Hayim, who felt his own status—which he owed entirely to his father's eminence—was under threat, and to the *nasi* himself, Joseph Benjamin. So these two representatives of the old leadership elite joined forces and began a series of attempts not only to prevent Kassin's installation as head of the rabbinic court, but to bring about his ejection from the city altogether.

Thus the Baghdad community split into two groups. One group appointed Kassin head of the rabbinic court in place of Halevi, hoping thereby to create a counterweight to the unrestrained power of the *nasi*. This group, known as the 'Kassini faction', included those *gevirim* who wanted to see an end to the system of rule by a *nasi*, joined by a considerable portion of the local rabbis. The other group, which opposed the replacement of Halevi by Kassin, was was known as the 'Abidi [from Obadiah] faction' and was headed by the *nasi*, Joseph Benjamin, and Elijah Hayim. This group also included the *nasi*'s close associates, including several rabbinic scholars of the first rank, such as David Hai Me'ir Joseph Nisim and Sason Elijah Halevi (Samokha), relatives of Elijah Hayim and students of his father.[28] The emissaries from Erets Yisra'el were, not surprisingly, divided between the two groups:[29] some supported Rabbi Kassin, hoping that he would improve their reception by the Baghdad community, while others hoped that if they supported the *nasi* they would be more likely to receive monetary gifts from him, which was important for the success of their mission.

According to the testimony of one emissary from Erets Yisra'el, Nisim Farhi, the *nasi* and his supporters laid false charges, supported by false testimony, against Rabbi Kassin and his supporters among the local scholars and the emissaries from Erets Yisra'el and sent these accusations to the *rishon letsiyon*, Abraham Hayim Gagin, in Jerusalem. At the same time, a rabbinic court in Baghdad headed by Rabbi Halevi declared a ban on Kassin. Kassin, who continued to have the support of the *gevirim* as well as that of a substantial part of the general Jewish community of Baghdad, responded by asserting that his accusers had acted improperly and that any such charges should be heard by three judges without any vested interest in the matter. He declared his commitment to abiding by whatever decision such a court reached. In the event, the broad public support Kassin enjoyed prevented the implementation of the *ḥerem* against him, forcing the members of the rabbinic court to

[28] See JNUL, DMA, V-736/224, where their signatures appear on an undated letter to Abraham Hayim Gagin.

[29] See Ben-Ya'akov, *Babylonian Jewry from the End of the Geonic Period* (Heb.), 157–8; id., *Babylonian Jewry in Recent Times* (Heb.), 167–8.

rescind it. In an attempt to restore peace in the community, Kassin agreed to the insulting demand of the members of the rabbinic court that he publicly ask forgiveness of the sages of Baghdad by declaring in person: 'I have sinned against the God of Israel and against the holy community of Baghdad.'[30] He nevertheless held fast to his position that the entire matter should be put before a disinterested court for clarification. Kassin's noble act of seeking public forgiveness, notwithstanding the refusal of the members of the Baghdadi court to allow him a fair trial, won him further supporters among the Jews of Baghdad; but it did not, as he had intended, restore harmony. The disputes between the 'Kassini faction' and the 'Abidi faction' deteriorated to the point of their exchanging blows in the synagogue.[31]

It is worth emphasizing at this point that sages from Aleppo enjoyed tremendous respect in Baghdad. The Aleppo community had exerted great influence upon the communities of Baghdad and Basra from at least the eighteenth century, and especially since Rabbi Sadkah Houssin of Aleppo had been appointed rabbi of Baghdad in 1744. Rabbi Houssin had in effect rebuilt the Baghdad community, which had disintegrated in almost all respects. The high point of his work there was his success in bringing about a spiritual revolution of far-reaching implications, which at a later stage transformed Baghdad into a major Torah centre.[32] Many Aleppan merchants settled in Baghdad, so that the city's wealthy elite came to include a good number of Jews of Aleppan origin; these evidently preferred to have a rabbi from Aleppo at the head of their community. In addition, wealthy laymen and merchants born in Baghdad who visited Aleppo in the course of their business travels found there a thriving group of Torah sages with strong connections among the wealthy men of the city.[33] The recognition accorded to the sages of Aleppo by the *gevirim* of Baghdad is reflected in the contributions they made to the printing costs of a significant number of books by these sages. They came to understand that in Aleppo, while the chief rabbi was nominal head of the community, and the Torah scholars enjoyed much respect, the community's material affairs were conducted, with its agreement, by the class of *parnasim*. Hence, when Raphael Kassin arrived in Baghdad, at a time when the institution of the *nasi* was on the brink of abolition as part of the programme of

30 Ben-Ya'akov, *Babylonian Jewry in Recent Times* (Heb.), 168.

31 See Ben-Ya'akov, *Babylonian Jewry from the End of the Geonic Period* (Heb.), 158 n. 13.

32 On the appointment and activity of Rabbi Sadkah Houssin see Ch. 1 above.

33 On the business relationships between tradesmen in Baghdad and in Aleppo see e.g. Dweck Hakohen, *Birkat eliyahu*, 93*b*, §6; Antebi, *Mor ve'aholot*, 92*b*, §11. On the origins of the earliest Aleppo group in Baghdad, see Yehudah, 'Transformations' (Heb.); id., 'Connections' (Heb.); and Ch. 1 above.

imperial administrative reform, the *gevirim* sought to imitate the Aleppan model of leadership by placing him at the head of the community.[34] Needless to say, Joseph Benjamin, the *nasi*, who had no intention of relinquishing his autocratic rule over the community, was opposed to this.

At the same time, there were certain rabbinic figures in Baghdad—such as, for example, Elijah Hayim—who sought to expand the reach of their authority into the material affairs of the community. While Rabbi Hayim and his supporters among the city's rabbis showed great respect for the sages and rabbis of Aleppo, they resisted total subordination to an Aleppan—all the more strongly because Hayim and his associates were both allies of the *nasi* and opposed to Kassin's appointment as the ally of the *gevirim* who sought to remove control of charitable funds from Hayim.

The Struggle to Obtain a Sultanic Appointment for the *Ḥakham Bashi*

The struggle between the Kassini group and the Abidi group remained unresolved. Some of the sources that comment on the affair assert that the opponents of Raphael Kassin, with the help of the local authorities, succeeded in having Kassin expelled from Baghdad in February 1847,[35] but other sources do not mention this at all; on the contrary, it appears from these accounts that, even though the *nasi* of the community bribed government officials in his attempt to bring down the rabbi from Aleppo, he did not succeed in doing so. Moreover, it seems clear that when Kassin left Baghdad for Istanbul that year, he did so with the explicit aim of obtaining a firman (edict) for his appointment as the first *ḥakham bashi* in Baghdad.[36] What appears to have happened, then, is not that Kassin was expelled from the city, but that his numerous confrontations with his opponents had led him and his supporters to the conclusion that they could not carry out the revolution in the leadership of the community they had hoped to achieve unless they had the backing of the authorities. They also understood that without such official endorsement Kassin would be unable to impose his own authority over the community in general. Hence he left for Istanbul on his own initiative, intending to return to Baghdad armed with a firman from the sultan confirming his appointment as *ḥakham bashi*. As a high-ranking government official bearing this new title—so he and his supporters believed—he would enjoy un-

[34] On the struggle in Aleppo between the elite and the rabbinic leadership, and the reconciliation between them at the end of the 18th century, see Ch. 2 above.

[35] See e.g. BZI, MS 3750. This version was also adopted by Ben-Ya'akov, *Babylonian Jewry from the End of the Geonic Period* (Heb.), 158.

[36] Y. Alfandari, *Porat yosef*, 64*b*–65*a*.

disputed standing as head of the community leadership, and his opponents would be effectively prevented from acting in opposition to his rulings. Accordingly, his supporters among the *gevirim* and rabbis of Baghdad gave him a letter to the *ḥakham bashi* in Istanbul, Rabbi Jacob Bekhor David, requesting that he use his influence with the Sublime Porte to have Raphael Kassin officially appointed *ḥakham bashi* of Baghdad.

Once the Abidi group became aware of what the Kassini group was doing, it too addressed a letter to the *ḥakham bashi* in Istanbul, asking that Rabbi Kassin not be appointed *ḥakham bashi* in Baghdad. This letter was indeed written with the support of, and in accordance with instructions from, the *rishon letsiyon*, Abraham Gagin, to whom Rabbi Kassin's opponents had previously appealed.[37] Some of those who had supported the candidature of Rabbi Kassin now recanted and signed his opponents' letter, possibly influenced by the express wishes of the *rishon letsiyon*. When this letter, signed by some of the people who had also signed the earlier letter in favour of Kassin, arrived in Istanbul it caused a good deal of confusion. The text of the letter attempted to clarify matters by arguing that those who changed sides had realized that Kassin had deceived them, telling them that he intended to leave Baghdad and asking for a letter of recommendation to show to the *ḥakham bashi* in Istanbul. Those who wanted to see him go were therefore happy to sign the letter. However, they claimed, once Kassin had arrived in the city of Mosul they heard a rumour that he was declaring that the whole point of his going to Istanbul was to receive an official appointment from the sultan as *ḥakham bashi* of Baghdad; therefore, they quickly signed the letter opposing this. Benjamin, who initiated the second letter, must have feared that, were Kassin to return to Baghdad with the title of *ḥakham bashi*, he would be able to strip the *nasi* of his function and status in the community. Hence he argued in the letter that Baghdad did not need a *ḥakham bashi* at all:

Behold, we the undersigned hereby declare our view before His Highness, the honour of His Torah, may God protect him, that we do not wish that there be a *ḥakham bashi* [here] at all, for this will cause great controversy within the entire community. Therefore we implore you, that if it be true that the above-mentioned Hakham Rabbi Raphael wishes to be *ḥakham bashi* in our city, that his Highness, the honour of his Torah, withhold this matter from him entirely, for we do not wish to have the above Hakham Rabbi Raphael over us as *ḥakham bashi*. For if we would wish to have

[37] See JNUL, DMA V-736/24, undated letter signed by twelve prominent figures from Baghdad to Rabbi Abraham Hayim Gagin. It appears from the letter that the contact between the opponents of Rabbi Kassin and the *rishon letsiyon* was the brother of Rabbi Elijah Hayim, Abdallah ben Rabbi Moses Hayim, who settled in Jerusalem in 1841. On him, see Ben-Ya'akov, 'Documents from Jerusalem' (Heb.).

a *ḥakham bashi*, we have among us—praise be to God—many wise and perceptive men.[38]

Should the sultan insist on appointing someone to the role of *ḥakham bashi*, Kassin's opponents of course had an alternative candidate to hand in the person of Elijah Hayim, who posed no threat to the status of the *nasi* and had shown no intention of changing the existing order in the community.

Once Kassin's supporters became aware of the existence of his opponents' letter, they quickly sent another letter of their own to Istanbul, setting out in detail how the hostility of the *nasi* and Elijah Hayim towards Rabbi Kassin had developed. Kassin's supporters further accused the two of them of having forged a number of the signatures on the letter opposing his appointment as *ḥakham bashi*. The *gevirim* reiterated their position: they were prepared to accept Raphael Kassin, and only him, as *ḥakham bashi*. To this letter, Kassin himself added a list of several points in which he detailed his complaints against his opponents. He claimed first that the *nasi* had threatened a number of his supporters, for which reason alone they had added their signatures at the end of his opponents' letter. He argued further that his own supporters represented a majority of members of the community. Two other points related to Elijah Hayim, the alternative candidate supported by his opponents: first, Kassin stated that Elijah Hayim did not deserve the appointment on his own merits; and second, he suggested that, if he wished to serve in place of his father by virtue of inheritance, the appropriate office for him would be that of rabbinic judge and not that of *ḥakham bashi*, a distinct office that had been introduced by the government. Kassin also put his arguments to other Torah scholars in Istanbul, requesting their support, and also the well-known *gevir* Abraham Kamondo, who had extensive connections and influence in the sultan's palace.[39]

For the Ottoman officials, the appointment of a *ḥakham bashi* at the head of the Baghdad community was an appropriate move, consistent with their plans for reform in the administration and control of the empire's minority communities. Baghdad had been under Ottoman rule since 1831, when Mameluke rule had been eliminated. Shortly thereafter the Ottoman central administration embarked on a series of reforms, beginning in 1839 with the order known as the Hatt-i şerif of Gülhane, aimed at improving the status of all the empire's subjects, especially that of the non-Muslim minorities.[40]

[38] Y. Alfandari, *Porat yosef*, 64*b*.

[39] Ibid. 65*a*; Ben-Ya'akov, *Babylonian Jewry from the End of the Geonic Period* (Heb.), 158. On Abraham Kamondo, see Asulin, *The Last of the House of Kamondo* (Heb.), 71–86.

[40] On the Ottoman reform, see Davison, *Reform in the Ottoman Empire*; cf. Lewis, *The Emergence of Modern Turkey*, 60–103; Tsur, *Introduction* (Heb.), 2.

These reforms also led, as noted above, to greater involvement of the imperial administration in the affairs of the Jewish communities. As the reforms were implemented, both the full autonomy which the Jews had enjoyed for centuries and the traditional framework of their communal leadership were disrupted, as the architects of reform sought to reshape the institutions of Jewish leadership in accordance with the patterns accepted in Ottoman law. As part of this process, the Ottoman authorities wanted to place a clergyman at the head of the community in Baghdad, as had been done in the other major communities of the empire.

As a result of this combination of factors, and with the assistance, advice, and recommendation of the *gevirim* of Istanbul, Kassin was officially appointed as *ḥakham bashi*, and returned to Baghdad on 9 January 1848, about a year after he had left, adorned in the robes of office with a decoration from the sultan. The institution of the *nasi* had been almost completely emptied of content, and was later formally abolished by the authorities.[41] For the first time, the Jewish community of Baghdad was headed by an ordained rabbi and renowned scholar of Torah, with extremely broad powers placed at his disposal by the government. In theory, there was a balance between his power and that of the *gevirim*, but in practice, at the beginning of his term of office, the rabbi was unable to take any significant action without the consent of the *gevirim*, who had helped to get him appointed.[42] However, over time the *ḥakham bashi* gradually began to consolidate his authority and to act as sole ruler of the community.

Rule, Conflict, and Deposition

Once Rabbi Kassin had returned to Baghdad armed with a firman from the sultan and the moral support of the rabbis of Istanbul, his position was beyond challenge. Kassin established himself and became part of Jewish life in Baghdad; he planned to settle there and even married a local woman, who bore him a daughter.[43] He set about the exercise of his new role energetically, introducing various edicts and changing established arrangements in order to set the community on a new path. Thus, for example, he succeeded in bringing about a major change in the attitude of the wealthy laymen of the community towards the emissaries from Erets Yisra'el. Travellers who passed through Baghdad noted that the *gevirim* began to open their homes and their hands generously to those who were in need.[44] On the other hand, the con-

[41] See Benjamin, *Travels of Israel* (Heb.), 45; *Hamagid*, 49 (22 Dec. 1875), 435.

[42] Benjamin, *Travels of Israel* (Heb.), 45.

[43] BZI, MS 3750.

[44] See Benjamin, *Travels of Israel* (Heb.), 47.

sciousness of finally being in a position of power seems to have led the *ḥakham bashi* to behave aggressively towards his opponents and even to take his revenge on them—starting with Obadiah Halevi, whom he removed from his position as head of the rabbinic court, appointing in his place a prominent local sage, Rabbi Jacob ben Joseph Jacob.[45] He also took another step of great public significance: on Shabat Hagadol and Shabat Shuvah, the sabbaths before Passover and Yom Kippur respectively, he gave the central sermon in the main synagogue himself, thereby forcing Rabbi Elijah Hayim, who had previously enjoyed the prerogative of giving these sermons, to deliver his address in a smaller synagogue. However, this move seems to have backfired. Despite the shortcomings attributed to Hayim, many people in the Baghdad community saw him as continuing his father's tradition and disapproved of his being humiliated in this way.[46]

Growing opposition to Kassin was fuelled by his arrogant behaviour. One observer described how he assumed the trappings of royalty when he went out into the streets of the city:

> And he was greatly honoured by the governor of the district, who placed at his disposal four soldiers as a fixed honour guard at the entrance to his home. In addition there were six Jews who were subject to his orders, whom he sent out to execute his commands. And whenever he went out of the gates of his home, the men of his honour guard rode before him on horses, as if before a prince of the country. As a sign of honour and greatness he carried on his heart the great sign of honour from the government . . . which very, very few Jews had ever received from the high government.[47]

Contrary to the hopes of the Baghdad *gevirim* who had supported his candidature, the new *ḥakham bashi* behaved in an overbearing manner, concentrated numerous powers in his own hands, and gave them no opportunity to become involved in his activities. His handsome appearance—'he had a striking face, his black beard flowing down upon his chest'[48]—and his superior bearing initially elicited admiration, but quickly became a source of murmuring and antagonism. This being the case, it is possible that more than a few disappointed *gevirim* who had initially supported him joined in the emerging demands for his deposition—but at the same time there were also rabbis who had previously opposed him, but later came to support him.[49]

[45] See Benjamin, *Travels of Israel* (Heb.), 45.

[46] BZI, MS 3750.

[47] Benjamin, *Travels of Israel* (Heb.), 45. For a somewhat different description, see BZI, MS 3750.

[48] Benjamin, *Travels of Israel* (Heb.), 45.

[49] Imprimaturs (*haskamot*) and some of his Torah innovations (*ḥidushim*) are cited in a number of books by the Baghdad sages. See Ben-Ya'akov, *Babylonian Jewry from the End of the Geonic Period* (Heb.), 160 n. 23.

Thus the composition of the groups respectively supporting and opposing Rabbi Kassin became confused. In the summer of 1851 his opponents succeeded in persuading the Ottoman governor to rescind his appointment, forcing Kassin to leave Baghdad and go to Istanbul to seek reappointment.

On his way to the capital Kassin passed through Aleppo, the city of his birth. The chief rabbi there, Abraham Antebi, ruled that those who had deposed him had not acted properly, and that therefore he was to be restored to office and paid his salary. Kassin also turned to the chief rabbi of Rhodes, Jacob Michael Israel, who concurred with Rabbi Antebi's ruling. An appeal was also sent to the leading sage of the Ottoman empire, Rabbi Hayim Palagi, who at this time was serving as a rabbinic judge in the community of İzmir. He too agreed that the office of *ḥakham bashi* in Baghdad should remain in the hands of Raphael Kassin. These rabbis were particularly troubled by the fact that Kassin's opponents had appealed to the non-Jewish authorities rather than to a Jewish court, perhaps seeing here a precedent that might threaten their own standing. Rabbi Palagi even called upon all the rabbis of the Ottoman empire, particularly the heads of the Istanbul community, to come out in support of Rabbi Kassin, who, he said, was being persecuted out of hatred and jealousy, and intercede on his behalf with the Ottoman authorities to have him restored to office.[50] Rabbi Palagi's ruling, which was signed on 10 August 1852, was also ratified by Rabbi Yehoshua Abraham Krispin, the *ḥakham bashi* of the community of İzmir.[51]

Rabbi Kassin, it seemed, had repeated his previous accomplishment—namely, gaining the moral support of the rabbis of the Ottoman empire. However, one component was lacking to make his success complete: this time, he failed to win the support of the *gevirim* of Istanbul, led by Abraham Kamondo.[52] It is possible that a number of his opponents among the wealthy men of Baghdad had preceded him to Istanbul, exploiting their business connections with the *gevirim* of the capital to pull them over to their own side. In any event, without the support of these prominent and wealthy laymen with connections in the sultan's court, the authorities were unwilling to act against what appeared to them to be the wish of the majority of the community, and declined to reinstate Kassin as *ḥakham bashi*.

Wanderings

Without a position and without a family—his wife and daughter having remained in Baghdad—Rabbi Raphael Kassin again turned to a life of wan-

[50] Palagi, *Ḥukot haḥayim*, 'Ḥoshen mishpat', 12*b*–13*a*, §3.

[51] Ibid. 13*a*.

[52] On the meeting between Hakham Kassin and Abraham Kamondo, see Ben-Ya'akov, *Babylonian Jewry from the End of the Geonic Period* (Heb.), 160 n. 24.

dering and literary polemic. His path from Istanbul led to İzmir, where he met up with his greatest supporter, Rabbi Hayim Palagi. On his earlier visit to Istanbul in 1847 he had published a book entitled *Derekh haḥayim*, in which he dealt at length with the anti-Jewish arguments of the Irish missionary Alexander McCaul in a work entitled *The Old Path* (published in Hebrew in 1839).[53] Now he made use of his time in İzmir, where a good deal of Christian missionary activity was taking place, to renew his anti-Christian writing. His study of comparative religion also led him to examine various schools within Judaism, both in ancient times and in his own day. In the course of his reading he became familiar, indirectly, with the Reform movement and its literature, through a fiercely polemical work against the movement entitled *Kin'at tsiyon*, written by Rabbi Israel Moses Hazan and endorsed by a number of rabbis from Erets Yisra'el.[54] Rabbi Kassin expressed himself with great intensity against the Reformers, who found support for their ideas in McCaul's book, referring to them as 'the ignorant group, a collection of evil-doers and council of traitors in the city of Braunschweig, where there gathered together all those lacking in knowledge and empty of all wisdom, and they raised their hands and profaned the holy things, saying to God, "Remove Yourself from us, for we do not wish knowledge of the Oral Torah . . . "'.[55]

Nevertheless, even though his tone is deeply hostile, his words reveal a certain degree of understanding of why some people were attracted by the idea of Reform. Kassin thought that the enthusiasm for Reform among certain parts of the Jewish public derived from the reluctance of those rabbis who were opposed to take up arms against Christian polemics—first and foremost McCaul's *The Old Path*, in which the rabbis were accused of distortion of the Torah. As he wrote in *Derekh haḥayim*:

Heaven forbid that I should justify this ignorant group mentioned. However, after they saw that four years had passed since the above-mentioned Satanic and Evil Urge book came out, and kept on cursing our holy rabbis, the masters of the Talmud, of blessed memory, and leading astray the people of Israel so that they do not believe in the Talmud . . . And when this collection of sinners, an ignorant gathering, saw that the sages of Israel—may God give them life and protect them—were silent, and that none of them encouraged himself in his soul with strength [Ps. 183: 3] to answer these corrupt lies and to refute them, arguing that they were utter emptiness, those people [the sinners] said that the sages of Israel were unable to

[53] On Raphael Kassin's anti-Christian polemics from the time of his arrival in Persia, see Harel, '"Likutei amarim"' (Heb.).

[54] On the book, its author, and the background for its writing, see Malachi, 'The Yishuv's Struggle' (Heb.).

[55] R. Kassin, *Derekh haḥayim*, 14*b*–15*a*.

answer McCaul's words, and all those people who were lacking in knowledge and ignorant gathered together and did what they did.[56]

Kassin argued that had the rabbis, particularly those living in European cities, refuted McCaul's arguments, the Reformers would not have come together and the Reform movement would not have gained momentum. In any event, his polemic was not directed primarily against the Reformers, but rather against Christianity.

Prompted by the practical need to arm the Jewish public against Protestant missionary activity, Kassin summarized the main anti-Christian arguments set out in his book *Derekh haḥayim* in a treatise of just 111 pages which he planned to circulate widely among the Sephardi communities. The treatise was called *Likutei amarim*, and was printed in a bilingual format, with Hebrew on one side and a translation into Ladino, Kassin's mother tongue, on the other. The book was endorsed by the *ḥakham bashi* of İzmir, Rabbi Hayim Palagi, who took steps to ensure that it was quickly published.

The book attracted the attention of the missionaries in İzmir. However, when one of them, the American Homer B. Morgan, asked Rabbi Palagi to give him a copy of the work, the latter denied its existence completely. Moreover, according to the testimony of the missionary—and it is not clear whether he was in fact telling the truth on this point or merely expressing his own wishes—Palagi was forced to stop the printing of an additional edition of the book and to return the remaining copies of the original edition to the author, together with a letter claiming that the Jewish community was not interested in a book of this type.[57]

Frustrated by the rejection of his literary work, Kassin set off on his wanderings once more. This time he headed for the countries of Christian Europe, taking with him a number of copies of *Likutei amarim* which he gave as gifts to the rabbis of the European communities through which he passed on his travels.[58] It would appear from the sources that he passed through France, but we have no confirmed details of the other countries and communities which he visited. However, it is reasonable to suppose that he visited the important Jewish centres about which he had heard, such as England and Germany. Here he would have become acquainted with the new Reform communities to which he had been so strongly opposed in the past, and

[56] Ibid. 15*b*.

[57] See *The Missionary Herald*, 51 (1885), 198–200.

[58] See e.g. the dedication in the copy in the Jewish National Library in Jerusalem: 'To his Highness, the Praiseworthy Rabbi, Teacher of the Place and Head of the Yeshiva in the city of Dijon, our Honourable Teacher, Rabbi Me'ir Sar Levi, may he enjoy a long life, until the priest stands with the Urim and Tumim [i.e. until the Temple is rebuilt], Amen, may it be His will. From me, the insignificant one, the young author, Raphael Kassin.'

learned about the Reform movement and its ideas at first hand. This direct experience seems to have brought about—it is not clear how—a revolution in his own attitude towards Reform, and he became strongly influenced by the Reformers' views and new ideas.

In 1862, after a decade of wandering following his ejection from Baghdad, Raphael Kassin returned to the city of his birth, Aleppo, where he sought to apply his new insights.

The Reform Rabbi of Aleppo

On 29 August 1862, the British consul in Aleppo reported to his ambassador in Istanbul on some ferment in the Jewish community. This had come about in the wake of some preaching in favour of anti-talmudic religious reform by a prominent rabbi who had returned to Aleppo after many years of wandering in India, Persia, and Europe. The consul does not refer to the rabbi in question by his full name, but calls him simply 'Hakham Raphael'. The rabbi is referred to in the same manner in an addendum attached to the consul's letter, containing a translation of the agreement to appoint him chief rabbi of a group which had accepted his leadership. The rabbi mentioned is undoubtedly Raphael Kassin, who had returned from his travels armed with the reformed religious approach he had acquired in Europe,[59] and found in Aleppo a public receptive to the message of change he brought from afar.

Even before Kassin's return, signs were already apparent in Aleppo of a weakening in the community's attachment to the traditional underpinnings of its religion, similar to that evident among the *maskilim*, the adherents of the Haskalah or Jewish Enlightenment in Europe. An increasing disregard, even contempt, for various laws of the Torah brought in its wake a lack of respect towards its representatives, the traditional Torah scholars and sages, and a diminution in their authority. We do not know the extent of this phenomenon or how serious it was. It is probable that the rabbis who preached against this tendency exaggerated it; be this as it may, their complaints indicate the areas in which a certain laxity was beginning to be apparent. From these we learn that commandments in respect of *tsitsit*, *tefilin*, the *mezuzah*, public prayer, and study of Torah were insufficiently strictly observed, and that prohibitions on eating food cooked by non-Jews, on gambling and games of chance, and on necromancy, were being flouted. At celebrations, family events, and other gatherings, men and women were mixing freely, there were musical groups that sang erotic songs, and women from the com-

59 For details of the proofs of Kassin's identity, see Harel, 'Spiritual Agitation' (Heb.), 29.

munity danced before the men. Women's clothing was not as modest as it had been in the past, and there were cases in which young men wore jewellery and grew their hair long in order to court girls. The laxity was said to have spread to commercial as well as religious and social life, with cases of cheating in weights and measures, and of violating the sabbath.[60]

What was happening was that the 'enlightened' (or, more accurately, educated) Jews of Aleppo—consisting largely of people from the middle and upper economic strata who had received a modern private education and had come into frequent contact with Europeans—were ceasing to believe in either the power or the authority of the rabbis.[61] Attributing the obedience of the masses to the sages to belief in their magical powers, including the power of their curses, they declared that, as enlightened and rational people, they did not believe in such powers and that the threat of excommunication (*ḥerem*) had no power to intimidate them. In accordance with modern European thinking, these Jews sought to place man at the centre of life and thought, and to minimize the role played by God in the running of the world.[62] Some of them threatened the rabbis; many refused to listen to them on subjects ranging from financial affairs to matters of personal life or family law, such as the prohibition on marriage between a *kohen* and a divorced woman.[63] By the middle of the nineteenth century, then, there existed in Aleppo a class of people, evidently with some economic means, who were drawn towards the Haskalah, who questioned the force of Jewish halakhah, and who sought to free themselves from its burden. It would appear that a part of this educated class was ready to listen to proposals for innovation and change in the traditional religious framework; and it was this segment of the public that served as Kassin's main base of support when he sought, in August 1862, to establish a separate Reform community in Aleppo.

It was not only the change in his own perspective that prompted Kassin to attempt this transformation of the community of Aleppo. It had been hard for him to come to terms with the loss of his position in Baghdad and of the

60 See Abadi, *Divrei mordekhai*, author's introduction; id., *Vikuaḥ na'im*, 7*a*, §23; A. Dayan, *Holekh tamim*, 27*a*–*b*, 54*a*–*b*, 56*a*; id., *Tuv ta'am*, 138, 141, 156, 200, 209–10, 218; id., *Zikaron lanefesh*, 18, 22, 39; Antebi, *Ḥokhmah umusar*, 7*a*–*b*, 13*b*–14*a*, 35*a*, 96*a*, 111*b*–112*a*, 115*b*, 116*b*–118*a*, 125*a*; J. Sutton, *Vayelaket yosef*, author's introduction; Laniado, *For the Sake of the Holy Ones* (Heb.), 165–6.

61 On the growth of the class of *maskilim* in Aleppo and its penetration by modern education, see Harel, *Syrian Jewry*, 80–91.

62 See e.g. A. Dayan, *Tuv ta'am*, 206. For more on the hatred of the *maskilim* in Aleppo towards the traditionalist rabbis, see id., *Zikaron lanefesh*, 65; Abadi, *Melits na'im*, 32–3, §261.

63 See A. Dayan, *Tuv ta'am*, 17*a*, §14; Labaton, *Nokhaḥ hashulḥan*, 'Ḥoshen mishpat', 96*b*, §33. On the weakening of tradition in the Syrian communities, see Harel, *Syrian Jewry*, 91–4.

benefits and signs of honour that accompanied it, and it seems that this later initiative was in part motivated by a desire to regain status and power. It is clear from the brief account of his youth given at the beginning of this chapter that Raphael Kassin, as the only son of his father, was accustomed to getting everything he wanted without any effort or trouble, and that his father had educated and encouraged him to believe that he was destined for greatness. The nature of his upbringing may perhaps explain his constant attempts to gain access to the courts of kings, such as the Persian shah and the Turkish sultan, his ceaseless struggles to achieve his own goals—first and foremost, appointment to the office of *ḥakham bashi* in Baghdad—and his high-handed manner of leading his community. Despite his acknowledged greatness as a scholar of Torah and his past as *ḥakham bashi* in Baghdad, he did not now enjoy any honour or special status in the city of his birth, and was not appointed to any position of formal leadership in the community. Hence his main preoccupation now was to find a way of regaining his elevated public status, specifically in Aleppo. But not a single person in the official leadership of the community was willing to yield his own position to this controversial figure who had been deposed as *ḥakham bashi* in Baghdad, who had been absent from his former home city for many years, and who had now returned to seek a position of authority.

The nature of the rabbinate in Aleppo was unique among the Jewish communities of the Ottoman empire. Until the 1880s, its leadership was not divided between two rabbis: the *ḥakham bashi* also served in practice as the highest spiritual authority, and it was he who headed the rabbinic court. The title by which this figure was usually known was *rosh al erets* [*aram tsovah*] *rabah*—'the head of greater [Aleppo]'; the Ottoman title, *ḥakham bashi*, was used only in contacts with people outside the community.[64] All taxpayers participated in the election of the rabbi; this important process thus involved a large proportion of the community and provided the middle class with a particularly prominent role. The rabbi's salary was paid from community funds—indeed, from a special fund set up for this purpose—thereby alleviating his dependence upon wealthy individuals.[65] Moreover, the fact that the *ḥakham bashi* was also accepted by the community as the highest spiritual authority gave his office greater force, and once appointed he generally held office for life. The successor chosen was usually the rabbi with the highest qualifications to serve as supreme spiritual authority. Under this system, the Aleppo community preserved relative stability.

At the beginning of 1858, Rabbi Hayim Mordecai Labaton was appointed

64 See e.g. A. Dayan, *Vayosef avraham*, 121*b*–122*a*; Labaton, *Nokhaḥ hashulḥan*, title page.

65 See Antebi, *Mor ve'aholot*, 'Ḥoshen mishpat', 100*b*, §13; id., *Ḥokhmah umusar*, 115*a*.

chief rabbi of the community of Aleppo, remaining in office until his death in 1869. Thus when Raphael Kassin arrived in the city in 1862 Rabbi Labaton had already been in post for four years. His term of office was a time of conservatism and stability, marked by activity to strengthen the status and authority of the Jewish court—primarily in response to the Ottoman reforms, which had threatened its status somewhat by restricting its remit to matters of personal status alone. The rabbi's greatness in Torah scholarship, the public's belief in his magic powers to bless and to curse, and the initial confusion surrounding the declaration of the reforms and the early stages of their application all worked to support the status of the chief rabbi and the force of halakhah in the community.[66]

Kassin understood that any direct campaign to win the leadership and the rabbinate was doomed to failure. Hence, taking advantage of the mood among the educated, modernizing segment of the population in Aleppo, he decided to create a separate Reform community, modelled on the separatist congregations with which he had become familiar in Europe, with himself at its head. In taking this initiative he was motivated in part by religious conviction, but also by personal ambition. He initially preached Reform in secret, but once he saw the number of those supporting him increasing, he openly called for the creation of a Reform community alongside the traditional community. Like a number of Reform thinkers in Europe, Kassin sought to diminish the importance of the Talmud and the words of the sages, to the extent of rejecting their authority.[67]

Armed with considerable expertise in the doctrines of different religions, as well as his own reforming zeal, Kassin sought the support of the heads of the Christian and Muslim communities in the city, evidently hoping that such support would strengthen the status of his new community as well as his own personal status vis-à-vis the established community and its rabbi. In other words, his erstwhile rivals, against whom he had composed many polemics, now became his supporters in the struggle within the Jewish community. Moreover, once it had been decided that a separate Reform community with Kassin at its head should be established, a contract was drawn up for his employment. This contract included conditions, benefits, and signs of honour similar to those he had enjoyed in Baghdad: absolute authority and the obedience of his community, a high salary, servants, and a residence commensurate with his status. By contrast, the traditional *ḥakham bashi* in Aleppo received

[66] Rabbi Labaton died on 22 June 1869 at the age of 84. On the legends and folk beliefs connected to him, see E. Yadid Halevi, *Shivḥei moharam*.

[67] Cf. e.g. the outlooks of Samuel Holdheim and Abraham Geiger as described in Meyer, *Between Tradition and Progress* (Heb.) 101–3, 135–6.

no such benefits.[68] This indicates that Kassin's supporters included people from the middle and upper classes who were able to fund his salary and expenses from their own pockets. It should be emphasized that the move to appoint Kassin as chief Reform rabbi was not led by the Francos: not being members of the community, they had no need to separate themselves from it in order to appoint a rabbi. It follows, therefore, that the move to break away from the traditionalist community and to create a new Reform community alongside it was led by prosperous educated elements within the community itself. Nevertheless, it is not impossible that some of the Francos were among Kassin's followers, as they were in any event not subject to the authority of the traditional *ḥakham bashi*.

In the wake of the creation of this separate Reform congregation, riots and controversies broke out in the Aleppo community, degenerating into fights in the marketplaces. However, in the end this episode was only a passing—and subsequently well-concealed—event in the history of the community. The Ottoman governor, Jawdat Pasha, was himself afraid that disorder of this kind might spread to other territories under his rule; also, the more conservative element within the community turned to him for help. He thus took the unusual step of intervening in an internal, autonomous Jewish matter, forbidding Rabbi Kassin to continue his attempts to win people over to his Reform approach.[69] From that point on, for the following nine years until his death on 22 February 1871, Raphael Kassin was pushed to the margins of the community—alone, persecuted, and considered to have lost his mind. A tradition relating to the pedigree of the Kassin family asserts that even back in his Baghdad days his mental balance had been fragile:

> A *shaykh* from among the Gentiles, out of jealousy, undermined the rabbi and made magic against him. To our hearts' distress, this worked upon the rabbi and caused him harm, for his mind became somewhat disturbed and he lost his wisdom, and from that time he had to return to the city of his birth, Aram Zova [Aleppo], and he spent the remainder of his days studying Mishnah and the Holy Zohar like one of the sages.[70]

The name of Hakham Raphael Kassin was no longer mentioned, his books were not published, and accounts of his life, especially the events towards its end, were all but eradicated from the chronicles of Aleppo, the city where he had been born.

[68] FO 78/1689, Heidenstam to Bulwer, Aleppo, 29 Aug. 1862, appendix.
[69] Ibid.
[70] J. Kassin, *Peri ets hagan*, 130–1.

CHAPTER FOUR

The Baghdad Community Torn between Rabbis Samoha and Dangoor

> Rabbi Yehoshua ben Kabousi said: All my life I fled from [positions of] authority. Now that I have entered one, I will come down upon anyone who tries to take it away from me like a teapot. Just as the teapot injures and splits and blackens, so will I come down on him.
>
> JT *Pesaḥim* 6.1

The Rule of Wealth in Baghdad

Having had a taste of power in the turbulence surrounding the appointment and downfall of *ḥakham bashi* Raphael Kassin,[1] the *gevirim* of Baghdad were reluctant to relinquish their new-found influence in the community. After the removal of the powerful, decisive, and energetic *ḥakham bashi*, these wealthy laymen took over at the helm, almost completely ignoring the rabbis. Thus, once Kassin had been removed, the *gevirim* of Baghdad reappointed Rabbi Obadiah Halevi—first as head of the rabbinic court, and thereafter as *ḥakham bashi*. To all appearances, the rabbi enjoyed great public prestige, confirmed during the summer of 1862 when he received a medal of honour from the sultan.[2] However, the uniting of the two offices in the hands of a single person who lacked any leadership ability seems to have been contrived in order to ensure that both posts were in weak hands and thereby to avoid the creation of a locus of power that might threaten the rule of the wealthy. Thus Jacob Obermeier, who moved to Baghdad after teaching in the school run by the Alliance Israélite Universelle in Damascus, wrote:

> The *ḥakham bashi* in Baghdad is the elderly rabbi Hakham Obadiah—may God protect him and give him long life—a native of Damascus who had previously lived

1 See Ch. 3 above.

2 See *Hamagid*, 49 (18 Dec. 1862), 388. Paradoxically his receiving the medal of honour, within the framework of medals being given to various bureaucrats and officials and men of other religions, prompted the reporter to call upon the Jews of Baghdad to select more suitable leaders.

in the Holy Land. He came here as the emissary of a *kolel* to collect money and the community appointed him chief rabbi, and he is a learned Torah scholar and extremely humble. One who has seen the *ḥakham bashi* in his glory in a great community such as Constantinople, İzmir, Salonica, Tunis, or Damascus; one who has seen the great honour which the Jews give to their kings, that is, their rabbis; one who has seen the greatness and glory surrounding the residence of the rabbi who was the leader of the community, will be astonished to see the sad state of the *ḥakham bashi* here, his lack of power and his inability to rule the public, the small degree of honour which they give him, and the grinding poverty under which he lives. It is true that the authorities call him the head of the community in Israel, but this title is an empty one that only exists on paper. The *ḥakham bashi* in Baghdad is a tool of the wealthy men of the community, whether they remove him from office or place him in it, whether they decrease his salary or increase it. At present his salary, including all his private income, amounts to about one hundred and twenty francs per month; he has children and grandchildren, and I know for an established fact that he lives a life of penury. How then can he not be fearful for his daily bread and not submit to those who have the power to remove him or to take the food out of his mouth or from the members of his household? For every person is concerned about his livelihood, acquiring which is as difficult as the splitting of the Red Sea, and I have seen with my own eyes the signs of fear and submission—so much so that one can justifiably say that the *ḥakham bashi* of Baghdad has no part in the leadership of the community, and that as a result of his poverty and his powerlessness, his authority is greatly reduced in the eyes of the mass of the people. If the *ḥakham bashi* walks through the marketplace or through the streets of the city, none of the Jewish people so much as moves from his place to even make a small gesture of greeting—and this is enough to indicate everything else, and one who is sensitive will take note.[3]

This combination of assertive *gevirim* and weak *ḥakham bashi* resulted in the wealthy laymen exercising unrestricted dominance over the community institutions and leadership. Moreover, having gained this control without any process of selection or endorsement by the community, this moneyed elite lost all sense of communal obligation and public duty. Once again, Jacob Obermeier describes the situation well, commenting here on how matters stood at the end of 1875:

The leadership of the community in Baghdad stands today, as it did during the times of the independent *pashas* [before the return of Ottoman rule in 1831], under the iron hand of the wealthy men of the community; the *ḥakham bashi* and the rabbinic judges and all the host of those who serve the community submit to them. . . . In these countries a person is not regarded as outstanding because of the goodness of his deeds or the breadth of his knowledge. Hence the masses of the people see no

[3] *Hamagid*, 2 (12 Jan. 1876), 13.

advantage to a person in his wisdom or his good deeds, and the majority of the people kowtow and submit to whoever is known to have more money than his neighbour, and he rules over them. And if on the next day, through some accident of fate, someone should lose part of his money to another person, then his honour and dominion are also taken from him and are given to one whose money bags are heavier than his own. For the appointment of the heads of the community in Baghdad is not a permanent thing and is not governed by law and halakhah, as it is in the other communities of Israel, but is no more than an accident of money. Hence these wealthy people may at their will make one person a head and another a tail. Sometimes they will say to the community: we are the rulers and you must accept our opinions regarding such and such a matter, and it is ours to command the officials of the community and to divide the burden of the taxes among them. And at another time, when the community is suffering troubles or if a poor man who suffers bangs on their doors they cry out: 'Who are we that you complain to us? Are we not like one of the community? Go to the *ḥakham bashi* and complain to him and he will act on your behalf!'[4]

In these circumstances the prestige of the court headed by the *ḥakham bashi* also declined, even though Rabbi Halevi and the two judges who sat with him, Sason Elijah Halevi and Nisim Hakohen, were expert in halakhah. During Halevi's term of office as *ḥakham bashi*, the Jews of Baghdad became accustomed to bringing their disputes before the Muslim judges. Nearly all monetary matters, particularly those involving the authorization of documents and the execution of notes of indebtedness, were brought to the *shari'a* court. The sages of the Jewish courts had to confine themselves mainly to discussion of marital questions, and occasionally responding to a request from the *gevirim* to approach government officials regarding some issue pertaining to the needs of the community.[5]

Rabbi Halevi's twenty-five-year term as *ḥakham bashi* was relatively tranquil. He posed no threat to the status of the wealthy, who did whatever they wished in the community. The rabbis, who were dependent for their livelihoods upon the moneyed elite, accepted the status and power that had been accumulated by this elite. Moreover, the wealthy elite produced some Torah scholars from within their own number, so that the learned included a number of individuals who were also successfully engaged in trade.[6] As a result the boundary between the mercantile and scholarly classes became blurred, and a

[4] Ibid.

[5] *Hamagid*, 3 (19 Jan. 1876), 22.

[6] The two explicit examples of this are of course, Rabbis Abdallah Somekh and Joseph Hayim. For comments by Israel Benjamin about the commercial activities of Rabbi Abdallah Somekh, see Benjamin, *Travels of Israel* (Heb.), 46. On Rabbi Joseph Hayim's involvement in commerce, see Ben-Ya'akov, *Babylonian Jewry from the End of the Geonic Period* (Heb.), 196–7, and below. See also Deshen, 'Baghdad Jewry', 193.

relationship of collaboration became established between the moneyed elite and the rabbinic leadership.

When Obadiah Halevi died on 23 Heshvan 5637 (10 November 1876), Rabbi Sason Elijah Halevi, known as Samoha, was appointed as his successor.[7] This appointment was made after a few months, with the approval of the government, and did not involve any great upheaval.[8] However, the economic and social changes that began to occur during the years following his appointment led to a new social alignment, which crystallized during the summer of 1879 when the fires of controversy between the various social groups within the community flared up once more.

The Community in an Age of Transformation

During the first half of the nineteenth century Jewish traders in the Ottoman empire were heavily involved in the large commercial caravans that travelled along the land routes between East and West, between the Persian Gulf and the Mediterranean. When the Moldavian traveller Benjamin the Second visited Baghdad in 1848 he found a flourishing, indeed growing, community, including many prosperous merchants whose activity contributed to the economic flourishing of the region as a whole.[9] However, over the following decades the increased use of steamships gradually transferred much trade to the sea, and the profits of those who engaged in land commerce slowly dwindled. The decline in the volume of overland trade was keenly felt in the Jewish community, where it had marked repercussions for the business dealings of the wealthy men of Baghdad. Even in 1860 when Yehi'el Fishel Kastilman, an emissary from Safed, visited the city, it seems from his descriptions that the economic situation of the Jews, who at that time numbered about 20,000, was not very good.[10]

[7] On Rabbi Obadiah Halevi's activity, see Ben-Ya'akov, *Babylonian Jewry from the End of the Geonic Period* (Heb.), 161–2. It would seem that an error was made in printing the date of the rabbi's death, as it is reported that he died in Heshvan 5636 (November 1875), and yet Obermeier reported at length from Baghdad during that same year about the *ḥakham bashi* and does not mention his death.

[8] It may be that, as Ben-Ya'akov wrote, Rabbi Sason Halevi only received the official uniform of office in 5639 (1879): see Ben-Ya'akov, *Babylonian Jewry from the End of the Geonic Period* (Heb.), 162 n. 44. However, his official seal as *ḥakham bashi* bears the date 1877. See ACRI, TR/Is/162*a*, Obadiah Sason Elijah son of Moses Halevi to the *ḥakham bashi* of Istanbul, Moses Halevi, Baghdad, 6 Tevet 5638.

[9] Benjamin, *Travels of Israel* (Heb.), 44–5, 47.

[10] Ya'ari (ed.), *Travels of the Emissary from Safed* (Heb.), 52. For a summary of sources relating to the demographic data of the Jews of Baghdad during the 19th century, see Kazaz, *The Jews in Iraq* (Heb.), 25–6.

The opening of the Suez Canal in 1869 was a key moment. On the one hand, it dealt a fatal blow to the caravan trade, to the detriment of traders on the inland stopping points along the route between Aleppo or Damascus and Baghdad.[11] On the other hand, it led to significant expansion in Baghdad of economic activity associated with maritime trade, primarily with the Far East. Some merchants withdrew almost completely from overland trade and invested most of their wealth in international marine trade with Europe and the Far East. Others were slower to react to the change in the economic order, continuing to invest in the old and familiar relationships and commodities, and it was these who gradually lost much of their wealth and property. As the maritime transportation networks were almost completely dominated by the British, Baghdad traders sought to become involved in the British trade, with a considerable degree of success.[12] The opening up of the new trade routes led many Jewish mercantile houses to establish branches throughout Europe and the Far East, which remained in close contact with the mother community in Baghdad.[13] Thus Iraq's location at the crossroads of many international trade routes saved the Baghdad traders from the marginalization suffered by their counterparts in Aleppo and Damascus.[14]

Moreover, during the second half of the nineteenth century Iraq experienced a period of stability under Ottoman rule. It is worth noting that 1869 is considered one of the most significant years in Iraqi historiography, indeed, a turning point in the history of the Baghdad region, owing to the appointment in that year of Midhat Pasha as governor of that region. The pasha, who was among the champions of the mid-century Ottoman reforms, set about attempting to apply these reforms fully in Baghdad. During the three years of his rule in the district, Midhat Pasha made significant achievements in implementing the policy of equality of all subjects before the law, in the development of the country, and particularly in the area of security, improving the observance of law and order.[15] Advances in security and communication encouraged the growing interest in Iraq on the part of the European powers, attracted by its location at a central point on the route towards India, a position of great strategic importance for gaining control of the Persian Gulf. European involvement in Iraq became ever deeper through direct financial investment, the creation of franchises, the establishment of factories, the development of transport and communications systems, and the quest for

[11] On the impact of the opening of the Suez Canal on the Jews of Syria, see Harel, *Syrian Jewry*, 48–9.

[12] Tsimhoni, 'Babylonian Jewry' (Heb.), 16–17.

[13] See Yehezkel-Shaked, *Jews, Opium, and the Kimono*; Ben-Ya'akov, *Babylonian Jewry in Recent Times* (Heb.).

[14] Neimark, *Journey in an Ancient Land* (Heb.), 67.

[15] See al-Najjar, *Ottoman Administration* (Arab.), 1–2.

the natural resources hidden beneath its soil. Western companies invested in developing the shipping lines and exploiting the river waters for irrigation and for energy.

All these enterprises offered opportunities for the Jews of Baghdad to undertake new investments, to create new connections, and to engage in new areas of business.[16] Also during this period they became involved in the development of credit and banking.[17] So, while the transition from overland to maritime trade may have caused a temporary decline in the economic status of Baghdad, it was soon followed by renewed growth and prosperity. Indeed, such was the attraction of the new economic opportunities in Baghdad that Jews from Kurdistan and even Persia came to try their luck there, either permanently or en route to the new centres in the Far East and the West. Thus there emerged a new stratum of *nouveaux riches* who wished to become involved in the Jewish community at higher levels and to exert influence over its affairs. At the same time, not all new business enterprises were successful and there remained many poor people in the community. Thus Baghdad's Jewish population took on a newly variegated character, divided along class and economic lines rather than by other social criteria, such as family ties or communal and ethnic connections. The rapid growth of the *nouveaux riches* and the tremendous wealth that continued to be accumulated by the families of the old elite sharpened the polarization of classes and the gap between rich and poor.[18]

Over these same decades another new social class emerged in Baghdad: that of the *maskilim*, the 'enlightened' Jews. This group came into existence as a result of the penetration of western culture into Baghdad by means of increasingly frequent personal contacts with European merchants and travellers. Initially, only the members of the economic elite received a modern education in addition to their studies in the communal institutions. Thus, for example, they learned foreign languages with private tutors in order more easily to engage in commercial dealings with the West. From the mid-1860s on, these beneficiaries of private education were joined by the graduates of the school of the Alliance Israélite Universelle, opened at the end of 1864.

[16] On the economic development of Iraq during this period, particularly in the area of foreign trade, see Hasan, *Economic Development* (Arab.), 337–45; Lloyd, *Twin Rivers*, 194–6; Longrigg, *Four Centuries*, 292–7, 317–19; Batatu, *The Old Social Classes*, 235–62.

[17] Hasan, *Economic Development* (Arab.), 337–45; al-Najjar, *Ottoman Administration* (Arab.), 118–19; Tsimhoni, 'Babylonian Jewry' (Heb.), 22–3.

[18] On social polarization and on the stratification of the people of Baghdad on the basis of wealth, see Deshen, 'The Jews of Baghdad', and see further ACRI, TR/Is/162*a*, the Chosen Committee of the Kollel in Baghdad to the *ḥakham bashi* in Istanbul, Moses Halevi, Baghdad, 21 Shevat 5640.

This school was one of the primary actors in preparing the younger generation—and not only the children of the elite—for work with the commercial firms that operated through the European consulates and to emigrate to the new economic and commercial centres. This education, with its western characteristics and its close contact with western companies, facilitated the penetration of modern western perceptions into the community.[19] The 'enlightened' thus began to take shape as a new bourgeois social class whose standing derived not from family pedigree or property ownership, but rather from its role in leading the community as a whole towards modernization. The moneyed elite needed these enlightened people to administer their businesses, while the rabbinic sages did not yet see modern education as a threat to the inculcation of traditional values, or the emerging class of *maskilim* as a threat to their own status in the community.[20] It is nevertheless worth emphasizing that this class was unable to realize its full potential within Baghdad, because many of its young people left the city of their birth to move abroad in search of the increasing economic opportunities awaiting them in London, Manchester, Marseilles, Istanbul, Bombay, Calcutta, and Hong Kong.

Economic growth also influenced the class of Torah scholars. The establishment of new communities in India and throughout the Far East created a demand for rabbis, religious functionaries, and judges competent to rule in religious courts. Moreover, as these new communities perpetuated the Baghdad tradition and culture, so Baghdad's importance as a spiritual centre for the more distant satellite communities grew.[21] The demand for talmudic sages led to the flourishing of institutions for training religious functionaries. Throughout the 1870s and 1880s the centre of Torah study in Baghdad was Midrash Beit Zilkhah, headed by Rabbi Abdallah Somekh. While Rabbi Somekh never held any official position in the community, he was recognized until his death on 18 Elul 5649 (14 September 1889) as the greatest sage in the city. This being so, the rabbinic court which he headed also served as a spiritual centre of the community. Over the course of time, this court became 'the High Court of appeal for all of the Jewish courts in Iraq and Kurdistan'.[22] So long as Rabbi Somekh lived, every rabbi appointed as *ḥakham*

[19] On Jewish education in Iraq, see Simon, 'Education' (Heb.); Gabbai; 'Education of Girls' (Heb.); Sehayik, 'Chapters' (Heb.), 22–3. For an approach which plays down the success of the Alliance in providing a French western education in Baghdad, see Yehudah, 'Babylonian Jewry and Cultural Changes' (Heb.).

[20] See Regev, 'The Attitude towards Enlightenment' (Heb.). On social changes in the Baghdad community, see Deshen, 'Baghdad Jewry'.

[21] Neimark, *Journey in an Ancient Land* (Heb.), 67–9.

[22] See Ben-Ya'akov, *Biography of Rabbi Abdallah Somekh* (Heb.), 22. See also the explanation

bashi knew that he was working in his shadow and that his support could help him to silence his opponents. His two disciples, Rabbi Sason Elijah Halevi and Rabbi Elisha Dangoor, rivals for office as head of the community from the end of 1879 on, were particularly keenly aware of this.

Given the pronounced class distinctions that characterized Jewish culture in Baghdad, the community conducted its affairs in accordance with general rules defining the status of each individual and each group therein. So long as there was peace between the *ḥakham bashi* and the hereditary and moneyed elites, there were no great upheavals in the manner of leadership of the community. However, during the period of Rabbi Samoha's leadership this equilibrium was upset by the demand that he be removed from office.

The Leadership of Rabbi Sason Elijah Halevi

Rabbi Sason Elijah Halevi (Samoha) was the first *ḥakham bashi* of Baghdad to have been born and brought up in the city. Samoha, who initially drew his authority both from the Ottoman government and from the Jewish community, was a forceful leader, who did not hesitate to confront its wealthy members when he judged their behaviour improper. This dictatorial attitude created enemies within the moneyed elite, who had become accustomed to running things themselves during the twenty-five years that Rabbi Obadiah Halevi, an outsider and a weak leader, had served as *ḥakham bashi*. These wealthy men soon came to regret Rabbi Samoha's appointment and to look for a propitious moment to get rid of him and to appoint another rabbi in his place. According to the rabbi's own testimony, although he had the power to arrest his opponents among the elite and even to have them imprisoned, he refrained from doing so; on the contrary, he took care to ignore their insults.[23]

The rabbi was not surprised that he had numerous opponents, accepting that it was not unusual for a religious court judge to have enemies.[24] Nevertheless, letters written by the rabbinic emissaries from Erets Yisra'el who were staying in Baghdad at the time noted the large number of enemies he had made within the community elite and attributed this to his unyielding

regarding the possible reasons for the non-appointment of Rabbis Abdallah Somekh and Joseph Hayim to the office of *ḥakham bashi* in S. Deshen, 'The Jews of Baghdad in the Nineteenth Century' (Heb.), 30–44.

[23] ACRI, TR/Is/162*a*, Rabbi Sason Elijah ben Moses Halevi to the *ḥakham bashi* in Istanbul, Moses Halevi, Baghdad, 22 Shevat 5640, 12 Iyar 5641.

[24] Ibid., Rabbi Sason Elijah ben Moses Halevi to *ḥakham bashi* in Istanbul, Moses Halevi, Baghdad, 22 Shevat 5640.

character.[25] It seems that in 1879, during the year prior to the outbreak of the dispute involving his tenure, Rabbi Samoha operated in complete disregard of the wealthy men of the community, some of whom were among the members of the steering committee. In fact, the *ḥakham bashi* neutralized the activity of this committee almost completely. According to Rabbi Samoha himself, the first attempt to depose him was made when he championed the poor people of the city who were suffering from the pressure exerted by the wealthy. Famine struck in 1879, and a number of wealthy people in the community exploited their position of economic strength to raise the price of wheat and other goods and thereby increase their profits. This led to agitation among the lower classes of the community. Rabbi Samoha described the episode as follows:

But when, due to our great sins of the past year, the Lord our God did not bring rain down upon the land of Babylon, rains of blessing and of generosity, and the land did not give its fruit, there were some people among the wealthy men of Babylonia who were cruel and evil-hearted and worsened this situation by storing up grain and raising its price to five and six times what it had been. And there was a great outcry throughout the city. And there were plaintive cries for grain and grapes and wine and olive oil, for they could not be had, and all the people from one end to another were filled with anger at those who were storing up the grain. And it happened that on Shabat Kalah[26] one of the sages from among those who were storing grain gave a sermon in the synagogue, and all the people who were in distress and were bitter of soul gathered together there, and cursed and shouted down the preacher with all kinds of curses and foul language, saying that he did not practise what he preached. And they wanted to beat him, and he ran away and went outside and hid himself. And after the end of Shabat all the community gathered together and made an agreement that, under pain of the ban, no person should store grain any more, and any person who violated this agreement would be separated and sent away from the community of Israel. And this was done in spite of and contrary to those who were gathering and storing up the grain, who were the cohorts of this preacher. And from that day on that preacher became an enemy of mine and he hated me all the days, saying that I had turned the heart of the people backwards to curse and excoriate him, and that if I had been on his side I would have put them under the ban and destroyed them under the heavens of the Lord.[27]

[25] Ibid., Rabbi Yitshak Arazi Hakohen to the *ḥakham bashi* in Istanbul, Moses Halevi, Baghdad, 33rd day of the Omer (18 Iyar 5640).

[26] The sabbath prior to Shavuot, which is one of the four sabbaths during the year on which the rabbi gave a special sermon. See below, n. 31.

[27] ACRI, TR/Is/162*a*, Rabbi Sason Elijah ben Moses Halevi to the *ḥakham bashi* in Istanbul, Moses Halevi, Baghdad, 22 Shevat 5640.

The alignment of forces within the community at the beginning of this controversy is clearly reflected in the above description, which highlights a number of aspects of the social structure of the Baghdad community and the tensions deriving from that structure. The gap between the upper classes and the lower classes was exacerbated by the actions of those who possessed great wealth and had control over the flow of basic goods. The wealthy had both business and family connections with certain individuals among the rabbinic sages, as a result of which the latter did not challenge their behaviour. These same sages were viewed by the masses as collaborators with the moneyed elite, a factor which aroused a great deal of strong feeling within the community. It seems clear that the *ḥakham bashi* tended towards the side of the poor and that it was at his encouragement that it was decided to impose the *ḥerem*, the ban, upon those who were inflating prices. He used extremely harsh language in criticizing those who used the grain trade to increase their own profit at the expense of the poor, speaking of 'the profit of the grains which they made from the blood of the poor and unfortunate people'.[28] The blurring of the boundary between the moneyed and learned classes, noted above, led to the organization of an opposition to Rabbi Samoha composed of people from both these social groups who had status and influence in the community.

It is worth noting here who the individuals were at the head of this alliance between the wealthy and the sages. Close examination of the record reveals that those who demanded the expulsion of Rabbi Samoha were led by Rabbi David Hai ben Me'ir ben Joseph Nisim, the head of the steering committee of the community. This man, who had served since 1868 as the treasurer of the Alliance Israélite Universelle in Baghdad, was among the most wealthy and most active members of the community, and was also a Torah scholar.[29] Some years earlier he had been involved in the campaign to depose Rabbi Raphael Kassin. He was also the uncle of Rabbi Joseph Hayim, serving as the younger man's mentor before he went to study at the *beit midrash* run by Rabbi Abdallah Somekh.[30] In his letters, Rabbi Samoha describes Rabbi David Hai as 'the mother's brother', that is, the uncle of the preacher whom the community had accused of collaboration with the grain hoarders. Moreover, the leader of the grain hoarders is identified in Rabbi Samoha's letter as

[28] ACRI, TR/Is/162*a*, Rabbi Sason Elijah ben Moses Halevi to the *ḥakham bashi* in Istanbul, Moses Halevi, Baghdad, 22 Shevat 5640.

[29] See AAIU, Irak, I.B., 3, Bagdad, David Hai Me'ir Joseph Nisim to Adolphe Crémieux, 4 Nisim 5640.

[30] See Ben-Ya'akov, *Babylonian Jewry from the End of the Geonic Period* (Heb.), 139–40, 158, 191.

Nisim, the preacher's brother. On the basis of these two familial identifications, combined with the fact that Rabbi Joseph Hayim was the permanent preacher in the great synagogue in Baghdad on the four main sabbaths of the year, and the only preacher in Baghdad on Shabat Kalah,[31] we can confidently identify the preacher who was an enemy of the *ḥakham bashi* as Joseph Hayim himself. And indeed, Rabbi Joseph Hayim, who was a sleeping partner in his brother's business, played a significant role in Rabbi Samoha's removal from office.

These key individuals were joined in their opposition to Samoha by several others. One of them was Rabbi Menahem Salman ben Menahem Daniel, the scion of a family of wealthy money-changers and landowners who wielded great influence in the community and had strong connections with the authorities, most of whose inherited wealth came from their intensive trade in grain.[32] Another was Ezekiel Moses Somekh, the nephew of Rabbi Abdallah Somekh and a member of both the moneyed and hereditary elites.[33] To these we must also add two more wealthy members of the community: Rabbi Joseph Shem-Tov, one of those who assisted the Alliance in its efforts to provide a western education to the younger generation;[34] and Salah Nisim Kashi.[35]

The First Stage in the Deposition

The campaign to depose Rabbi Samoha began during the summer of 1879, in the wake of his threat to use the ban against those who were raising the price of grain. According to Rabbi Samoha's account, those who sought his removal from office were led by members of the elite who, in seeking revenge for his earlier criticisms of their conduct, made common cause with the grain

[31] The Hayim family held the prerogative of preaching in the Baghdad community on the four special sabbaths of the year: Shabat Kalah (before Shavuot), Shabat Zakhor (before Purim), Shabat Hagadol (before Passover), and Shabat Shuvah (before Yom Kippur), on all of which Rabbi Joseph Hayim was the only preacher from the year 1859 onwards. As early as the time of Rabbi Raphael Kassin there was an outcry when Rabbi Elijah Hayim, Joseph Hayim's father, was replaced in this role by the new *ḥakham bashi* himself, who preached in his place on Shabat Hagadol. See Chapter 3 above. See also Ben-Ya'akov, *Babylonian Jewry from the End of the Geonic Period* (Heb.), 158 n. 12, 191–2; id., 'Rabbi Joseph Hayim' (Heb.), 12. Cf. ibid. 33; also Regev, 'Homiletical and Ethical Literature', 35–6. On his brother Nisim and his influence in the areas of business and relationships with the authorities, see Ben-Ya'akov, *Babylonian Jewry from the End of the Geonic Period* (Heb.), 129.

[32] See Ben-Ya'akov, *Babylonian Jewry from the End of the Geonic Period* (Heb.), 182.

[33] See Ben-Ya'akov, *Biography of Rabbi Abdallah Somekh* (Heb.), 84.

[34] Ben-Ya'akov, *Babylonian Jewry from the End of the Geonic Period* (Heb.), 191–2, 288.

[35] On Salah Nisim Kashi, see ibid. 188, 365–7.

merchants. One of the grounds on which they chose to attack his reputation among the community at large, including the poor people whom he had supported, was the collection of the *'askariyya*, the tax paid in commutation of military service.

The Hatt-i Hümayun reform decree of 1856 allowed the drafting into the army of members of non-Muslim minorities throughout the Ottoman empire. The Jews did not welcome this move, seeing it not as part of the advance in their civil status towards full equality, but as a potential threat to the observance of their faith. The primary source of Jewish opposition to military conscription was the fear that, during the period of army service, they would be required to violate religious laws such as sabbath observance or *kashrut* which, in turn, would be likely to lead towards assimilation. The Christians in the Arab provinces of the Ottoman empire likewise expressed dissatisfaction at the possibility of being drafted into the sultan's army.

The unwillingness of the minorities to accept these new obligations, along with the reluctance of Muslims to serve in the army alongside 'heretics' and the combined inability and lack of will on the part of the imperial authorities to deal with the complex of problems that would be raised by the drafting of non-Muslims into the army, prompted the search for a compromise to resolve the problem. The solution was found in the form of a special tax that served as a form of compensation for the exemption of non-Muslim subjects of the empire from military service. The tax was accepted reluctantly by the Jewish community, and over the years it gave rise to many intracommunal disputes. As Jacob Obermeier wrote:

> Every year the congregation is required to pay a fixed tariff of thirty-five thousand francs to the treasury in exchange for the exemption of Jews from military service. This sum is divided among various Jewish officials and among all the people of the community, each one according to his status and his property, and all of them are required by the government to pay whatever has been imposed upon them by the above-mentioned officials. This has become a great stumbling block to the community, because no one among them is happy to pay his valuation nor is anyone willing to pay more than others. And numerous quarrels and disputes ensue as a result, nor do the officials give a clear accounting . . . and many times some of them were arrested by the authorities, thereby profaning the name of Israel. Another evil that comes in the wake of the tariff evaluations is that many of the people who consider themselves to be exploited in this respect refuse to pay voluntarily to any mitzvah, but take revenge against the tax officials through the poor people of the community.[36]

[36] *Hamagid*, 4 (26 Jan. 1876), 30.

According to the *ḥakham bashi*, because many businessmen who had fallen on hard times were unable to pay their share of the tax, a wide gap opened up between the total sum gathered by the community and the amount demanded by the authorities. To fill this gap, the payments due from individuals unable to make them had to be met by other members of the community, even though they had already paid their own share of the tax. The opponents of the chief rabbi (again according to his account), led by Rabbi Joseph Hayim's uncle David Hai, whipped up ill feeling against him by alleging that the shortfall was in fact the result of his embezzling monies that had been collected to pay the tax. Rabbi Samoha further claimed that his opponents told the credulous masses that the drought that had caused the rise in grain prices was divine punishment for his corruption, promising them that if the *ḥakham bashi* were removed from office abundance would return to the land, and the hated *'askariyya* tax would also be abolished. These opponents, he said, also threatened his supporters, forcing them to add their own signatures to the document calling for his removal from office.[37]

Rabbi Samoha accused the sages who had joined in the calls for his expulsion of being crazed by hostility towards him, and of being tempted by the promises made by his enemies that they would inherit his authority, through appointment as rabbinic judges, and his income. In his view, these rabbis were not men of real stature in either halakhic or worldly matters, having been appointed as rabbinic judges only so that they might 'be submissive to the wealthy men of Babylonia who are storing up the grain'.[38] In other words, the *ḥakham bashi* saw the move to seek his expulsion as a renewed and sophisticated attempt to ensure the domination of the community by the wealthy elite while weakening both his own position and that of the other genuinely learned rabbis. He further accused those who were calling for his removal of having set up a steering committee of twelve people who were unfit to lead in community matters. These people, he alleged, were using the communal treasury to serve their own needs and withholding his salary from him.[39]

The version of events put forward by those calling for his expulsion was of course completely different. They claimed after the event not to have felt any personal animosity towards the *ḥakham bashi*, saying that events had taken on a momentum of their own and moved swiftly once they discovered the corruption of the *ḥakham bashi*, including the embezzlement of

[37] ACRI, TR/Is/162*a*, Rabbi Sason Elijah ben Moses Halevi to the *ḥakham bashi* in Istanbul, Moses Halevi, Baghdad, 22 Shevat 5640. [38] Ibid.

[39] Ibid., Rabbi Sason Halevi to the *ḥakham bashi* in Istanbul, Moses Halevi, Baghdad, 2 Sivan 5640.

community funds, the acceptance of bribes, and the giving of biased judgments.[40] On the basis of their testimony, a petition for deposition, signed by the vast majority of the community, was signed and presented to the Ottoman governor. He instructed them to send the petition to the Sublime Porte in Istanbul requesting confirmation of Rabbi Samoha's removal from office and the appointment of the new *ḥakham bashi* whom they had chosen, Rabbi Elisha Nisim Dangoor.[41]

As well as these two contradictory testimonies as to the reasons for the deposition by the parties to the affair, we also have the testimonies of the Ashkenazi and Sephardi emissaries from Erets Yisra'el who were staying in Baghdad at the time of the controversy in order to collect money for the communities in their respective cities. These emissaries all supported Rabbi Samoha, despite the fact that in doing so they risked losing contributions as most of those likely to make donations were among his opponents. Their support for the *ḥakham bashi* derived from the fact that, as Torah scholars themselves, they felt closer to the *ḥakham bashi* and to his version of events than they did to that of his opponents. It should nevertheless be emphasized that emissaries did not automatically support an incumbent *ḥakham bashi*, for their position could also be affected by personal considerations.[42] Nevertheless, they stressed that, as foreigners, they had no interest in supporting one side or the other in the controversy. According to their account, they reached a common position only at the end of a two-month stay in Baghdad, and only after they had carefully examined the claims of both sides.[43] Their conclusion was that the entire attempt to depose the *ḥakham bashi*, Rabbi Samoha, was no more than a conspiracy by a number of interested parties, whom they referred to as the 'ten traitors'.[44] These men, they asserted, were members of a moneyed and hereditary elite who sought to rule the community in order to strengthen their own position at the expense of the poor, who made up the overwhelming majority of its members.

40 ACRI, TR/Is/162*a*, the representatives of the Va'ad Kolel, Baghdad, to the *ḥakham bashi* in Istanbul, Moses Halevi, Baghdad, 21 Shevat 5640.

41 For an extended treatment of Rabbi Elisha Nisim Dangoor, see Ben-Ya'akov, *Babylonian Jewry from the End of the Geonic Period* (Heb.), 163–9; see also Dangoor, *Gedulot elisha*, 'Introduction' (Heb.), and further below.

42 See e.g. Harel, 'The Overthrow of the Last Aleppan Chief Rabbi' (Heb.), 124–5; on the position of the emissaries against an incumbent *ḥakham bashi* see also id., 'The Relations' (Heb.), 70–1.

43 ACRI, TR/Is/162*a*, Yitshak Arazi ha-Cohen, emissary from Tiberias, and Yudel Aaron Zalz ben Rabbi Avraham Hirsh of Tiberias to the *ḥakham bashi* in Istanbul, Moses Halevi, Baghdad, 20 Av 5640.

44 Cf. Jer. 9: 1; and compare in the text there *atseret bogdim* and *aseret bogdim*.

However, the *ḥakham bashi*'s opponents won the day, and Rabbi Samoha was deposed from office in Av 5639 (1879).

The Class Struggle Worsens

In Shevat 5640 (1880), about six months after the deposition of Rabbi Samoha, the poor people of Baghdad came to realize that, in supporting his removal, they had played into the hands of the moneyed elite. Their economic situation did not improve, the yoke of taxation was not eased, and no rain fell to relieve the drought. Moreover, the grain hoarders and their supporters were maintaining their iron grip on the community and its institutions by means which had previously been neither prevalent nor acceptable in Jewish society, such as denouncing their opponents to the authorities and imprisoning them. In retrospect it appeared that the oligarchy that had gained control over the community was concerned, as it had been in the past, exclusively with its members' own interests and well-being and those of their sycophants. Having reached this conclusion, the community at large raised a petition to restore the deposed *ḥakham bashi* to his office. The signatories included virtually all the poorer members of the community, who called upon Rabbi Samoha to resume his office and take up the reins of community leadership once more.[45]

For his part, Rabbi Samoha accused his opponents of making threats in the synagogues to deter people from signing the petition. He even claimed that a number of his supporters had been imprisoned on a variety of pretexts, particularly on trumped-up charges of having evaded paying the *'askariyya* tax, and accused the rabbis who supported his opponents of having been bribed with funds from the communal coffers. He also testified that, in the light of these factors, he had asked his supporters to refrain from signing the petition in order to avoid accusations of stirring up controversy.[46] Moreover, he argued, initially he even refrained from complaining to the Ottoman governor so as to avoid *ḥilul hashem*, profaning God's name among non-Jews.[47] Only after he saw with his own eyes threatening notes distributed in the synagogues did he take one of these notes, translate it into Turkish, and present it to the governor. The governor advised the deposed *ḥakham bashi* to

[45] ACRI, TR/Is/162*a*, Yitshak Arazi Hakohen to the *ḥakham bashi* in Istanbul, Moses Halevi, Baghdad, 33rd day of the Omer [18 Iyar] 5640.

[46] Ibid., Rabbi Sason Halevi Samoha to the *ḥakham bashi* in Istanbul, Moses Halevi, Baghdad, 27 Av 5640.

[47] Ibid., Rabbi Sason Elijah to the *ḥakham bashi* in Istanbul, Moses Halevi, Baghdad, 22 Shevat 5640.

bring his complaints against his opponents to court. Rabbi Samoha preferred not to do this, and instead appealed to the *ḥakham bashi* in Istanbul for instructions on how to act. Meanwhile his opponents began to gather signatures on their own petition opposing his return to office, prompting Rabbi Samoha to claim further—a claim supported by the testimony of the emissaries from Erets Yisra'el who were present in Baghdad—that these signatures were gathered under threat and that they included many signatures of his own supporters that had been forged.[48]

Rabbi Samoha appealed once more to the governor, who responded that he could not take any position on an internal Jewish matter until he had received instructions from Istanbul. This answer strengthened Rabbi Samoha in his determination to seek the support and influence of Rabbi Moses Halevi, the *ḥakham bashi* in Istanbul. He had also to contend with another problem, namely the withholding of his salary by his opponents among the wealthy elite of Baghdad. This vindictive measure was a serious matter for the *ḥakham bashi*, who was not financially independent and therefore depended entirely upon remuneration from the public purse. The salary paid to him from the public coffers amounted, according to his statement, to more than 2,000 Turkish *kuruş* per month. The *ḥakham bashi*'s main sources of income were the *gabilah* (meat tax), fees for writing legal documents and divorce writs, and fees for placing the seal of the rabbinate upon various legal documents.[49] As his reinstatement to office, and the income that went with it, required the approval of the Sublime Porte, Rabbi Samoha wrote requesting support for his claim from the *ḥakham bashi* in Istanbul, the most senior Jewish figure in the Ottoman government.[50]

Rabbi Samoha's opponents also understood that the key to dominance over the community lay in the hands of the *ḥakham bashi* in Istanbul. Once they saw that support for Rabbi Samoha's reinstatement was growing, and having heard from the governor that the appointment of Rabbi Dangoor as *ḥakham bashi* required approval from Istanbul, they too turned to Rabbi Halevi to seek his confirmation of the deposition of Rabbi Samoha and the appointment of Rabbi Dangoor in his place.[51]

[48] ACRI, TR/Is/162*a*, testimony of Yitshak Arazi Hakohen of Tiberias, Yehoshua ben R. Ya'akov of Jerusalem, and David ben Yitshak of Safed, Baghdad, 4 Iyar 5641.

[49] Ibid., Rabbi Sason Halevi Samoha to the *ḥakham bashi* in Istanbul, Moses Halevi, Baghdad, 27 Sivan 5641.

[50] Ibid., Rabbi Sason Halevi Samoha to the *ḥakham bashi* in Istanbul, Moses Halevi, Baghdad, 27 Av 5640.

[51] Ibid., the Elected Members of the Va'ad Hakolel in Baghdad to the *ḥakham bashi* in Istanbul, Moses Halevi, Baghdad, 21 Shevat 5640, 16 Iyar [5640].

The Involvement of the *Ḥakham Bashi* in Istanbul

The *ḥakham bashi* in Istanbul was considered by the Ottoman rulers the official head of the Jewish millet throughout the empire, and it was he who represented all the Jews in the empire at official ceremonies. However, he did not outrank the chief rabbis of the various other communities of the empire, nor did he have any authority to intervene in their internal affairs. Every large community in the Middle East could choose its own *ḥakham bashi* and conduct its affairs in a completely autonomous manner. It is true that until the 1870s the chief rabbis in the cities of the empire were appointed at the request of the *ḥakham bashi* in Istanbul, but this was a purely formal arrangement, and generally speaking his approval was merely a rubber stamp confirming the wishes of the respective communities. Nevertheless, the *ḥakham bashi* in Istanbul was also considered by the other Jewish communities of the empire to function as a kind of mediator between themselves and the Sublime Porte. According to the accepted norm, a community which wished the government authorities to confirm its choice of *ḥakham bashi* or to depose him turned in the first instance to the *ḥakham bashi* in Istanbul, and not directly to the Sublime Porte.[52]

Those who had sought to depose Rabbi Samoha had departed from this practice, choosing to bypass the chief rabbinate in Istanbul and to obtain permission for the appointment of a new *ḥakham bashi* directly from the Sublime Porte. This action seems to have caused some astonishment in the corridors of Ottoman power, where officials were used to dealing with all issues relating to the rabbinates in individual Jewish communities through the *ḥakham bashi* in Istanbul. It also angered the *ḥakham bashi* in Istanbul himself, Rabbi Moses Halevi, who sent a furious letter to the new committee in Baghdad in which he took them to task. The committee apologized, in effect transferring the blame for their action to the local Ottoman governor: according to them, he had instructed the committee to send the decision about appointing a new *ḥakham bashi* directly to the Sublime Porte for his approval.[53] Once it became clear to the members of the new committee that they could not make headway without the backing of the *ḥakham bashi* in Istanbul, they fell into line with his directions, setting out in specific detail their request to Rabbi Halevi and the substantial resources—payments to the government authorities and to the *ḥakham bashi* himself—which they were willing to devote to achieving

[52] See Levy, 'The Founding of the Institution of the *Ḥakham Bashi*' (Heb.), 47.

[53] ACRI, TR/Is/162*a*, the Elected Members of the Va'ad Hakolel in Baghdad to the *ḥakham bashi* in Istanbul, Moses Halevi, Baghdad, 21 Shevat 5640.

their goal: namely, recognition by the Ottoman rulers of the appointment of Rabbi Elisha Dangoor as *ḥakham bashi* in Baghdad.[54]

In Shevat 5640 (1880), some six months after his deposition, Rabbi Samoha wrote once again to Rabbi Halevi, requesting that he instruct the authorities in Baghdad to set up a committee of seven leading laymen of the community, whose function would be to examine the entire episode and come to a decision that all parties to the dispute would be obliged to accept.[55] When the news of Rabbi Samoha's latest appeal to Istanbul became widely known, his opponents reacted with an appeal of their own. Then, in an attempt to discredit those opponents, Yitshak Arazi Hakohen, a rabbinic emissary from Tiberias, wrote to the *ḥakham bashi* in Istanbul that the opponents were resolved to reject any involvement of the rabbinate in Istanbul unless it supported their own view.[56]

Rabbi Halevi took his time in responding to these various approaches. The detailed petitions from both sides, the letters from the emissaries staying in Baghdad, and the lobbying by various other people in Istanbul on behalf of the different sides made it very difficult for him to reach a decision. At the same time, members of the steering committee in Baghdad rejected Rabbi Samoha's proposal to set up a mediating committee drawn from within the community; instead, they told the *ḥakham bashi* in Istanbul that they were prepared to appear at a hearing against Rabbi Samoha at the mixed court of the district, on which both Jewish and non-Jewish judges sat. Their determination to get the outcome they wanted was reflected in their hinting to the *ḥakham bashi* in Istanbul that, if he would not help them to appoint Rabbi Elisha Dangoor as *ḥakham bashi* in Baghdad, they would find other ways to achieve this end.[57]

Rabbi Samoha continued to send letters and appeals to Istanbul. Increasingly, these related to his problems of everyday livelihood since his deposi-

[54] ACRI, TR/Is/162*a*, the Elected Members of the Va'ad Hakolel in Baghdad to the *ḥakham bashi* in Istanbul, Moses Halevi, Baghdad, 21 Shevat 5640. See also ibid., the Elected Members of the Va'ad Hakolel in Baghdad, 17 Iyar [5640]. It was accepted practice to pay for the firman; however, the addition of further payment for the trouble taken by the *ḥakham bashi* Moses Halevi might be interpreted as an attempt to bribe him or to encourage him to support their position.

[55] Ibid., Rabbi Sason Elijah to the *ḥakham bashi* in Istanbul, Moses Halevi, Baghdad, 22 Shevat 5640. At a certain stage the *ḥakham bashi* in Istanbul proposed sending an investigating committee composed of two rabbis from the capital city in order to clarify the claims of both sides. However, this did not materialize. See ibid., Rabbi Sason Elijah to the *ḥakham bashi* in Istanbul, Moses Halevi, Baghdad, 27 Sivan 5641.

[56] Ibid., Yitshak Arazi Hakohen, and Yudel Aaron Zalz, son of Rabbi Avraham Hirsh of Tiberias, to the *ḥakham bashi* in Istanbul, Moses Halevi, Baghdad, 20 Av 5640.

[57] Ibid., the Elected Members of the Va'ad Hakolel in Baghdad, 17 Iyar [5640].

tion. As noted above, those who had opposed him suspended the payment of his salary as a means of forcing him to leave his office, leaving him without any means of support.[58] Now, once he became aware that his opponents had rejected his proposal for mediation, he began petitioning for a firman which would reaffirm his status as *ḥakham bashi* in Baghdad.[59]

Both sides in the dispute, as well as the Ottoman governor, awaited the answer of Rabbi Moses Halevi in Istanbul. In effect, at this point the entire affair seemed to depend upon the decision which would be taken in the capital city. Finally, in the month of Nisan 5641 (spring 1881), the answer of the *ḥakham bashi* in Istanbul arrived: Rabbi Sason Elijah Halevi was to be restored to office. The Ottoman and the regional *majlis* accepted the decision and officially declared Rabbi Samoha the *ḥakham bashi* in Baghdad. His rule was once again recognized by the authorities, and the rabbinic court composed of scholars who were opposed to him ceased to function.[60]

The Involvement of Rabbi Joseph Hayim

While the authorities accepted Rabbi Halevi's decision, Rabbi Samoha's opponents refused to give in, arguing that he was corrupt and that it would be contrary to divine law to leave the leadership of the community in his hands. Needless to say, Rabbi Samoha thought their real motive was somewhat different: namely, fear that his return to office would deprive them of the benefits they had enjoyed at the expense of the lower classes. His opponents' economic power, their control over the communal coffers and the system of tax collection (which they had now maintained for over a year), and their close connections with various figures in the local government all strengthened their position, and they continued to put pressure both upon people in the community and upon various government figures. These opponents were joined by those Torah scholars who were enemies of Rabbi Samoha, who upon his reinstatement lost both their status and their income from the communal coffers. In retaliation, Rabbi Samoha's supporters were forced to absorb a significant increase in the rate of the *'askariyya* tax; some were even thrown into gaol, while others were placed under *ḥerem*, excommunication

[58] Ibid., testimony of Yitshak Arazi Hakohen of Tiberias, Yehoshua Ben-Ya'akov of Jerusalem, and David ben Yitshak of Safed, Baghdad, 4 Iyar 5641. This source also contains the wording of the community agreement and the warning to the community not to pay Rabbi Elijah Halevi from the public coffers.

[59] Ibid., Rabbi Sason Elijah to the *ḥakham bashi* in Istanbul, Moses Halevi, Baghdad, 2 Sivan 5640.

[60] Ibid., Rabbi Sason Elijah to the *ḥakham bashi* in Istanbul, Moses Halevi, Baghdad, 12 Iyar 5641.

from the community. Rabbi Samoha also alleged that his opponents falsified petitions to the Ottoman courts, presenting the demand to depose him as if it were backed by the community as a whole.[61]

The Ottoman governors set up a committee to examine the entire issue. According to Rabbi Samoha, the committee's conclusions confirmed his own position and refuted the arguments of his opponents. However, he knew he could not face down the wealthy elite and override their influence in the community even if most of the ordinary community members were on his side. On more than one occasion he expressed his suspicions that his opponents were bribing government officials in Baghdad to take sides against him.[62] His greatest fear was that those officials would succeed in altering the decision of Rabbi Halevi in Istanbul. These fears prompted Rabbi Samoha to use unprecedentedly strong language in his next letter to the *ḥakham bashi* in the capital, cursing his opponents every time he mentioned their names. This was a marked departure from his previous practice; he even went as far as accusing Elisha Dangoor of murdering his own brother. He wished to show not only that Rabbi Dangoor was undeserving of the position of *ḥakham bashi* but that to select him would be contrary to the Ottoman empire's own rules governing appointments to this office as set out in the Jewish millet decree of 1864–5.[63] Rabbi Samoha put forward two specific objections: first, that Rabbi Dangoor was of Persian rather than Ottoman origin; second, that he was guilty of murder. To this he added various other insults. The following extract from his letter gives an indication of its tone and content:

> And now the sinful people who have been mentioned—may their name and memory be erased—wish [to appoint] Hakham Elisha Dangoor. And it is known that the above-mentioned Hakham Elisha had been uprooted from the cities of Persia, as several elderly people will relate and testify; moreover, those above-mentioned wicked people have chosen evil like themselves in Hakham Elisha, for he beat his brother with a stone and he died. And his father, may he rest in Paradise, did not wish to publicize this matter to the Emperor, may his glory be exalted, as is known to the entire holy congregation of Baghdad—may the Almighty establish it, Amen. Moreover, his mother's brother converted and became a *sufi*[64] and he is called Haji Salman—may his name and memory be erased. And though the above-mentioned Hakham Elisha is a murderer, he was chosen to be *ḥakham bashi* and judge.[65]

[61] ACRI, TR/Is/162*a*, Rabbi Sason Elijah to the *ḥakham bashi* in Istanbul, Moses Halevi, Baghdad, 12 Iyar 5641.

[62] Ibid.

[63] See the Jewish millet decree as cited by Barnai, 'The Jews in the Ottoman Empire' (Heb.).

[64] A member of a mystical ascetic Muslim sect.

[65] ACRI, TR/Is/162*a*, Rabbi Sason Elijah to the *ḥakham bashi* in Istanbul, Moses Halevi, Baghdad, 12 Iyar 5641. These accusations were confirmed by the emissaries from Erets Yisra'el,

To his astonishment, about two weeks after he sent this letter of accusation to Istanbul, Rabbi Samoha received a telegram from *ḥakham bashi* Moses Halevi bearing the following message: 'I have troubled myself greatly over this matter so that he [i.e. the addressee] might remain in his [position of] greatness, but I did not succeed in doing so. And now Elisha Efendi [Rabbi Elisha Dangoor] has been written by the government.'[66] Rabbi Samoha replied the same day in a bitter letter to Rabbi Halevi complaining of the latter's fickle and contradictory treatment of the entire incident. The rabbi was particularly angry that the *ḥakham bashi* in Istanbul had changed his decision and agreed to his deposition in favour of Rabbi Dangoor without waiting for the conclusions of the committee set up in Baghdad, which judged Rabbi Samoha's behaviour to have been faultless.

By this point, Rabbi Samoha had been struggling to survive without his salary for nearly two years, from its suspension by the *parnasim* at the moment he was deposed during the summer of 1879 to the confirmation of his deposition by the *ḥakham bashi* in Istanbul in spring 1881. From now on, this problem was the focus of Rabbi Samoha's further letters to Istanbul.[67]

The *ḥakham bashi* in Istanbul had found it impossible to continue supporting Rabbi Samoha against the united front of *gevirim* and Torah scholars in Baghdad.[68] The wealthy laymen imposed pressure using their political and economic connections, while the Torah scholars added an important dimension of spiritual authority and moral backing to the act of deposition.

One of Rabbi Samoha's leading opponents throughout this affair was Rabbi Joseph Hayim; and yet, for reasons best known to himself, he never mentioned Hayim by name in his letters to Rabbi Halevi, alluding to him only indirectly as 'the Preacher'. Rabbi Joseph Hayim was extremely active in the move to depose Rabbi Samoha, without disclosing his direct interest in the matter through the business activities of his brothers, in which he was

Yitshak Arazi Hakohen, Yehoshua Ben-Ya'akov, and David ben Yitshak, by their signatures in the margins or at the bottom of the letter, after receiving testimony from 'God-fearing elders who fear God and consider His name'.

66 Ibid., Rabbi Sason Elijah to the *ḥakham bashi* in Istanbul, Moses Halevi, Baghdad, 25 Iyar 5641. The telegram was written in Turkish and the quotation is a translation by Rabbi Samoha.

67 Ibid.; see also ibid., Rabbi Sason Elijah to the *ḥakham bashi* in Istanbul, Moses Halevi, Baghdad, 27 Sivan 5641, 10 Av 5641; ibid., TR/ Is/162*b*, Rabbi Sason Elijah to the *ḥakham bashi* in Istanbul, Moses Halevi, Baghdad, 29th day of the Omer [14 Iyar 5642], 22 Iyar 5642, 5 Tamuz 5642, 4 Av 5642, 18 Av 5642.

68 According to the testimony of Moses Halevi himself, in a letter to Rabbi Joseph Hayim and Joseph Ezra Gabbai published in the weekly Calcutta Jewish newspaper *Peraḥ*, he changed his opinion only after one of the *gevirim* of Istanbul, Avraham Agiman, had recommended that he accept the opinion of those who were opposing Rabbi Samoha, testifying to their honesty. See Ben-Ya'akov, *Babylonian Jewry from the End of the Geonic Period* (Heb.), 163 n. 46*.

himself a partner. It would appear that the letters to the *ḥakham bashi* in Istanbul from Hayim, who was already well known as one of the leading rabbinic leaders in the Ottoman empire and as an eminent Torah scholar, influenced Moses Halevi's actions, helping to persuade him to change his decision and confirm the deposition.[69]

Communications between those who opposed Rabbi Samoha and the *ḥakham bashi* in Istanbul took place through two parallel channels: on the one hand, through the steering committee created after the deposition, and on the other through Rabbi Joseph Hayim, representing the class of Torah scholars, and Joseph Ezra Abraham Gabbai, the leading Jewish merchant in Baghdad during that period.[70] The sultanic firman ordering the appointment of Rabbi Elisha Dangoor as *ḥakham bashi* in Baghdad was sent specifically to these two individuals, and not to the community board. The two of them thanked Rabbi Moses Halevi for his decision and confirmed—with a view to removing any lingering doubt in his mind—that Rabbi Samoha was universally despised.[71] They added to their own letter one from the steering committee stating the impossibility of continuing to pay the deposed *ḥakham bashi* his salary from the communal coffers.[72] They also appended copies of the agreement of the members of the community to this measure, warning the steering committee not to pay Rabbi Samoha so much as a single cent from the community coffers, and not to make any future attempt to restore him to office. According to their testimony, this agreement was signed by 'all the sages and the heads and leaders of the community and was signed by most of the people of our city'.[73] Rabbi Joseph Hayim and Moses Ezra Gabbai knew that this would not please Rabbi Moses Halevi; they therefore promised in their own letter to attempt to persuade the community leaders nevertheless to set aside a certain sum of money for the deposed *ḥakham bashi*.

Rabbi Joseph Hayim's direct interest in this affair—as a result of his family and business connections with Rabbi Samoha's opponents—certainly influenced the position he took in it. But it would appear that the main determinant of that position was his position in the community. Like his teacher, Rabbi Abdallah Somekh, who also supported the deposition of Rabbi

69 For the opinions of the rabbis about him, and for references to responsa and his Torah narratives which were published in the books of the rabbis of the period, see Ben-Ya'akov, *Babylonian Jewry from the End of the Geonic Period* (Heb.), 191.

70 On Gabbai, see ibid. 177–8.

71 ACRI, TR/Is/162*a*, Rabbi Joseph Hayim son of Elijah son of Moses Hayim and Joseph Ezra Abraham Gabbai to the *ḥakham bashi* in Istanbul, Moses Halevi, Baghdad, 16 Sivan 5641.

72 Ibid., the Elected Members of the Va'ad Hakolel in Baghdad to the *ḥakham bashi* in Istanbul, Moses Halevi, Baghdad, 16 Sivan 5641.

73 ACRI, TR/Is/162*a*, copy of the agreement of the community.

Samoha, Rabbi Joseph Hayim did not hold any official position as rabbi or halakhic decisor in the community.[74] He enjoyed an assured income from his business and had no need of support from the public coffers. He was nevertheless respected as an important *posek*—that is, as an authority in halakhic matters. Moreover, rather surprisingly, even though during the last quarter of the nineteenth century there were numerous learned people in Baghdad who were capable of ruling in halakhic matters, there were only two individuals who were known as rabbinic *posekim* and as authors of responsa: Rabbi Abdallah Somekh and Rabbi Joseph Hayim. According to Solomon Deshen, the other Baghdad sages were reluctant to serve in such a capacity, as only the very greatest sages, who enjoyed economic independence, were considered deserving of such authority. Deshen argues that this self-abnegating view prevented other sages entering into positions of religious leadership.[75] It is also worth noting the view of Jacob Obermeier, expressed several years prior to this dispute, that Rabbi Joseph Hayim's haughty attitude towards the other Torah scholars was attributable to his great wealth:

> There is wealth which is kept by its owners to their own ill [Eccles. 5: 12]. The two thousand gold coins which he had in his purse were clearly to his disadvantage, in that they led him to behave as he did, acting arrogantly towards all the innocent and poor sages who were around him.[76]

It is therefore quite possible that Rabbi Joseph Hayim disliked Rabbi Samoha because of the independent and disinterested halakhic position the latter took against those who wielded political and economic power in the community, and that this dislike reached a peak when Samoha placed a ban on Hayim's brothers among those who inflated grain prices. However, Rabbi Joseph Hayim did not ask to be appointed *ḥakham bashi* in place of Rabbi Samoha, but instead lobbied for the appointment of another rabbi who had a weaker personality, and who would therefore not challenge or present any threat to his own position.

The Decline in the Status of the Rabbinate

After two years of controversy over the deposition of Rabbi Samoha, Rabbi Elisha Dangoor, a disciple of Abdallah Somekh, was confirmed as *ḥakham bashi* in Baghdad. On 16 Sivan 5641 (13 June 1881), the new incumbent sent a

[74] In the documents which were available to me there is no mention of Rabbi Abdallah Somekh's stance on this incident. However, from the source cited by Ben-Ya'akov it appears that this was indeed the case. Ben-Ya'akov, *Babylonian Jewry from the End of the Geonic Period* (Heb.), 162 n. 46.

[75] Deshen, 'Baghdad Jewry', 35. See also Agassi, *Imrei shimon*, 237.

[76] *Hamagid*, 7 (16 Feb. 1876), 58.

letter of gratitude to the *ḥakham bashi* in Istanbul, Moses Halevi, for the firman and robes of office the latter had provided on behalf of the Sublime Porte, and began to take up his official duties.[77] Despite the explicit orders of Rabbi Halevi, the Baghdad community only paid Rabbi Samoha his stipend after an entire year had elapsed since Dangoor's appointment, and only after the *ḥakham bashi* of the capital had threatened that he would retract his decision if his instructions were not carried out.[78]

The removal of Rabbi Samoha markedly lowered the status of the chief rabbinate in Baghdad, both in the eyes of the Ottoman authorities and in the eyes of the community at large. The weakening of Jewish legal autonomy found expression in a challenge made to the validity of a registration of land ownership (*tabu*) in the Jewish court. The Ottoman land law of 1858 and 1874 required all land ownership to be registered in the imperial property records. In the past, all property deals between Jews had been recorded and authorized in documents of the Jewish court, which were considered valid in the regional or district court. If a dispute between Jews involving the ownership of a particular piece of property was brought to the district court, the judges would base their position upon documents signed by the rabbinic court of the Jewish community. However, during the course of the dispute between Rabbi Samoha and his opponents, the approach of the Ottoman district court changed: it ceased to accept the documents of the Jewish court as legal, and demanded that the witnesses who had signed the original documents appear personally and testify to the transaction orally before the Ottoman court. This new procedure may have derived from the necessity for official registration of land deals under the new legislation, but it is not impossible that the timing of its implementation—at the very height of the struggle over the office of *ḥakham bashi*—was influenced by the controversy between Rabbi Samoha and his opponents, one aspect of which was the question of who would have possession of the official seals of the community. During the course of this dispute, the seals were taken from Rabbi Samoha by deceitful means, thereby severely damaging the credibility of the Jewish court.[79] After this episode, not only was the Jewish court increasingly bypassed in matters of land ownership but—and far more seriously—instances of dishonesty, cheat-

[77] ACRI, TR/Is/162*a*, Rabbi Elisha Nisim to the *ḥakham bashi* in Istanbul, Moses Halevi, Baghdad, 16 Sivan 5641.

[78] Ibid., the Elected Members of the Va'ad Hakolel of Baghdad to the *ḥakham bashi* in Istanbul, Moses Halevi, Baghdad, 16 Sivan 5641; see also Ben-Ya'akov, *Babylonian Jewry from the End of the Geonic Period* (Heb.), 163 n. 46*.

[79] Ibid., Rabbi Sason Halevi to the *ḥakham bashi* in Istanbul, Moses Halevi, Baghdad, 26 Sivan 5641.

ing, deception, and evasion of obligations and mortgages in property dealings began to appear within the Jewish community.[80]

During the second half of the nineteenth century, cultural changes began to take place in the community of Baghdad, the main common feature of which was the abandonment of Jewish tradition and a move towards secularism. From the 1870s onwards, reports in the Jewish press of contempt for the commandments and defiance of instructions issued by the religious leadership in Baghdad became increasingly frequent. The decline in the status and spiritual authority of the rabbis was further aggravated by disputes involving the greatest talmudic sages of the community. As for the authority of the *ḥakham bashi*, this was almost fatally damaged, to the extent that the local authorities ceased enforcing his decisions or those of the rabbinic court. The weakening in religious observance became apparent in public violations of Jewish law and of edicts promulgated by the rabbis. One of the regulations which was widely violated was the prohibition against a man taking a second wife without permission from the rabbinic court.[81]

As the power and status of the rabbinic court in Baghdad continued to decline precipitously, even to the point where it became common for litigants to address curses to the members of the court,[82] so the personal stature of the incumbent *ḥakham bashi*, Elisha Dangoor, suffered accordingly, and calls began to be heard for his removal and for a replacement to be appointed in his stead.

The Proceedings to Depose Rabbi Dangoor

A number of the wealthy lay leaders who had hoped to benefit from the removal of Rabbi Samoha and the appointment in his place of of Rabbi Dangoor were disappointed when they saw those benefits accruing not to themselves but to others among their number. The same held true for the scholarly class, who no longer presented a unified front on questions of leadership and control within the community. As a result of these divisions, the long-standing alliance between the wealthy laymen and the rabbinic sages finally broke up. The cessation of co-operation between these two groups, as expressed in the failure of the *gevirim* to give public backing to the decisions

[80] Ibid., Rabbi Elisha Nisim to the *ḥakham bashi* in Istanbul, Moses Halevi, Baghdad, 25 Tamuz 5641. On a similar phenomenon in Syria, see Zohar, *Tradition and Change* (Heb.), 153–85.

[81] Ibid., Rabbi Elisha Nisim to the *ḥakham bashi* in Istanbul, Moses Halevi, Baghdad, 25 Tamuz 5641. On the growth of the phenomenon of secularism, see Deshen, 'Baghdad Jewry', 195–6; id., 'The Jews of Baghdad in the Nineteenth Century' (Heb.), 38–41.

[82] Hayim, *Rav pe'alim*, 'Ḥoshen mishpat', pt. 7, §1.

of the scholars (as they had done in the past) was, in the eyes of a number of Torah scholars, the main reason why they lost their influence over the public.[83] In place of the traditional co-operation between the wealthy laymen and the rabbinic leadership, new alliances and partnerships were formed based upon common interests, leading to numerous disputes and frictions, with parties seeking to undermine each other and to take revenge for damage they considered to have been inflicted on them and their interests. The public agenda was no longer dominated by the welfare of the community, but rather by the welfare of certain interest groups in its upper levels.

In the month of Iyar 5643 (May 1883), a new dispute broke out in Baghdad, this time between the supporters of *ḥakham bashi* Elisha Dangoor and those who by now were regretting the removal of Rabbi Samoha and sought to restore him to office. Eventually, the stubborn and persistent refusal of Rabbi Samoha's opponents to pay him the monies which he claimed they owed him led to his appealing to the sultan's vizier, 'Abd al-Rahman Pasha, and to the Ottoman minister of justice. In the end, with the assistance of the *ḥakham bashi* in Istanbul, Moses Halevi, he obtained an order from the ministry of justice requiring the *wali* of Baghdad to ascertain that the Jewish community had paid Rabbi Samoha his stipend as due.[84] It is conceivable that this 'victory' of the deposed *ḥakham bashi* over his rivals in the community encouraged him and his supporters to act more forcefully in their attempts to restore him to office. However, Rabbi Dangoor refused to carry out the order and to disburse the funds to Rabbi Samoha. According to the latter, when Rabbi Dangoor saw that some two thousand members of the community had signed a petition calling upon him to pay the former *ḥakham bashi* his salary, he announced in the synagogues that whoever supported Rabbi Samoha would be banned from the synagogue and had sixteen people who had signed the petition in his favour arrested by the authorities. Others, Rabbi Samoha claimed, were imprisoned on various false charges—that they were thieves and criminals—while still others were subjected to additional tax demands and then, when they proved unable to pay, were arrested and detained for long periods.[85]

Among those who took Rabbi Samoha's part at this juncture were three wealthy laymen: Salah Daniel, his son Menahem, and Joseph Garji, all of whom became active in opposition to the elected steering committee. According to Rabbi Dangoor, the former two were close to the deposed

[83] Agassi, *Imrei shimon*, 208–9.

[84] ACRI, TR/Is/162*b*, Rabbi Sason Elijah to Rabbi Moses Halevi, Baghdad, 5 Tamuz 5642, 4 Av 5642, 18 Av 5642.

[85] Ibid., Rabbi Sason Elijah to Rabbi Moses Halevi, Baghdad, 26 Sivan 5643.

ḥakham bashi and supported his demand that his salary be restored, while Joseph Garji joined them because the rabbinic court headed by Rabbi Dangoor had ruled against one of his relatives in a certain dispute.[86] According to another source, Joseph Garji demanded that the steering committee and the spiritual committee require all young men in the community to marry before the age of 25 and punish anyone who failed to do so. This demand was rejected by Dangoor on the grounds that it was not enforceable.[87] The three were also joined by the *gevir* Hayim Gabbai, a British protégé, whom the steering committee refused to exempt from paying taxes on the grounds that he had been born in Baghdad and that his British protection did not affect his liability.[88] This quartet presented the *wali* with a petition signed by numerous members of the community calling for the deposition of Elisha Dangoor from the office of *ḥakham bashi*. This alliance was rooted in a coincidence of interests between the previous *ḥakham bashi* and the three *gevirim*. Rabbi Samoha wanted to be restored to his old office; for their part, the *gevirim* wished to control the steering committee, and in order to do so they needed first to remove the *ḥakham bashi* because, according to the Jewish millet decree, he was the only one with the power to disband the elected committees.[89] In response to this move, the official leadership of the community—that is, the members of the spiritual committee and the steering committee—presented the *wali* with a counter-petition, according to which the community was very satisfied with Rabbi Dangoor as *ḥakham bashi*. Both sides also sent telegrams and letters to the *ḥakham bashi* in Istanbul, Moses Halevi, and to the imperial government in the capital.

The wealthy laymen opposed to Dangoor—possibly in order to appease the latter's supporters who did not want to see Rabbi Samoha reinstated as *ḥakham bashi*—organized two petitions to the *ḥakham bashi* in Istanbul and set about trying to collect signatures from members of the two groups. One petition declared that the community did not want a *ḥakham bashi* at all. As this was an administrative and not a religious office, it was suggested that the community appoint in his place an individual who would work directly with

[86] Ibid., Elisha Nisim Sason Dangoor, Yehezkel Moses Halevi, and Abraham Moses Hillel to Rabbi Moses Halevi, Baghdad, 24 Iyar 5643. Since Ben-Ya'akov has described this incident in great detail on the basis of sources that were available to him but to which I did not have access (Ben-Ya'akov, *Babylonian Jewry from the End of the Geonic Period* (Heb.), 164–8), I have not repeated his account here. I cite only material that can add to the picture or cast it in a different light from that in which it appeared to Ben-Ya'akov, on the basis of those sources that were available to me and not to him.

[87] BZI, MS 3750, 58. For a description of one of the incidents in which Joseph Garji disagreed with the rabbinic courts see Dangoor, *Ma'aseh beit din*, 54–60, §14.

[88] BZI, MS 3750, 58.

[89] Ibid.

the government authorities. This amounted to a desire to return to the older system of the *nesi'im* which had existed in Baghdad prior to the arrival of Rabbi Raphael Kassin, and once more to separate the office of the *nasi* —which had been filled by a layman, a *gevir*—from that of head of the rabbinic court, who would be a rabbinic scholar. The supporters of Rabbi Elisha Dangoor described this initiative as follows:

Joseph Garji gathered together most of the wealthy people and said to them, 'Why do we place upon ourselves a *ḥakham bashi*? Are we not as good as our forefathers, who never appointed a *ḥakham bashi*? Hearken now to my advice and, in place of the *ḥakham bashi*, appoint one of the ordinary people, not one of the sages, but someone who knows how to deal with the rulers regarding the concerns of the community, and he will be called the Official of the Community.[90]

The second petition dealt with the issue of the steering committee. Here too a return to the old ways was proposed, with the suggestion that the elected committee be disbanded and replaced by 'seven good people of the city'. Many of Rabbi Dangoor's supporters initially signed this petition, but subsequently withdrew their support, explaining that they had given it only to avoid quarrelling with the wealthy man to whose home they had been invited in order to sign the document. They further claimed that all the demands set out in this petition were in contravention of the Jewish millet decree and consequently not legal.[91]

In response to these petitions, Dangoor's opponents became more outspoken in their letters to Rabbi Moses Halevi, criticizing in great detail the *ḥakham bashi*'s conduct both as leader of the community and as a rabbinic judge. According to them, he had been drunk on more than one occasion, even when sitting with the *gevirim* to discuss communal matters. Old accusations were raised again, including the charge that Rabbi Dangoor was a murderer, as well as allegations that he had spilt blood, and that in his court a woman had been beaten to death and that the assault had never been investigated.[92]

In a letter of his own to Rabbi Moses Halevi, Rabbi Samoha represented Rabbi Dangoor and his supporters as acting to the detriment of the *ḥakham*

90 BZI, MS 3750, 58.

91 ACRI, TR/Is/162*b*, the sages and rabbis of the city and the elected people of the community headed by Rabbi Abdallah Abraham Joseph Somekh to Rabbi Moses Halevi, Baghdad, 24 Iyar 5643. It is worth noting that in this letter, as in other letters which pertain to this incident, the signature of Rabbi Joseph Hayim does not appear. See also ibid., Rabbis Elisha Nisim Dangoor, Yehezkel Moses Halevi, and Abraham Moses Hillel to Rabbi Moses Halevi, Baghdad, 24 Iyar 5643.

92 Ibid., anonymous letter to Rabbi Moses Halevi, Baghdad, 13 Sivan 5643.

bashi in Istanbul by failing to obey his orders, including the instruction to pay Rabbi Samoha the money that was due to him. In requesting his reinstatement, he emphasizes both his loyalty to Rabbi Halevi and the will of his own community:

Listen to me, O master; you who are the Prince of God: Expel this one before you, and do not allow [the number of those] servants who break out against their masters to multiply, but acquire for yourself a faithful servant . . . For I place myself under your banner and everybody knows that your name is called upon me. And may our Teacher and Master know that I have another petition, on which are the signatures of more than a thousand people who want me to be the *ḥakham bashi* instead of the Hakham Elisha and to restore me to my previous strength.[93]

As in so many cases where rival parties are vying for popular support, the faction that supported Rabbi Samoha attempted to win over the public by means of promises for the future. One of these was that when *ḥakham bashi* Dangoor was deposed, and control of the community passed into the hands of his opponents, the collection of payments for the *'askariyya* tax would be abolished, and the money to pay the tax—which had been tripled that year at the instruction of the government—would be paid from the income collected through the meat tax (*gabilah*).[94] According to another account, Rabbi Samoha's supporters attempted to abolish the *gabilah*, so as to deprive the majority of the rabbinic scholars, who had supported Rabbi Dangoor, of their main source of income.[95] They also spread rumours in the city that they had been promised the support of the *ḥakham bashi* Moses Halevi and of the other *gevirim* of Istanbul who were close to the sultanate, including notable figures such as Yitshak Kamondo.[96]

The depth of hostility between the two groups found expression in arguments and physical violence. Fights broke out and members of both groups were imprisoned with the help of the authorities. Matters came to a head on Wednesday, 26 Av 5643 (29 August 1883), when two Arabs assaulted Rabbi Elisha Dangoor on his way to the synagogue and beat him up severely. One of them even drew a knife, apparently intending to murder him. Passers-by who saw what was happening hastened to help the *ḥakham bashi*, and the attackers ran away. In an investigation of this incident, the suspicion was

93 Ibid., Rabbi Sason Elijah to Rabbi Moses Halevi, Baghdad, 26 Sivan 5643.

94 AAIU, Irak, I.C., 2, Baghdad, J. Luria and M. Cohen au Président de l'AIU, 20 Nov. 1885.

95 BZI, MS 3750, 63.

96 ACRI, TR/Is/162*b*, the sages of Baghdad and its *gevirim* headed by Rabbi Abdallah Abraham Joseph Somekh to Rabbi Moses Halevi, Baghdad, 27 Sivan 5643. For an almost identical letter signed by Rabbi Abdallah Somekh and Nisim ben Yehezkel to the *gevir* Yitshak Kamondo, see Ben-Ya'akov, *Babylonian Jewry from the End of the Geonic Period* (Heb.), 190–1.

raised that supporters of Rabbi Samoha had hired the Arabs to attack Rabbi Dangoor. Rabbi Samoha's sons, Elijah, Ezekiel, and Ezra, were arrested, along with a number of his supporters. After several days the Jewish prisoners were released and only the Arabs who had carried out the actual attack were imprisoned, remaining in gaol for some time. However, the accusation regarding the attempted murder of the *ḥakham bashi* continued to hang in the air.[97]

The new alignment of forces that eventually led to the deposition of *ḥakham bashi* Elisha Dangoor was no longer based upon an explicit class division. While most of the Torah scholars in the city tended to support Rabbi Dangoor, if only because of Rabbi Abdallah Somekh's support of his continued rule, the two rival groups both included wealthy laymen, rabbinic scholars, and sections of the broader population. In 1883, with the dispute at its height, the Jewish traveller Ephraim Neimark passed through Baghdad and noted:

> The behaviour of our brethren in this city is puzzling, as for some eighty years[98] they have been divided into two parties regarding the election of the *ḥakham bashi*—namely, the 'Party of the Sages' and the 'Party of the Laymen'. They are known by those names, but there are also sages and wealthy men in both parties. Whoever is chosen by the one, the other hates, and whoever is brought close by the latter, the first pushes away; and each one finds satisfying arguments.[99]

The community remained irreconcilable in its inability to agree upon a suitable candidate for the office of *ḥakham bashi*. At the end of Elul 5643 (1883), orders came from Istanbul to suspend Elisha Dangoor's term in office and to appoint in his stead a temporary replacement—Rabbi Abraham Hillel—until a final decision could be made in the matter. But only Dangoor's supporters agreed to this solution; the backers of Rabbi Samoha did not recognize the appointment of Rabbi Hillel, nor did the local authorities.[100] In Heshvan 5644 (November 1883), the *ḥakham bashi* in Istanbul tried to persuade Rabbi Elisha Dangoor to resign, pointing out that the rabbi's opponents had succeeded in convincing the governor that only his removal could calm the atmosphere in Baghdad. Under increasingly intense pressure to fire Rabbi Dangoor, Rabbi Moses Halevi offered the Baghdad *ḥakham bashi* an honourable way out: to resign of his own free will.[101] Dangoor refused the

[97] BZI, MS 3750, 63.

[98] Something of an exaggeration: 'forty years' would be more accurate.

[99] Neimark, *Journey in an Ancient Land* (Heb.), 61. On the subsequent repercussions of this incident, see Ben-Ya'akov, *Babylonian Jewry from the End of the Geonic Period* (Heb.), 164–9.

[100] BZI, MS 3750, 64.

[101] Letter of Rabbi Moses Halevi to Rabbi Elisha Dangoor, published in the weekly *Perakh*,

suggestion, and within months was shocked to discover, in Iyar 5644 (May 1884), that the governor of Baghdad had received a directive from Istanbul to remove him conclusively and appoint another person in his place. The deposed *ḥakham bashi* appealed to the members of the community in a personal letter, in which he charged his opponents with ulterior motives:

Listen now, my dear brethren . . . What is this and for what reason are you gathering? And against whom are you gathered? Is it to seek a remedy for the embittered and poor ones? Or is it to make law and order in matters of the community? . . . Rather, you are walking with closed eyes after the advice of your Evil Urge to strengthen talebearers who wish to turn things upside down. And when your children say to you tomorrow [cf. Exod. 13: 14], 'For what reason did you agree to remove Elisha from his office? What was his sin? What was his transgression?' . . . Who among you does not know that I have only occupied this office reluctantly and not to my own benefit? Whom have I exploited, and whom have I mistreated, and from whom have I taken any bribe? [cf. 1 Sam. 12: 3]. May the Lord see and judge, that you have ruined my 'fragrance' in the eyes of the government without any crime on my hands, and may my vengeance be taken from those who rise up against me for evil and who pursue me to the point of destruction.[102]

On 21 Iyar 5644 (16 May 1884) Rabbi Samoha's supporters gathered to reappoint him as *ḥakham bashi*. This step was accompanied by a demonstration of physical power. Tough-looking men went around the synagogues and warned the rabbis who supported Rabbi Dangoor not to incite the community against the reappointment of the former *ḥakham bashi*. A week passed until the group of rabbis headed by Rabbi Abdallah Somekh agreed to publish once more the document setting out the agreement of the community, attained some years earlier, never again to appoint Rabbi Samoha to any public office. The sages who supported Rabbi Dangoor wrote numerous protests to Istanbul against the involvement of the *wali* in the deposition of the *ḥakham bashi*, which ought to have been a matter entirely internal to the autonomous Jewish community, declaring their categorical opposition to the renewed appointment of Rabbi Sason Samoha. Thus Baghdad was witness to a strange spectacle: the renewed appointment of Rabbi Samoha by his supporters and its repudiation by his opponents. The verbal confrontations between the two camps brought in their wake further acts of violence, and members of both parties reported one another to the police. Rabbi Samoha's

6/32 [27 Tevet 5644], and reproduced in Ben-Ya'akov, *Babylonian Jewry from the End of the Geonic Period* (Heb.), 192–3.

102 BZI, MS 3750, 65–6. The letter also appears in Ben-Ya'akov, *Babylonian Jewry from the End of the Geonic Period* (Heb.), 194.

supporters even denounced Rabbi Abdallah Somekh because he refused to accept the government order deposing Rabbi Dangoor.[103]

The emissaries from Erets Yisra'el were divided between the two sides; some even attempted to make peace between the two camps.[104] By contrast, those people associated with the Alliance Israélite Universelle gave tacit support to Rabbi Samoha, seeing Rabbi Dangoor and his supporters—that is, the members of the steering committee and most of the rabbis in the city—as opponents of enlightenment and progress. They were particularly disturbed by Rabbi Dangoor's opposition to the establishment of a modern school for girls.[105] They also believed that the members of the steering committee were obstructing their activities, fearing that the Alliance would extend its patronage to the large *talmud torah* of the city. Hence the representatives of the Alliance admitted that they were not troubled by the removal of the chief rabbi nor by the disbanding of the steering committee.[106]

It was only in Nisan 5645 (spring 1885), several months after the two sides had reached a degree of mutual appeasement, understanding that the continuation of the struggle would be utterly destructive to the community, that instructions arrived from Istanbul that after all Rabbi Samoha was not to be reappointed to the office of *ḥakham bashi* and that Rabbi Dangoor was to be temporarily returned to office. But just two months later, on 19 Sivan 5645 (2 June 1885), Rabbi Dangoor, evidently psychologically broken by the long struggle, requested permission to stand down.[107] The authorities, greatly perplexed by what was happening in the community, ordered that no replacement as *ḥakham bashi* be appointed and that no new steering committee be assembled (the existing committee having been dissolved during the course of the struggle between the rival groups).[108] Thus the community was left broken and divided, with neither a *ḥakham bashi* nor a steering committee. Once again a state of complete anarchy prevailed. Rabbi Dangoor continued

[103] BZI, MS 3750, pp. 67–71. See also what Dangoor wrote after the imprimatur (unnumbered page).

[104] See Ben-Ya'akov, *Babylonian Jewry from the End of the Geonic Period* (Heb.), 166–7, and the sources cited there.

[105] See the letter of opposition to the establishment of such a school from the sages of Baghdad, written in Adar Alef 5646, cited in Schlesinger, *Ma'aseh avot* (Heb.), 77–81.

[106] AAIU, Irak, III.E, Bagdad, 75*a*, J. Luria and M. Cohen au Président de l'AIU, 25 Nov. 1885.

[107] Ben-Ya'akov thinks that Rabbi Dangoor finally resigned on 19 Sivan 5646: Ben-Ya'akov, *Babylonian Jewry from the End of the Geonic Period* (Heb.), 168. However, there are many indications from that year that the community of Baghdad was already without a *ḥakham bashi* in the month of Sivan 5645. This matter requires clarification.

[108] AAIU, Irak III.E., Bagdad, 75*a*, J. Luria and M. Cohen au Président de l'AIU, 25 Nov. 85.

to serve as the head of the rabbinic court and to control the communal coffers without any supervision whatsoever. Wealthy laymen on both sides preferred to concentrate on their own business and completely neglected the needs of the community. Many members of the community stopped paying their taxes and responded with violence to unwelcome decisions of the rabbinic court. The head of the rabbinic court was unable to impose the *ḥerem*, as according to the Jewish millet decree the *ḥakham bashi* alone had the power to wield this sanction. Thus, when members of the rabbinic court headed by Rabbi Dangoor attempted to discipline those who dared to disobey them by this means, the latter complained to the authorities that the court was acting illegally.[109]

With the communal institutions disintegrating around them, representatives of the Alliance encouraged those young educated people who had graduated from their school and had remained in Baghdad rather than migrating overseas to organize themselves and to take the running of community affairs into their own hands. With their encouragement, an association called Kaveh Le'atid (Hope for the Future) was set up, which it was hoped would set the community back on the path of progress; sadly, this initiative failed to yield the desired results.[110]

Rabbi Dangoor was the last *ḥakham bashi* of the Baghdad community until Rabbi David Pappo arrived—towards the end of 1905, armed with an official firman from the sultan. Without that official seal of approval from the Sublime Porte, the rabbis who filled the position in the interim served only as a kind of accepted stopgap or temporary substitute. Rabbi Elisha Dangoor died on the sabbath of 27 Adar 5655 (23 March 1895); Rabbi Samoha outlived him by many years, dying on 22 Kislev 5671 (23 December 1910) at the age of 90.

[109] ACRI, TR/Is/162*b*, Rabbis Elisha Nisim Sason Dangoor, Yehezkel Moses Halevi, and Abraham Moses Hillel to the *beit din* in Istanbul, 27 Heshvan 5646.

[110] On this association, its organization, and its purposes, see AAIU, Irak, III.E., Bagdad, 75*a*, J. Luria and M. Cohen au Président de l'AIU, 20 Nov. 85. See also Meir, *The Socio-cultural Development of Iraqi Jewry* (Heb.), 398–400.

CHAPTER FIVE

Abraham Dweck Hakohen (Khalousi): The Last *Ḥakham Bashi* Born in Aleppo

> 'And it came to pass in the days that the judges judged'—Woe to the generation that judges its judges, and woe to the generation whose judges must be judged.
>
> *Ruth Rabbah* 1

The Creation of Models of Leadership

One of the surprising aspects of the events described and analysed below—namely, those surrounding the deposition in 1895 of the *ḥakham bashi* Abraham Dweck Hakohen in Aleppo—is the absolute silence on them in all printed texts from the time, and the denial that it ever happened in the testimony of the elders of the city.[1] At the time his removal from office was the cause of great turmoil and controversy, not only in Aleppo but also in Istanbul and Jerusalem. It was brought to the attention of the broader public and reported in the newspapers. Yet notwithstanding the contemporary attention devoted to the episode, it was subsequently deliberately erased from the annals of the Jewish community of Aleppo—evidently owing to the fear that it would have a negative effect on the image of the community as a traditional body that respects its rabbis.

In the middle of the nineteenth century there was no model of regional communal organization in Syria. Jewish leadership in the region was decentralized, with no official position of 'chief rabbi' of all the communities of the region. Each of the larger communities, and quite a few of the smaller ones as well, tended to appoint its own chief rabbi, whose authority was limited to the members of his particular community. There are no extant records docu-

[1] See Laniado, *For the Sake of the Holy Ones* (Heb.), 2. Cf. the account of the deposition by the traveller Adler, who visited Aleppo some three years later. According to his account, which is evidently based upon information provided to him by the community, Dweck was deposed by the local governor. There is no mention at all of the community's involvement in the act of deposition. See Adler, *Jews in Many Lands*, 166.

menting the appointment of a communal rabbi, making it difficult to determine the precise extent of his authority or the full range of privileges granted to him by virtue of that office. Nevertheless, we do have the document from 1862 by which Rabbi Raphael Kassin of Aleppo was appointed rabbi of a group set up outside the authority of chief rabbi Mordecai Labaton. From this document one may tentatively draw certain conclusions regarding the appointment certificates of other rabbis. True, the powers given to Rabbi Kassin were almost unlimited, but it would appear that most community rabbis enjoyed far-reaching authority.[2] On the face of it, the community was almost completely dependent upon its rabbi, although in practice the relationship was not as one-sided as that might imply.

For centuries, the leading rabbis in the Syrian communities had been chosen or appointed as was customary throughout the Ottoman empire—that is, by the community itself, without any involvement on the part of the imperial authorities. The chosen spiritual leaders were partners in the leadership of the community alongside the moneyed elite and sometimes also the hereditary elite. There was always a sense of mutual dependence between the rabbis and their partners in leadership, alongside an element of tension and the consequent intermittent crises.

During the second quarter of the nineteenth century, the empire re-examined its relationship with its non-Muslim minorities within the framework of the administrative reforms introduced at that time. The minorities were organized in autonomous religious communities known as millets.[3] While the various millets enjoyed the official recognition of the Sublime Porte, this recognition came at the price of increased government involvement in their internal affairs. In the case of the Jewish communities, this involvement reached a peak with the introduction of the Jewish millet decree of 1864–5, which laid out the procedure for the election of the chief rabbi—the *ḥakham bashi*—in Istanbul, and confirmed his status as head of the Jewish millet. The decree also spelt out the obligations and authorities of the *ḥakham bashi* as the key figure in all matters pertaining to the relationship between the Jews and the government, and as the person responsible for carrying out the instructions of the Sublime Porte within his community. The same law also established community institutions enjoying a certain limited authority alongside the *ḥakham bashi* and prescribed a set procedure for elections to these institutions.[4] Alongside the primary public functions of the chief rabbi,

[2] See Harel, 'Spiritual Agitation' (Heb.), 33–4.

[3] Much ink has been spilt on the precise significance of this term. See Levi, 'Changes in the Leadership' (Heb.), 266.

[4] See Davison, *Reform in the Ottoman Empire*, 129–31.

he was also deemed responsible for collecting imperial taxes from members of the community and handing them over to the authorities, and given the power to impose special internal taxes on the community as needed. Arrangements similar to those regarding the central Jewish leadership were also introduced in respect of the leadership in the various other Jewish communities throughout the empire, so that each main centre would have its own *ḥakham bashi*.

Several of the rules relating to the election of the *ḥakham bashi* were of a democratic nature, such as the use of a secret ballot. However, the greatest innovation was the provision whereby the successful candidate was granted official recognition by the sultan. This made the state, rather than the community, the ultimate source of the chief rabbi's authority, and opened up the possibility of an individual's holding the office by virtue of government recognition while failing to achieve the confidence and trust of community members. Notwithstanding these formal innovations, the government's involvement in such appointments did not take the same form, nor did it occur at the same time, in Baghdad, Damascus, and Aleppo.[5] Moreover, during the period in question the newly democratic manner of selecting the *ḥakham bashi* was not implemented in practice in any of the communities in Syria or Iraq, where the *ḥakham bashi* continued to be chosen by the old oligarchies: 'It is known that at the time when the people of the city wish to appoint a Torah scholar as judge or as leader [*parnas*], the wealthy nobility of the community gather together and take counsel with one another as to whom to appoint.'[6]

The Undermining of the Office of *Ḥakham Bashi*

In Aleppo the *ḥakham bashi* did not need any special political talents, primarily because of the particular role played here by the Jewish consuls, all members of the Picciotto family, who provided the main political support of the community.[7] The Picciottos were Francos, and as such were not involved in the election of the chief rabbi, the Francos remaining apart from the communal framework with its privileges and obligations. For that reason, and because the political power they enjoyed by virtue of the consular status of

[5] It is also worth noting that obtaining governmental recognition of a chief rabbi could cost the community a lot of money. See e.g. ACRI, TR/Is/162*a*, the *gevirim* of Damascus to Rabbi Moses Halevi, Damascus, 18 Elul 5634.

[6] Dweck Hakohen, *She'erit ya'akov*, 31*a*; cf. Abulafia, *Penei yitsḥak*, iii, 39*b*, §9; Antebi, *Ḥokhmah umusar*, 115*a*.

[7] For a list of the Jewish consuls in Aleppo, see Ch. 10 below; also Harel, *Syrian Jewry*, 225–34. For more detail on the Francos, see Ch. 2 above.

the Picciotto family, the Francos of Aleppo did not see the *ḥakham bashi* as a rival for positions of power. As for the wealthy laymen of the community, given the dominance of the Francos their political activity was in any event limited, and they did not see the *ḥakham bashi* as a competitor—unlike, for example, their counterparts in Damascus. Hence, in Aleppo, scholarly erudition and greatness in Torah, rather than political skills, continued to be the most important characteristics expected of candidates for the office of *ḥakham bashi*. The rabbi appointed to this office also served as 'head of the spiritual ones', in addition to serving as head of the community's rabbinic court. Another rabbi usually served alongside the *ḥakham bashi*, both as his deputy on the rabbinic court and to represent the community in dealings with the outside world. For example, Rabbi Moses Sutton functioned as deputy to chief rabbi Hayim Mordecai Labaton during the 1860s, and also conducted the foreign relations of the community from the mid-1850s until his death on 23 July 1878.[8]

It is not clear whether the chief rabbis of Aleppo enjoyed the recognition of the Ottoman authorities prior to 1880. Rabbi Abraham Antebi served as the community's chief rabbi from 1817,[9] with Rabbi Hayim Mordecai Labaton as his deputy for many years. In January 1858, shortly after Rabbi Antebi's death, Rabbi Labaton was appointed chief rabbi, holding the position until his own death on 30 May 1869.[10] The circumstances by which Rabbi Labaton was succeeded by Rabbi Saul Dweck Hakohen, rather than Rabbi Moses Sutton, who had been Labaton's deputy, are not known. Around the time of Rabbi Saul Dweck Hakohen's appointment the Aleppo community was both suffering a severe economic crisis and experiencing the effects of the Ottoman reforms, which had begun to penetrate into the fabric of life and to disrupt the traditional communal framework. It is therefore possible that the selection of Rabbi Saul Dweck Hakohen resulted from internal struggles within the community that led to disorder or irregularities in its administration.[11] According to Nisim Behar, a representative of the Alliance Israélite Universelle in Aleppo, Rabbi Saul Dweck Hakohen did not enjoy a

[8] On Sutton's activity and his connections as representative of the community with external actors, see his notebook, BZI, MS 3724; also his numerous letters to the Alliance, e.g. AAIU, Syrie, I.B., Alep, 1, 3 Adar 5635, his recommendation to the Alliance that it support the appointment of the French official Alexander Lucciana as the French consul in Aleppo, because of his positive relations with the Jews.

[9] See Antebi, *Mor ve'aholot*, 'Even ha'ezer', 54*b*, §12. Rabbi Abraham Antebi died on 14 January 1858, aged 93.

[10] On the characteristics of the period of Rabbi Abraham Antebi and Rabbi Hayim Mordecai Labaton, see Ch. 3 above.

[11] See *Bulletin*, 1st sem. 1873, pp. 84–5.

particularly respected position in the community, and his influence over events therein was negligible.[12]

It would seem that the appointment of a rabbi lacking both charisma and leadership ability, who served in the position for a period of four years, was a turning point in the status of the chief rabbinate in Aleppo, marking the beginning of the institution's decline. Following the death of Rabbi Saul Dweck Hakohen on 22 January 1874, differences of opinion within the community over which of the local scholars would be the most suitable successor came to the surface once again. The solution found was the return of Rabbi Menasheh Sutton, who had left Aleppo four years earlier to serve as the rabbi of Safed.[13] He was not particularly successful in gaining acceptance within an increasingly divided community, and in 1876, two years after his return, he resigned and accepted an invitation to serve as rabbi of the community of Alexandria in Egypt.[14] In his place Rabbi Aaron Choueka was appointed chief rabbi of Aleppo; evidently a compromise candidate, he was more readily accepted by the modernizing, educated, prosperous segment of the community than by the traditional scholars. Saul Somekh, an emissary of the Alliance in Aleppo, described him as 'deserving of renown and praise; having a relatively liberal consciousness, he defended the school against the attacks of narrow-minded people and zealots'.[15] It may be that it was because of his open-minded approach that Rabbi Choueka did not enjoy the support of the Torah scholars; it is also possible that the Francos incited them against him, provoked by his implacable opposition to their plans for the Alliance school: the Francos wanted this institution to be an elitist one, whereas the rabbi

[12] See AAIU, Syrie, III.E., Alep, 21, Behar, 22 Aug. 1870. A contrary impression is given by Rabbi David-Sion Laniado, who praises Rabbi Saul Dweck in exaggerated fashion: Laniado, *For the Sake of the Holy Ones* (Heb.), 79. However, it would seem that Behar's words are more reliable, both because they are based upon first-hand testimony and because they do not attempt to praise the rabbis of Aleppo, as Laniado does.

[13] See M. Sutton, *Maḥberet pirḥei shoshanim*, 'Introduction by the Author's Grandson' (Heb.). On his title as chief rabbi of Aleppo as early as May 1874, see Benayahu, 'The Rabbinic Emissary' (Heb.), 185.

[14] Rabbi Menasheh Sutton never reached Alexandria, dying on his way there, on 13 September 1876. See M. Sutton, *Maḥberet pirḥei shoshanim*, 'Introduction by the Author's Grandson' (Heb.); Laniado, *For the Sake of the Holy Ones* (Heb.), 45; also Ze'ev, 'A Description' (Heb.), 86.

[15] AAIU, Syrie, X.E., Alep, 83, Somekh, 8 July 1880. For more detail on this struggle see Harel, *Syrian Jewry*, 84–7. Rabbi Choueka made his living by selling drinks, and so was known as Sharbati. See Abadi, *Mikra kodesh*, 54–5. He died on 12 July 1881; see Laniado, *For the Sake of the Holy Ones* (Heb.), 10. Cf. FO 195/1154, for his signature as *ḥakham bashi* of Aleppo, confirming the testimony of the sages of Aleppo on the British citizenship of members of the Dweck family, 24 Tevet 5637.

wanted it to be a more popular school. He was evidently forced to leave his position in 1880, at which point Rabbi Moses Hakohen was appointed as *ḥakham bashi* and Rabbi Moses Swed as his deputy.

Moses Hakohen is the first chief rabbi in Aleppo whom we definitely know to have received the approval and recognition of the Ottoman authorities, expressed in their sending a royal firman and a special set of robes from the sultan.[16] This recognition created in Aleppo, at least in theory, an official division of the community leadership between two rabbis: the *ḥakham bashi*, who represented the community to the authorities, and the head of the spiritual committee, who served as head of the rabbinic court. However, in practice Rabbi Moses Hakohen continued to serve as head of the court, and it was only after his death in 1882, when Rabbi Abraham Dweck Hakohen—the brother of Rabbi Saul Dweck Hakohen—was appointed as *ḥakham bashi*, that an actual separation was made between the two functions. There was an interim period immediately after Rabbi Moses Hakohen's death when Rabbi Moses Swed, who had previously served as head of the community's rabbinic court, also assumed the title of *ḥakham bashi*—evidently without an official firman—but he did not remain in office for long.[17] Testimonies from 1883 already mention Rabbi Abraham Dweck Hakohen as being recognized as *ḥakham bashi* by the authorities, referring to Moses Swed only as head of the rabbinic court.[18]

From Aleppo to Antioch and Back

Abraham Dweck Hakohen is first mentioned in the extant sources as the youngest of the Torah scholars supported by a fund devoted to the sages of the yeshiva in Aleppo.[19] Thereafter his name does not appear among the signatures of city's sages until 1883, the year in which he was appointed *ḥakham bashi* of the community. The reason for the disappearance of his name is that he moved to Antioch, where he served for more than thirty years as that community's rabbi.[20] Attaching great importance to the backing of the government authorities, he took the trouble to obtain an official appointment as

16 AAIU, Syrie, X.E., Alep, 83, Somekh, 8 July 1880; ACRI TR/Is/162*a*, Rabbi Moses Hakohen to Rabbi Moses Halevi, Aleppo, 5640. See also *JC*, 13 Aug. 1880, p. 13.

17 For his signature as *ḥakham bashi*, see JNUL, DMA, Arc. 4to, 1271/617, Swed to Elyashar, Iyar 5642 and 13th day of the Omer, 5643.

18 See Neimark, *Journey in an Ancient Land* (Heb.) 55; cf. *Ḥavatselet*, 36 (17 Av 5644), 283.

19 See Laniado, *For the Sake of the Holy Ones* (Heb.), 168. The date of the agreement in which his name is mentioned was evidently close to 5607 (1847), the year of Rabbi Ezra Hakohen's death. See E. Laniado, *Degel maḥaneh efrayim*, 66.

20 See JNUL, DMA, Arc. 4to, 1271/614, Dweck to Elyashar, 17 Av 5655.

ḥakham bashi of Antioch and attempted to establish his status as equal to that of the heads of the Christian churches in the city.[21] In December 1866, the Antioch community received a firman from the sultan officially appointing him rabbi of the community with the status of *qayimaqam* (provisional) *ḥakham bashi*. It was unusual for so small a community to receive an official appointment of this type, and its conferral in this instance was evidently attributable both to the political activity of the rabbi and to efforts made on his behalf by his relatives, wealthy merchants who paid the fee required for the firman to be issued.[22] Rabbi Dweck Hakohen expanded the realm of his activities beyond the specifically religious framework and energetically pursued contacts with the government. He did not consider himself inferior to any of the leaders of other religious communities, not even the Muslim *qadi* (judge). Thus, when the *qadi* wished the Jews to follow Muslim law in the matter of inheritance, the *ḥakham bashi* insisted that the Jews be allowed to follow their own laws, and that this right be affirmed in a firman from the sultan.[23] His activity in the Jewish community of Antioch is described as follows:

There was a certain learned man who was a *shoḥet* [ritual slaughterer] and led the holy community in all those matters required for the wellbeing of the city, and he also taught their children the words of our ancient sages, of blessed memory . . . And he lived in Antioch for a number of years, as the spokesman and leader, and the majority of the people in the community were his students, and he acted on their behalf vis-à-vis the nations of the world. He would not rest and was not silent if one of them was imprisoned, be it because of some money matter or some libel, until he released him from prison.[24]

We do not have many details about the circumstances of Rabbi Abraham Dweck Hakohen's appointment as *ḥakham bashi* in Aleppo. It would seem that his relationship with the community in Antioch was not an easy one, so that when the office in Aleppo became vacant he saw an inviting opportunity to move.[25] First he needed to convince the community leaders that he was a suitable candidate, and to this end he emphasized his rich experience in leading the community of Antioch. He was described at the time of his appoint-

[21] See ACRI, TR/Is/162*a*, Rabbi Abraham Dweck Hakohen to Rabbi Moses Halevi, Antioch, 22 Nisan 5640, 22 Sivan 5640.

[22] For the firman itself, see Galante, *Histoire*, 370–1. On the manner of appointing rabbis in the satellite communities of Aleppo, see Harel, *Syrian Jewry*, 69–70.

[23] See ACRI, TR/Is/162*b*, Abraham Dweck to Moses Halevi, 15 Shevat 5646.

[24] S. Dweck Hakohen, *Emet me'erets*, 27*a*–28*a*, §4.

[25] On the dispute that broke out between him and the community of Antioch, see ibid. 27*a*, §4.

ment as 'Abraham Dweck, who from the beginning excited the people with his smooth tongue so as to raise up the position of Israel and the flag of the nation, who "would go out before them and would come in before them" regarding the laws of the government, and he rose up like a lion, to be their leader and head'.[26] This appointment sowed the seeds of controversy which eventually led not only to his deposition but also to the reunification of the two separate functions of head of the spiritual committee and *ḥakham bashi*.

The Weakening of Rabbinic Authority

One of the striking features of the Jewish communities of Syria during the second half of the nineteenth century, particularly that of Aleppo, was the large number of ethical (*musar*) treatises that were written and disseminated among their members.[27] One of the principal reasons for this was the growing and increasingly open disregard for the traditional Jewish way of life. This in turn led to a decline in the status of the Jewish rabbinic court and other established community institutions. Rabbi Abraham Dayan, in attempting to trace the factors leading to the weakening of Aleppo Jews' allegiance to the traditions of their religion, describes the situation in the community around the middle of the nineteenth century as follows:

> Today there are many servants who rebel against their master, the Lord in heaven, and do not wish to do His will. Each one builds himself a high place to do whatever their Evil Urge desires; they run about and are lenient with themselves and with others in everything they do—and I do not know whom they take as their authority.[28]

The status of the rabbinic court as the exclusive source of authority within the community was gradually challenged, as more and more people appealed instead to the Ottoman and consulate courts. Instances of contempt for the rabbinic court, expressed in defying its rulings and instructions, became more common. Popular belief in the magical power of the rabbis and in their ability to curse and to impose bans gradually weakened. When Rabbi Raphael Kassin attempted in 1862 to establish a Reform community in the city, the Torah scholars saw the Reform group as an organization of western-educated people posing an ideological threat to traditional Judaism and to their own religious hegemony. They responded by banding together to strengthen their supervision of individuals' behaviour and to seek the backing and support of the wealthy members of the community. In doing so, the sages

26 JNUL, DMA, Arc. 4to, 1271/622, Safdeyé to Elyashar, 27 Av 5654.

27 See Harel, *Sifrei erets* (Heb.), index.

28 A. Dayan, *Tuv ta'am*, 205.

sought to emphasize their unique status and cohesion as a group. These efforts gave rise to the image of the Aleppo community as an observant, traditionalist community whose rabbis had full powers of enforcement over individuals and whose court enjoyed authority of the highest order.[29] But in fact the rabbinic class in Aleppo was in constant danger of losing its authority both in principle and in practice, as a result of which it was perpetually engaged in an uncompromising struggle against those who challenged its standing.

Within the context of this struggle, the sages of Aleppo rejected any new approach to the interpretation or understanding of Judaism, waging an unforgiving battle against any literature that seemed likely to arouse debate among the educated classes within the community. Matters came to a head in 1865 with the burning of the book *Em lamikra* by Rabbi Elijah Benamozegh of Livorno. In this book, which is primarily a commentary on the Torah, Benamozegh tried to prove that there is a similarity, a parallel—at times even identity—between the principles underlying the faiths, customs, and traditions of ancient peoples. When the Aleppo sages saw the book, they burned it publicly, and the rabbis of Damascus followed suit. It would seem that Benamozegh's book accentuated the existing conflict between the educated *maskilim*, who had already shown themselves receptive to modern reformist ideas, and the Torah scholars. Thus it seems that the extremity of the Aleppo sages' opposition to such ideas derived more from the social reality within their community than from a purely intellectual and spiritual world-view.[30]

The contempt exhibited towards the rabbinic leadership in Aleppo grew ever more pronounced, as is apparent from the measures successive chief rabbis took in attempting to counter it. In 1880, when Rabbi Moses Hakohen was appointed *ḥakham bashi* in Aleppo, one of his first acts was to ask the government authorities to grant him extraordinary powers to impose his authority over those who refused to pay communal taxes, and against those who contradicted or disobeyed him or did not behave in accordance with the tradition. He even turned to the *ḥakham bashi* in Istanbul, Rabbi Moses Halevi, asking him to obtain a firman that would enable him to send the rebels to the city's prison—a very serious and unusual move in the context of the communal tradition.[31]

Nevertheless, so long as the rabbi who headed the rabbinic court also represented the Jewish community in dealings with the government, his own

[29] See Zohar, *Tradition and Change* (Heb.), 38, 68–9.

[30] For a fuller treatment of this incident, see Harel, '"The Edict to Destroy"', 57–60.

[31] ACRI, TR/Is/162*a*, Rabbi Moses Hakohen to Rabbi Moses Halevi, *parashat* 'that his days may last long over his kingdom', 5640.

central position in the life of the community was assured. However, once a split was introduced between the office of *ḥakham bashi* and that of the head of the spiritual committee, who also served as head of the rabbinic court, the *ḥakham bashi* began to overshadow his colleague to a marked degree. Saul Somekh, the headmaster of the Alliance school in Aleppo, paints a gloomy picture of the status of the rabbinic court and of its head, Rabbi Moses Swed, during the first half of the 1880s. According to him, the power of the spiritual leadership was in sustained decline. As the judges were elected by the community and derived their authority from its members—without any involvement or affirmation on the part of the government—the court's ability to act and to exert its authority depended on the goodwill of the Jewish public and their continuing demand for its services.[32]

When Abraham Dweck Hakohen was appointed *ḥakham bashi*, a complete split occurred between himself and Moses Swed. It seems plausible that Rabbi Swed was hurt by the fact that he had been bypassed as a candidate for the office of *ḥakham bashi* in favour of Rabbi Dweck Hakohen. In any event, he prohibited him from serving as a member of the rabbinic court, thereby excluding him from any involvement in the spiritual life of the community. There ensued an open battle of words, in which both men set out to slander one another and to draw the support of the community to their own side. According to Somekh, this struggle resulted only in yet greater contempt for the rabbis on the part of the wider community.[33] Rabbi Dweck Hakohen, not content with the sultanic firman he had received in Antioch, now sought to strengthen his position even further. He implored Moses Halevi, the *ḥakham bashi* in Istanbul, to obtain on his behalf a special firman and crown as *ḥakham bashi* in Aleppo, thereby hoping to establish his own status in the eyes of the government as equivalent to that of the heads of the other religious communities.[34] In fact, the struggle between the two heads of the community, both of whom belonged to the group of Torah scholars, contributed more than a little to the growing feeling in some segments of the community that communal matters should no longer be left in the hands of religious figures, leading to demands that an official steering committee be set up alongside the *ḥakham bashi*.

During the latter decades of the nineteenth century the economic situation of the Aleppo community began to decline. The opening of the Suez Canal in 1869 and the bankruptcy of the Ottoman government in 1875 were both damaging to the interests of the city's merchants, and although the com-

[32] AAIU, Syrie, X.E., Alep, 83, Somekh, 10 Apr. 1884. [33] Ibid.

[34] ACRI TR/Is/162*b*, Abraham Dweck to Moses Halevi, 15 Shevat 5646.

munity as a whole was still prosperous, many individuals suffered losses as a result of these events.[35] At the beginning of the 1880s most imports into Aleppo were in Jewish hands, while exports were mostly controlled by Muslims and Christians. Most of the Jews within the community earned their livelihoods through trade, handicrafts, and services on a small to medium scale.[36] Until 1894, the communal government was led by the *ḥakham bashi* alongside a small number of wealthy householders. These *gevirim* were not elected by the community, but served by virtue of their wealth and status, or personal connection with Rabbi Abraham Dweck Hakohen. All of the community's expenses, with the exception of the *'askariyya* tax, which was a personal or poll tax, were met from two sources: contributions from the wealthy men of the community, based on a 'valuation' calculated by the chief rabbi and other prominent individuals; and voluntary contributions made by the Franco families, who remained outside the communal framework until the mid-1910s.

The decline in the community's economic situation affected the ability of the *gevirim* to fund its expenses, and the leaders of the community felt a need to spread the burden of financing it more widely across its members. At the same time, some within the community saw the decline in the power and influence of the *gevirim* leading to an excessive concentration of power and influence in the hands of the *ḥakham bashi*. Both these factors fuelled widespread demands for the establishment of an elected steering committee, of the type customary in other communities in the Ottoman empire, to lead the community and its institutions. A propitious moment for such a change came in summer 1894, with the appointment of Hasan Haki Pasha as *wali* of the Aleppo district.[37] Later, when the new steering committee sought to depose the *ḥakham bashi*, it was supported in this demand by the Torah scholars, who felt themselves to have been damaged by his activities.

Also among the groups demanding change at this time was a new social class, whose members drew their power not from money or pedigree, but rather from education. This class, which emerged in the Aleppo community over a period of some twenty-five years, was composed of graduates of the Alliance school, founded in Aleppo in 1869. By the 1890s members of this educated class occupied important positions in the municipal councils, in the

[35] On the economic situation of the Aleppo community before 1880, see Harel, *Syrian Jewry*, 54–7.

[36] On the economic situation in Aleppo at this time, see Neimark, *Journey in an Ancient Land* (Heb.), 27; *Ḥavatselet*, 12 (24 Tevet 5635), 97; 34 (2 Tamuz 5640), 255.

[37] On Hasan Haki Pasha and the circumstances of his appointment, see *Ḥavatselet*, 41 (15 Tamuz 5654), 211.

courts, and in the government offices.[38] These *maskilim* now joined forces with the growing number of middle-class merchants who had begun to displace the wealthy householders in positions of influence to demand changes in the structure of the communal leadership.

Tension between the Torah Scholars and the *Ḥakham Bashi*

As we have seen, although Rabbi Abraham Dweck Hakohen had served as the spiritual leader of the community in Antioch as well as its representative to the authorities, in Aleppo he was not a member of the rabbinic court—unlike his predecessors as *ḥakham bashi*, who had also served as head of the court. This exclusion explains Rabbi Dweck Hakohen's repeated attempts to interfere in the activities of the spiritual committee, which over time prompted most of the community's scholars to align themselves with the powerful laymen of the community in the campaign to depose him. It will suffice here to note briefly four cases in which the *ḥakham bashi* directly interfered in the court's work in such a way as to nullify a ruling or prevent its execution, with resultant damage to the authority of the court.

The first case occurred in 1888, when the court, headed by Rabbi Moses Swed, declared a certain woman to be a *moredet*—that is, a rebellious wife. The *ḥakham bashi* and two other rabbis ruled in favour of the woman and against the husband. Rabbi Ezra Eli Hakohen, one of the judges in the communal court, described the situation created by the conflict between these two rulings:

> There flared up the fire of controversy and opposition to rabbinic sages—these prohibit, and those permit—and the outcome was that people did not listen to the rabbis. As for ourselves, we are greatly pained by this controversy, and particularly the defamation of God's Name, Heaven forbid, for [people] say there is no judgment below [i.e. in this world], for at this time the Law is like clay in the hands of the potter, who turns it about whichever way he likes.[39]

Seeing the *ḥakham bashi* attempting to interfere in areas which until then had been outside his jurisdiction, people began to fear that the force and authority of the rabbinic court as the final arbiter in matters of halakhah within the community would be weakened. The dispute became increasingly intense, to the point where both sides presented their arguments to Rabbi Jacob Saul Elyashar in Jerusalem, seeking his support. Rabbi Abraham

[38] See *JC*, 25 July 1884, 11; *Ḥavatselet*, 45 (15 Av 5654), 362.

[39] Elyashar, *Ma'aseh ish*, 'Even ha'ezer', 45*b*, §1. On Ezra Eli Hakohen, see Laniado, *For the Sake of the Holy Ones* (Heb.), 68.

Dweck Hakohen and his rabbinic supporters were accused, at least by implication, of distortion and outright lies. It would appear that during this period the *ḥakham bashi* still enjoyed the support of the wealthy men of the community, so he had no qualms about establishing a committee to resolve the dispute, headed by the Austrian consul, Moses de Picciotto.[40]

The second case took place in Iyar 5654 (1894), when Rabbi Solomon Safdeyé was serving as head of both the spiritual committee and the rabbinic court. It concerned a well-to-do individual, a member of the Dweck family, who had taken property that belonged to his son-in-law, in defiance of a ruling by the communal judges. He refused to appear before the rabbinic judges, relying on the support of both the British consul and the *ḥakham bashi*. Rabbi Solomon Safdeyé commented: 'There are among us certain learned people who are not fair-minded people . . . and they go to the litigants and teach them arguments and show them halakhic works [with arguments] that may be used in their favour, and strengthen their heart so as not to listen to the voices of the teachers [i.e. rabbis].'[41]

The third case, in Av 5654 (1894), related to a number of members of the community who had had sexual relations with a non-Jewish woman: the sages and rabbis of Aleppo wished to take steps against them, but the *ḥakham bashi* prevented them from doing so.[42]

The fourth case was without doubt the main cause of the rabbis' demands that the *ḥakham bashi* be removed from office. It revolved around the fitness of Saul David Sutton Dabah, a young Torah scholar, to serve as a ritual slaughterer for the community. About thirty years earlier he had used subterfuge to learn the skill of slaughtering animals, bribing one of the *shoḥatim* to teach him, despite the prohibition on his doing this work that had been imposed upon him in the 1860s when Mordecai Labaton had been *ḥakham bashi*. The scholars in the community denounced him, saying that since he had first been banned from slaughtering animals he had committed many violations of religious and moral laws, including eating non-kosher food, stealing, cheating, and generally displaying contempt for the commandments. There were even accusations that on one occasion when Sutton had been sent on a mission

[40] See NLIS, Arc. 4to, 1271/133, Ezra Eli Hakohen to Elyashar, 20 Tamuz 5648; ibid. 1271/48, Abraham Dweck to Elyashar, 5 Av 5648. On Moses de Picciotto, see Gaon, *The Jews of the East* (Heb.), 545; Harel, *Syrian Jewry*, index.

[41] JNUL, DMA, Arc. 4to, 1271/622, Safdeyé to Elyashar, Aleppo, 4 Av 5654; 1271/623, Yitshak Shrem to Elyashar, 11 Iyar 5654; Pinto to Elyashar, 11 Iyar 5654. On Rabbi Solomon Safdeyé, see Laniado, *For the Sake of the Holy Ones* (Heb.), 88.

[42] JNUL, DMA, Arc. 4to, 1271/610, heads of the community to Elyashar, Aleppo, 22 Av 5654.

involving the use of *hekdesh* (communal funds) to help the orphans of the Antioch community, he had behaved dishonestly, accepting bribes and causing great monetary loss to the orphans. As early as 1887 Rabbi Moses Swed had attempted to disqualify him, but without success. In 1891, new charges were raised against Sutton, regarding improper slaughtering and adultery. Realizing that many of the scholars were attempting to disqualify him from practising slaughtering, he set up an investigating committee, composed of five rabbis (including members of the rabbinic court), other learned scholars, and wealthy laymen, with the *ḥakham bashi* Abraham Dweck Hakohen at their head. The committee examined the evidence against him and ultimately gave him permission to resume his activities as slaughterer. This ruling sparked a storm of controversy in the community, relating as it did to questions of ritually prohibited foods that concerned everyone. The community split into two camps, one of which accepted that Sutton was a legitimate slaughterer, and another that refused to eat meat from animals he had slaughtered. Both sides sent their halakhic rulings for the approval of rabbis in Erets Yisra'el. The slaughterer obtained a judgment pronouncing him qualified to slaughter from Rabbi Elijah Mani of Hebron, while his opponents elicited a ruling disqualifying him from Rabbi Jacob Saul Elyashar of Jerusalem.[43] The investigating committee itself sent letters to the rabbis of Jerusalem and, in the final analysis, obtained the agreement of Rabbi Elyashar that Sutton be permitted to engage in slaughtering under certain conditions. Notwithstanding this outcome, the community remained divided.[44]

The controversy flared up a second time in summer 1894 with new accusations against Saul Sutton. The rabbis who opposed him testified that many people had ceased to eat meat from animals slaughtered by him because they feared the slaughtering had not been done in accordance with Jewish law: 'but the honourable rabbinic court do not take heed of these words because they are afraid of him, as he is a violent person'.[45] This was an extremely serious accusation, implying an almost total loss of trust on the part of the community in the rabbinic court and its ability to exert its authority in the face of actual or potential threats of violence. The *ḥakham bashi*'s support for this slaughterer placed him in opposition to the majority of the Torah scholars of Aleppo, who were now united in denying the *kashrut* of animals slaughtered by Sutton.[46] It was this dispute that, at a later stage, led to the overwhelming majority of the community coming out in opposition to Rabbi Abraham

[43] See Elyashar, *Ma'aseh ish*, 'Yoreh de'ah' 27*a*, §13; Yadid Halevi, *Yemei yosef*, 'Yoreh de'ah', 14*b*, §1.

[44] See S. Sutton, *Diber sha'ul*, 'Yoreh de'ah', 41*a*, 'Yoreh de'ah', §8.

[45] JNUL, DMA, Arc. 4to, 1271/24, anonymous letter to Elyashar, 18 Av 5654.

[46] Ibid. 1271/618, Silvera to Elyashar, 23 Heshvan 5655.

Dweck Hakohen's continuing to serve as *ḥakham bashi*. His main supporters were those whom he had backed against the rulings of the rabbinic court—first and foremost the slaughterer Saul Sutton—and they evidently stirred up the controversy until it span out of control. As a result, the demands that the *ḥakham bashi* be deposed and that Sutton be disqualified from serving as a ritual slaughterer went hand in hand.

The Attempt to Reorganize the Community

The Jewish community in Aleppo, like others in the Ottoman empire, was required to pay the *ʿaskariyya* or military commutation tax. This tax was divided among members of the community on the basis of a 'valuation' made by the *mukhtariyya*, a group of people appointed to this function by the *ḥakham bashi*. At this time the Aleppo community did not use taxes such as the *gabilah* to fund the needs of the community; as noted above, the community's expenses were met primarily from various kinds of voluntary contributions. These expenses included the salaries of the *ḥakham bashi*, of the rabbinic judges (*dayanim*), and of the ritual slaughterers; maintenance of the two central synagogues and charitable institutions; and contributions to emissaries from Erets Yisra'el.[47]

The fact that the amount of *ʿaskariyya* tax to be paid by each member of the community was determined by an arbitrary group, not subject to any outside review or control, aroused a great deal of discontent, particularly among the poorer members, who found themselves without anyone to protect their interests and in a situation of economic distress. The *ḥakham bashi* and the *mukhtariyya* were accused of arbitrary and inequitable division of this tax burden. In 1892 several distinguished members of the community attempted to persuade Rabbi Abraham Dweck Hakohen to change the system of tax collection as part of wider improvements in the running of the community, but this attempt ended badly: the *ḥakham bashi*, who saw in their initiative an attempt to challenge his authority, denounced them to the government authorities, and they were forced to ransom themselves by handing over a large sum of money.[48] It is worth emphasizing that Rabbi Dweck's appointment as *ḥakham bashi* had been ratified in 1891, and that he exercised his authority in a dictatorial fashion. According to other leading figures in the community, he used the powers given him by the government indiscriminately, exploited his closeness to senior officials within the Ottoman judiciary and military to act

[47] See *Havatselet*, 34 (2 Tamuz 5640), 255–6; and Elyashar, *Ma'aseh ish*, 27*a*.

[48] See JNUL, DMA, Arc. 4to, 1271/610, heads of the community to Elyashar, 22 Av 5654; 1271/612, Alkutser to Elyashar, 27 Av 5654.

against his opponents, and even compelled the community to make him the permanent preacher in the synagogue, throwing anyone who dared to oppose him into prison.[49]

As mentioned, the appointment of the new *wali*, Hasan Haki Pasha, was seen as a good opportunity to change the structure of the community leadership in such a way as to enable it better to meet its needs and also to bring it into line with the provisions of the Jewish millet decree—specifically, to set up a steering committee to work alongside the *ḥakham bashi*. In order to prevent Rabbi Dweck Hakohen from opposing this step, it was taken in consultation with him.

It would appear that the rabbi, who was by now aged 75, initially agreed to this because he thought that such a committee could be of assistance to him as he grew older. It is also reasonable to assume that the *ḥakham bashi* hoped that by accepting the change he would improve his relationship with the people of the community, which had been strained for a long time, notwithstanding his powerful position in the eyes of the rulers.

The steering committee was duly established, consisting of ten distinguished members of the community, selected by lot, who would serve for one year only. Their election even received the approval of the local officials. The committee's first act was to appoint a new *mukhtariyya* to collect the *ʿaskariyya* tax. Its second was to set up two additional rabbinic courts, which, along with the existing court, would sit in rotation for four months each, following the system used in Jerusalem. A spiritual committee was also appointed, consisting of ten rabbinic sages, to oversee matters relating to ritual prohibitions in the life of the community.[50]

The Origin and Development of the Dispute

There are several differing accounts of the origin of the controversy that led to the demand that the *ḥakham bashi* be removed from office, expressing the viewpoints of the two sides. According to the members of the steering committee, which was supported by the sages and rabbis of Aleppo, two things prompted them to oppose Rabbi Abraham Dweck: first, the document of

[49] Ibid. 1271/610, heads of the community to Elyashar, 22 Av 5654. Cf. 1271/612, Alkutser to Elyashar, 27 Av 5654. On the confirmation of his appointment as *ḥakham bashi*, see *Hamagid*, 25 (25 June 1891), 197–8. It is worth mentioning that Rabbi Dweck Hakohen's forceful approach in his office helped the community innumerable times in its confrontations with the authorities and with the Christian and Muslim communities. See e.g. *Ḥavatselet*, 4 (7 Heshvan 5649), 31.

[50] JNUL, DMA, Arc. 4[to], 1271/610, heads of the community to Elyashar, 22 Av 5654.

partnership the *ḥakham bashi* had drawn up between himself and the *mukhtariyya*, and second, his attempt to undermine the authority of the steering committee and to obstruct its work. In their account, in 1890 the *ḥakham bashi* had entered into a secret arrangement with the *mukhtariyya*, set out in a document of partnership, concerning the division of profits from all monetary collections within the community, such as fees collected for registration of property via the *tabu* and payments towards the *ʿaskariyya* tax. According to them, the committee's appointment of a new *mukhtariyya* affected the income of the old *mukhtariyya* and that of the *ḥakham bashi*, and the latter took some steps to protect his profits.[51] It is important to recall that control over the collection of the *ʿaskariyya* in effect gave complete control over the community, as individuals were afraid to oppose the collector openly lest a heavier tax burden be imposed upon them. In practice, it appears that in this the *ḥakham bashi* was a tool in the hands of his supporters, led by the *shoḥet* Saul Sutton, a situation of which the members of the steering committee were well aware:

The source of the confusion and imprecations came from his deputy, Hakham Saul [Sutton] Dabah, the uprooter of Israel, knowing that if he [the *ḥakham bashi*] were to fall, he could not rise again . . . And if God is with them, and they are victorious over the *ḥakham bashi*, he [Sutton] will immediately be removed from his office of ritual slaughterer. Therefore, he and those close to him should not rest nor sleep and not be silent, to help the *ḥakham bashi*. And they obtained a number of signatures from the poor people of the land, who do not know their right hand from their left. And as Heaven is my witness, the rabbis and the other individuals who are God-fearing and all those with intelligence are filled with contempt for the *ḥakham bashi*, and all await the final redemption and deliverance from his hand. However, there are a number of individuals, including Khawaja [Mr] Ezra Dweck . . . who refuses to give the inheritance of his daughter to his son-in-law; and the sons of Khawaja Reuben Gabbai . . . who for many years have not borne the yoke together with the public, and do not give charity either to the poor or to the emissaries from Erets Yisra'el . . . And they are among the wealthy ones of the people, and for the sake of a thousand coins that they give every year to the *ḥakham bashi* he supports them and they support him, and they impose terror upon the public, not for the sake of Heaven.[52]

The Gabbai family, with whom the members of the steering committee were in dispute, were British subjects, and it was on this basis that they were

[51] JNUL, DMA, Arc. 4to, 1271/610, heads of the community to Elyashar, Av 5650. See also AAIU, Syrie, IX.E., Alep, 70*b*, Raffoul, 12 July 1895.

[52] JNUL, DMA, Arc. 4to, 1271/618, Silvera to Elyashar, 23 Heshvan 5655. Cf. ibid. 1271/610, heads of the community to Elyashar, 22 Av 5654, 4 Tishrei 5655; 1271/620, Pinto to Elyashar, 24 Tishrei 5655.

exempted from paying community taxes. While they were not Francos, their wealth bought them special status within the Jewish community of Aleppo—a status further strengthened shortly before the outbreak of the controversy when one of its members was appointed Persian consul for the Aleppo district.[53] It is reasonable to assume that, with the support of the *ḥakham bashi*, the Gabbai family sought to preserve the old system of leadership, according to which the chief rabbi acted with the support of a group of dignitaries. This attitude aroused the opposition of people within the community, but enjoyed the backing of the *ḥakham bashi* who, as the passage quoted above points out, received part of his salary from this family.

For his part, the *ḥakham bashi* saw himself as a victim of circumstances. He described his opposition to the way in which the steering committee worked as deriving not from personal considerations but from his position as *ḥakham bashi*. He argued in his defence that he had initially co-operated with the committee, had asked the government authorities to recognize it, and had even announced in the synagogue that the members of the committee were the leaders of the community—but the government had refused to recognize the new committee, as had rivals of the committee members within the community. As a result of this, he argued, both sides saw him as their enemy.[54] Rabbi Dweck Hakohen went on to describe the document of partnership with the *mukhtariyya* as having been made with the knowledge of the heads of the community, on the understanding that the monies gathered were intended to cover communal expenses.[55]

As noted above, in the past the Ottoman rulers had been accustomed to avoid involvement in the internal affairs of the Jewish community, including the election of the *ḥakham bashi*. But this time, in the light of repeated requests of both sides, the *wali*—who both sides agreed 'does not show favour and not show respect to the great one . . . is clean of hands and hates bribery'[56]—was forced to intervene. From his perspective, the main goal was to keep the peace in the district under his jurisdiction. To this end, he initially gave unqualified backing to the *ḥakham bashi*, who like himself was a government official, and instructed the complainants to present their grievances in writing to himself and to the authorities in Istanbul. The opponents of Rabbi Dweck Hakohen, who wanted him removed from office immediately, used various arguments in their attempts to incriminate him. First, they exagger-

[53] *Ḥavatselet*, 26 (22 Adar II 5654), 205.

[54] JNUL, DMA, Arc. 4[to], 1271/614, Dweck to Elyashar, 17 Av 5655. Cf. ibid., Dweck to Elyashar, 29 Tevet 5655; 1271/621, ruling of Dweck, n.d.

[55] See ibid. 1271/610, receiving testimony before the representatives of the *ḥakham bashi* in Istanbul, 27 Kislev 5655.

[56] Ibid., sages of Aleppo to Elyashar, 22 Av 5654.

ated his age, claiming that he was 80 years old and that as a result his mind was confused through senility. They also argued that, along with his partners in the old *mukhtariyya*, he had misused tax monies that were intended for the government. They also accused him of illegal activity in respect of the import of sacred books, which were subject to a high tariff unless intended for the poor. The committee accused the *ḥakham bashi* of deceiving the government; in its view, he imported such books claiming that they were intended for the poor, when in fact he sold them on the open market for great profit.[57]

In the *ḥakham bashi*'s view, the controversy revolved around the definition of the committee's status and remit. He therefore attempted, on his own initiative, to bring about a compromise between the community and the government by writing to the governor, without consulting with the committee, stating that it was not a steering committee, but rather a temporary committee to take care of the needs of the community. The committee interpreted this as a proposal to disband it altogether—and at the same time discovered Rabbi Dweck Hakohen's document of partnership with the *mukhtariyya*. All these things aroused the anger of the heads of the community, leading to their demand that the *ḥakham bashi* be deposed.

At this point the governor declined to accept the committee's ruling without the approval of the Sublime Porte; hence, all the prerogatives involving leadership of the community and the administration of its financial affairs were once again in the hands of the *ḥakham bashi*. It is worth emphasizing that the Ottoman authorities were sensitive to the establishment of any new organization at this juncture, and that their reaction must be understood against the background of the Armenian revolutionary movement, which at this time was seeking national independence. The governor's cautious approach stemmed from his fear that revolutionary activity might spread in the area under his jurisdiction—a fear which the *ḥakham bashi* later exploited for his own ends, warning the authorities that the committee was likely to cause disturbance in the city, as the Armenians had done.[58]

On the basis of the extant documentation, there seems no doubt that the *ḥakham bashi* appealed to the government because he felt that he lacked support among the leading figures within the community. As noted above, in the

[57] JNUL, DMA, Arc. 4to, 1271/614, Dweck to Elyashar, 17 Elul 5655; JNUL, DMA, Arc. 4to, 1271/614, Dweck to Elyashar, 17 Av 5655; 1271/610, testimony received before representatives of the *ḥakham bashi* in Istanbul, 27 Kislev 5655.

[58] On the Armenian movement in the 1890s, see Lewis, *The Emergence of Modern Turkey*, 333–4, 348–51. For reports on Dweck Hakohen, see JNUL, DMA, Arc. 4to, 1271/612, Alkutser to Elyashar, 27 Av 5654; 1271/620, Pinto to Elyashar, 24 Tishrei 5655; 1271/610, rabbis of Aleppo to Elyashar, 24 Heshvan 5655. See also AAIU, Syrie, IX.E., Alep, 70*b*, Raffoul, 12 July 1895.

Ottoman empire the *ḥakham bashi*'s authority derived from two sources: his voluntary acceptance by the community and the recognition of the Sublime Porte by means of an official firman confirming his appointment. As Rabbi Dweck Hakohen's authority within the community dwindled, so he turned to the government authorities to strengthen his position as a senior government official and his hold on the office of *ḥakham bashi*. Among other things, he asked the authorities to arrest and to send into exile the members of the steering committee together with eight rabbis, including the head of the spiritual committee, Rabbi Solomon Safdeyé, on the grounds that these rabbis, having been appointed judges paid by the steering committee, had joined the ranks of his opponents.[59]

The leading members of the committee, well aware of the connections between the *ḥakham bashi* and the authorities, did not hesitate to make their own approach to the Ottoman government. With the approval of the *wali* a petition was submitted, signed by 350 individuals in the community, demanding the *ḥakham bashi*'s removal from office. In addition, several members of the committee who also enjoyed a certain status within the institutions of the district government, such as membership of the regional *majlis*, used their power and influence to present their side of the argument.[60]

The conflict was a bitter one, with denunciations, threats, and intimidation on both sides. In its wake, an atmosphere of fear dominated the Aleppo community, especially among the opponents of the *ḥakham bashi*. Evidence of this may be seen in, for example, the absence of the signatures of Isaiah Dayan and Yitshak Bekhor Mizrahi, both members of the rabbinic court headed by Rabbi Solomon Safdeyé, from any of the letters written in opposition to Rabbi Dweck Hakohen. Rabbi Dayan did not sign them because he was being blackmailed by the supporters of the *ḥakham bashi*: he owned a printing shop that operated without a permit, and was threatened with denunciation to the authorities by the *shoḥet* Saul Sutton if he spoke out against either himself or Rabbi Dweck Hakohen. Mizrahi, in turn, refrained from signing the letters out of deference to Rabbi Dayan, who was more senior than him.[61]

[59] JNUL, DMA, Arc. 4to, 1271/622, Safdeyé to Elyashar, 27 Av 5654; 1271/610, heads of the community to Elyashar, 22 Av 5654, 4 Tishrei 5655; 1271/614, Dweck to Elyashar, 29 Tevet 5655; AAIU, Syrie, IX.E., Alep, 70*b*, Raffoul, 12 July 1895.

[60] See JNUL, DMA, Arc. 4to, 1271/610, heads of the community to Elyashar, 22 Av 5654; 1271/612, Alkutser to Elyashar, 27 Av 5654; 1271/620, Pinto to Elyashar, 24 Tishrei 5655.

[61] See ibid. 1271/610, heads of the community to Elyashar, 22 Av 5654; 1271/622, Safdeyé to Elyashar, 28 Iyar 5655; 1271/611, testimony of Rabbis Isaiah Dayan and Yitshak Bekhor Mizrahi against the *ḥakham bashi*, given in camera before Rabbis Ya'akov Hayim Alfia and Ezra Lofez, 22 Av 5654. On Rabbi Isaiah Dayan, see Laniado, *For the Sake of the Holy Ones* (Heb.), 41;

The atmosphere of fear and threat is apparent from many of the letters sent from Aleppo at this time, some of which express the reluctance of certain people to sign the letters or petitions, and some of which contain an appeal to the addressee not to show the letter or to reveal its contents to anyone. The following, for example, is an extract from one letter written by Rabbi Solomon Safdeyé to the head of the Jewish community in Erets Yisra'el, Rabbi Jacob Saul Elyashar:

I present my request before the throne of the splendour of your greatness, that this letter of mine be hidden away in a cleft of a rock, that it not be seen or found by anyone, neither those far away nor even more those who are close, for I am fearful of the wrath, knowing that he [the *ḥakham bashi*] and his offspring have tongues like a well-honed arrow, to harm me both bodily and in my money. And I am old, my strength has waned, I cannot stand against them! And I have heard from those that tell the truth that last Friday he wrote a hateful document against the committee, the honourable householders . . . and against eight rabbis, from among the sages and rabbis of Aram Zova, to the governor, asking that they be sent into exile away from their land, to forgotten cities in houses where none dwells.[62]

Faced with the two conflicting accounts, the authorities were inclined to accept the *ḥakham bashi*'s version. Thus, a ruling was made against the steering committee stating that its members would be exiled if they refused to accept the authority of Rabbi Dweck Hakohen and make their peace with him. The community leaders had no choice but to submit and accept the ruling—but they did so in form only, with no intention of admitting defeat. Some time earlier, the controversy had broken out beyond the narrow confines of Aleppo, with both sides calling upon outside forces, in addition to the local authorities, for support in their struggle over the leadership. In the next section we shall consider four such external actors, one group and three individuals, that exerted a decisive influence upon the development of the controversy up to its denouement with the removal from office of the *ḥakham bashi* Rabbi Dweck Hakohen. These are, first, the Francos in Aleppo; second, Benjamin Alkutzer, a rabbinic emissary from Jerusalem; third, Jacob Saul Elyashar, the *ḥakham bashi* in Jerusalem; and fourth Moses Halevi, the *ḥakham bashi* in Istanbul.

On Rabbi Yitshak Bekhor Mizrahi, see ibid. 37. On threats against Rabbi Isaiah Dayan, see Dayan, *Imrei no'am*, author's introduction; cf. Harel, *Sifrei erets* (Heb.), 24–5; Ya'ari, 'Hebrew Printing' (Heb.), 102.

[62] JNUL, DMA, Arc. 4to, 1271/622, Safdeyé to Elyashar, 27 Av 5654; and cf. ibid. 1271/612, Alkutser to Elyashar, 2 Heshvan 5655; 1271/24, Gada to Elyashar, 2 Heshvan 5655, 7 Kislev 5655; 1271/618, Silvera to Elyashar, 3 Heshvan 5655; 1271/610, sages and rabbis of Aleppo to Elyashar, 24 Heshvan 5655.

The Role Played by External Actors in the Controversy

The Francos in Aleppo, as noted above, were families who had come to the city from Europe, assumed prominent economic and diplomatic positions, and preserved their independence in relation to the community until the beginning of the twentieth century. Although by the 1890s their numbers had markedly declined—in part through intermarriage with local Jewish families, in part as a result of emigration—the Francos remained outside the community organization, and in consequence of this independence were of potential importance to both the *ḥakham bashi*'s supporters and his opponents. The situation of the Francos at the time of this controversy was described by one of their number:

It is well known that among the people of Aram Zova there are certain families who are called Signores Francos . . . who do not belong to and are not involved in the holy community of Aram Zova at all, and do not pay taxes with them, nor do they pray with them or volunteer with them, and the fruit of their charity is set aside as they will, for visiting the sick and for the *talmud torah* of the poor orphans. Regarding the other charities, if they wish to do so they give, and if not, there is nobody who can oblige them to do so. Such has been their law from earliest times until now. At present there are six families of the Francos: Picciotto, Silvera, Ancona, Altaras, Belilios, and Lopez—may God protect them and give them long life. The three latter families are very few, numbering just three people—may they multiply. Not so the former three families: among them there are princes and distinguished people, wealthy people, wise and sage people, and God-fearing people—and they all hold fast to the custom of their forefathers not to be involved in the community in any matter, and they pray in their own homes or their own study houses, and they have a special *shoḥet*, like a community in its own right. And a sign of this is that they give separate contributions to the emissaries from Erets Yisra'el. Likewise, when the distinguished individuals and rabbis gather together [under] the rule of the holy community—may He give it life and protection—our souls do not come into their council, and we do not enter into their edicts or agreements, and the rabbis themselves do not pay attention to us, as it has been since the days of the early rabbis.[63]

This explanation of the separate status of the Francos in relation to the community at large was prompted by the *ḥakham bashi*'s claim that the Francos, under the leadership of the Picciotto family, supported him and his remaining in office.[64] The Francos' insistence that this was not the case, and

[63] Ibid. 1271/618, Silvera to Elyashar, 23 Heshvan 5655. On the arrival of the Francos in Aleppo and the dispute regarding their status, see Ch. 2 above.

[64] See JNUL, DMA, Arc. 4[to], 1271/618, Silvera to Elyashar, 23 Heshvan 5655. It would seem that Rabbi Dweck Hakohen based this argument upon the fact that his translator was

that they were not involved in any community matters, suggests that their sympathies were in fact with the steering committee against the *ḥakham bashi*, and that it was in this spirit that they attempted to act and to exert influence. In the past, the Francos' involvement in community life had only accentuated their separation; they had been asked to intervene as mediators in disputes within the community specifically because they were distinct and separate from it. Their monetary donations to the community were likewise seen as emphasizing their great generosity, for as a group that was separate from the community they were not obliged to pay these taxes. It may thus be inferred that the dispute between the community and *ḥakham bashi* Rabbi Dweck Hakohen led to greater involvement of the Francos in the issue of community leadership. This involvement increased further at the beginning of the twentieth century, reaching its peak in their full participation in the appointment of Rabbi Hezekiah Shabetai as *ḥakham bashi* in Aleppo.[65]

Given the proximity of Syria to Erets Yisra'el, every rabbinic emissary who left Palestine on a mission to Turkey or 'Arabistan' (i.e. Syria and Iraq) passed through its communities. It seems virtually certain that these emissaries were never sent specifically to the communities of Syria, but stopped there on their way to or from Turkey.[66] Moreover, the mystique that surrounded the emissaries in countries that were more distant from Erets Yisra'el was less evident in Syria, where the 'Holy Land' was something concrete and close by, rather than an abstract, remote, and lofty concept. Nevertheless, the emissaries still played an important role in the communities of Syria: various testimonies record emissaries being added to the composition of a local rabbinic court to give extra force to its rulings, or being asked to make a *tikun* for the sins of certain individuals, or giving their approval to halakhic rulings of local rabbis.[67]

Thus when Rabbi Benjamin Alkutser, an emissary of the Sephardi communities in Hebron and Jerusalem, arrived in Aleppo during August 1894, the two rival sides both sought to involve him in the dispute.[68] Each side presented him with its own version of the facts, while also attempting to influence him by means of gifts and contributions, coupled with promises of

Rafael de Picciotto, who also acted on his behalf during the dispute. See ibid. 1271/621, ruling of Rabbi Dweck Hakohen, n.d.; ibid. 1271/610, testimony received before the delegates, 3 Tevet 5655.

[65] See Ch. 10 below.

[66] On the various types of mission, see Ya'ari, *Emissaries from Israel* (Heb.), 20–1.

[67] Abulafia, *Lev nishbar*, ii. 68*b*; Labaton, *Nokhaḥ hashulḥan*, 78*b*; Y. Sassoon, *Keneset yisra'el*, p. 6*b*; Azriel, *Kapei aharon*, 111*a*.

[68] On Rabbi Benjamin Alkutser, see Gaon, *The Jews of the East* (Heb.), 88.

future contributions once the dispute had been resolved in their favour. While the emissary attempted to play down the influence of these financial incentives on his opinion, it is hard to avoid the conclusion that they had some effect.[69]

Initially, Alkutser did no more than send a letter to Rabbi Elyashar in Jerusalem, in which he described the events unfolding in Aleppo, emphasizing that the steering committee, rather than the *ḥakham bashi*, was in the right. The emissary did not mince his words:

> But unfortunately a number of wicked people, headed by the *ḥakham bashi*, Rabbi Abraham Dweg [*sic*], have risen up as opponents to them; every leprous person who had a grievance joined their company . . . For this destructive lion has imposed fear and terror upon all the inhabitants of the land, for he has no fear of God—stealing, oppressing, doing violence; and there is none who can say to him, 'What do you do?' For who shall endanger his soul to enter into conflict with him, since everyone knows that he informs on people [i.e. to the Ottoman government], and that on more than one or two occasions he has denounced 'great ones' in Israel . . . And if I were to tell your honour one part in a thousand of what my ears have heard about this wild ass of a person, or give testimony before you about the terrible scandals which my eyes have seen, my lips would be silent . . . And I testify before heaven and earth, by the life of the Lord of Hosts, that it is permitted to murder the above-mentioned *ḥakham bashi* just as one slaughters a pig [even] on Yom Kippur that falls on the sabbath, for he has brought low the banner of our Holy Torah, cursed and shamed the Rock of Jacob, and dragged the Israelite nation down to the dust.[70]

There is no doubt that language of this kind, which he probably also used before the members of the steering committee, would have done little to defuse the tension, to say the least. Indeed, Rabbi Dweck Hakohen explicitly accused Rabbi Alkutser of inciting the people against him: 'Then this sage, Benjamin Kutsri, came and confused the land, and made it like a seething pot . . . and caused the fire to flare up within the land [i.e. Aleppo] . . . and that Hakham Benjamin mentioned bears responsibility for the damage.'[71]

Alkutser's enthusiasm for polemic found expression in his willingness to go to Istanbul to give eyewitness testimony before the *ḥakham bashi* there, Moses Halevi, against the *ḥakham bashi* in Aleppo. From the sources available, it seems possible that the emissary himself initiated this trip, which was not included in his original itinerary, in exchange for a promise that the

[69] See JNUL, DMA, Arc. 4[to], 1271/614, Dweck to Elyashar, 29 Tevet 5655; 1271/612, Alkutser to Elyashar, 27 Av 5654, 2 Heshvan 5655; heads of the community to Elyashar, 12 Tishrei 5655; 1271/24, Gada to Elyashar, 2 Heshvan 5655.

[70] JNUL, DMA, Arc. 4[to], 1271/612, Alkutser to Elyashar, 27 Av 5654.

[71] Ibid. 1271/614, Dweck Hakohen to Elyashar, 29 Tevet 5655.

income of the *kolelim* of Hebron and Jerusalem would not suffer as a result. Or perhaps Alkutser secretly hoped that, once Rabbi Dweck Hakohen had been deposed, the Jews of Aleppo would call upon him to serve as *ḥakham bashi* in his place. Alkutser was also chosen for this mission because his departure from the city would not arouse the suspicion of the *ḥakham bashi* and his party, as an emissary from Erets Yisra'el would be expected to travel a good deal. Even so, the arrangements for his trip were made in great secrecy.[72] Once in Istanbul, Alkutser gave the *ḥakham bashi* Moses Halevi a petition bearing the signatures of 300 Jews from Aleppo, demanding the removal of Rabbi Abraham Dweck Hakohen from office.

Alkutser's involvement in this incident almost led to his imprisonment. Upon his return from Istanbul to Aleppo, the supporters of the *ḥakham bashi* complained to the authorities that he was an agitator who was stirring up rebellion within the community. As a result, soldiers were sent to the home of Raphael Silvera, where he was staying, to arrest him. Such an act, sending the authorities against a rabbinic emissary, was unprecedented, contravening the most sanctified values of the Aleppo community. It did great damage to the authority of the incumbent *ḥakham bashi*, and also to the aura of holiness that usually surrounded the office of emissary from Erets Yisra'el—as Alkutser himself complained, in describing the dangers to which he was subjected:

> And their hands were also upon me, and they denounced me before the court, and I was greatly pained by this, not for myself, but because of the defamation of our holy land in general, and for the honour of its sages and rabbis in particular. And the people of Aram Zova raised a loud and bitter cry, but in vain, for they are unable to speak a single sentence to them, for they fear for their lives, saying that if these people dared to denounce an emissary from Jerusalem and did not heed the great rabbis and sages of Jerusalem, what will become of them?[73]

But Alkutser escaped the danger. Raphael Silvera was an Italian subject; therefore he appealed to the Italian consulate, requesting it to extend its protection to the emissary, as representing an Italian citizen from Jerusalem.[74]

The rabbis and rabbinic courts of Jerusalem, with its *ḥakham bashi* at their head, were held in great esteem by the sages and rabbis of the Jewish communities of Syria. Correspondence with Jerusalem concerning matters of Jewish law, and requests for approval of judicial rulings, appear extensively in the writings of the Syrian rabbis during the nineteenth century. The rabbinic

[72] See JNUL, DMA, Arc. 4to, 1271/618, Silvera to Elyashar, 3 Heshvan 5755; 1271/612, Alkutser to Elyashar, 2 Heshvan 5655; 1271/24, Gada to Elyashar, 2 Heshvan 5655.

[73] See ibid. 1271/612, Alkutser to Elyashar, 22 Tevet 5655.

[74] See ibid. 1271/618, Silvera to Elyashar, 22 Tevet 5655.

court in the holy city, known as 'the High Court in Jerusalem', was considered the highest religious authority, and it was here that disputes among different courts, or cases which required the imposition of a rabbinic ruling over wealthy and powerful members of the community, were referred for resolution.[75] To all those involved in the Aleppo dispute, then, it was of paramount importance to obtain the support of the *ḥakham bashi* of Jerusalem, Jacob Saul Elyashar, known as the Yisa Berakhah, and that of the rabbinic courts in Jerusalem, in order to give ethical and halakhic force to their position. The sages and rabbis of Aleppo justified their turning to Rabbi Elyashar in a letter to him, saying: 'for the Lord has placed you supreme over the land, as a faithful shepherd over our brethren, the Sephardi children of Israel, and particularly over the cities of Syria'.[76] In this they effectively repudiated the authority of the local *ḥakham bashi*, implying that there was a higher ethical authority than him. The leaders of the steering committee, with the support of the sages and rabbis of Aleppo, asked Rabbi Elyashar to take three steps in particular against Rabbi Abraham Dweck Hakohen: first, to instruct the rabbinic court in Jerusalem to issue a ruling against him; second, to issue another ruling instructing his removal from office; and third, to send letters to the *ḥakham bashi* in Istanbul, Moses Halevi, supporting the request by the leaders of the community that Rabbi Dweck Hakohen be removed from office and the head of the spiritual committee, Solomon Safdeyé, be appointed in his place. The emissary Benjamin Alkutser supported these requests, adding to them his own:

> I therefore appeal to Your Honour that you do not rest and be not silent until these evildoers are recompensed according to their evil—namely, the tyrannical and miscreant *ḥakham bashi*, and the well-known denouncer Ezra Nehmad, and the accursed scoundrel Saul [Sutton] Dabah. May they be subject to the great ban at the Western Wall, before the Divine Presence; may the text of the ban be circulated here in print in 200 copies, in order to publicize their shame. And if His Honour does not wish to sign his name, he may write it simply in the name of the rabbis, for if Your Honour is silent regarding this matter and does not have pity on his own honour and on that of the sages and rabbis of Jerusalem—may it speedily be rebuilt—and particularly to the desecration of Jerusalem, there will result from this matter a very great defamation of the Name.[77]

Rabbi Dweck Hakohen likewise attempted to obtain the approval of the Yisa

[75] See Palagi, *Ḥukot haḥayim*, 1*b*. For examples of requests for approbations, see e.g. Antebi, *Mor ve'aholot*, 145*b*; Abulafia, *Penei yitsḥak*, vi. 3*b*.

[76] JNUL, DMA, Arc. 4[to], 1271/610, Torah scholars to Elyashar, 12 Tishrei 5655.

[77] See ibid. 1271/612, Alkutser to Elyashar, 22 Tevet 5655. On Ezra Nehmad and his activities, see ibid. 1271/621, anonymous letter to the courts in Erets Yisra'el, Aleppo, n.d. Cf. ibid.

Berakhah, and thereby to establish moral support and validation for his position. He organized his arguments in the form of a rabbinic ruling, for which he sought Rabbi Elyashar's approval.[78]

Eventually, after much hesitation, indecision, investigation, and examination of numerous sources, Rabbi Elyashar agreed to issue a ruling indicating the need to remove Rabbi Dweck Hakohen from office as *ḥakham bashi* in Aleppo. He even sent letters on the subject, under his own signature and with the signatures of the judges in the four rotating courts of Jerusalem, to Rabbi Moses Halevi in Istanbul. It would nevertheless appear that the Jerusalem courts did not declare a ban against the *ḥakham bashi*.[79] When Rabbi Dweck Hakohen saw that the rabbis of Jerusalem were not favouring him, and that in their letters to Aleppo they were supporting the steering committee, he attempted to dissuade them from becoming involved in a controversy that was not their own, and even threatened to take them to the rabbinic court. This failure to gain the support of the highest spiritual authority for Jews in the Ottoman empire evidently forced Rabbi Dweck Hakohen to rely increasingly upon the support of the government authorities and to threaten his rivals with retribution through government sanctions.[80]

The only person with the power to order the deposition of the *ḥakham bashi* or his remaining in office was the *ḥakham bashi* in Istanbul, Moses Halevi. He alone could recommend to the Ottoman authorities that they nullify the firman given to Rabbi Dweck Hakohen. Thus, alongside and in parallel to the attempts to gain the halakhic and ethical support of the *ḥakham bashi* in Jerusalem, great effort was also expended on persuading the rabbinate in Istanbul to take the side of the steering committee, so that its ruling might be carried out in practice. The eyewitness testimony given by the emissary Benjamin Alkutser on his mission to Istanbul led to the direct involvement of Moses Halevi, the *ḥakham bashi* in the capital, who sent an investigating team to Aleppo composed of his brother Rabbi Shabetai Halevi and Hezekiah Hatim, secretary of the Council of Chief Rabbis in Istanbul.[81] The two men arrived in Aleppo at the end of December 1894, charged first

1271/823, 28 Av 5652, document of obligation prohibiting Ezra Nehmad and his son Abraham from engagement in communal matters on grounds of suspicion of spying and denouncing Jews to the authorities.

[78] See JNUL, DMA, Arc. 4to, 1271/621, ruling of Abraham Dweck Hakohen, n.d.; 1271/622, Safdeyé to Elyashar, 11 Kislev 5655.

[79] Ibid. 1271/610, sages and rabbis of Aleppo to Elyashar, 24 Heshvan 5655; 1271/62, Safdeyé to Elyashar, 11 Tevet 5655.

[80] See ibid. 1271/614, Dweck Hakoen to Elyashar, 29 Tevet 5655.

[81] *Ḥavatselet*, 8 (2 Kislev 5655), 54. On Hezekiah Hatim, cf. *Ḥavatselet*, 1 (12 Tishrei 5651), 4.

and foremost with clarifying the facts—including which of the two sides had first turned to the authorities—and then with making peace between the rival camps.

From the testimonies presented to the investigators, it is clear that the overwhelming majority of the community did not want the *ḥakham bashi* to continue in office. Nevertheless, given the support provided to Rabbi Dweck Hakohen by government officials, and the governor's fears that the controversy would escalate to insurrection, the delegates were unable to act on their conclusions immediately. Instead, on 3 January 1895 they returned to the capital city to present their findings to Rabbi Moses Halevi.[82] Their departure without publishing their conclusions created suspicion among the leaders of the community, on the one hand, and satisfaction and a desire for revenge among Dweck Hakohen's supporters on the other. As noted above, the latter had already attempted to have the rabbinic emissary Alkutser imprisoned or arrested, and the heads of the steering committee and the rabbis, beginning with Rabbi Solomon Safdeyé, sent into exile.[83] For his part, the governor would not take any action without instructions from the Sublime Porte.

Then, on the eve of Passover, a telegram came bearing the recommendation of Rabbi Moses Halevi that Rabbi Abraham Dweck Hakohen be removed from office as *ḥakham bashi* and that Rabbi Solomon Safdeyé be appointed in his place as acting *ḥakham bashi*. On 4 April Rabbi Safdeyé was duly announced as *wakil ḥakham bashi*, reuniting the offices of *ḥakham bashi* and 'head of the spiritual ones', in the latter capacity also serving as head of the rabbinic court. A few months later the steering committee was also confirmed as the official leadership body of the community.[84]

Between Intrigue and Revolution

Socio-economic transformations in late nineteenth-century Aleppo, including the emergence of a prosperous and educated middle class and the decline of the class of wealthy householders upon which the institution of the rabbinate had relied for many generations, created an urgent need for a

82 For copies of the testimonies supporting the *ḥakham bashi* given before the investigating committee and approved by those close to him, see JNUL, DMA, Arc. 4to, 1271/614, Dweck to Elyashar, 29 Tevet 5655. For copies of the testimony before the committee from 27 Kislev 5655 and 3 Tevet 5655, see ibid. 1271/610.

83 See ibid. 1271/618, Silvera to Elyashar, 22 Tevet 5655.

84 Ibid. 1271/622, Safdeyé to Elyashar, Rosh Hodesh Iyar 5655; 1271/613, Gada to Elyashar, 5655 (no day or month given): *Hatsevi*, 17 (16 Iyar 5655), 64; *Hatsevi*, 30 (19 Av 5655), 115; AAIU, Syrie, IX.E., Alep, 70*b*, Raffoul, 12 July 1895.

comprehensive reorganization of community leadership and institutions. The ascent of new forces within society, the distress of the weaker classes, the decline in influence of those families who had constituted the old leadership—and with whose support almost unlimited power and authority had been concentrated in the hands of the *ḥakham bashi*—all led to unrest throughout the Jewish public and a widespread desire for participation in running the affairs of the community. In practice, then, the deposing of the *ḥakham bashi* served a clear goal: to limit the power of the individual holding that office and to transfer some of it into the hands of the steering committee. This being so, the removal from office of Rabbi Abraham Dweck Hakohen—if only because of its consequences—can be seen as representing a revolution in the order of communal leadership, not merely the result of intrigue and conspiracy based upon personal hostility.

Revolution, by its very definition, entails the nullification or abolition of an existing form of government in order to establish a new one. In this case, its most obvious manifestation was the establishment of the steering committee alongside the *ḥakham bashi*. The approval and official recognition of the steering committee by the Ottoman authorities—notwithstanding their suspicion of any change that might upset the delicate balance needed to preserve peace and calm throughout the empire—strengthened the committee's position. It derived its authority both from the community and from the government, and as a result detracted from that of the *ḥakham bashi*, who ceased to be the exclusive representative of the Jewish community before the authorities. In this sense, the steering committee achieved its goals even more comprehensively than it had initially intended, for the new *ḥakham bashi*, Rabbi Solomon Safdeyé, was elderly, in poor health, and utterly inexperienced in organizing and leading the community. The consequent strengthening of the 'secular' elements within the community leadership stands out even more strongly in the light of the simultaneous decline in the status of the office of *ḥakham bashi* in the eyes of the authorities. For many years, those who followed Rabbi Abraham Dweck Hakohen in this office did not receive official confirmation of their appointment in the form of a sultanic firman and the accompanying ceremony, and were regarded in practice as merely acting occupants of the office. This affected their status in the eyes of the community and enabled the steering committee to concentrate power within its own hands.[85]

The fact that the committee was an elected body represented another revolution in the life of the Aleppo community—a traditional community

[85] Elyashar, *Ma'aseh ish*, 55*a*; *Hatsevi*, 30 (19 Av 5655), 115.

which had been led for centuries by an unelected and self-perpetuating aristocracy of money and pedigree. While election to the committee was on the basis of lot and not by ballot, no restrictions were placed on candidates, so that anyone could present himself for election. Proof of this may be seen in the fact that most of those chosen to sit on the steering committee were not from upper-class families. In its first incarnation it was headed by Yom-Tov Gada, and its key members included among others the brothers Moses and Siman-Tov Menashe and David Farhi—almost all of them practical men who belonged neither to the aristocracy of pedigree, such as the Dayan or Laniado families, nor to the aristocracy of money, such as the Asses, Sutton, Sasson, Gabbai, or Dweck families.[86]

The traditional leadership chose to give their support to those who had worked to depose the *ḥakham bashi*, despite their realization that—given the establishment of the steering committee—they would never regain their previous status and that the old order of things in the community would never return. The old aristocratic families did not marshal their forces to attempt to halt a process that threatened their superior position, and may perhaps have understood, in the light of the stance of most members of the community, that such change was inevitable. They may also have believed their position to have been damaged by the actions of Abraham Dweck Hakohen, who had concentrated power in his own hands and appointed his closest supporters to key positions in the community, thereby violating the historical alliance between the elite families and the rabbinic leadership. For whatever reason, ultimately the traditional aristocracy, with the exception of the Gabbai family and a few other individuals who were close to Abraham Dweck Hakohen and personally dependent upon him, did not support the *ḥakham bashi*.

Another of the features of the deposition and its consequences that elevated it from mere conspiracy to revolution was its role in accelerating the decline in the status of the rabbis and the rabbinate, after many centuries during which they had enjoyed a position of superiority to ordinary people and authority to lead the community and take decisions on all that happened within it. The very position of the chief rabbi as both religious figure and head of the communal leadership was testimony to the high status of the rabbinic class within the community and its leadership. The class of Torah scholars would have been expected to support Rabbi Abraham Dweck Hakohen, as he had come from their own ranks. In choosing to oppose him, for their own reasons, they failed to grasp that the communal leaders' campaign against the *ḥakham bashi* was designed to gain political power in the community at

[86] *Hatsevi*, 30 (19 Av 5655), 114–15.

the expense of the religious authorities, and thereby failed also to foresee the ultimate results of their own struggle against the *ḥakham bashi*.

The decision by the Torah scholars to join forces with the powerful laymen in the community against Rabbi Dweck Hakohen was originally motivated by personal opposition to him and his attempt, as they saw it, to violate the prerogatives of the rabbinic court, which had previously been under their exclusive authority. At that time the status of the rabbinic court was in any event becoming progressively weaker, as elements in the community were ceasing to consider it the repository of ultimate authority. In requesting that Rabbi Solomon Safdeyé, the head of the spiritual committee, be appointed as *ḥakham bashi*, the Torah scholars sought to reunite the two offices of *ḥakham bashi* and head of the spiritual committee and rabbinic court, and thereby restore the status of the court. However, in the event this change damaged the office of *ḥakham bashi* itself, bringing in its wake a further decline in the status of the rabbinic sages and their authority with regard to any matters concerning the leadership and administration of the community. From now on, the Torah scholars had to confine themselves to a greater degree than in the past to dealing with the 'four ells of Torah'—that is, with the strictly religious realm. The rule of halakhah in the community became progressively weaker, as expressed in the growing number of cases brought before the Ottoman and consular courts, reflecting a loss of popular faith in the power of the sages as well as a clear decline in the material support for students of Torah.

The rabbinic sages attempted to bolster their dwindling status by issuing edicts reasserting their position in the community, both on the organizational and on the ideological and religious levels.[87] Nevertheless, the ranks of rabbinic scholars in the city progressively diminished. In earlier times, some Torah scholars had left Aleppo for Jerusalem, but these were mostly older individuals who had not attained the first rank of scholarship. By contrast, during the years following the deposition of Rabbi Dweck Hakohen there was a striking increase in both the numbers and the quality of rabbis emigrating from Aleppo. In the course of a few years, Aleppo lost many of the leading rabbis who had been involved in the dispute, including among others such figures as Yitshak Labaton, Jacob Hayim Alfia, Yitshak Shrem, Moses Harari, Me'ir Laniado, and Abraham Ades. They moved to Jerusalem, where they played an active role for many years, laying the foundations for the strictly Orthodox and conservative nature of the Aleppo community there. Their

[87] It is against this background that one needs to understand the regulation cited by Laniado (*For the Sake of the Holy Ones* (Heb.), 88), which was instituted a few weeks after the deposition of the *ḥakham bashi* Abraham Dweck Hakohen. See also Zohar, *Tradition and Change* (Heb.), 62–4.

spiritual activity and creativity, the recognition of their authority in halakhic rulings, and the very fact of their dwelling in Jerusalem dimmed the glory of Aleppo, which had in the past been a centre of learning recognized as boasting outstanding Torah scholars.

The Aleppo community never fully recovered from this dispute and from the consequent departure of the most important rabbis in the community, nor did it succeed in restoring the glory and dignity of the office of *ḥakham bashi* to its former heights. Until 1908, no *ḥakham bashi* was given the full appointment with a firman from the sultan, Dweck Hakohen's successors being considered only substitutes. In that year, when the time came to choose a new rabbi for this office, the community of Aleppo, once described as 'a city of sages and scribes', was unable to overcome its internal disputes sufficiently to agree on a rabbinic personality of sufficient stature to lead the community. Hence, for the first time a rabbi from outside the community was chosen for the position: Rabbi Hezekiah Shabetai from Jerusalem, who had previously served as *ḥakham bashi* in Tripoli, Libya.[88] Thus Abraham Ezra Dweck Hakohen was the last *ḥakham bashi* to have been born in Aleppo.

[88] See Ch. 10 below.

CHAPTER SIX

Yitshak Abulafia's Troubled Path to Rabbinic Office in Damascus

Rabbi Johanan said: Woe to the rabbinate, which buries its occupants.

BT *Pesaḥim* 87*b*

The Balance of Power in the Damascus Community

The institutional structure of the Jewish community of Damascus and the basic patterns of its activity had been laid down over the centuries, following models that had existed in the Jewish world since the talmudic period. During the mid-nineteenth century the communal institutions were restructured under the influence of the Ottoman reforms of this period. As in Baghdad and Aleppo, this reorganization took place largely under the guidance and encouragement of the Ottoman authorities, but at the same time reflected internal social ferment accompanied by criticism of the traditional arrangements for communal leadership.

In Damascus the rabbi's salary was paid by the community, but in practice the main burden of funding fell on the shoulders of the wealthy class. As a result, the rabbi was often dependent for his livelihood on a small group of men. On more than one occasion the wealthy *gevirim* attempted to appoint a particular individual as rabbi, not necessarily because he was 'suitable and decent in terms of wisdom and character and wholeness',[1] but rather because he was not financially independent, thereby ensuring their influence over him. They sought to perpetuate a situation in which, while the rabbi would officially be the leader of the community, the strings of leadership would in effect be pulled by those who chose him. Thus the economic elite attempted to translate their financial power into political power—and often succeeded in doing so. One example of this was the appointment of Rabbi Jacob Antebi as rabbi of the Damascus community in 1809. He was put forward to stand against Rabbi Hayim Nisim Abulafia, who was superior to him in wisdom, in

[1] Abulafia, *Penei yitsḥak*, iii. 39*b*, §9.

age, in family background, and in wealth—making him an unwelcome candidate for the wealthy men of the community.[2]

Indeed, from the moment that Jacob Antebi was appointed as rabbi of the Damascus community, he was dependent upon the goodwill of the wealthy members of the community, headed by the Farhi family.[3] The weakness of his position at the end of the 1830s is clearly implied in his own words: 'I am unable to do anything, because they have made judgments upon me, the like of which are unheard of.'[4] The members of the Farhi family did not hesitate to act forcefully whenever they felt that the rabbinic court, headed by Rabbi Antebi, was about to decide against them in some legal matter—even to the extent of bribing government officials to place the rabbi under house arrest.[5]

Similarly, members of the Harari family, one of the most distinguished and wealthy in Damascus, withheld payment of the rabbi's salary for two and a half years because he opposed their laxity in religious observance and their refusal to accept his halakhic authority.[6]

In general, then, in all matters pertaining to communal leadership, the chief rabbis of Damascus acted in accordance with the dictates of the wealthy members of the community. However, without the official approval of the rabbis the decisions of the *gevirim* lacked legal force. Thus, in practice all agreements and regulations were made with the agreement of both sides. Any departure from this norm could not be sustained for long. For example, at the end of the 1860s *ḥakham bashi* Jacob Perets imposed, evidently with the agreement of the wealthy members of the community, an indirect tax on kosher meat, the *gabilah*. In 1872 one of the wealthy householders tried to persuade the *ḥakham bashi* to abolish this tax so as to lower the price of kosher meat, which was double the price of the meat sold by Christian and Muslim butchers. When the *ḥakham bashi* refused to do so, the *gevir* began to supply kosher meat to all the Muslim butchers' shops, which could then sell it to the Jews at their lower prices, thereby in practice doing away with the *gabilah*.[7]

The Division in the Rabbinic Leadership

Towards the end of 1840, after Ottoman rule had been restored to Syria following the military withdrawal of the Egyptian ruler Mohammed Ali, the leadership of the Jewish community in Damascus found itself in deep crisis.

[2] On Jacob Antebi, see Gaon, *The Jews of the East* (Heb.), 523. On Hayim Nisim Abulafia, see ibid. 7.

[3] On the Farhi family, see Philipp, 'The Farḥi Family'.

[4] Palagi, *Ḥukot haḥayim*, 'Ḥoshen mishpat', 7*a*, §2.

[5] Ibid. 7*b*, §2.

[6] See Alhalel, 'An Important Original Document' (Heb.), 42.

[7] FO 78/2242, Green to Rumbold, Damascus, 15 Apr. 1872.

Prominent figures in the communal leadership had only recently been released from prison, shattered in both body and spirit, having been incarcerated in the wake of the Damascus blood libel, in which they were accused of slaughtering a Christian priest and his servant in order to use their blood for the Passover matzah.[8] The *ḥakham bashi*, Rabbi Jacob Antebi, who was among those who were brutally tortured, had just completed thirty years of service in the rabbinate and wished to retire to Jerusalem for the rest of his days. In the summer of 1842, he did just that, and spent the rest of his life in the holy city.

The great weakness of the chief rabbi as spokesman for the Jewish community was particularly apparent during the Damascus blood libel—in part because, as a local citizen, he was helpless in relation to the rulers. Realizing this, the leading figures in the community concluded that the most important function of the official head of the community was to create connections with the rulers—and particularly with the foreign consuls who represented various European countries and had proved their political power when coming to the defence of the Jews at the time of the libel. Hence, as the time of Rabbi Antebi's retirement approached, the people of Damascus set their hearts on Rabbi Hayim Maimon Tobi, a British subject born in Gibraltar. Described by one missionary as a wise, educated, and well-mannered man, he had lived in Damascus for some time, at least since 1825, evidently pursuing his own business interests.[9] It was hoped that his foreign citizenship, combined with his other sterling qualities—which did not necessarily include expertise in Torah scholarship—would enable him to represent the community to the authorities more successfully than his predecessor. And indeed, Rabbi Tobi's British citizenship proved useful in his negotiations with the imperial government, and even more so in his attempts to engage the British consul in action on behalf of the Jewish community of Damascus.[10] Nevertheless, with regard to all intracommunal affairs he was still cowed by the wealthy laymen, above all by the Farhi family. Even though at the time most members of this family were preoccupied by their own financial difficulties—in part owing to commercial factors, in part to the numerous quarrels involving the inheritance of Hayim Farhi—Rabbi Tobi still held back from intervening in such matters on several occasions. Even before his appointment, he was reluctant to sign halakhic rulings relating to members of the Farhi family 'because the fear of

[8] For a detailed account of the Damascus blood libel, see J. Frankel, *The Damascus Affair*.

[9] Wilson, *The Lands of the Bible*, ii. 330; Woodcock, *Scripture Lands*, 47.

[10] A testimony from 1825 describes Hayim Maimon Tobi as a respected merchant and a friend of the English, and as enjoying good relations with the French consular representative, Beaudin. See Madox, *Excursions in the Holy Land*, ii. 122–3, 137–8.

Mordecai [Farhi] had fallen upon him and, according to them, he already knew which way the law was tending, and he removed himself out of fear'.[11]

Rabbi Hayim Maimon Tobi retired from the leadership of the Jewish community in Damascus in 1849, evidently on grounds of old age.[12] His place was taken shortly thereafter by Rabbi Hayim Romano, who was considered the greatest Torah scholar in the city and the mentor and teacher of those rabbis who served after him.[13]

Why Rabbi Romano retired so soon from practical leadership of the community to concentrate on spiritual pursuits is not entirely clear. Poor health may well have been one reason, but it seems probable that, like his predecessors, he found his position difficult in relation to the wealthy members of community—including members of the Farhi family, who had denounced him to the authorities in 1847—prevented him from continuing to serve as spokesman for the community. Despite his withdrawal from active life, the chief rabbis who succeeded him allowed him, out of respect, the privilege of signing letters addressed to Jewish communities in Europe, and even to sit at the head of the rabbinic court whenever he was present in Damascus (he was frequently absent on fundraising journeys).[14] However, once again it was clear that prowess in Torah scholarship was no guarantee of capacity to represent the community adequately in dealings with its imperial government.

In the early 1850s, perhaps because it had realized that scholarly and political ability were not to be found in the same person—or perhaps because it did not wish to concentrate excessive power in the hands of one rabbi—the Damascus community created a dual model of leadership, headed by two rabbis. One rabbi, who held the official Ottoman title of *ḥakham bashi*, was responsible for the community's relations with the authorities; the other, who was selected on the basis of his status as the best of the Torah scholars, served as rabbinic judge, issued halakhic rulings, and engaged in study and teaching. His job was to preserve the religious framework of the community, including the status of the rabbinic court. This rabbi's authority derived not from

[11] Labaton, *Nokhaḥ hashulḥan*, 'Ḥoshen mishpat', 78*b*, §25.

[12] See JNUL, DMA, V-736/248, Hayim Maimon Tobi to Hayim Nisim Abulafia, Damascus, Iyar 5609. Rabbi Tobi died on 18 January 1857.

[13] L. A. Frankel, 'To Jerusalem' (Heb.), 116. See Rabbi Romano's signature under the title, 'moi Premier Rabin', kept in AECADN, Constantinople, Correspondance avec les Echelles, Damas, 1846–53, Levi à Garnier, 4 Apr. 1849.

[14] Rabbi Romano was evidently a self-appointed emissary. On the relations between the rabbis of Damascus and Jerusalem and Rabbi Hayim Romano, see e.g. JNUL, DMA, 8vo 5655, 12*b*. Rabbi Romano was also the first signatory on Galante's endorsement (*haskamah*).

official recognition, but rather from his scholarly prestige and his recognition by the community as its highest religious authority. The authority of the *ḥakham bashi*, by contrast, derived from two sources: on the one hand from the community which appointed him, and on the other hand from the Ottoman authorities, who ratified his appointment. The backing of the rulers was intended to strengthen his position, to give him full authority, and to enable him to call upon their assistance in any confrontation with rivals or opponents from within.

Jacob Perets was the first rabbi in Damascus whose appointment as *ḥakham bashi* was confirmed in this way by the government. Alongside him, Rabbi Aaron Jacob Benjamin Baghdadi, whose name is indicative of his origins, served as spiritual leader of the community. A document from 1856 attests that '[regarding] the Sage Aaron and the Sage Jacob Perets—may they have long lives—the second was placed on his throne by the government of the Ishmaelites [Muslims]'.[15] At this point, for the first time, arrangements were made for the payment of both rabbis' salaries by the community, so that neither was entirely dependent for his livelihood upon those who appeared before him as litigants.[16] Perets's status in particular, both in the eyes of the community and in those of the inhabitants of Damascus generally, increased when, in December 1861, he was publicly awarded—alongside government officials and Christian clergymen—the sultan's medal of honour.[17] As for Rabbi Benjamin, his halakhic authority and power were beyond question: every rabbi in Damascus who ruled on a matter of halakhah would write in the margins of his ruling that it was valid only on condition that it received the approval of Rabbi Benjamin.[18]

Rabbi Benjamin not only received his salary from the community but was himself a wealthy man, and so (unlike most of the other rabbis of Damascus) was not dependent upon the goodwill of the wealthy householders. This financial independence no doubt contributed to his ability to take up independent positions without fear of reprisals.[19] Nevertheless, the status of the community's rabbinic leadership was still weak relative to that of the *gevirim*. As noted above, the Ottoman authorities tended not to involve themselves in affairs internal to the Jewish community; moreover, even in those cases where they were forced to do so they tended to favour the wealthy laymen—upon whose money they were also dependent—over the rabbis. Moreover, the two

15 L. A. Frankel, 'To Jerusalem' (Heb.), 116. For colourful descriptions of Rabbis Jacob Perets and Aaron Baghdadi, see *Halevanon*, 11 (8 Sivan 5625), 169; Bost, *Souvenirs d'orient*, 36.

16 See *Halevanon*, 7 (13 Nisan 5626), 102.

17 *JC*, 4 Apr. 1862, p. 3.

18 Abulafia, *Penei yitsḥak*, i, 'Even ha'ezer', 100*a*, §16.

19 AAIU, Syrie, XVII.E., Damas, 160, Heymann, 12 Jan. 1866.

rabbis' salaries, although now paid by the community, were not particularly generous, so that they still needed other sources of income. Thus the *ḥakham bashi* still remained dependent to a degree upon the wealthy laymen of the community.[20]

Jacob Perets and Aaron Jacob Benjamin served together for more than twenty years in their respective positions, co-operating fully with each other. Despite their relative weakness, they knew how to lead the community wisely while trying to keep a balance between the interests of its various component groups, thereby ensuring for both themselves and the community as tranquil and secure a life as possible. They avoided conflict with the wealthy families, whose allegiance to traditional religious observance had begun to weaken. They trod a careful diplomatic path, co-operating with the Ottoman authorities—unlike the Christian minority, who sought to create a common front with the Jews to protect the rights of the minorities—and at the same time avoiding any conflict with the Protestant missions that might lead to confrontation with the British consulate, thereby enabling the community to continue to enjoy the protection of the British consul.[21]

The Abulafia Family in Damascus

The Abulafia family enjoyed considerable status within the Jewish communities of the Middle East. Branches of this family had lived in Damascus since the earliest times, although there is no record of when they arrived there. It is reasonable to assume that additional branches of the family settled in Damascus in the early nineteenth century after Rabbi Joseph David Abulafia was brought from Tiberias to serve as chief rabbi. His appointment marked a break in the previously uninterrupted sequence of chief rabbis from the Galante family.[22] When Rabbi Joseph David Abulafia left office a relative of his, Rabbi Hayim Nisim Abulafia, who was both a great Torah scholar and a wealthy man, hoped to inherit the position—indeed, he had apparently moved from Aleppo to Damascus with that end in view.[23] However, as noted above, the wealthy men of the city were reluctant to appoint as their chief rabbi a person who combined Torah learning with worldly stature, for fear that he would be excessively independent in his views; hence they chose instead Rabbi Jacob Antebi.

On his failure to gain the chief rabbinate in Damascus, Rabbi Abulafia

20 *Halevanon*, 7 (13 Nisan 5626), 102.

21 On this, see Harel, *Syrian Jewry*, 223–5.

22 See JNUL, DMA, 8vo 5655.

23 See Toledano, 'On the History of the Jewish Settlement in Tiberias' (Heb.), 57.

moved to Tiberias, and thence to Jerusalem where, on 21 October 1854, following the death of the *rishon letsiyon*, Yitshak Kovo, he was appointed chief rabbi of Jerusalem to succeed him.[24] Meanwhile, at least two of his sons remained in Damascus or returned there a few years after their father's departure. The eldest, Jacob, became one of the most respected figures within the community and, by virtue of this status, was chosen on more than one occasion to serve as mediator in disputes within the wealthy class.[25] The second son, Moses, a learned sage and a respected merchant, also belonged to the community leadership. It was his prominence within the community that led to his arrest at the time of the Damascus blood libel in February 1840. Broken by interrogation and torture, and under threat of death, Moses Abulafia eventually submitted to conversion to Islam, and later gave 'expert testimony' concerning the alleged use by the Jews of human blood for ritual purposes.[26] Following the end of this affair Moses Abulafia returned to Judaism, but we may assume that he had irretrievably lost any standing in the community.[27]

Moses' wife Oro (Gold) gave birth to their son Yitshak Abulafia in Damascus some fifteen years before the blood libel, in about 1825. As a result of the events of 1840 and the atmosphere to which they gave rise, the teenage Yitshak was removed from his father's home and sent to stay in Tiberias with his grandfather, Rabbi Hayim Nisim Abulafia, who would be the young man's teacher and mentor for some twenty years.[28] When Hayim Abulafia moved to Jerusalem in 1847, he was accompanied by his grandson.

In 1848, when he was 23 years old, Rabbi Yitshak Abulafia was sent on his first mission as a rabbinic emissary, on behalf of the Tiberias *kolel*, to Tunisia and Tripoli.[29] Two years later he was sent to North Africa on behalf of the Safed *kolel*.[30] It seems that it was on his return from this mission in the spring of 1861 that he realized that the time had come for him to return to his ancestral home and birthplace in Damascus. The timing of this decision may have been connected with his grandfather's death in January 1861, after serv-

24 See Gaon, *The Jews of the East* (Heb.), 7, and below. On Rabbi Yitshak Kovo, see Gaon, *The Jews of the East* (Heb.), 615.

25 On his role as a mediator in disputes involving the inheritance of the *gevir* Hayim Farhi, see JNUL, DMA, V-736/218, statement of the sages and laymen of Damascus, 14 Adar 5607. Jacob Abulafia was among the Jewish dignitaries who were imprisoned after the massacre of Christians in July 1860 on charges of having co-operated with the Muslim rioters. See *JC*, 23 Nov. 1860, p. 6; 30 Nov. 1860, p. 6.

26 For an evaluation of his character as reflected in his letters, see Toledano, *Otsar genazim*, 122–5.

27 Moses Abulafia seems to have died in 1863. See Laniado, *For the Sake of the Holy Ones* (Heb.), 51.

28 Abulafia, *Lev nishbar*, 55*b*, §6.

29 See Ya'ari, *Emissaries from Israel* (Heb.), 654.

30 See ibid. 677.

ing as chief rabbi of Jerusalem for six years. Rabbi Yitshak Abulafia's signature as a member of the rabbinic court in Damascus appears for the first time in June 1861.[31] It would appear that for a few years thereafter he divided his time between Tiberias and Damascus, but that around 1865 he settled permanently in Damascus.

There seems little doubt that Yitshak Abulafia's renown as a scholar of Torah and his position as the scion of a notable rabbinic family, particularly as grandson of the *rishon letsiyon*, assured him a position of the highest dignity and honour upon his return to Damascus, in the first rank of the scholars in the city. There was, however, yet another significant family connection, and this one would help to establish him among the wealthy people of the city. His grandfather, Rabbi Hayim Nisim Abulafia, had not only served as *rishon letsiyon* himself; he was the father-in-law of Rabbi Shalom Moses Hai Gagin, son of an earlier chief rabbi of Jerusalem, Rabbi Abraham Hayim Gagin. By virtue of this connection, Yitshak Abulafia was also indirectly related to one of the great Jewish bankers of Damascus—Shemaiah Angel.

The Banker Shemaiah Angel

Shemaiah Angel was a member of a prominent Sephardi family that had settled in Damascus and was considered among the leaders of the community during the mid-nineteenth century. In addition to the high status conferred upon him by his great wealth, he was also very well connected, his father-in-law being the *rishon letsiyon* Rabbi Abraham Hayim Gagin.[32]

Contemporary opinions of Angel's business skills and personality varied. There is no doubt that he was involved in many worthwhile communal enterprises: he assisted rabbinic emissaries from Erets Yisra'el and supported Jewish settlement there; he used his influence and his numerous connections in the corridors of power to advance the interests of the Jewish community; and he contributed to many charitable enterprises.[33] He also played a notable role when Jews were accused, in July 1860, of assisting Muslims in the massacre of Christians: he proved the innocence of the Jews who were imprisoned, visited them in gaol every day over a period of two months, and took the trouble to ensure that they were provided with kosher food while in custody.[34]

The news of Shemaiah Angel's great wealth and well-appointed residence

[31] See Hazan, *Nediv lev*, 28*b*.

[32] See Gagin, *Yismaḥ lev*, author's introduction.

[33] See Ya'ari, *Emissaries from Israel* (Heb.), 743.

[34] On the Jews' involvement in these events, see Harel, *Syrian Jewry*, 174–83. On Shemaiah Angel's involvement, see *JC*, 30 Nov. 1860, p. 6.

extended as far as Europe. His home was open to distinguished Jewish travellers visiting Damascus, who were greatly impressed by both his surroundings and his civilized manners. Thus, for example, Ludwig August Frankel describes his visit to the Angel home in Damascus while on his way to set up a modern school in Jerusalem:

On the sabbath day we were . . . invited to feast by Mr Angel Shemaiah. They placed bread in a spacious courtyard, near a flowing fountain surrounded by a marble wall, under the shade of a verdant tree. And Mr Shemaiah loves rhetoric, and supports all of the pleasant singers, who gather in his home every sabbath singing songs of faith and melodies from all over the world, in Hebrew and Arabic and Spanish.[35]

Shemaiah Angel was also renowned for his support and respect for learned scholars and for the elderly.[36]

Shemaiah Angel's family originated in Venice, and he himself held Austrian citizenship. In 1865 he was the preferred candidate of the Austrian foreign ministry to serve as Austrian vice consul in Damascus, although in the end he was not appointed to this position, apparently because of the excessive payment which, according to the Austrians, he demanded in exchange for his services.[37] He also enjoyed the regard of the Ottoman authorities of Damascus, who on more than one occasion needed the credit he extended to them to finance their military and administrative expenses.[38] His reputation extended as far as the court of the sultan, ʿAbd al-ʿAziz, who granted him the title *efendi* and the first order of the Majjidi medal.[39]

When Shemaiah Angel died in April 1874 at the age of 73, his elaborate funeral was described in the Jewish press:

All of the sages and rabbis of the city, the great and honourable members of the Jewish community, walked before his bier holding wax candles. Behind them walked all of the children from the *talmud torah* and the schools and other teachers and tutors, singing songs of praise to God. The great prince, the *wali*, governor of the province of Syria, and all the distinguished figures of the government and the consuls of European governments, heads of the Christian churches, and distinguished citizens of the city, all dressed in black, walked behind his bier. Two hundred soldiers dressed in battle uniform surrounded his coffin, with the barrels of

[35] L. A. Frankel, *To Jerusalem* (Heb.), 119.

[36] JNUL, DMA, V-736/242, Abraham Galante to Shalom Moses Hai Gagin, 3 Shevat 5638.

[37] HHSTA, Adm. Reg., F8/38, Weckbecker, Beirut, 7 Aug. 1864; Weckbecker, Wien, 23 Feb. 1865; Prokesch, Constantinople, 18 Aug. 1864, 11 Oct. 1864; Angel, Damascus, 6 Apr. 1863. On the Jews of Syria and the European consulates, see Harel, *Syrian Jewry*, 211–25.

[38] On loans that the authorities received from the Jews of Damascus, see Harel, *Syrian Jewry*, 49–53.

[39] J. Frankel, *The Damascus Affair*, 210.

their rifles turned down as a sign of mourning. Sounds of weeping and wailing were heard from every direction: 'Woe, woe,' they cried, 'for the crown is removed from our heads, and glory has been stolen.'[40]

There seems no doubt that a demonstration of this sort in honour of a prominent Jewish layman was a rare sight in an orthodox Muslim city such as Damascus. Eulogies in his memory and honouring his activities were also delivered in many Jewish communities throughout the Ottoman empire.[41]

The description above—echoed in extensive and prominent coverage in the Jewish press, and also in those few brief biographies that have been written of Shemaiah Angel—creates the impression of a good-natured, public-spirited, and blameless person motivated by sound moral principles and a wish to assist his brethren in distress. However, there are other, less well-known statements that represent Shemaiah Angel in an entirely different light. These may explain the positions he took and the intrigues in which he was involved, as we shall see below, in the struggle over the rabbinate in Damascus.

The most important of these accounts is that of Heymann, the first representative of the Alliance Israélite Universelle in Damascus, who for a year and a half ran the Alliance school that was founded at the end of 1864.[42] Heymann arrived in Damascus on 22 January 1865, to a warm reception by the French consul and leaders of the Jewish community. Prior to this, Shemaiah Angel had promised the Central Council of the Alliance that he would personally ensure the construction of a suitable building in which to house the school, and had even worked on its behalf to raise money from wealthy Jews in London, Paris, and Istanbul.[43] Upon arriving in Damascus, however, Heymann discovered that most of the wealthy laymen in the community were indifferent to the material needs of the school. Shemaiah Angel alone supported its establishment, even contributing 60,000 French francs from his own pocket towards that end. Impressed, Heymann described Shemaiah Angel as 'a warm-hearted Jew who runs about, worries, and exerts pressure to build the school established by the Alliance', while the other wealthy laymen sat with folded hands.[44]

Heymann did not initially understand why Shemaiah Angel's 'good

40 *Ḥavatselet*, 36 (18 Tamuz 5634), 108, 273–4.

41 See e.g. Rabbi Jacob Saul Elyashar's eulogy of Shemaiah Angel, cited in Elyashar, *Ma'aseh ish*, introduction.

42 On the circumstances of the opening of this school, see Harel, *Syrian Jewry*, 81–2.

43 AAIU, Syrie, XI.E., Damas, 94, Hequard, 27 May 1864.

44 Ibid. XVII.E., Damas, 160, Heymann, 9 Feb. 1865.

deeds' were not appreciated by the Damascus community, and why they even elicited opposition and lack of goodwill from the other *gevirim* of the community.[45] However, over the course of time Heymann came to realize that the apathy of the other *gevirim* and their refusal to assist the school derived not from any hostility towards himself or the Alliance, but from their own tense relations with Angel. Once Angel began to make his financial support conditional upon the fulfilment of certain requirements that he imposed regarding the running of the school—for example, that the children of the other *gevirim* should not study there—Heymann understood that he was using the institution as a tool in his struggle against the other wealthy men of the community.[46] It became clear to Heymann that behind Angel's deeds and contributions was not so much a 'warm Jewish heart' but a desire for self-aggrandizement and increased control over the community. Angel's defaulting on all his promises to the Alliance only confirmed this conclusion.[47]

Matters came to a head in October 1865, when a cholera epidemic broke out in Damascus. The wealthy men of the city fled to their summer homes in the villages outside the city or in Lebanon, while the poor people remained in the city without any food. In its distress, the community sent a delegate to Shemaiah Angel, who at the time was living in his home in a village some five miles outside Damascus, requesting a loan of 9,000 francs to finance the needs of the poor people. 'This man of charity', wrote Heymann with heavy irony, 'agreed to provide the money, on condition that he be given as security all the silver *rimonim* and crowns [decorations on the Torah scrolls] from all the synagogues in the city.'[48]

This situation drove Heymann to despair, and he decided to leave Damascus. Giving up his position as its representative there, he wrote to the Alliance:

> Mr Shemaiah, upon whom you pinned your greatest hopes, is a man lacking in compassion, whose wealth comes from sources of which an honest man would not know. His piety is superficial, and if he performs a deed of kindness, it is done in a demonstrative manner. His main passion is to make a name for himself, but his greed for money prevents this.[49]

The Stambuli Family

Notwithstanding the Jewish millet decree, until the end of the nineteenth century there were no formal elections in Damascus for the steering committee, which was intended to act alongside the chief rabbi in seeing to the day-

45 AAIU, Syrie, XVII.E., Damas, 160, Heymann, 13 Apr. 1865.
46 Ibid.
47 Ibid., 21 May 1865, 11 July 1865.
48 Ibid., 21 Oct. 1865.
49 Ibid., 12 Jan. 1866.

to-day administration of the material affairs of the Jewish community, such as collecting taxes, running charitable institutions, dealing with government officials, and so on. Wealth, and at times also family lineage, were usually the factors that gained an individual a place of honour in the leadership of the community and on its executive bodies; and this continued to be the case even after elections were introduced according to the provisions of the decree. The hereditary and moneyed elites were highly protective of their status and disinclined to allow other elements in society to become involved in the communal leadership. It must nevertheless be remembered that such involvement not only conferred a certain prestige but also entailed considerable financial expenditure on behalf of the public. For this reason, it was in the community's interest that leadership was exercised by the wealthy—which in 1856 meant the Stambuli, Lisbona, Angel, Harari, Farhi, and Picciotto families, who ran the community's affairs alongside the *ḥakham bashi*.[50]

It is worth noting that, according to the Jewish millet decree, it was the task of the steering committee to supervise the *ḥakham bashi* and to assist him in fulfilling his tasks. The lack of an elected body, recognized by the authorities, detracted from the ability of the civil leadership of the community to fulfil its task of serving as a supervisory body. The disputes among the wealthy members of the community, which usually had their roots in commercial as well as personal tensions, also interfered with the proper running of the community.

The opposition to Shemaiah Angel's attempts to dominate the community was led by the Stambuli family. This family had apparently come to Damascus from Istanbul and was held in very high esteem. Various accounts describe the heads of this family as forceful people, to the extent that they threatened the judges of the community.[51] Nevertheless, Nathan Halevi Stambuli was known as 'a proper, God-fearing person, who loved the Torah and those who studied it, who loved justice and was not, Heaven forbid, a violent man'.[52]

Members of the Stambuli family played a significant role in numerous suits brought against the Farhi family in the 1840s.[53] During the course of these disputes, members of the Farhi family were not above bribing witnesses

[50] L. A. Frankel, *To Jerusalem* (Heb.), 116.

[51] See e.g. Palagi, *Ḥikekei lev*, 'Ḥoshen mishpat', 175*b*, §53.

[52] Ibid. 176*a*. On the Stambuli family, including Nathan Halevi Stambuli, see Hyamson (ed.), *The British Consulate*, i. 354–5.

[53] These demands were indirectly related to the dispute that erupted within the Farhi family concerning the estate of the *gevir* Hayim Farhi. See e.g. JNUL, DMA, V-736/218, members of the Jewish court in Damascus to Rabbi Abraham Hayim Gagin, 14 Adar 5607.

and persuading them to alter their testimonies; according to Nathan Stambuli, they were assisted in this by Shemaiah Angel.[54] This may have been the origin of the personal rivalries between the Stambuli family and Shemaiah Angel, which quickly became a struggle for control of the community and its institutions.

The Dispute between Rabbis Abulafia and Gagin

Yitshak Abulafia and Shalom Moses Hai Gagin first met and became friends in Jerusalem during their youth. The close ties of friendship forged in those years were further strengthened when their families became connected through Gagin's marriage in 1847, when he was 15 years old, to the daughter of Rabbi Hayim Nisim Abulafia.[55] In later years Gagin made frequent visits to Damascus, where he would stay in the home of his brother-in-law, Shemaiah Angel, or in that of his friend and relative by marriage, Rabbi Yitshak Abulafia. During one of these visits, in October 1868, Rabbi Abulafia authorized him to serve as an expert *shoḥet*, showering him with extravagant praise.[56] When Abulafia in turn visited Jerusalem, he often stayed at Gagin's home. Although older than his friend, Abulafia was in the habit of consulting him or asking his opinion on halakhic decisions he had made or responsa that he had written.

On one such occasion, while staying in Jerusalem, Abulafia showed Gagin a halakhic decision of his concerning a dispute that had occurred in 1847 between two branches of the Farhi family regarding the ownership of a promissory note from one of the Catholic monasteries in Jerusalem. It is worth noting that this question had initially been raised for discussion before Gagin's father, Rabbi Abraham Hayim Gagin, and Abulafia's grandfather, Rabbi Hayim Nisim Abulafia—a fact whose importance will become clear below.[57] On this occasion Shalom Gagin did not agree with Yitshak Abulafia's responsum. When Abulafia published the first volume of his book *Penei yitsḥak* in 1871, containing the ruling in question, he also cited Gagin's words and attempted to show that his opposition to the ruling was mistaken.[58] Gagin was infuriated by this public repudiation of his ruling, and levelled

[54] See JNUL, DMA, V-736/50, Nathan Halevi to Abraham Hayim Gagin, Rosh Hodesh Sivan 5606.

[55] See Abulafia, *Lev nishbar*, 53*a*.

[56] The writ of ordination is preserved in JNUL, DMA, V-736/252.

[57] See Abulafia, *Penei yitsḥak*, i, 'Ḥoshen mishpat', §22; Gagin, *Yismaḥ lev*, 'Ḥoshen mishpat', 38*a*, §10. On the loan made to monasteries in Jerusalem, see Gerber, 'Jews and Moneylending' (Heb.), 171, and the references there.

[58] See Abulafia, *Penei yitsḥak*, i, 'Ḥoshen mishpat', §22.

four substantial charges against Abulafia. His first and main argument was that Rabbi Abulafia had shown him his own ruling on the assumption that he would agree with it, but that once he realized that Gagin in fact disagreed with him, he had altered the texts of both his own halakhic ruling and of Rabbi Gagin's reply, printing the falsified version in order to demonstrate that he was right. Second, in addition to the accusation of falsification and lying, Gagin argued that Abulafia had hurt him by representing him as disagreeing with his own father. The third charge related to the harm caused by Abulafia to his father, Rabbi Abraham Gagin; for, he said, even though Rabbi Abraham Gagin had served as *rishon letsiyon* prior to Rabbi Hayim Nisim Abulafia, Yitshak Abulafia had in his responsum placed the words of his own grandfather before those of the elder Rabbi Gagin. His fourth and final accusation was that Rabbi Yitshak Abulafia had injured not only himself but the other rabbis of Jerusalem by his use of arrogant and haughty language against them and by altering their words in order to prove that he was right and that he possessed superior expertise in halakhah.[59]

There seems no doubt that Gagin put these arguments to his brother-in-law, Shemaiah Angel, who immediately ceased to be an intimate friend and supporter of Abulafia and became his implacable enemy. Abulafia himself, conscious not only of having aroused the hostility of a central figure in the Damascus community but also of rumours that many of the sages of Jerusalem were angry about what he had said of them in his book, decided to go back to Jerusalem as soon as possible with the intention of resolving the dispute. Not only did he want to restore good relations with his old friend Rabbi Gagin—and indirectly also with Shemaiah Angel—but, according to Gagin, above all he wished to appease the sages of Jerusalem in the wake of their angry reaction to his book.[60]

Upon his arrival in Jerusalem, Abulafia went promptly to Gagin's *beit midrash*, and began to enter into discussion with him in the presence of many of the other sages of the city—including the *rishon letsiyon*, Abraham Ashkenazi, who tried to bring about a compromise and make peace between

[59] Gagin, *Yismaḥ lev*, 'Ḥoshen mishpat', 38*a*, §10; 50*b*, §11. This claim is supported by the fact that Rabbis Rahamim Joseph Franco (Heharif) and Elijah Hazan likewise accused Rabbi Abulafia of 'loving arguments' and of distorting their words and arguments in his books. See Abulafia, *Penei yitsḥak*, i, 'Ḥoshen mishpat', 189*a*, §24; 196*b*, §24; Franco, *Sha'arei raḥamim*, 'Ḥoshen mishpat', 23*a*, §13. Rabbi Yitshak Abulafia apologized for insulting Rabbi Elijah Hazan (on the circumstances of his apology, see Hazan, *Ta'alumot lev*, 'Even ha'ezer', 41*a*–51*b*, §2). Hazan published this apology in his book *Zikhron yerushalayim*, a fact that further strengthens the claim against Abulafia; and cf. below.

[60] Gagin, *Yismaḥ lev*, 'Ḥoshen mishpat', 50*b*, §11.

the sides.[61] According to Gagin, the sages of Jerusalem took his side, urging Abulafia to 'send ten people to ask forgiveness at the grave of the rabbi the *gaon*, my [i.e. Gagin's] father, of blessed memory; and to obligate himself by a handshake, in place of an oath, to print this statement within two years, and to publish it throughout the Jewish world'.[62]

In September 1872, Rabbi Jacob Saul Elyashar formulated a statement of apology, which Rabbi Abulafia signed, in which he apologized for expressing himself improperly towards Rabbi Shalom Gagin and for offending the memory of his father, Rabbi Abraham Gagin, and asked the younger Gagin for forgiveness. The statement also mentions the ten people whom he sent to ask forgiveness at Rabbi Abraham Gagin's grave. But this apology was in fact never published.[63]

Abulafia, for his part, thought that all these moves on the part of the Jerusalem sages were initiated by Gagin, even though he had not in any way intended to harm his friend.[64] According to him, he signed the statement and organized the mission to Abraham Gagin's grave solely to pacify Shalom Gagin, and never agreed to publish an apology. However, he did give Gagin the statement, and he also published a similar statement in Elijah Bekhor Hazan's book *Zikhron yerushalayim*.[65] In fact, the statement in *Zikhron yerushalayim* served not to heal but to perpetuate the feud between Abulafia and Gagin—a dispute that was later to have repercussions for the struggle over the rabbinate in Damascus. Gagin thought that Abulafia had agreed to publicize a statement identical to that which he had been given privately, with all of the clauses mentioned above, whereas the version published in Hazan's book amounted only to a simple apology to Rabbis Hazan and Gagin for having expressed himself too strongly and requesting forgiveness for this. Rabbi Abulafia evidently considered this sufficient to put an end to the dispute;[66] however, the lack of a public apology for the offence against Gagin's father or a statement that he had sent ten men to ask forgiveness at his grave was perceived by Gagin as a failure to honour his commitment. This point was to become a thorn in Rabbi Abulafia's side two years later, when he sought to be

[61] On Ashkenazi, see Gaon, *The Jews of the East*, 121–2.

[62] Gagin, *Yismaḥ lev*, 'Ḥoshen mishpat', 50*b*, §11.

[63] For the full text of the statement as it was supposed to have been disseminated, according to Gagin, see ibid.

[64] Abulafia, *Lev nishbar*, author's introduction, s.v. *akh haḥakham einav*.

[65] See Hazan, *Zikhron yerushalayim*, 128–9.

[66] See JNUL, DMA, Arc. 4to 1271/606, letter of Rabbi Yitshak Abulafia to Rabbi Jacob Saul Elyashar, 2 Heshvan 5633. The letter was written following his return from Jerusalem, and in it he asks sends greetings to the rabbis of Jerusalem, especially Rabbi S. M. H. Gagin.

appointed head of the rabbinic court in Damascus, only to find that Shemaiah Angel had marshalled all his considerable influence to oppose his appointment.

The First Crisis of the Rabbinate: 1873–1875

The deaths within little more than a year of the two leading rabbis of Damascus, Aaron Jacob Benjamin and Jacob Perets—the one in February 1873, the other in March 1874—led to a storm of conflicts for status and prestige in the Damascus community. The main struggle occurred on the death of Rabbi Benjamin regarding the question of his successor as head of the spiritual leadership and head of the rabbinic court. Ranged against one another here were, on one side, the Stambuli, Lisbona, and Farhi families, who supported Abulafia's appointment in his place, and on the other Shemaiah Angel and his supporters. Over the course of ten months, it was agreed by both sides that those opposed to the appointment of Rabbi Yitshak Abulafia as head of the court would select two other judges to sit with him. However, thereafter Shemaiah Angel attempted to create 'facts on the ground' in order to obtain complete hegemony over the community. He called a meeting without the knowledge of his rivals which chose a steering committee consisting of six members, including his own son Eleazar. Among the steering committee's powers was the right to appoint the community's judges. According to the testimony of Jacob Halevi Stambuli, the members of the committee promised that they would not change the status quo and that Rabbi Abulafia would in all events be appointed as judge, alongside two others. But in the event the committee appointed three new judges and announced in the synagogues that anyone who dared to bring litigation before any other judges would be punished by the ban and by imprisonment. The supporters of Rabbi Abulafia responded by electing three other judges, including himself.[67]

Shemaiah Angel and his supporters then tried a new tack: they sought to involve the government authorities and the sages of Jerusalem in the opposition to Abulafia's appointment. According to Abulafia's supporters, Shemaiah and Eleazar Angel recruited the support of the governor of Syria, who owed them large sums of money and hoped that, in exchange for his support, they would annul his debt.[68] Shemaiah Angel also sent a letter to the *rishon letsiyon*, Rabbi Abraham Ashkenazi, portraying Rabbi Abulafia as a thoroughly corrupt person who, in exchange for bribes, did not hesitate to give rulings

[67] JNUL, DMA, V-736/221, Jacob Halevi to [Rabbi Abraham Ashkenazi?], Damascus, n.d.

[68] ACRI, TR/Is/162*a*, 'Megilat setarim', people of Damascus to Rabbi Moses Halevi, n.d.; TR/Is/160*a*, Jacob Halevi, Solomon Halevi, Aaron [?], Me'ir Lisbona, Ezra Abadi, Solomon

contradicting all the other sages of Damascus, thereby damaging their authority and upsetting the order of the community.[69] Shemaiah Angel presumably knew that his brother-in-law, Rabbi Shalom Gagin, would support his account in relaying it to the *rishon letsiyon*.

From the rival camp, Jacob Halevi Stambuli sent letters to the Jerusalem sages supporting Abulafia and casting doubt upon the motives of his opponents:

> And he is most suitable and upright, more so than all the other Torah scholars here . . . And it is our truthful testimony that whatever was written about him by Signor Shemaiah and his son is all lies and deceit . . . On the contrary, he is a righteous and honest person, as is widely known . . . For they [the rumours against him] are all emptiness and hot air and [the result of] jealousy and hatred and rivalry. And the honourable Rabbi Yitshak—may God give him life and protect him—is pure and upright in his deeds, righteous and pious in all his ways, as is known, and we are not prepared to accept any judge and rabbinic teacher other than him . . . And the entire purpose of the *gevir* [i.e. Angel] and his son is to take vengeance and to fulfil their will and desire, and they pay no heed to the desecration of the honour of our teacher Rabbi Yitshak, nor of the honour of his Torah nor the honour of his family.[70]

Abulafia's supporters asked the *rishon letsiyon* to mediate and to attempt to make peace between the two sides.

Then, on 18 February 1874, Shemaiah Angel fell seriously ill, and one month later he died. His departure from the scene encouraged hopes that it might now be possible to calm the situation down. Preliminary steps were taken towards conciliation, including a recommendation by the *rishon letsiyon*, Rabbi Abraham Ashkenazi, that Rabbi Shalom Gagin, who was related to both the Angel and the Abulafia families, should go to Damascus to attempt to make peace between the two sides.[71] It should be emphasized that, from the time of the so-called reconciliation between Rabbis Gagin and Abulafia until 1875, Gagin had refrained from any public expression of hostility towards Abulafia, expressing his feelings only in private to his friend and relative Shemaiah Angel, thereby strengthening the latter's desire to take vengeance against Abulafia by undermining his appointment as chief rabbi of Damascus.

Shortly before Shemaiah Angel's death, the *ḥakham bashi*, Rabbi Jacob Perets, also died, further exacerbating the crisis of community leadership.

Yitshak Farhi, Me'ir Raphael Farhi, Moses Lisbona, Nisim Abadi, and Rahamim Ma'aravi to Rabbi Moses Halevi, Damascus, 25 Av 5634.

69 JNUL, DMA, V-736/219, Shemaiah Angel to Rabbi Abraham Ashkenazi, Damascus, n.d.

70 JNUL, DMA, V-736/221, Jacob Halevi to [Rabbi Abraham Ashkenazi?], Damascus, n.d.

71 JNUL, DMA, V-736/145, Jacob Halevi to Rabbi Abraham Ashkenazi, Damascus, Rosh Hodesh Sivan 5634.

The issue now was not only who would fill the office of the senior rabbinic judge, but also who would take over as *ḥakham bashi*. Eleazar Angel, who was evidently aware of Rabbi Gagin's true feelings about Rabbi Abulafia, continued his father's attempts to dominate the community, gaining the backing of the governor and the provincial *majlis* for the election of a new steering committee. He also succeeded in persuading the government to issue an order stating that the judges to be chosen by the new committee would serve in their position until the appointment of a new *ḥakham bashi*. Needless to say, Yitshak Abulafia was not among them. Eleazar Angel further persuaded the governor of Damascus to ask the *rishon letsiyon* in Jerusalem to send a scholar of his choosing to serve as *ḥakham bashi* in Damascus.[72] It is not impossible that Angel's purpose in doing this was to contrive the installation of Shalom Gagin.

Abulafia's supporters continued to demand that he be appointed as Rabbi Benjamin's successor. Nevertheless, they were willing to compromise and to appoint Rabbi Solomon Sucari, the candidate of the rival camp, alongside him as joint head of the rabbinic court.[73] Regarding the selection of a new *ḥakham bashi*, their position was that, whether he came from Damascus or from outside, the appointment had to be made with the agreement of the majority of members of the community. Jacob Halevi Stambuli was even more explicit, telling the *rishon letsiyon* that should he accede to the request of the governor and appoint a *ḥakham bashi* without majority support, the community would refuse to recognize him as their rabbi and would not pay his salary. Stambuli further demanded that, whoever was eventually chosen as *ḥakham bashi*, Rabbi Abulafia should serve alongside him as the senior judge and as rabbi of the community.[74]

Rabbi Abulafia himself, who as the focus of this storm was the target of more than a few insults, at one point sought to withdraw his candidacy for the headship of the rabbinic court; however, his supporters refused to stand down and concede victory to the rival camp, and placed heavy pressure upon him to stand firm. In order to block the possible appointment of a *ḥakham bashi* from outside Damascus, they also sought to reunite the two offices, that of *ḥakham bashi* and that of head of the rabbinic court, in the hands of a single rabbi,

[72] Ibid.

[73] Sucari was the son-in-law of Jacob Antebi. On him, see Laniado, *For the Sake of the Holy Ones* (Heb.), 55. Cf. R Antebi's approbation of Jacob Sucari's book *Vayikra ya'akov*, and cf. S. Sucari, *Ateret shelomoh*, Son's Introduction; Jacob Sucari, *Vayikra ya'akov*, 2; id., *Yoru mishpateikha*, 16, 19, 23.

[74] JNUL, DMA, V-736/145, Jacob Halevi to Rabbi Abraham Ashkenazi, Damascus, Rosh Hodesh Sivan 5634.

namely, Yitshak Abulafia. But the fact that Abulafia was a French citizen at the time worked against him. Evidently, his opponents managed to persuade Halat Pasha, the governor of Syria, to turn to his superiors in Istanbul and ask them to send a suitable *ḥakham bashi* to Damascus. The governor explained that, according to Ottoman law—specifically, the Jewish millet decree—Abulafia could not serve in this office owing to his foreign citizenship. He also wrote that the debts of the Jewish community to the authorities were growing, and there was an urgent need to appoint a *ḥakham bashi* who would see to paying them off.[75]

Once Abulafia's supporters became aware that the governor had been persuaded to refer to his superiors in the imperial government, they in turn wrote to the capital—in their case to the *ḥakham bashi*, Rabbi Moses Halevi. Writing secretly, so as not to be seen to be opposing Halat Pasha, they argued that Ottoman law permitted a rabbi who held foreign citizenship to be appointed as *ḥakham bashi*, provided that he committed himself in writing to be subject to Ottoman law and to act exclusively in accordance with its directives. This letter was accompanied by a petition to the Sublime Porte requesting that Abulafia be appointed as *ḥakham bashi* and asking Moses Halevi, as *ḥakham bashi* in Istanbul, to ensure that all official directives on the subject be made in the name of the Sublime Porte, so that the governor of Syria would have no pretext for objecting to the appointment. Abulafia also agreed to relinquish his French citizenship and to return to his previous status as an Ottoman subject. His supporters added that the matter of collecting monies due was not the concern of the *ḥakham bashi*, but rather the business of what they called the *mukhtar al-yahud*.[76]

The *ḥakham bashi* in Istanbul nevertheless decided, for reasons of his own, that it would be best for the Damascus community to have as *ḥakham bashi* an individual who was not involved in disputes between rival groups. Hence he put forward a relatively unknown rabbi from Istanbul named Hayim Yitshak Kimhi. This appointment was ratified by the Ottoman authorities, but his firman gave him only provisional, temporary status as *qayimaqam ḥakham bashi*.[77] The inability to agree upon the appointment of a local rabbi and the compromise expressed in the appointment of a *ḥakham bashi* from outside was a turning point in the history of the Damascus community,

[75] ACRI, TR/Is/162*a*, people of Damascus to Rabbi Moses Halevi, 'Megilat setarim', n.d.

[76] Ibid. This title appears to be similar to that given to the head of the community in the Jewish communities at the centre of the Ottoman empire in Turkey. See Ben-Na'eh, 'The Organization' (Heb.), 360.

[77] On the confusion in the community, see AAIU, Syrie, XI.E., Damas, 94, Halfon, 19 May 1874.

signifying the beginning of its decline. That process was greatly accelerated when, in October 1875, shortly after the arrival of Rabbi Kimhi, the wealthiest men of the community went bankrupt. This financial collapse brought the community down to its lowest ever level, after a long period of flourishing.

Rabbi Kimhi's tenure as *ḥakham bashi* did not leave much of an impression on the community; nor did he last long in office. His lack of a local power base, opposition to him within the community, his unfamiliarity with the local language, his economic dependence upon the wealthy men of the community, and thereafter their own bankruptcy and the division of the community into rival factions struggling for control of its institutions—all these factors led Rabbi Kimhi, at the end of 1878, some three years after his appointment, to resign his position.[78]

The bitter conflicts within the community also prevented the election of a rabbi to serve as head of the spiritual leadership. As a figure acceptable to the majority of the community could not be found, until 1880 this position was occupied jointly by Rabbis Yitshak Abulafia and Solomon Sucari.

The Renewal of the Dispute between Rabbis Gagin and Abulafia

In the autumn of 1874, Rabbi Shalom Gagin publicly declared that he had never really accepted Abulafia's apology. His continuing hostility towards his former friend was articulated in a halakhic ruling that he wrote, sprinkled with numerous insults, opposing one by Abulafia. He even went so far as to send this ruling to the sages of Damascus, including Rabbi Abulafia himself. It was clear to Abulafia that, so long as his rival was living in Jerusalem, he would continue to incite the sages of that city against him. He therefore decided that he would no longer send his own rulings to the sages of Jerusalem for their approval. Abulafia also feared that his enemies in the Damascus community would send false documents in his name to the sages of Jerusalem.[79] In December 1874 he wrote to his friend Rabbi Jacob Saul Elyashar about Shalom Gagin's continued enmity towards him:

And certainly, because of his great hatred towards me, Rabbi S. M. H. [Gagin] will do their will to reject my words, even with a straw [i.e. a palpably false and weak

[78] See *JC*, 3 Dec. 1880, p. 12. Rabbi Kimhi did not contribute much to the halakhic record either. His isolated responsa are scattered in a few places in the literature: see e.g. Gagin, *Yismaḥ lev*, 'Even ha'ezer', 39*b*–40*b*, §17; 'Ḥoshen mishpat', 65*b*, §18; 69*b*, §19; Navon and Elyashar, *The Sons of Benjamin* (Heb.), 105*a*, §44.

[79] A question of this type was printed in Azriel, *Kapei aharon*, 2, 'Ḥoshen mishpat', 101*a* ff., §5. The author of the book, Rabbi Aaron Azriel, who himself spoke in sharply censorious terms

argument] . . . And since they do not really know the facts of the case and all the details of its development, may possibly agree with him to do his will and that of Signor Eleazar, my great enemy, who constantly pursues me and seeks to uproot my honour and that of my father's house, and to reduce me to dust, and to lift up those who are smaller than me in wisdom and in age. And as for myself, the Lord knows and Heaven is my witness that I do not hate any person in the world, and that every night I forgive whoever has angered me apart from him.[80]

In 1878, fuelled by two separate events, the struggle over the rabbinate in Damascus erupted again. The first of these events was the resignation of Rabbi Kimhi and the vacancy thereby created in the office of *ḥakham bashi*. The second was the publication of the book *Yismaḥ lev*, in which Rabbi Gagin set out for all to read the whole history of the dispute between himself and Yitshak Abulafia, but this time publicly representing the latter as a forger and liar, a man lacking in all decency who insulted Torah scholars and who failed to fulfil his promise to publish the statement of apology and restitution that he had given to Gagin in 1872.[81]

The publication of so inflammatory an account of this dispute—and specifically at a time when there was renewed competition for the highest rabbinic office in Damascus, and when Rabbi Abulafia was, in practice, the leading candidate for this office—hit Abulafia like a thunderstorm on a clear day. True, he knew that Gagin had never genuinely put aside his animosity towards him, and that for years he had been inciting the sages of Jerusalem and his relatives in the Angel family in Damascus against him, but he had not imagined that he would resort to such a blatant and brutal public excoriation. In his eyes, this indicated that Gagin, the members of the Angel family, and their supporters had all entered into a conspiracy to remove him from the rabbinic office in Damascus. He wrote of his shock on reading Gagin's attack:

Now recently, not many days ago, the world turned black for me. I have been eviscerated, and my [rabbinic] seat has been shaken by the rabbi, author of the book *Yismaḥ lev* . . . He said harsh things against me, tough as sinews . . . with shame and arrogance and insult I have been devoured and astonished, insulted and abused and cursed and humiliated with harsh and vile and bitter words, and they have come against me with libel and pretext and imaginary and false things, which the mind and thought cannot accept. His tongue spat out poison like a scorpion, and he spilt

about Rabbi Yitshak Abulafia, states that it was Eleazar Angel who sent the question. The harsh terms Rabbi Azriel uses are surprising in the light of the rebuke he gave S. M. H. Gagin concerning the language he used against Abulafia in his book *Yismaḥ lev* (see n. 85 below).

[80] JNUL, DMA. Arc. 4to, 1271/606, Rabbi Yitshak Abulafia to Rabbi Saul Elyashar, Rosh Hodesh Tevet 5635.

[81] Gagin, *Yismaḥ lev*, 'Ḥoshen mishpat', 50*b*, §11.

his anger like fire, destroyed in his rage, slaughtered without mercy to achieve his will and the will of his like, who hated me with a destructive hatred and have waged war against me for no reason and sought my humiliation . . . And he removed the mask of shame from his face to insult a Torah scholar who is dust and ashes like myself, and in his own mind came against me with a great libel . . . And he has done as he planned, and his sins and transgressions are with me, written with his hand and inscribed with an iron and lead pen, and he distributed that book throughout all the cities of Israel, near and far, in order to insult and humiliate and curse me and to make me shameful in the eyes of all Israel,[82] and particularly in the eyes of the people of my own city, among whom I had been accepted as rabbi and as righteous teacher, and to reduce my honour in their eyes.[83]

Abulafia decided to fight back. What was now at stake was not only the chief rabbinate in Damascus, which was important in its own right, but the question of his reputation and image in the world of Torah. Notwithstanding the considerable financial outlay involved, and even though he was about to publish the second volume of his own book *Penei yitsḥak*, Abulafia decided to publish a tractate defending his good name against Gagin's onslaught. The name of this tractate, *Lev nishbar* (A Broken Heart), had a double meaning: on the one hand, as the author himself declared, it referred to the anguish and pain he had experienced upon reading the words of his relative and rival: 'May it be His will that there be fulfilled in me the verse, "A broken and contrite heart God will not despise"' [Ps. 51: 19].'[84] On the other hand, it also echoed the title of Gagin's book, *Yismaḥ lev* (The Heart Will Rejoice), suggesting a desire to refute the words of its author.[85]

In his own book, R. Yitshak Abulafia enumerates and answers, one by one, all of Gagin's arguments and allegations, regarding both matters of halakhah and the details of the dispute between them. Abulafia sent no fewer than twenty copies of this book to the sages and rabbis of Jerusalem in order to vindicate his position.[86]

82 Rabbi Gagin cynically sent a dedicated copy of his book to Rabbi Abulafia himself. See Abulafia, *Lev nishbar*, author's introduction, s.v. *beram me'akhar vehidpis*.

83 Ibid., s.v. *vehen atah mikarov*.

84 Ibid., s.v. *uvekhen hineni*; cf. Ps. 51: 19.

85 Gagin's attack on Abulafia was a grave irritant to many of the sages in Jerusalem and in other Jewish communities throughout the Middle East. Thus, for example, in Rabbi Asher Kovo's book *Sha'ar asher* there is a harsh rebuke from the sages and rabbis of Salonica to Gagin and the language he used against Abulafia in his book. They also testify there that Rabbi Aaron Azriel, head of the kabbalistic yeshiva Beit El in Jerusalem, returned the copy of the book *Yismaḥ lev* sent him by Gagin, with a rebuke. See Kovo, *Sha'ar asher*, last page.

86 See JNUL, DMA, Arc. 4to, 1271/606, Rabbi Yitshak Abulafia to 'Yisa berakhah', Damascus, 25 Tishrei 5645.

The Authorities' Involvement in the Appointment of the *Ḥakham Bashi*

As we have seen on several other occasions discussed above, the Ottoman authorities did not usually involve themselves in the internal affairs of the non-Muslim communities. However, the weakness of the Damascus Jewish community at this juncture and its inability to choose a new *ḥakham bashi* for itself led the governor, Midhat Pasha, to intervene in the selection of a candidate for this office. Thus, towards the end of 1879 he imposed upon the Jews of Damascus Rabbi Ephraim Mercado Alkalai. The two men knew one another from the period when Alkalai was *ḥakham bashi* in Niš in Serbia, while Midhat Pasha was governor of the province of the Danube. Like his predecessor, Rabbi Alkalai was not a native Damascene, but unlike his predecessor he was a wealthy man with a great deal of property and as a result not at all dependent upon the community for his livelihood. Moreover, Rabbi Alkalai enjoyed the full backing of Midhat Pasha in a manner that enabled him to deal effectively with his opponents.[87] According to Rabbi Alkalai's own testimony, the situation of the community was so bad—lacking in leadership, divided, and involved in internal disputes—that had it not been for the pressure of Midhat Pasha and the members of the community, he would not have sacrificed his own inclination to remain for the rest of his life in Jerusalem. To the *ḥakham bashi* in Istanbul he wrote:

> And I give witness that it is very difficult for me to leave the holy place . . . particularly since that city [Damascus] has been abandoned for several years, during which they did not have a preacher and leader to guide the people in the proper path. Therefore the poor people of the city have broken the boundaries of decent behaviour . . . and they are lacking in a number of important things and good regulations. So that even in the smallest city in Turkey one can almost find better regulations and manners and proper conduct than in this city.[88]

Alkalai's acceptance of his new role, with the backing of the governor, brought a new spirit to the community. Its institutions were reorganized and co-operation between the *ḥakham bashi* and the steering committee was re-established. The crowning achievement of Alkalai's activity on behalf of the community was the reopening of the Alliance school in 1880. His term in office was thus considered successful—so long as Midhat Pasha continued to serve as governor of Syria. However, when Midhat Pasha was forced out of

[87] Harel, 'Midhat Pasha', 340–1.

[88] ACRI, TR/Is/162*a*, Rabbi Ephraim Mercado Alkalai to Rabbi Moses Halevi, Damascus, 17 Kislev 5640.

office in 1881, Rabbi Alkalai's position weakened and he became less active. Frustrated by the absence of government backing and the resurgent confrontations and disputes within the community, the *ḥakham bashi* left Damascus in February 1883 and returned to Jerusalem.[89]

Rabbi Abulafia as Sole Candidate for the Office of *Ḥakham Bashi*

Rabbi Alkalai's abandonment of Damascus paved the way for Rabbi Abulafia's ascent, at last, to the office of *ḥakham bashi*. Despite his being a man of exceptional Torah learning and the scion of a distinguished rabbinic family, his appointment to this office, to which he was eminently suited, had been delayed for more than ten years, owing to disputes with his own relatives, his family connections with Rabbi Shalom Gagin, and the wealthy laymen Shemaiah and Eleazar Angel. However, in 1883 he had no rivals for the office in Damascus, while his sworn enemies in the Angel family had temporarily left the city for Istanbul. While divisions in the community persisted, at this point the position of Abulafia's supporters was stronger than that of his opponents and he was appointed, in addition to his existing position as head of the religious court, to the office of *ḥakham bashi* of Damascus.

[89] See JNUL, DMA, V-736/261, Alkalai to Gagin(?), Damascus, 5643. Rabbi Alkalai died in Jerusalem on 11 Heshvan 5655 (10 November 1894).

CHAPTER SEVEN

The Appointment and Deposition of Rabbi Yitshak Abulafia

> 'My master Moses, restrain them!' [Num. 11: 28]. What is meant by 'restrain them'? He said to him [Joshua to Moses]: Impose upon them [responsibility for] the needs of the public, and they will be destroyed by themselves.
>
> BT *Sanhedrin* 17*a*

Restoring the Old Order

The appointment of Rabbi Ephraim Alkalai, which, as noted in the previous chapter, was imposed upon the Jews of Damascus at the end of 1879 by the *wali*, Midhat Pasha, was an attempt to force a reorganization of the Jewish community from outside and to place it on a new path. This was consistent with the Ottoman reforms, in whose implementation Midhat Pasha was one of the main figures. This being the case, Rabbi Alkalai's success or failure depended upon the backing he received from the secular powers in Damascus—which, as we have seen, diminished with the departure of Midhat Pasha. This revolutionary and unprecedented attempt by the authorities to involve themselves directly in the internal affairs of the Jewish community in such a way as to influence its conduct suffered a decisive setback with Rabbi Alkalai's departure from Damascus. While one or two things were done during his relatively brief term in office to improve the condition of the community, the communal institutions were not organized in such a way as to enable them to thrive after the economic collapse that followed the Ottoman government's declaration of bankruptcy on 6 October 1875.[1]

The appointment in February 1883 of Rabbi Yitshak Abulafia as successor to Rabbi Alkalai signalled the return of the old order. The remnants of the old elite, who had begun to recover somewhat from the economic crisis and continued to serve as leaders of the community, wished to appoint a rabbi

[1] On the bankruptcy of the wealthy men of Damascus, see Harel, *Syrian Jewry*, 53. On the appointment of Rabbi Alkalai, see Ch. 6 above.

with local roots, who would both have political talents and be regarded as a figure of major stature in the rabbinic world. High hopes were pinned on Rabbi Abulafia, who was considered a decisive person as well as being recognized as a halakhic authority of the highest order.

At the time of Abulafia's appointment to the office of *ḥakham bashi*, the Damascus Jewish community numbered 2,224 households—around 10,000 people. Most of these were artisans or craftsmen, small merchants and businessmen, while a minority were street vendors or completely impoverished. Only ten individuals were still considered to be wealthy.[2] Thus Abulafia's term as chief rabbi was devoted primarily to preserving that which existed and preventing the community from declining any further. There were nevertheless certain areas in which the rabbi made breakthroughs and even brought about revolutionary change. Although his appointment was never confirmed through an official firman from the sultan, Rabbi Abulafia's relations with the government were excellent, as were his relations with the leaders of the Christian and Muslim communities. During his term in office the number of Jews who served in Ottoman government institutions increased. Me'ir Lisbona, the honorary president of the local committee of the AIU, was appointed as a member of the regional *majlis*; Yitshak Halphon, one of the first graduates of the Alliance school, was appointed as a member of the appeals court; Yitshak Ades was appointed as a member of the municipal court; and Hayim Laniado, Rabbi Abulafia's son-in-law, was appointed a judge in the commercial court.[3] Within the community, the conduct of affairs proceeded without renewed conflict, particularly after several of Abulafia's opponents among the hereditary elite emigrated from Damascus, lost their money, or died. Nevertheless, the rabbi still had to negotiate a path among various groups both within and outside the community. Apart from the government institutions and heads of the other religious communities, these groups included, on the one hand, the supporters of the AIU in Damascus and, on the other hand, some of the more zealous Torah scholars. We therefore turn next to consider Rabbi Abulafia's tenure in relation to the activity of the Alliance and to the issue of modern education, as this manifested itself with the renewal of the society's activity in Damascus in 1880.

Rabbi Abulafia as Leader of an Educational Revolution

The first emissary of the AIU to Damascus arrived on 22 January 1865. The Torah scholars of the city, led by chief rabbis Jacob Perets and Aaron Jacob

[2] See *Ḥavatselet*, 42 (29 Elul 5642), 328. For the results of the Ottoman census from the 1880s, see Karpat, 'Ottoman Population Records', 265.

[3] See *JC*, 28 May 1886, p. 14*b*.

Benjamin, welcomed the Alliance's interest in Damascus and co-operated with its representative in furthering the society's aim of disseminating modern education among the community's children. Rabbi Abulafia, who was at the time a member of the community's rabbinic court, was one of those who supported the Alliance's activity among the younger generation from the very outset. Among the explicit expressions of his support was his agreement to join the committee set up to oversee the establishment of the school, which was intended to combine sacred and secular studies. However, notwithstanding the widespread admiration of the Alliance and support for the introduction of modern education into the Damascus community, towards the end of 1869 the director of the school had to leave Damascus—for personal reasons, as well as differences of opinion with the wealthy laymen of the community, albeit not with its rabbis.[4]

Thereafter, the Alliance's official activity in Damascus ceased for a period of ten years, although in practice its values and principles continued to be articulated in Damascus through the work of three graduates of the school. These people set up a society known as La Société de jeunes gens à Damas (Society of Young Men in Damascus), whose goal was to act in the spirit of the Alliance. These individuals saw education and enlightenment as the highest values; hence, with the financial help of the Alliance, they established a library in Damascus and began to teach themselves Turkish which, as the language of the government, was of particular importance. They tirelessly spread the message and principles of the Alliance among the members of the community, and distributed the contents of the society's newsletter, *Bulletin de l'Alliance Israélite Universelle*, in Damascus. Throughout this decade, they constantly appealed to the Alliance to re-establish its school in the community.[5] Thanks to their persistence, the Damascus community retained a connection with the Alliance, and the chief rabbis continued to turn to it with various requests for assistance.[6] Moreover, after the wealthy laymen of Damascus went bankrupt, and in consequence could no longer support the students of Torah, the entire class of Torah scholars turned to the Alliance with an appeal to support them and their families:

[4] On the beginnings of the Alliance's activity in Damascus, see Harel, *Syrian Jewry*, 80–3. On the approach of the Middle East sages to enlightenment and the revolution which took place in their approach, see Harel, 'From Openness to Closedness' (Heb.).

[5] See AAIU, Syrie, XI.E., Damas, 94, Halfon, 2 Aug. 1872, 7 Jan. 1874; Syrie, I.B., 5, Damas, Halfon, 8 Jan. 1873, 20 Dec. 1875; Syrie, I.B., 5, Damas, Balillios, 1 May 1879.

[6] See e.g. AAIU, Syrie, I.B., 5, Damas, Rabbi Kimhi to the Alliance, end of Nisan 5635; rabbis of Damascus to the Alliance, Rosh Hodesh Heshvan 5637.

And because of our sins this terrible rebellious act of Satan has succeeded, for individuals within our community have lost their wealth and property and the work of their hands, their silver and gold, have all descended to oblivion at the hand of the king and the princes, as is known . . . And they remain naked and destitute . . . and this caused them to cease supporting the Torah scholars, and the livelihood [of the latter] ceased, and their income stopped utterly, and the doors of the study houses and yeshivot were sealed shut, and goodness ceased from the world . . . And the rabbinic sages sit in shock, confused and pressured, furious and enveloped in hunger, for they had never previously known how to do any kind of labour . . . and the lack of money is very harsh . . . and their homes are bereft of all goodness . . . and the creditors have come up to their necks . . . and they nearly despaired of their lives because of the oppression . . . We beg you . . . by your desire and willingness to perform kindness and compassion with all flesh and spirit, and particularly with those who are here today, the poor and unfortunate, destitute and miserable . . . And we place our trust in their love and compassion, that they will do with us doubly good. Blessed be the Lord, God of Israel, who has not withheld from us a redeemer.[7]

This heartfelt appeal, expressing the profound respect and admiration of the class of Torah scholars for the Alliance, also enjoyed the approval of the spiritual leaders of the community, Rabbis Yitshak Abulafia and Solomon Sucari.

In 1880 the *wali*, Midhat Pasha, put all his authority behind a campaign to promote public education in Damascus. Nevertheless, the Jews and Christians were still reluctant to send their children to the public school out of fear that they would be humiliated there.[8] Midhat Pasha also directly supported an initiative to reopen the Alliance school in Damascus. Following his appeal to the Alliance and to Agudat Ahim, the Anglo-Jewish Association in London, these two groups allotted funds for a school for boys in the city, to be opened under the directorship of the AIU. This imposition of a modern Jewish–European educational enterprise by the secular governing authority was an unusual step. Rabbi Ephraim Alkalai, who at the time was the *ḥakham bashi* in Damascus, and had worked intensively with Midhat Pasha for the reopening of the school, was placed at the head of the school committee, alongside two or three other dignitaries.[9] Most of the rabbinic scholars in the city gave their blessing to the initiative. Moreover, even those who served as *melamedim* in the *talmudei torah*, and whose livelihood was therefore presumably threatened by the opening of the modern school, initially chose not to oppose the Alliance's initiative but instead requested that it extend its sponsorship to their own *talmudei torah*.[10] During the years that followed, the

7 AAIU, Syrie, I.B., 5, Damas, 31 sages from Damascus to the Alliance, Heshvan 5640.

8 FO 195/1514, Dixon, Damascus, 12 Nov. 1885.

9 On this episode see Harel, 'Midhat Pasha'.

10 See AAIU, Syrie, I.B., 5, Damas, teachers of small children in Damascus to the Alliance,

spiritual heads of the Damascus community would visit the school to test the knowledge of its students. It appears from a letter sent by Rabbis Yitshak Abulafia and Solomon Sucari to the heads of the Alliance, following their own visit to the school about a year after it was reopened, that their impression was extremely positive. They were effusive in their praise for the students' knowledge of Jewish subjects, for the management of the school, and for its curriculum which, in addition to Jewish studies, also included 'languages, and secular studies'.[11]

The Alliance's emissary in Damascus at this time, Moses Fresco, saw the reopening of the school as a turning point, from which progress would be made to end ignorance among the community's youth. However, he also identified numerous problems associated with the introduction of modern education to the people of Damascus. According to him, the tuition fees were too high, making less wealthy families reluctant to register their children in the new school. On the other hand, he alleged that some of the Jews of Damascus were exploiting the recent bankruptcy of the wealthy men of the community to avoid paying for tuition and to demand that the Alliance enable pupils to study in their institutions without any payment. Fresco complained that twelve years earlier the community had been wealthy but did not want education; now it wanted education, but did not have the means to pay for it.[12] In order to encourage members of the community to sacrifice some of their meagre incomes in order to give their sons a modern education, Fresco called on the heads of the community—and particularly the senior Torah scholars and the judges, who were the highest ethical authority—to give the school their explicit support. Their backing was particularly important because a degree of opposition to the Alliance was starting to emerge among the second level of Torah scholars, particularly those who taught in the *talmudei torah*, as some of them began to see the activity of the association as a threat to their own monopoly over the education of the very young.[13]

Rabbi Abulafia continued to give his explicit support to the activity of the Alliance, as did his colleague Rabbi Sucari. In addition to recognizing the great importance of the children studying secular subjects as well as sacred texts, they understood that modern education was the key to the progress of

received 29 June 1880. The Alliance responded to the request and, in co-operation with the Agudat Ahim society of London, began to provide annual support to the *talmudei torah*. Finally, in 1885, the *talmudei torah* were moved to the full supervision of the Alliance. See *Bulletin*, 2nd sem. 1885–1st sem. 1886, p. 49; 2nd sem. 1886, p. 35; and see below.

[11] AAIU, Syrie, XI.E., Damas, 96, Abulafia and Sucari to the Alliance, Damascus, received 29 May 1881.

[12] AAIU, Syrie, XV.E., Damas, 146, Fresco, 3 Nov. 1880.

[13] AECCC, Damas, vol. 7, p. 169, Gillois, 20 Jan. 1893.

Jewish society and the improvement of its status in the eyes of the surrounding non-Jewish society. As the rabbis and *gevirim* of Damascus wrote to the Alliance:

Every single day our eyes see tender children, the youth of the children of Israel, increasing in their study of the perfect Torah of the Lord, adding wisdom and understanding and knowledge, and writing the languages of the nations and *derekh erets* [secular studies] . . . The mouth cannot tell the great joy of our hearts, in going on the day set for examination of these charming students, and together with us were princes and great people of the nations, who honoured and praised the wisdom of these youths, the children of the Hebrews, that within a few days [of coming to the school] the children of Israel had light in their dwellings.[14]

The perception of modern education as 'light' led Rabbis Abulafia and Sucari to take another very significant public step: immediately upon their appointment as spiritual leaders of the community, they joined the Alliance Israélite Universelle themselves, as regular members.[15]

This was a development of some significance. European Jewish education led to a change, even perhaps a revolution, in the cultural life of the Jews of Damascus as well as in the schooling of their children. The Alliance school was the first to present theatrical productions to the Jewish community. These plays were usually European ones, although some were dramatized stories from the Bible. The soirées at which these performances were presented constituted a high point in the cultural life of the Damascus elite, to which leading figures were invited from the government and the military, as well as foreign consuls, senior officials, and municipal dignitaries. These illustrious guests all came to the soirées sponsored by the Alliance school in order to enjoy a taste of Europe, this institution being one of the few strongholds in Damascus of French culture, so greatly valued by the city's elites. It is interesting to note that the chief rabbi and other Jewish dignitaries also went to see the plays alongside these secular figures. In other words, the educational revolution which Abulafia encouraged, not only by giving it his moral support but also by being present at the theatrical productions, indirectly led to an expansion of the cultural world of Damascene Jews to include social encounters with non-Jews. Visiting governors and military officers, dignitaries and consuls, Muslim and Christian clergymen, even kings, became a frequent sight at the Alliance school in Damascus, both during the hours of study and at cultural events.[16]

[14] AAIU, Syrie, XVIII.E., Damas, 175, Lisbona, Damascus rabbis and *gevirim* to Alliance, received 27 Mar. 1882. Cf. Syrie, XI.E., Damas, 96, Aboulafia, Damascus rabbinic judges to the Alliance, 12 Iyar 5641.

[15] See *Bulletin*, 1st sem. 1883, p. 82.

[16] See e.g. ibid., 2nd sem. 1884–1st sem. 1885, p. 34.

After Rabbi Abulafia was elected to the office of *ḥakham bashi* he continued to give the Alliance not only moral support but also tireless practical assistance. He served as a valuable role model: as noted above, he took meticulous care to renew his membership every year.[17] Dozens of members of the community joined the society in his wake. But he did not confine himself to symbolic steps. One area in which he gave significant support to revolutionary change within the community was that of women's education. The received wisdom in the Orient—not only within the Jewish world—was that there was no value or benefit in educating girls. Since a woman's concerns were exclusively within the home, she had no need for education beyond the imparting of household skills; her only functions were to please her husband and to care for their children. Women had no authority within the home, let alone within the community. As a result, until the middle of the nineteenth century there were no educational institutions for girls in the Syrian communities, and the vast majority of girls did not even learn how to read or write. August Frankel describes the behaviour of the women in a Damascus synagogue in the mid-1850s during the taking out of the Torah scrolls: 'Not a single one of them had a prayer book in her hand, since they do not know how to read a book; their entire share in the Divine service is to move their hands and stand up from their seats.'[18] Only among the wealthy families, in which there was greater openness to different ideas, were girls allowed to study in a private framework or in missionary institutions for young women.

The opening of Protestant missionary educational institutions for girls in the 1850s led to a revolution in ideas about female education. More and more families began to send their daughters to these institutions in order to acquire some learning—particularly as there were no tuition charges. Indeed, in many cases not only were the students themselves provided with all the supplies they needed, but their families were given gifts and monetary grants as well.[19] With concern growing that girls who attended these Protestant institutions would be drawn into the Christian churches, and with the intervention of the French consul, the Alliance agreed to establish the first school for Jewish girls in Damascus.[20] When it opened its gates at the beginning of November 1883 it had eighty students between the ages of 6 and 16, some

[17] *Bulletin*, 1st sem. 1883, p. 82; 1st sem. 1884, p. 104; 2nd sem. 1885–1st sem. 1886, p. 134.

[18] L. A. Frankel, *To Jerusalem* (Heb.), 115.

[19] On Protestant missionary activity in Damascus until 1880, see Harel, *Syrian Jewry*, 186–93, and below.

[20] AAIU, Syrie, XI.E., Damas, 94, heads of the Damascus community Musa Farhi, Abraham Pinto, David Atiyah, Me'ir Lisbona, Moses Lisbona, Jacob Halevi, Joseph Lisbona, Moses Elias, Moses Atiyah, and Solomon Farhi to the Alliance, received June 1883.

of whom had transferred from the Protestant school. The curriculum included the usual subjects taught to boys, such as French, arithmetic, and Hebrew, but also what were considered explicitly 'feminine' skills such as drawing, weaving, and music.[21]

The willingness of parents to send their daughters to school at all, irrespective of whether it was Protestant or Jewish, amounted to a revolution. This was testimony to the process of change in what had until that time been the dominant world-view with regard to the status and function of girls and women in society. There was as yet no question of equality between men and women; the vast majority of the inhabitants of Damascus, male and female, Jews and non-Jews, continued for many more years to see women as lowly creatures without any authority in the family or the community, whose purpose began and ended with caring for their husbands and children.[22] Nevertheless, the very act of sending girls to study at school entailed a new acceptance that women did have influence within society. A girl who had been educated would be both a better mother in terms of the education that she could give her own children, and better able to contribute to the progress and development of the community.[23] The tension between the desire to advance the Jewish woman and the expectation that she fulfil her traditional obligations found expression in the request made by the heads of the community to the Alliance that they teach the girls French—but also handicrafts.[24]

The opening of a girls' school within the Jewish community was thus, while only a minor revolution, one of immeasurably great importance. The support of the *ḥakham bashi*, Rabbi Abulafia, was essential. Without his stamp of approval for the school, and the change it signified in the status of women, the innovation would have been impossible.

One immediate result of the establishment of a school for girls was the setting up of a committee of Women of the Alliance in Damascus. This committee consisted of fifteen women from the social and economic elite of the city's Jewish community, including Rabbi Abulafia's daughter, Bolisa Nehamah.[25] This was the first organized communal activity of Jewish women in Damascus, and as such it too represented a revolution.

Within a year of its opening, the great success of the school for girls led to the establishment of what was, from the viewpoint of the Alliance, another

[21] *JC*, 17 Aug. 1883, p. 7*b*; 8 Feb. 1884, p. 10*a*.

[22] These ideas had long been dominant in many sections of Damascus society. See e.g. AECCC, Damas, vol. 7, p. 169, Gillois, 20 Jan. 1893.

[23] Ibid.; cf. Rodrigue, *De l'instruction*, 81–2.

[24] AAIU, Syrie, XI.E., Damas, 94, heads of the Damascus community to the Alliance, received June 1883.

[25] *Bulletin*, 2nd sem. 1885–1st sem. 1886, p. 56.

pioneering institution in Damascus—a new framework for vocational training for young women. Encouraging Jews to take up economically productive work was a fundamental element in the world-view of the Alliance. Thus, following the establishment in 1870 of the agricultural school Mikveh Yisra'el near Jaffa in Palestine, it began to establish a network of vocational schools and training programmes in artisanship for Jewish youth. As part of this enterprise, in November 1884 the Alliance established a workshop for young women in Damascus—its first workshop for women anywhere, and opened in advance of its apprenticeship programme for young men in Damascus, launched in May 1885. On these schemes, apprentices were assigned to work with Muslim or Christian artisans who were paid by the Alliance to teach their craft. The Alliance subsequently established workshops adjacent to its own schools, in which the apprentices worked and sold the goods they had made. Once the young men had completed their period of training, the Alliance provided them with loans, enabling them to buy the tools and equipment they needed to begin to establish themselves.[26] Even though, as a rule, the vocations learned were not modern ones but traditional arts and handicrafts, this initiative was greatly valued by the people of Damascus, as it directly helped them to diversify and improve their sources of income. The apprenticeship project for girls enjoyed particular prestige as the community came to realize that girls were capable of earning their own living and so need not always be a burden upon the men of their families, as they had been in the past. Over a period of years, this enterprise led to a total revolution for Jewish women in Damascus, who acquired an autonomous status, independent of the men around them.[27]

Some of the Alliance's activities in Damascus were oriented towards short-term ends, while others aimed at longer-term goals. On the one hand, the depressed economic situation required that children be prepared to cope with the everyday exigencies of earning a living; the emissaries of the Alliance admitted that it was not their goal to train academic professionals such as teachers, lawyers, and engineers, but rather skilled, hard-working, and honest manual workers. On the other hand, the educators of the Alliance wished to encourage change in the customs, patterns of thought, and way of life of the local Jews, and this, they believed, could best be done through graduates of the Alliance schools disseminating ideas of progress and modern culture within their own families.[28]

[26] *Bulletin*, 2nd sem. 1885–1st sem. 1886, p. 56; AECCC, Damas, vol. 7, p. 169, Gillois, 20 Jan. 1893.

[27] See Harel, 'On the Jewish "Singing Women"' (Heb.).

[28] *Bulletin*, 2nd sem. 1886, pp. 64–5.

Rabbi Yitshak Abulafia supported the activities of the Alliance, both because of his own world-view—within which there was no harm in teaching secular subjects to young people—and by virtue of his understanding that, as leader of the community, his first task was to help the younger generation, both boys and girls, to escape the poverty and backwardness that were the lot of most of the Jews of Damascus. He thanked the Alliance for its educational work, significantly mentioning the girls before the boys:

> I have come now to offer them double thanks for the great things they have done with us and with the people of our community, here in our city of Damascus, may God protect it, to help and to benefit the schools of the girls and the boys, and the *talmudei torah* of our city. This is my obligation, and I will give them thanks for all their goodly activity which they have done, which they do, and which they shall continue to do in the future.[29]

From the time the school reopened, its principal, Moses Fresco, and the advisory committee attempted to acquire suitable premises for it, considering the construction of a new building for the purpose.[30] Rabbi Abulafia, shortly after he took up the position of *ḥakham bashi*, applied himself wholeheartedly to the effort, even suggesting that the Alliance purchase the most beautiful group of houses in the Damascus community, the residences of the Farhi family.[31]

At the time of the bankruptcy, the traditional educational system in the Damascus community was composed of several *talmudei torah*. These institutions were primarily intended for the children of the poor, as the offspring of the wealthy families tended to study in Christian institutions or with private tutors. The curriculum in the *talmudei torah* consisted primarily of the study of Hebrew and of Holy Scripture, at the most basic level. Until the economic collapse of 1875, the community supported the *talmudei torah* through money given by the *gevirim*, the wealthy laymen; but thereafter the rabbis who taught in them began to run them as private businesses, without any supervision or communal control. The premises were dark, damp, and neglected, sanitation was inadequate, and the students were often sick. As the teachers' income was not assured, they were forced to compete with one another for students. According to one contemporary testimony, this competition lowered them to the level of servants of the students.[32]

[29] AAIU, Syrie, XI.E., Damas, 96, Aboulafia, Rabbi Yitshak Abulafia to the Alliance, 18 Av 5644.

[30] Ibid., Syrie, XE.E., Damas, 146, Fresco, 23 Nov. 1880, 3 Dec. 1880.

[31] Ibid., Syrie, XI.E., Damas, 96, Aboulafia, Rabbi Yitshak Abulafia to the Alliance, 18 Av 5644.

[32] AECCC, Damas, vol. 7, p. 169, Gillois, 20 Jan. 1893.

The Alliance representatives were shocked by the situation of the *talmudei torah* and sought to help them, beginning with advice on improving their sanitary conditions. They taught new habits of cleanliness, which rapidly brought about a dramatic decline in the rate of illness among the students.[33] When the economic situation worsened further, so that the support of the *talmudei torah* by individuals within the community ceased altogether, the teachers appealed to Yitshak Astruc, headmaster of the Alliance school, with the request that he take their schools under the full sponsorship of the society:

> We have come to beseech your holiness to return his supervision over us for our good, to be our spokesman and leader as he was originally. And particularly now that the Holy Society under whose shadow we had taken shelter has removed its supervision over us, and we are left like flock without a shepherd. And we wish that the conduct of the *talmud torah* be like that which your honour introduced initially, both in terms of the cleanliness of the place where the *talmud torah* is held—may the Almighty establish it Amen—and in terms of guidance of the students—may the Rock protect them and give them life—as we have seen that there is a great gap between the manner in which your honour behaved with us, giving us all kinds of goodness, and our condition since then. We have asked but one thing, that you not turn us away empty-handed; that you complete the good deed you have begun.[34]

Even though they did not make the request explicitly, the *melamedim* who signed this letter also hoped that their salaries would be paid by the Alliance.

At the end of 1885 Rabbi Yitshak Abulafia gave his final approval for most of the *talmudei torah* to be taken under the aegis of the AIU. This was without doubt the most revolutionary move ever made by a *ḥakham bashi* in Damascus in the field of Jewish education. At a single stroke, 450 pupils were exposed to the world of modern education: reforms were made in both the administration and the curriculum of the *talmudei torah*, new teaching materials were introduced, a new accountant was appointed, and the rabbis' salaries were assured—thereby quashing opposition to the change. The curriculum came to include the study of Arabic, French, and other basic subjects, and Hebrew studies were immeasurably improved. Astruc employed regular cleaners and put the collection of tuition fees on an organized footing. With the help of contributions from Europe, particularly from the Alliance and the Agudat Ahim society of London, one of the ramshackle buildings was repaired and its pupils, who had previously had to sit on the floor, were now

[33] AAIU, Syrie, XII.E., Damas, 106*b*, Astruc, schoolteachers to Astruc, received 26 Jan. 1886.

[34] Ibid., schoolteachers to Astruc, 2 Shevat 5646.

able to sit on benches.[35] In this manner the *talmudei torah* were transformed from a backward institution, in which only religious subjects were studied, to a modern academy in which secular subjects were taught alongside religious studies.

Rabbi Abulafia's support of this move played an important role in the conceptual revolution undergone by many of the parents in Damascus. Even the most conservative among them were now able to give their children a broader education within the framework of the traditional *talmud torah*, without feeling that they were handing their children over to European Jewish teachings. Within a few months, the number of students in the *talmudei torah* increased from 450 to 650.[36] During the years that followed, the *talmudei torah* became a preparatory school for full entrance into the modern educational system. Once every six months the outstanding students were transferred from the *talmud torah* to the Alliance school for boys.[37] In the mid-1880s the Alliance was at the height of its success, and the number of those joining its ranks was constantly increasing.[38] Rabbi Abulafia's trust in its motives and intentions also increased. In his eyes, the French Jewish society was not suspect; he believed that it was both able and willing to assist the community's Torah scholars in expanding and developing the teaching of various kinds of Jewish studies. Thus, when he came to publish the second part of his book *Penei yitsḥak*, he had no hesitation in turning to the Alliance with a request for its support, thereby giving full expression to what he saw as the proper combination of secular and sacred.[39]

Spiritual Decline and Religious Zealotry

One of the striking features of Jewish communities in the Ottoman empire at the end of the nineteenth century was the growing contempt for the traditional Jewish way of life. In Damascus as in other communities of the region, this phenomenon led to a decline in the status of the Jewish rabbinic court and a weakening of the Jewish establishment within the city.[40]

As people increasingly disregarded the laws of the Torah, so they also began to treat its representatives, the traditionally learned Torah sages, with

35 *Bulletin*, 2nd sem. 1885–1st sem. 1886, p. 49.

36 Ibid., 2nd sem. 1886, p. 35; 1st–2nd sem. 1888, p. 51.

37 AECCC, Damas, vol. 7, p. 169, Gillois, 20 Jan. 1893; *JC*, 12 Apr. 1895, p. 18*a*.

38 *Bulletin*, 2nd sem. 1885–1st sem. 1886, p. 134.

39 AAIU, Syrie, I.C., Damas, 5, Rabbi Yitshak Abulafia to the Alliance, 2 Nisan 5647.

40 J. Frankel, *The Damascus Affair*, 111; Abulafia, *Penei yitsḥak*, ii. 68*a*–*b*, 76*b*; Elyashar, *Yisa ish*, 'Ḥoshen mishpat', 78*b*, §5; S. E. Alfandari, *Teshuvot hasava kadisha*, ii, 'Oraḥ ḥayim', 12, §1.

less respect. In Damascus this phenomenon derived not so much from ideological change as from the dictates of convenience and a desire to throw off what came to be seen as the burdensome yoke of tradition. The first group to break with the norm of obedience to the Jewish court, as early as the mid-nineteenth century, was that of the wealthy laymen (*gevirim*): their desire to enjoy the pleasures of life without restriction led them repeatedly to behave in ways that were not in accordance with halakhah. Moreover, those who succeeded in attaining foreign citizenship could seek legal approval outside the halakhic structure: they ceased to make exclusive use of the Jewish court and took many of their concerns to the consular court for adjudication.[41] Nevertheless, the wealthy laymen continued to support the Torah sages; the main struggle between the lay leaders of Damascus and its rabbis did not involve matters of religion, but centred upon issues of political power within the community.

Another group that allowed itself to ignore rabbinic rulings and the orders of the Jewish court consisted of those Jews with Ottoman citizenship who were involved in the government bureaucracy. Members of this group enjoyed the protection of the authorities; thus if any clash arose between the law of the state and the laws of the community, they could with impunity ignore the instructions of the community institutions.[42] However, during Rabbi Abulafia's term as *ḥakham bashi*, the number of Jews with European citizenship who exploited their status to avoid subjugation to the community and its regulations decreased sharply. By the 1880s, most of those with foreign citizenship were Algerian Jews under French protection, who saw themselves as fully belonging to the local community.[43]

Among the community at large, disregard for the commandments derived primarily from ignorance and, until the mid-1880s, did not threaten the status of the religious and spiritual leadership. This leadership continued to be respected and accepted; indeed, the uneducated masses continued to fear what they believed to be the magical powers of the Torah scholars. As a result, the rabbis of Damascus were not forced to exert their full authority, as the phenomenon of secularization *per se* did not involve any challenge to their status or to the validity of their religious authority. However, towards the end of the 1880s the Torah scholars began to feel that their public status as a distinctive group within Damascus Jewish society was being increasingly challenged, and in an effort to reassert themselves they began to take more zealous and intransigent positions.

[41] See e.g. FO 195/1765, Eyres to Clare-Ford, Damascus, 19 May 1892.

[42] See e.g. Abulafia, *Penei yitsḥak*, v, 'Ḥoshen mishpat', 129*a*, §3; vi. 1*b*, §1.

[43] See Harel, 'The Citizenship of the Algerian-Jewish Immigrants', 299–302.

One of the phenomena which most troubled the Torah scholars, as an expression of the wider challenge to the authority of halakhah and its representatives in the community, was the increase in the number of Jews—primarily women—who converted to another religion: the majority to Islam and a smaller number to Christianity. Most of these conversions were motivated by the desire for economic betterment;[44] in many instances, Jewish girls converted to Islam in order to marry Muslim men.[45] There were also a considerable number of Jews who visited Protestant institutions and listened to the preaching of missionaries. Even though these missionaries were not generally successful in their goal of converting Jews to Christianity, they took heart from the very presence of more than a few Jews among their audience, listening to their words about Jesus and his gospel.[46]

The extensive missionary activity within his community was one of the motivations for Rabbi Abulafia's unflinching support for the institutions of the Alliance. During the 1890s there were already two Protestant missionary schools active in Damascus that had been established with the intention of attracting Jewish students, both boys and girls, as well as the schools of the various Catholic religious orders which admitted Jews.[47] Jewish visitors to Damascus were astonished to observe the extensive educational and cultural activity of the Christian orders, which enjoyed the support of European states and of the United States. The temptation to study in Protestant schools was particularly great because they did not charge for tuition, and needy families even received a degree of financial support. The Protestant school thus served as a meeting place for children from both ends of the Jewish social spectrum: the children of the poor, attracted by the financial support offered, and the children of the well-off, whose parents wished them to enjoy a European education with consequent economic benefits.[48] The people of the Alliance implored Rabbi Abulafia to dissuade members of the community from sending their children to the missionary schools, and he responded positively:

This is my obligation, and I will do it . . . And my teachers, the 'kings of the land', may believe me that from the day that I sat upon the throne of the rabbinate of the holy community of Damascus—may God protect it—from some twenty years ago

[44] Tarab, *Milei de'ezra*, 'Even ha'ezer', *66b*, §3.

[45] A report from 1898 testifies to the conversion to Islam of at least one Jewish girl each month. See AAIU, Syrie, XIX.E., Damas, 190*a*, Ouziel, 7 Aug. 1898.

[46] On the beginnings of missionary activity in Damascus, see Harel, *Syrian Jewry*, 186–91.

[47] For details of the schools, see AECPC, Turquie, Damas, vol. 17, pp. 85–109, Bertrand, 10 Oct. 1893.

[48] AECCC, Damas, vol. 7, p. 169, Gillois, 20 Jan. 1893; *Bulletin*, 2nd sem. 1886, p. 65.

until this day, I have stood on watch not to allow any person from Israel go to them. But my hand is not so strong at present, now that freedom and choice have been granted by the government—may His Majesty be exalted—and each person does that which is right in his own eyes, and no one can say to them, 'What are you doing?' And this is particularly so because poverty has not passed over many, thus causing the poor people to violate the word of their Creator. Nevertheless, I use every possible subterfuge to rebuke them with the staff of admonition that they not go to them. For thanks be to God who has not left us bereft of a redeemer—[namely,] your honour, who is learned in Torah—who has established and set up for us schools, a *talmud torah* and a [modern] school and good and proper teachers to lift up the banner of Israel and the banner of our holy Torah, to teach to the youth of Israel all matters of wisdom and ingenuity and language and writing [i.e. script] of the nations, and to uplift the Torah and make it glorious.[49]

The challenge presented by Christian missionary activity and conversion troubled other communities in the Middle East, too; but, in contrast to the situation in Europe, it never constituted an existential threat to the community.[50] This important fact influenced attitudes towards modern education in Jewish communities across the region. In Europe, suspicion of the deleterious influence on Jewish identity of encroachment by the Christian environment through modern education led communities to close in upon themselves and to distance themselves from general education. By contrast, in the Muslim Middle East, in which there was no danger of assimilation within Christian society, fear of the Christian educational influence led not to a comprehensive repudiation of modern education, but rather to activity specifically intended to counter its influence. This approach led to the expansion of modern Jewish education, under the supervision of the rabbis.

Nevertheless, the first seven years of Rabbi Abulafia's term of office as *ḥakham bashi* were marked by improved relations with the local Christians. Thus, for example, the prizegiving for students at the Alliance's schools, both boys and girls, was honoured by the presence not only of the commander of the military, a representative of the district government, and almost all the foreign consuls—as would have been expected on such an occasion—but also of representatives of various other educational institutions, such as the principal of the Imperial Military School and his teachers, the headmaster of the Lazarite school and his teachers, the headmaster of the Greek (Melkite) Catholic school, and the headmasters and teachers of the Jesuit and Francis-

[49] AAIU, Syrie, XI.E., Damas, 96, Aboulafia, Rabbi Yitshak Abulafia to the Alliance, Damascus, 29 Nisan 5652.

[50] See e.g. Bornstein-Makovatzki, 'The Activity of the American Mission' (Heb.). On common features of the Alliance and of the mission, see Zohar, 'On the Influence of the Alliance' (Heb.).

can schools.[51] Accounts from the 1880s portray a situation in which the local Christians, hitherto predominantly hostile towards the Jews, became more civil, and in which some signs of real friendship between Christians and Jews were evident.[52]

As noted above, there was a great upsurge in Protestant missionary activity during Abulafia's term as *ḥakham bashi*. Dozens of Jews came into contact with the missionaries and were subject to some degree of influence. The missionary activity included preaching and conversation, distribution of bibles and missionary literature, and the work of educational institutions in which the emphasis was placed on study of the New Testament. Public prayer meetings were organized at which some of the prayers were read in Hebrew. Several of the missionaries were apostate Jews with Jewish surnames, such as Segall—a factor which helped them in attracting the attention of Jews. The missionaries also exploited the absence of a Jewish hospital in Damascus to open, in 1895, a mission-run clinic in the heart of the Jewish district.

The *ḥakham bashi*'s struggle against the missionaries, notwithstanding the strength of his views as expressed, for example, in the passage reproduced above, was not always reflected in practical matters. Thus, for example, following the accepted practice in Damascus and other cities with Jewish communities, Rabbi Abulafia allowed people to rent houses in the Jewish quarter to Christians, and even to missionaries—a practice to which the rabbis who preceded him had not objected.[53] He was also accustomed to hosting Christian travellers in his home and conversing with them, to the extent that he acquired a reputation as a 'Christian lover'.[54] These permissive tendencies aroused the hostility of the more traditional Torah scholars of Damascus, who at the beginning of the 1890s launched an all-out war against the missionaries, and against the *ḥakham bashi* himself.[55]

Those Torah scholars who held a jaundiced view of Rabbi Abulafia's approach to educational matters found strongholds in two traditionalist educational institutions. One of these was the communal school, which was for all practical purposes a *talmud torah* and not under the supervision of the Alliance. Five rabbis taught in this school, earning their living directly from tuition fees collected from the students. According to a contemporary account, the building in which the school was housed was ugly and neglected,

51 *JC*, 24 Oct. 1884, p. 6*a*.

52 *Bulletin*, 2nd sem. 1886, pp. 65–6.

53 Abulafia, *Penei yitsḥak*, v, 'Yoreh de'ah', 15*b*, §1.

54 'Love of Christians' was ascribed to all the rabbis of the Abulafia family who lived in Tiberias; see Weld, *Sacred Palmlands*, 281.

55 On the activity of the mission, its success, and the struggle against it at the beginning of the 1890s, see Gidny, *The History of the London Society*, 459–63, 558–60.

and its curriculum consisted exclusively of religious subjects. When the Alliance offered to sponsor this institution as well as all the other *talmudei torah*, it encountered severe opposition from the rabbis—who, according to the French consul in Damascus, preferred to decline in misery rather than to accept the authority of a heretical approach.[56] The other educational institution run by Rabbi Abulafia's opponents was the orphanage established by the *gevir* Raphael Halevi-Stambuli, which housed about a hundred children. During the lifetime of their patron the orphans were properly cared for, but in 1892 Stambuli died without having taken measures to ensure the continued existence of the institution after his death.[57] At that point the orphanage would have been closed had it not been for the support of several generous families. The staff of this institution consisted of three *melamedim*, who taught religious subjects only; offers of sponsorship from the Alliance met with fierce opposition from conservative Torah scholars.[58]

Why did religious zealotry grow to such an extent in Damascus during the second half of the 1880s, to the point where the community was described as one of the most backward in the Middle East? At the beginning of the 1890s the French consul described the community as one characterized by superstition and blind religious zealotry, whose members followed the practices of their religion by rote, without understanding its values. According to him, the fanaticism and distinctive way of life of the Jews cut them off from the rest of the population, so that the only connection Jews had with non-Jews was on the level of practical business: that is, in the commercial bargaining that occurred in the marketplace.[59]

One of the explanations offered is that the promise of modernization and progress offered by the AIU was not fulfilled. This failure stands out particularly strongly in the light of the general educational situation in Damascus at the end of the nineteenth century. This was a time when general education in Damascus was very open and progressive—so much so that the city was considered a major educational centre, comparable to Cairo.[60] Signs of disillusion with the activity of the Alliance began to appear in the years following the opening of the school for boys. Many parents anticipated that, after a few

[56] AECCC, Damas, vol. 7, p. 169, Gillois, 20 Jan. 1893. Cf. AECPC, Turquie, Damas, vol. 17, pp. 85–109, Gillois, 10 Oct. 1893.

[57] On the wealthy layman Raphael Halevi Stambuli, see *Halevanon*, 14 (20 Tamuz 5625), 216.

[58] AECPC, Turquie, Damas, vol. 17, pp. 85–109, Gillois, 10 Oct. 1893; AECCC, Damas, vol. 7, p. 169, Gillois, 20 Jan. 1893.

[59] Ibid.

[60] AECPC, Turquie, Damas, vol. 17, pp. 85–109, Gillois, 10 Oct. 1893; and cf. Tibawi, *A Modern History*, 194–5.

years of study in the 'European' school, their sons would emerge as teachers, engineers, or lawyers, or as clerks in the Ottoman Bank, in a European commercial firm, or in the government tobacco company. According to Astruc, the principal of the school, the parents did not understand that it would be difficult for their sons to get such positions, owing to the requirement that they work on the sabbath. Several parents, disappointed with the results of the education their older children had received, were not prepared to pay further to educate their younger children in the Alliance school.[61]

The Alliance schools also suffered from a lack of persistence or diligence on the part of their students, many of whom left before completing a course of education. This problem was particularly severe among girls, who continued to marry in early adolescence, as a result of which they were unable to complete their education. Teenage boys from rich families also tended to drop out early from their studies, as their income was assured and they could go into their parents' businesses without completing their studies. The children of poor families, on the other hand, abandoned their studies the moment they were able to assist in providing for their family's income.[62]

Another problem was that of emigration, especially of young educated Jews. Most of the students who stayed in the Alliance schools were those from the middle class, who placed a high value on education. Accounts of the time describe how these young people began to depart from the old ways and develop a lively curiosity. According to Astruc, the horizons of these students broadened, and they developed a desire to know what was taking place in the wider world beyond Damascus and its environs. Thus a number of the school's graduates struck out in new directions. Their modern education enabled the merchants who employed them to make connections with the large industrial and commercial centres in Europe.[63] Their familiarity with European culture and commerce, on the one hand, and their realization that Damascus did not have much to offer graduates of a modern Jewish education on the other, prompted many young, educated people to leave Damascus. Hence, the education provided by the Alliance school did not revive the Damascus community but, on the contrary, helped to create an expatriate community overseas.[64] At the same time, the departure of a large number of young educated people left power in the hands of those more conservative elements in the community who remained behind. These were now able to

61 *Bulletin*, 2nd sem. 1886, pp. 64–5.
62 AECCC, Damas, vol. 7, p. 169, Gillois, 20 Jan. 1893.
63 *Bulletin*, 2nd sem. 1886, p. 65; 1st–2nd sem. 1890, p. 52.
64 On immigration, its motivations, and its results, see Harel, *Syrian Jewry*, 250–3.

emphasize the damage, as they saw it, caused by the Alliance education rather than the promised benefits.

The decline in the level of Torah studies in Damascus also fuelled the rise of religious zealotry. It has been widely observed that ignorance leads to extremism and fanaticism, especially when accompanied by erosion of a traditional way of life and growing tolerance towards deviation from the tradition.[65] Disregard for the commandments began to assume the dimensions of an accepted popular norm. Even those commandments hitherto strictly observed by the Damascus Jewish public were now coming to be held in contempt.[66]

The low level of the religious scholarship in Damascus left Rabbi Abulafia almost completely alone in terms of Torah knowledge and erudition. While there were a few other Torah scholars of stature in the city, even they were not on a par with him. This being so, his main halakhic discourse was with other scholars of comparable stature elsewhere in the Middle East.[67] Hence he gained a reputation for being a strong-minded rabbi, who did not take into account the opinion of the other rabbis in his own city, and even became known as one who 'does not allow any other rabbi to settle in Damascus'.[68] Clearly, this approach did not do much for his popularity in the city. It is nevertheless important to bear in mind that, like other rabbis in the Near Eastern communities who occupied political positions of similar importance, Rabbi Abulafia understood the needs of the time and was therefore open-minded in his approach to modern education and ideas. On the other hand, for the majority of the local Torah scholars—who were not confronted with the practical challenges of providing for the community's survival and well-being in the light of both the demands of the imperial authorities and the pressures of modernization, and so were able to ignore the constraints under which the official leaders of the community operated—the preservation of the traditional framework came to be of overriding importance, to the exclusion of all else.[69] The disappearance of the old elites who had been more open to European culture likewise led to an increase in the extremism and narrow-mindedness of the sages. This tendency was diametrically opposed to the world-view of Rabbi Abulafia, whose openness to western culture simply exacerbated the hostility of the Torah scholars towards his exercise of his

[65] See Friedman, 'Religious Zealotry'.

[66] See Harel, 'The Damascus Community' (Heb.), 143.

[67] See throughout his writings (Abulafia, *Penei yitsḥak*, i–vi). His halakhic deliberations and responsa are cited in almost all the responsa works of the period, from Alexandria to Salonica.

[68] Goldstein, *Travels in Jerusalem* (Heb.), 289–90. Rabbi Abulafia also became involved in confrontations with other sages; see Ch. 6.

[69] See Harel, 'From Openness to Closedness' (Heb.), 39.

duties as *ḥakham bashi*. In their view, his seemingly tolerant attitude towards those who threatened the tradition was worse than simple deviation from the tradition since, as spiritual leader of the community, it was his responsibility to set an example; ordinary members of the community were likely to conclude from his tolerance that such views and behaviour were not so reprehensible.

In Damascus, as in other communities in the Middle East towards the end of the nineteenth century, the internal dynamic of religious zealotry eventually led to confrontation between the zealots and the established religious leadership—the *ḥakham bashi*.[70] This confrontation took place in a context that saw the Jewish community losing ground within Damascus society overall. The relations of Jews with Christians, which had fluctuated during the years since the 1840 Damascus blood libel, reached a new nadir in the early 1890s, expressed in the renewal of the blood libel. Rabbi Abulafia's way of dealing with this problem attracted sharp criticism from his opponents, leading even to acts of violence and calls for his removal from office.

Blood Libels, Bribery, and Falsification

The bankruptcy of the wealthy Jewish householders in the mid-1870s and the consequent collapse of the communal framework occurred at a time of relative calm in relations among the three monotheistic religions in Damascus. Attacks on Jews by Muslims were few and relatively mild, while the Christian population was still licking its wounds from the slaughter and destruction of the Christian quarter by Muslim rioters in July 1860.[71] Following these events, blood libels occurred only infrequently in Damascus, and did not generally elicit a public response.[72] However, at the beginning of the 1890s a change came about that exacerbated feelings of alienation on the part of Damascus's Jews and, in one blow, returned them to the dark days of terror and torment they had known in the year 1840—the days of the most notorious such accusation in modern Jewish history, the Damascus blood libel.[73]

[70] See e.g. Friedman, *Society and Religion* (Heb.), 17–21. On the question of the sages of the Middle East and religious zeal, see Brown, 'Sages of the East' (Heb.); id., '"European" Modernization' (Heb.); Zohar, 'Orthodoxy' (Heb.).

[71] On relations between Muslims, Christians, and Jews in Damascus, see Harel, *Syrian Jewry*, 169–93.

[72] On failed attempts to revive the blood libels see e.g. *JC*, 21 Jan. 1870, p. 10*a*; *JC*, 3 Aug. 1877, p. 13*a*. On Muslim religious zealotry which threatened to harm the Jews, see FO 195/1113, Elliot to Dickson, Damascus, 15 Apr. 1876; AECPC, Turquie, Damas, vol. 11, pp. 46–8, Guys, Damas, 12 Apr. 1876.

[73] On this libel, see J. Frankel, *The Damascus Affair*.

In 1890, Christian Easter occurred at the same time as the Jewish Passover. On 7 April, the second intermediate day of Passover, 6-year-old Christian child disappeared; the Jews were accused of murdering the child and using his blood for their religious rituals. Quarrels broke out and acts of violence ensued, including Christian attacks on Jewish funerals. The child's body was found two weeks later in a well. An autopsy revealed a number of circumstances that seemed to confirm the belief of the Christian masses that the Jews had indeed slaughtered the child for ritual purposes: for example, the body was drained of blood, and one of the arms bore cut marks. It was ultimately established that the child had drowned rather than being murdered, and that the Jews were innocent; however, this did not appease the Christian population in Damascus. The French consul's refusal to support the Christian accusations against the Jews, the British consul's openly joining forces with him to defend the Jews against these accusations, and the local authorities helping to protect the Jews from attacks by Christians[74] all strengthened the Christian consciousness—and in no small measure that of the Muslims as well—that, as in the past, the guilty Jews were contriving to evade punishment thanks to the political power and influence of their brethren in Europe.[75]

Why did this new blood libel emerge specifically at this time, on the threshold of the twentieth century? It is worth remembering that the story of the Damascus blood libel had remained alive in Christian consciousness throughout the half-century that had passed since its occurrence. The popular belief that the Jews of Damascus used human blood for ritual purposes was also widespread and strong among quite a few Muslims too.[76] During the final decade of the nineteenth century the Christian community had begun to recover from the devastation of 1860 and to regain its strength, both in

[74] On more than one occasion, the legal authorities in Damascus refused to investigate, even during subsequent years, similar accusations against the Jews. This, they claimed, was because of the existence of a firman from the sultan prohibiting them from taking testimony about the murder of Christians by Jews for ritual purposes. See *JC*, 12 Aug. 1882, p. *6a*. On this firman and the circumstances of its publication, see Kushner, 'A Firman' (Heb.). For a concrete explanation of the governor's taking the side of the Jews, see AECPC, Turquie, Damas, vol. 15, pp. 392–3, Gillois, 4 May 1890. The British consul Dickson, in the very middle of the libel, visited the home of the *ḥakham bashi*, Yitshak Abulafia, to assure him that he would protect the Jews—an act for which he received a letter of thanks from the various British Jewish organizations. See BofD, Minute Book, ACC/3121/C11A/001, protocol of the joint committee for external matters of Agudat Ahim and Emissaries of the Communities, 9 June 1890.

[75] On the blood libel of 1890, see AECPC, Turquie, Damas, vol. 15, Gillois, 19 Apr. 1890, 25 Apr. 1890, 4 May 1890; FO 78/4290, Dickson to Marquess of Salisbury, Damascus, 26 Aug. 1890; *JC*, 16 May 1890, p. *9a*.

[76] See AECPC, Turquie, Damas, vol. 15, Gillois, 4 May 1890.

the economic sense and in terms of its public standing in Damascus. This strengthening of the Christians' position, which continued until the eve of the First World War, took place largely at the expense of the Jews, who were displaced from key economic positions.[77] Moreover, the Jews were a central target for attacks in the Christian press, whose centre was in Beirut. Thus, for example, at that time the weekly *al-Bashir* published an article endorsing the belief that the Jews made use of Christian blood for Passover rituals. This weekly, which was the organ of the Jesuits in Lebanon, had an explicitly French Catholic orientation and consistently expressed hostility towards the Jews.[78] Thus, even if the approach of France's official consular representative in Damascus was neutral, its clerical representatives unequivocally took the part of the anti-Jewish Christian population. The approach of the Christian press was thus consistent with the antisemitism beginning to penetrate the Middle East under the influence of French clergymen and other antisemites.[79] At the time of this new blood libel its foundations were strengthened by two antisemitic tracts that were distributed in the cities of the Middle East. One was written by a Christian Lebanese journalist living in Egypt and was published in Arabic in Cairo; the other was written by a French priest and was published in Paris under the title: *Tué par les Juifs: Histoire d'un meurtre rituel* (Killed by the Jews: The Story of a Ritual Murder).[80] This incitement, attributable to French Catholic inspiration, reinforced the ferment within the Christian population, leading to attacks and beatings of Jews in the streets of Damascus. A few days after the festival of Passover, two priests, members of the Capuchin order in Damascus, incited the Christian mob to riot against the Jews. Jewish stores were looted, many Jews were beaten, and one girl was even kidnapped by a priest and imprisoned for purposes of interrogation.[81]

Blood libels took place in Damascus almost every year during the first half of the 1890s.[82] Some of these died down quickly and left no impression, while others ended in outbursts of violence which reached the point of Jews being stabbed in the streets.[83] Christian hostility also exacerbated a deterioration in relations between Muslims and Jews. Rabbi Abulafia described Christian attacks upon Jews in the wake of the blood libels:

[77] Almaleh, *The Jews in Damascus* (Heb.), 22.

[78] See *Ḥavatselet*, 28 (19 Iyar 5650), 217. On the Christian press in Beirut, see Sehayik, 'The Dreyfus Affair' (Heb.), 192.

[79] On this, see Harel, 'In the Wake of the Dreyfus Affair'.

[80] AECADN, Constantinople, Correspondance avec les Echelles, Damas, 807 (1890–1), Carton 15, Gillois, 24 Jan. 1891.

[81] *JC*, 16 May 1890, p. 9*a*.

[82] See e.g. AECPC, Turquie, Damas, vol. 16, pp. 34–7, Gillois, 3 Feb. 1891; *JC*, 12 Aug. 1892, p. 13*a*; *Ha'or*, 38 (3 Elul 5652), 150; 3 (14 Tishrei 5653), 10.

[83] *Bulletin*, 1st–2nd sem. 1891, p. 60.

Yet nevertheless their hands are still outstretched with a high arm to hit every man and woman, youth and elder, who may on occasion set foot within their territory and inside their walls, whether in the city or in the field, and . . . several of our people—may the Rock protect them and give them life—suddenly fell into their hands, and were in great danger because of the injuries and riots, with [people using] spears and daggers and other weapons, in addition to their cursing the law and religion of the Torah and the flag of the Talmud, calling them names upon the earth—and the page is too short to describe it all, for we have neither help nor assistance, neither friend nor neighbour.[84]

The Alliance representative in Damascus made every attempt to confute the blood libels. He confronted the local French consul, who was trying to remain neutral throughout these events, and arranged for him to receive letters from the heads of the Alliance in Paris imploring him to take sides against the Christians on the matter of the blood libels.[85]

Throughout the period of the blood libels the *ḥakham bashi* maintained close contact with the governor, Mustafa Azim Pasha, in the attempt to ensure the security of the Jewish quarter. However, some of his contacts with Christians angered his opponents. They were particularly incensed by his relationship with Ibrahim Mishaqa, one of the local physicians who had been involved both in examining the body of the child in the 1890 libel and in the new libel raised against the Jews in 1894. According to Rabbi Abulafia's opponents, Mishaqa was well known in Damascus as an enemy of the Jews. According to them, he had told the authorities in 1890 that the Jews were guilty of the murder of the child for ritual purposes, and had testified against the Jews again in the libel of 1894, thereby fomenting Christian hatred of the Jews and outbursts of violence against them. Moreover, they claimed that Mishaqa had asked the leaders of the community to sign a document stating that he treated poor Jews without charge, and that when they refused to do so he turned to Rabbi Abulafia. The *ḥakham bashi*—so they claimed—accepted a bribe from the physician in return for the desired testimony, given not only in his own name but in that of the other rabbis and community leaders, concerning services to the poor people of the community.

The *ḥakham bashi*'s opponents thus accused him of four extremely serious acts: giving support to a Jew-hater; taking bribes; falsifying documents; and ignoring the opinion of the other members of the communal leadership. On these grounds they appealed to Rabbi Moses Halevi, the *ḥakham bashi* in

[84] AAIU, Syrie, XI.E., Damas, 96, Aboulafia, Rabbi Yitshak Abulafia and others to the Alliance, Damascus, 17 Av 5654.

[85] AECPC, Turquie, Damas, vol. 16, pp. 34–7, Gillois, 3 Feb. 1891, 6 Mar. 1891, 19 Mar. 1891, 2 Apr. 1891, 5 May 1891.

Istanbul, requesting that he depose Rabbi Abulafia and appoint another *ḥakham bashi* in his place: 'For he does not even fear regarding things he said which cause damage to the entire people because of the money [that he took]; all the more so regarding a matter that pertains to every individual, that the pen cannot describe—that for one silver coin he destroys an entire palace so that he might have that [payment].'[86]

It is possible that the accusation against Rabbi Abulafia contained a veiled suggestion that he was behaving in a manner similar to his father, Moses, who during the period of the previous Damascus blood libel had converted to Islam and given testimony against the leaders of the Jewish community. It is worth remembering in this context that Ibrahim Mishaqa also had a direct family connection with the 1840 blood libel: his father, Dr Michael Mishaqa, had been among the physicians who examined bones found in the sewerage in the Jewish quarter and determined that they were the bones of a monk whom the Jews had been accused of murdering for ritual purposes.

Needless to say, Rabbi Yitshak Abulafia represented these matters in a completely different light. According to his account, Ibrahim Mishaqa had in fact always treated poor Jewish patients free of charge. Becoming aware that the British were about to set up a hospital in Damascus, and hoping to get a job there, Mishaqa asked the *ḥakham bashi*—through the mediation of Rabbi Moses Perets, son of the previous *ḥakham bashi*, Jacob Perets—to recommend him, in the light of his sympathetic attitude towards poor Jews. According to Rabbi Abulafia, when his opponents heard about this they accused him of giving his recommendation to a doctor who hated Jews.

The *ḥakham bashi* stood firm in his support for the Christian doctor against his own opponents among the rabbis and community leaders, even though in doing so he attracted further hostility and threats. He described the atmosphere of violence against himself and his supporters within the community:

And all this is a false libel which they made up against that uncircumcised [person], for I clearly know that such things never took place. But these evil people say so in order to place guilt upon us, claiming that we gave him a document or testimonial, and they fanned the flames and excited the hearts of the violent ones among our own people to insult and curse Rabbi Moses [Perets] . . . and they curse him continuously, Heaven forbid. And he is hiding in my home, for they have taken counsel together to beat him with deathly blows.[87]

86 JNUL, DMA, Arc 4to, 1512/269, sages and rabbis and individuals in the Damascus community to *ḥakham bashi* Moses Halevi, Damascus, end of Sivan 5654.

87 Ibid. 1271/606, Rabbi Yitshak Abulafia to Rabbi Jacob Saul Elyashar, Damascus, 27 Sivan 5654.

The Breaking of Alliances and the Establishment of a New Front

Twenty years before this episode, a considerable number of Torah scholars in Damascus had supported the *gevir* Shemaiah Angel in his hostility towards Rabbi Yitshak Abulafia.[88] Following Angel's death, his son Eleazar continued the feud, continually challenging Rabbi Abulafia's halakhic authority and encouraging other Torah scholars to oppose his rulings. In 1881 Eleazar Angel was appointed to the regional executive council and awarded a medal of honour from the government; secure in this strengthened public position, Eleazar Angel gradually increased his influence over the internal affairs of the community.[89] The disputes among the rival groups became so severe that those scholars who opposed Rabbi Abulafia refused to sit with him in halakhic discussions.[90]

The opposition to Rabbi Abulafia among the Torah scholars had been growing slowly and gradually from the time he was put forward by the old elites for the position of *ḥakham bashi*, until now most of the scholarly class was ranged against him. That initial preference for Abulafia may have been felt particularly strongly by members of the Cohen–Maslaton-Tarab family, which had produced many Torah scholars, first and foremost Rabbi Ezra Hakohen Maslaton-Tarab. Indeed, the sources suggest that this rabbi was Yitshak Abulafia's main rival, heading the scholars' opposition to the *ḥakham bashi*.[91]

Matters came to a head when Rabbi Abulafia publicly supported the remnants of the old moneyed elites in their attempt to impose an indirect tax, the *gabilah*, on the sale of meat in order to fund payment of the taxes imposed by the authorities. Specifically, they wished to lighten the burden imposed upon them by the *ʿaskariyya* tax and to spread it over a larger number of people within the community. In essence, whereas in the past the wealthy laymen had balanced the budget of the community in exchange for a senior role in its leadership, they now wished to enjoy that senior position without having to meet its financial obligations.[92] These *gevirim* were opposed by the tradi-

88 See Ch. 6 above.

89 See CZA, J41/83, Yitshak Halfon, Damascus, 23 July 1881.

90 See Abulafia, *Penei yitsḥak*, ii. 105*b*. On the involvement of Eleazar Angel in these tensions, see Tarab, *Sha'arei ezra*, 118*a*.

91 On the opposition of the class of rabbinic sages—led by Rabbis Ezra Hakohen Maslaton-Tarab, Netanel Habuba, and Yehudah Mahadib—to Rabbi Yitshak Abulafia, see e.g. Abulafia, *Penei yitsḥak*, ii. 95*b*–99*a*; Tarab, *Sha'arei ezra*, 117*b*–118*b*. Rabbi Maslaton-Tarab died on 28 Shevat 5680 (17 February 1920). On him, see Laniado, *For the Sake of the Holy Ones* (Heb.), 53.

92 In the second half of the 19th century the issue of the *gabilah* became a point of contention that influenced the struggles over leadership in almost all the main Jewish communities of the

tional scholars, who claimed to represent the vast majority of the community, who in turn were likely to bear the brunt of the new tax.

The Torah scholars were concerned first and foremost with their own personal benefit, as up to this point they had been exempt from all taxes imposed upon the community. Their own economic situation had declined in the wake of the bankruptcy of 1875, exacerbating their unwillingness to pay their share of the tax burden. Consequently, most of them opposed Rabbi Abulafia's wish to impose the *gabilah*.[93] The claim of the lay leaders of the community that income from the *gabilah* would also serve to fund the *talmudei torah* carried no weight with them, as they were opposed to the reforms that had been made in these schools with Rabbi Abulafia's encouragement and support.[94] The Torah scholars further argued that the community's difficulties in paying the taxes demanded by the Ottoman authorities derived not from a lack of money, but rather from the dishonest practices of the wealthy laymen, who had made false declarations concerning their own property. According to the scholars, the *gevirim* had abolished the arrangements for tax collection that had been accepted in the past out of a desire to avoid paying their dues in full.[95]

These disputes reflected a deep crisis in relations between the rabbis and the communal leadership. The alliance that had existed for generations between the economic elite and the learned class, allowing the two groups to rule the community between themselves, was now broken. Faced with this rift, Rabbi Abulafia took an uncompromising position in support of the old elite—to whom he owed his appointment to the office of chief rabbi and possibly also his salary—and against the traditional Torah scholars, and particularly against the halakhic ruling which they had published on the matter of taxation. The *ḥakham bashi* affirmed the claims of the wealthy laymen, point by point, on the grounds that the rabbis who opposed him did not understand the economic situation properly, whereas 'I come from the battle [1 Sam. 4: 16] and know very clearly that they [the *gevirim*] are unable to cover the expenses and debts in question from their own funds without the assistance of the *gabilah*'.[96] In doing so, he was acting in accordance with the old order, based upon an alliance between the secular leadership and the spiritual leadership. However, as the secular leadership had by now lost the trust both of

Ottoman empire. See Levi, 'Changes in the Leadership' (Heb.), 243–60. For discussion of this affair, see also Zohar, *Tradition and Change* (Heb.), 34–5.

[93] He did, however, have the support of a few rabbinic scholars. See JNUL, DMA, Arc. 4to, 271/606, Rabbi Yitshak Abulafia to Rabbi Jacob Saul Elyashar, Damascus, 27 Sivan 5654.

[94] Elyashar, *Yisa ish*, 'Ḥoshen mishpat', 78*b*, §5.

[95] Ibid.

[96] Ibid. 79*a*.

the masses and of the rabbinic sages, this pitted him against the vast majority of the community, cutting him off from the social class to which he naturally belonged—that of the Torah scholars.[97]

The chief rabbi and the old elites also found themselves in opposition to another new group, in addition to the traditional class of scholars. The self-consciously modernist nature of this group found expression in the explicitly French name its members chose for it: the Union Israélite (Ahdut Yisra'el). Its members included several graduates of the first Alliance school in Damascus, which had been opened in 1865 and closed four years later, as well as graduates of the first intake of the second Alliance school, opened in 1880. They represented the first shoots of the modern intellectual elite in Damascus. This elite, which emerged from the middle class of the community, now demanded a significant role in selecting the community leadership, in order that it might be run according to the modern values they had imbibed through their education. The members of this new society include hardly any names from the old aristocratic families, most of whose members, impoverished by the collapse of 1875, had either emigrated to Beirut or overseas, or had simply passed away. In 1894, the Union Israélite confirmed its modernist allegiance by uniting itself with the Alliance Israélite Universelle. This act, along with the members' social attitudes, their education, and their familiarity with French culture, immediately won them the friendship of the Alliance's emissary in the city.[98]

Even before the establishment of the Union Israélite, some of the educated young people from the middle class had set up an administrative committee with the intention of reforming the communal framework in Damascus. The very establishment of this committee signified a lack of trust

[97] See AAIU, Syrie, XXI.E., Damas, 213a, Somekh, 24 Apr. 1894; Elyashar, *Yisa ish*, 'Ḥoshen mishpat', 77*a*–78*a*, §5; Tarab, *Sha'arei ezra*, 'Ḥoshen mishpat', 152*b*, §37.

[98] AAIU, Syrie, XXI.E., Damas, 213*a*, Somekh, 24 Apr. 1894; *Bulletin*, 1st–2nd sem. 1894, p. 156. At the beginning of the 1880s, the names of the old aristocracy, such as Lisbona and Stambuli, still appear in the list of dignitaries of the city; see Neimark, *Journey in an Ancient Land* (Heb.), 50–1. By contrast, in the list of 'sages, rabbis, *ge'onim*, wealthy people, and philanthropists of the great city in Israel, Damascus' who in Tamuz 5663 (1903) contributed to the fund created in Tiberias in order to maintain the holy place around the grave of Rabbi Me'ir Ba'al Hanes (cited in Alhadif, *Yatsev gevulot*, 39–40), one finds only isolated names from the old aristocracy, while the names of those who in the future would take the leadership of the community are prominent, such as Totah, Pinso, Katran, Atar, and Sakal. For more on the changes of families in the Jewish leadership in Damascus, see Rivlin, 'Sir Shemaiah Angel' (Heb.). The Totah family, which held the leadership of the community throughout the second decade of the 20th century, is mentioned in the list of Jewish dignitaries prepared by British intelligence, where it appears as a family of bankers and moneylenders. See FO 371/6455, 'Who's Who in Damascus, 1919' (Secret), 10.

in the old leadership and its institutions. That incumbent leadership, including *ḥakham bashi* Abulafia, placed various obstacles in the path of the committee and the implementation of the reforms it proposed in order to improve the running of the community, including reform of the system of tax collection. According to Saul Somekh, the Alliance's emissary in Damascus, the measures taken by the old elite, which included falsification and embezzlement, led to the breakdown of the new committee. Somekh believed that the wealthy elite was motivated simply by a desire to avoid paying taxes and instead to impose the burden of payment upon the broad public, and accused the oligarchy of selfishness and systematic cruelty towards the poor. Somekh reported that Rabbi Abulafia was accused of co-operating with the wealthy members of the community because they supported him, thereby earning the hatred of both the public and the other rabbinic sages of the city. The accusations of taking bribes and falsifying documents levelled against Rabbi Abulafia led to curses against him by the public, in the synagogue and by demonstrators outside his home, and nearly to his arrest by the authorities—who, according to this testimony, took a very lenient approach towards the rabbi.[99]

In the final analysis, the controversy between the Torah scholars and the *ḥakham bashi*, seen against the background of the deteriorating economic situation and the virulent criticism directed against him, damaged the Torah scholars' own authority—and, to an even greater extent, that of the rabbinic court. The violent opposition to Rabbi Yitshak Abulafia and his supporters was not confined to the political realm, but also spilled over into threats and pressures imposed upon the judges in the rabbinic court to rule in a manner that would satisfy one side or the other.[100] Contempt for the rulings of the Torah scholars grew ever more widespread, and their inability to enforce their authority led in turn to increasing numbers of Jews choosing to ignore halakhah and its spokesmen in the community. The sages' authority was further weakened by the breakdown of their co-operative relationship with the wealthy laymen, even if many people continued to be afraid of their magical powers.[101]

How did two such radically different social groups—the traditional Torah scholars and the new educated class—come to join forces? Was their common goal sufficient to bridge the tremendous differences in world-view between those who tended towards conservatism and the innovators, or modernizers, who sought to take over the dominant role in the leadership of

99 AAIU, Syrie, XXI.E., Damas, 213*a*, Somekh, 24 Apr. 1894.

100 See Zohar, *Tradition and Change* (Heb.), 73–5.

101 See Almaleh, *The Jews in Damascus* (Heb.), 25; *Ha'aḥdut*, 8 (15 Kislev 5671), 14.

the community and to re-establish it on modern foundations? The answer is to be found in the mutual dependence of the two groups. On the one hand, the educated classes understood that, without the backing of the Torah scholars, they would be unable to gain a hearing from those external actors who could bring about the removal of Rabbi Abulafia—namely, the *ḥakham bashi* in Istanbul and his counterpart in Jerusalem. On the other hand, the Torah scholars, as representatives of the traditional intellectual elite, understood that by breaking the alliance between themselves and the old elites of family and money, and in the light of their own increasingly difficult economic situation, they were at risk of becoming marginalized within Jewish society. This being so, they joined forces with the enlightened group in an attempt to acquire some control over the highest official position within the community—that of *ḥakham bashi*. Moreover, the class of Torah scholars, notwithstanding their opposition to all the attitudes and ideals of the modernizers, understood that they were dependent upon the latter group in all matters pertaining to the external relations of the community. In the final analysis, the traditionalist rabbis understood that it was the members and supporters of the Alliance who had acted on behalf of the community during the period of the blood libels at the beginning of the 1890s; it was they who maintained contacts with the consuls, with the European governments, and with important groups of Jewish philanthropists such as members of the Alliance in Paris or the Agudat Ahim in London. Thus it was that these two disparate groups came together in a somewhat revolutionary alliance—a joining of forces between young educated people and traditional Torah scholars in a determination to take over the leadership of the community.

The Involvement of External Forces

In seeking outside assistance in the effort to depose Rabbi Abulafia, his opponents appealed to two key figures. One was Rabbi Moses Halevi, the *ḥakham bashi* in Istanbul. Rabbi Halevi was perceived by the Ottoman authorities as the highest rabbinic authority in their territories, with the power to recommend the appointment and removal of rabbis throughout the Jewish communities of the empire. As such, his response to any request to depose Rabbi Abulafia and to name a new *ḥakham bashi* for the Damascus community would be decisive. The other key figure was the *rishon letsiyon* in Jerusalem, the *ḥakham bashi* Jacob Saul Elyashar, head of the most important Jewish spiritual centre in the Middle East. It was of the greatest importance to Abulafia's opponents that they obtain the approval of this rabbi, with his considerable ethical authority, as well as that of the other sages of Jerusalem. Both sides in

Damascus sent letters to both Halevi and Elyashar, but it would seem that Abulafia placed his primary reliance upon the sages of Jerusalem—both because of his long-standing personal acquaintance with them, and because he was himself the descendant of a distinguished rabbinic dynasty.[102] From them he sought both ethical support and their agreement to exert their influence on his behalf with the *ḥakham bashi* in Istanbul, so that the latter would not act against him in the official context. Each side attempted to demonstrate that it had majority public support and that its opponents were few and marginal within the community.

To Rabbi Elyashar in Jerusalem, Abulafia wrote:

> And though the time is unreliable . . . those who rise up against me to do evil are all laymen and ignorant people, for all the great people of the city and most of the holy community of our congregation, may the Rock protect them and give them life, of the intermediate class and the masses of people—almost all of them are with me. Nonetheless, when they see that the opposing side does not listen to me, and stand up against me, they go in their own way and their own concerns, and they think evil of me, to uproot my honour and the honour of my father's house. But I trust in my Creator and in the virtue of my holy fathers, that their hands will not gain any benefit at all.[103]

According to Abulafia, his opponents would stoop to any means of defaming him. They even attempted to bribe the son-in-law of *ḥakham bashi* Moses Halevi to call for Abulafia's deposition. But Rabbi Halevi was not tempted, telling them that if they wanted a new *ḥakham bashi* they should approach the *rishon letsiyon* in Jerusalem themselves, without any intervention on his part. For his part, Abulafia tried to strengthen Rabbi Elyashar's opposition to the attempt to depose him, explaining to him that his supporters, who included many of the wealthy men of the city, would refuse to finance the salary of his replacement. He also emphasized that his own connections with the authorities, and particularly with the governor, Ra'uf Pasha, remained firm, and that the *wali* himself was opposed to his deposition. In effect, having lost the active support of most members of his own community, Abulafia now sought, in presenting his case to the *rishon letsiyon*, to build up the second source of his authority—namely, his recognition by the Ottoman authorities. He also implored Rabbi Elyashar to convince the *ḥakham bashi* in Istanbul that there was no substance to his opponents' allegations against him.[104]

[102] Although Rabbi Yitshak Abulafia had lived in Damascus for many years, he continued to gain support from Jerusalem, which considered him one of its own. See JNUL, DMA, Arc. 4to, 1271/606, Rabbi Yitshak Abulafia to Rabbi Jacob Saul Elyashar, Damascus, 25 Tishrei 5645.

[103] Ibid., Rabbi Yitshak Abulafia to Rabbi Jacob Saul Elyashar, Damascus, 9 Sivan 5654.

[104] Ibid., Rabbi Yitshak Abulafia to Rabbi Jacob Saul Elyashar, Damascus, 27 Sivan 5654.

As in cases reviewed in other chapters, so in this case too the opinions of the rabbinic emissaries present in the city at the time of the controversy were of great importance. In summer 1894, when the dispute between the two parties reached its peak, Rabbi Benjamin Alkutser and the grandson of Rabbi Elyashar, Rabbi Raphael Kalamaro, were both in Damascus.[105] Given their overriding objective of procuring as many contributions as possible for the *kolelim* in Jerusalem, their priority in the controversy within the community was to navigate their course between the rival groups in such a manner as not to harm their own income. As their letter of introduction as emissaries was addressed to the *ḥakham bashi*, Abulafia, his was the first address to which they turned in Damascus. According to his own account, he received them and offered them hospitality in his home; but in the end they submitted to pressure from his opponents and took the contrary side. Believing that the *ḥakham bashi*'s opponents would provide them with larger sums, they not only abandoned him but encouraged their new allies to take the most serious steps against him. The decision of the rabbinic emissaries to come down on the side of Abulafia's opponents clearly provided them with the ethical support for which they had been hoping; but Rabbi Abulafia's greatest fear was that the recommendation of these emissaries would tip the view of the *rishon letsiyon* against him.[106]

In the summer of 1894 Rabbi Yitshak Abulafia was finally removed from the office of *ḥakham bashi*—an office surrounded by anger and controversy from the beginning of his period in Damascus. Some tried to put a favourable gloss on the event: Rabbi Abraham Palagi, rabbi of İzmir, portrayed the *ḥakham bashi*'s departure as an act of voluntary retirement, which did not damage his great stature as a halakhic authority, and insisted that Rabbi Abulafia maintained his position as the most respected Torah scholar in Damascus, to whom many people turned for advice.[107] But that is not the way things were, especially not after Rabbi Solomon Eli'ezer Mercado Alfandari was appointed in his place.

[105] On Rabbis Benjamin Alkutser and Raphael Kalamaro, see Gaon, *The Jews of the East* (Heb.), ii. 88, 626.

[106] JNUL, DMA, Arc. 4[to], 1271/606, Rabbi Yitshak Abulafia to Rabbi Jacob Saul Elyashar, Damascus, 27 Sivan 5654.

[107] Abulafia, *Penei yitsḥak*, v, introduction by Rabbi Abraham Palagi.

PART III

RABBIS OF THE REVOLUTION

CHAPTER EIGHT

The Appointment and Removal of Rabbi Solomon Eli'ezer Mercado Alfandari in Damascus

> An elder to whom something happened is not removed from his greatness, but rather we say to him: Be honoured and sit at home.
>
> JT *Mo'ed katan* 3: 1

The Ruling Regarding the Deposition of the Rabbi of Hamadan

Once it became clear to Rabbi Yitshak Abulafia that the leaders of the Damascus community and its Torah scholars were bent on removing him from office, he attempted to forestall this process by issuing a halakhic ruling prohibiting this removal.[1] He described the events surrounding his own position in detail but disguised the identifying features. He wrote as if he were not an interested party but presenting a quite separate case: specifically, of the wish of the Jews of Hamadan in Persia to depose their rabbi, who had served that community for more than twenty years, and to appoint another rabbi in his place. The match between this account and the process described in the last chapter confirms the view that this halakhic ruling, allegedly addressing the issue in Hamadan, in fact concerned Rabbi Abulafia's own deposition from office in Damascus.[2] In it, Abulafia sharply criticized those who organized themselves to bring about their rabbi's deposition, especially his rabbinic colleagues, whose attitude towards him was tantamount to excommunication:

I was asked by the holy community of Teheran—may the Rock preserve them and give them life—the following question: Reuben had been accepted as judge and righteous teacher in the holy community of Hamadan—may God protect it—for twenty years or more. And during all those years that the above-mentioned has

[1] On the events leading up to the deposition, see Ch. 7 above.
[2] For the deciphering of this disguise, see Ben-Zvi, 'An Exchange of Letters' (Heb.).

been on the rabbinic seat, he has judged the poor with righteousness and nobody ever had any suspicion of him, and all the people answered 'holy' after his word. And indeed, he was in truth and justice a person who was great in Torah, and his name was known in the gates, in all the cities of Israel in the kingdom of Persia, as is known. But then several people, who are not decent, turned against him as enemies; the Torah scholars in that city, his scholarly brethren, upon seeing that they were not appointed as judges and rabbis, were also jealous of him and hated him for no reason: they hated him because of their jealousy, and could not speak peaceably unto him. And their tongues went about in the land, to speak false things of him before the householders, members of the community, saying that he deliberately issued legal rulings that were contrary to the law, and that he took money from its owners wrongfully, by error or for his own benefit, Heaven forbid. Therefore, in their opinion, he is unfit to sit as judge between man and his fellow, and he should be pushed aside and removed completely and another named in his place. And so that the members of the community would believe what they say about Reuben, the scholars, great and small, whoever was called *ḥakham*, conspired together in a strong conspiracy against Reuben, the above-mentioned rabbi: all these rabbis wrote and sealed an agreement, that they would not go to the house of Reuben at all, and would not speak with him and would not sit with him, even in the homes of the members of the community, and would not listen to any sermon or words of Torah from his mouth in any place at all. And in this matter too they seduced and led astray several of the householders among the people of the city who were beloved to them, who believed their evil words and made a conspiracy with them, as mentioned. And they voted and decided to remove and to bring down Reuben from the rabbinate, and to curtail his income and livelihood. And they spent a huge amount of money to bring a *ḥakham* from another place, and they stood closely together, hoping that they would bring another sage, as they had plotted.

Now look and behold, you sages of Israel from every city and from every country, come and see: has there ever been the like of this evil thing in any of the cities of the diaspora: to remove a judge and righteous teacher who had already merited the position for more than twenty years? Who has seen such a thing? Who has heard of such a thing, and not felt their hearts being torn! And we must ask who allowed them to remove and to bring him down from office and to truncate his livelihood in his old age.[3]

According to this account, as the class of Torah sages had united against him, Abulafia's main complaints were addressed to members of this intellectual elite, who he felt had become his greatest enemies. How was it, he asked, that, if he had indeed issued biased and illegitimate judgments while sitting on the court, no one among the sages had objected during all the previous years he had served as judge and *ḥakham bashi*? Rabbi Abulafia accused the

[3] Abulafia, *Penei yitsḥak*, v, 'Ḥoshen mishpat', 119*a*, §1.

Torah scholars who opposed him of being motivated not by concern for the welfare of the public, but rather by personal considerations—namely, their hope of inheriting his place as judge and leader of the community. He also alleged that his opponents hated him because he had ruled against them on the question of the *gabilah* tax.

According to Rabbi Abulafia, his deposition amounted to a defamation of the divine name (*ḥilul hashem*) in the eyes of society, as everyone would think that the rabbi had been removed from office for acts of corruption. He also feared losing his livelihood: loss of the office of *ḥakham bashi* would make him entirely dependent upon his son-in-law, Hayim Moses Laniado, one of the wealthy members of the community.[4] He completely rejected the claim that he had made erroneous halakhic rulings and decisions in court cases, and warned that the injury done to the *ḥakham bashi* through his removal and public embarrassment would, in the final analysis, damage the status of Torah scholars generally.[5]

Attempts to Import a New *Ḥakham Bashi*

At the time when Rabbi Abulafia wrote his Hamadan ruling, his opponents were negotiating with Rabbi Moses Halevi for a new *ḥakham bashi* to be sent from the capital. These negotiations began during the spring of 1894, with appeals from the scholars and modernizers of Damascus for a new *ḥakham bashi* who was not just a scholar of stature, but also the recipient of a firman from the sultan. In their initial appeals to Rabbi Moses Halevi, indeed, they offered to pay any price for the appointment of a new *ḥakham bashi* and for the firman that he would bring with him.[6] What they wanted was a chief rabbi who would derive his authority first and foremost from the Ottoman authorities, and thereby enjoy strengthened standing within the community and in Damascus public life generally. It is possible that the young educated people, who joined with the traditional scholars in their attempt to depose Abulafia, did not want one of those local scholars as the new *ḥakham bashi* because they felt a certain contempt for them, whereas the Torah scholars themselves chose to forgo the chance of succeeding Rabbi Abulafia themselves so that their complaints against him would not be perceived as stemming from self-interest. Both groups, it seems, hoped that a new chief rabbi appointed from the capital city would bring with him new approaches and

[4] For Rabbi Abulafia's remarks about his son-in-law, see Abulafia, *Penei yitsḥak*, iv, title page, author's introduction.

[5] Ibid. v, 'Ḥoshen mishpat', 123*a*, §1.

[6] JNUL, DMA, Arc. 4to, 1512/269, sages and rabbis of Damascus to the *ḥakham bashi* Moses Halevi, Damascus, end of Sivan 5654.

stronger connections with both the local government and the central government in Istanbul, paving the way for a revolution in the running of the community that would advance its interests and and lead it to a better future.

Rabbi Abulafia, by contrast, was convinced that his opponents were motivated by personal animosity towards himself. In his view, the entire attempt to acquire a new chief rabbi armed with a royal firman was no more than an exercise to win over the Damascus Jewish community to his opponents' side; by the same measure, he argued, his own position at the head of the community could have been greatly strengthened had the community taken the trouble to attain a royal firman for him.[7]

Notwithstanding all these considerations, Rabbi Abulafia's opponents were not uniformly enthusiastic about the idea of bringing in a chief rabbi from Istanbul. Such an appointment would entail a substantial financial outlay which the people of the Union Israélite were not sure they would be able to meet, particularly as most of the wealthy members of the community did not support them. Hence, when *ḥakham bashi* Moses Halevi did not reply promptly to the initial request, the members of Union Israélite seriously considered bringing one of the sages of Jerusalem to serve as chief rabbi of Damascus, asking Rabbi Elyashar to recommend a candidate.[8] When Rabbi Elyashar likewise failed to reply, they wrote to a native of Damascus who had moved to Istanbul some years earlier, asking him for help in their search for a rabbi. This person recommended to Rabbi Halevi that he appoint Rabbi Solomon Eli'ezer Mercado Alfandari, the rabbi of his own community, Ortaköy. At the time Rabbi Alfandari was already more than 50 years old and, according to his contemporaries, had never even dreamed of appointment to such high office.[9] Halevi officially recommended Alfandari's candidacy to the community of Damascus, alongside another candidate, Rabbi Shabetai Hali. Both rabbis asked for a salary of 100 gold coins a year, a tremendous amount for a community that had not yet recovered from the bankruptcy of twenty years earlier. Rabbi Abulafia's opponents wrote once more to Rabbi Elyashar in Jerusalem, asking him to choose a rabbi for them from among three Jerusalem sages.[10]

We do not know who these three candidates were, or why none of them

[7] Abulafia, *Penei yitsḥak*, v, 'Ḥoshen mishpat', 124*b*, §1.

[8] JNUL, DMA, Arc. 4to, 1271/44, Union Israélite Damas to Rabbi Jacob Saul Elyashar, Damascus, 20 Tamuz [5654].

[9] AAIU, Syrie, XXI.E., Damas, 213*a*, Somekh, 25 Oct. 1894; and see Gaon, *The Jews of the East*, ii. 85–6.

[10] JNUL, DMA, Arc. 4to, 1271/44, Union Israélite Damas to Rabbi Jacob Saul Elyashar, Damascus, 20 Tamuz 5654.

was chosen by Rabbi Elyashar. It would appear that, notwithstanding the pleas of the people of Damascus, Elyashar deliberately refrained from helping the rivals of Rabbi Abulafia, with whom he enjoyed a good relationship.[11] With no recommendation from Jerusalem to counter that from Istanbul, the choice ultimately settled on Rabbi Alfandari.

Significantly, the appointment of the new *ḥakham bashi* was confirmed with an official firman from the sultan. This contributed substantially to his standing in the eyes of both the community and the surrounding society. At the end of October 1894 Alfandari arrived in Damascus, where the community had great hopes of him.[12] He continued to enjoy the unqualified support of the government, and a year and a half later the sultan gave Rabbi Alfandari, along with other rabbis throughout the Middle East, a medal of honour.[13]

But, great as the hopes were, so were the disappointments. Just two weeks after Rabbi Alfandari's arrival in Damascus complaints were already beginning to be heard regarding his shortcomings and his comprehensive lack of ability in modern community administration. The new *ḥakham bashi* had not even the most basic skills required of a political leader, such as the ability to conduct a negotiation with the local government. He was not fluent in Arabic, the language of the country, in which most of the community's business was conducted, both internally and between itself and its immediate environment.[14] Nor did he have proper command of Turkish, the language of the senior government officials. Thus from the outset there was a gulf between himself and the community on the one hand, and between himself and the local officials on the other.

The local rabbis therefore decided to appoint, alongside the new *ḥakham bashi*, additional preachers and judges.[15] Rabbi Yitshak Abulafia's position as head of the rabbinic court was filled by Rabbi Ezra Maslaton-Tarab.[16] The sermons of the four central sabbaths of the year—Shabat Shuvah, Shabat Zakhor, Shabat Hagadol, and Shabat Kalah—were usually given by various learned rabbis in Arabic.[17] Most of the public did not understand Rabbi Alfandari's sermons, and a sense of estrangement grew up between the community and its chief rabbi. It is also possible that the fact that the new *ḥakham*

[11] Later on friendly relations were also established between Rabbis Alfandari and Elyashar. See e.g. S. E. Alfandari, *Teshuvot hasava kadisha*, i, 'Even ha'ezer', 142, §29.

[12] AAIU, Syrie, XXI.E., Damas, 213*a*, Somekh, 25 Oct. 1894.

[13] See *Hamagid*, 22 (4 June 1896), 178.

[14] For his dependence upon the services of translators, see S. E. Alfandari, *Teshuvot hasava kadisha*, i, 'Even ha'ezer', 107, §25.

[15] Abulafia, *Penei yitsḥak*, v, 'Ḥoshen mishpat', 124*b*, §1.

[16] A proof of this is that the registry of divorces of the rabbinic court of Rabbi Ezra Tarab begins on 4 Av 5694. See Tarab, *Sha'arei ezra*, 93*b*.

[17] For the sermons of Rabbi Ezra Hakohen Maslaton-Tarab, see Tarab, *Sefer ezra*.

bashi was not appointed to lead the rabbinic court created tensions between him and the local Torah scholars.

In addition to the language problems, members of the community were troubled by the considerable expense involved in the appointment of Rabbi Alfandari. The official firman from the sultan cost 2,000 francs, while the rabbi's annual salary came to 2,300 francs. This was an extremely heavy burden on the community, which was already under considerable economic strain.[18] The Damascus community might nevertheless have borne the cost had it not been for the fact that Rabbi Alfandari became embroiled in arguments and disputes with nearly all the groups around him, both within and outside the community. One of the main reasons for these disputes was the centralization that the rabbi had introduced, reflecting his lack of administrative skills. The opposition to Rabbi Alfandari was of course led by Rabbi Yitshak Abulafia.

Friction between Rabbi Alfandari and Rabbi Abulafia

Rabbi Yitshak Abulafia remained frustrated and embittered by his removal from office, and the inevitable rivalry between himself and the new rabbi did not enhance the latter's authority in the community, to say the least.[19] At times, the two were called upon to issue halakhic rulings on the same subject: when litigants were unsatisfied with the ruling delivered by one of them, they would present the question to the other. Thus, during the early years of Alfandari's tenure there was intense hostility between the two personalities—expressed, especially by Rabbi Alfandari, in insulting language, to the extent of accusations of lying and deceit.[20]

A serious dispute broke out between the two over whether Jewish women were permitted to go out in public wearing a wig, or whether this failed to satisfy the halakhic requirement that a woman cover her hair. Rabbi Abulafia, in opposition to the ruling of Rabbi Alfandari, allowed women to wear wigs, and indeed his own wife was accustomed to do so. This amounted to a repudiation of the *ḥakham bashi*'s authority, to which Alfandari was not disposed to turn a blind eye. He gave the following account of the clash with his predecessor:

And I issued a declaration throughout the city, that all the women are required to wear a scarf and that all the hairs of their heads must be covered, and there was not a single woman who failed to cover her hair, apart from one—the wife of the rabbi

[18] AAIU, Syrie, XXI.E., Damas, 213*a*, Somekh, 11 Dec. 1894.
[19] See Goldstein, *Travels in Jerusalem* (Heb.), 289–90.
[20] S. E. Alfandari, *Teshuvot hasava kadisha*, ii. 160–1.

[Yitshak Abulafia][21]—who alone remained with a wig, and I could not speak with him about this for reasons that I shall keep to myself. But as I was concerned that after a period of time matters would begin to deteriorate, so that all of them [i.e. the women] would return to their old ways, some of them wearing wigs and some of them going about with uncovered hair, I cried out to them, and they all answered with words of no substance. Some, whose wives went about with uncovered hair, said that as others, including those who hold fast to the Torah, had returned to the old practice and did not listen to the voice of teachers [Torah scholars], they did not succeed in persuading their wives. And other people of the city said that, if there were an equal edict upon all the women of the city that they must wear a scarf and cover their hair, they would accept this equitably, but since there were women who remained without hair covering, their wives would not listen to them and would not accept this from them. In the end they said that this permission came from the rabbi [i.e. Yitshak Abulafia], and therefore they are not to be punished, and the blame rests on his shoulders . . . I said, I will keep my mouth sealed for the present, but then after a certain period of time I spoke sweetly with the rabbi, and asked why and wherefore he permitted his wife to do such-and-such, and others inferred from her that it was permitted . . . I therefore asked of him, for the honour of God and that of His holy Torah, that he command his elderly wife to cover her hair with a scarf, so that she would not serve as a pretext for others.[22]

In his disappointment with Rabbi Alfandari, Rahamim Ouziel, the emissary of the AIU in Damascus, became an ally of Rabbi Abulafia. With his encouragement, Abulafia turned to the leadership of the Alliance in Paris to request financial assistance in printing his books, and in the course of this correspondence he also related the story of his deposition. Some of those who had acted against Abulafia were now having second thoughts, although, like Ouziel's support for the former *ḥakham bashi*, their regret derived less from 'love of Yitshak' than from the widespread disillusionment with his successor.[23]

As time passed, however, the hostility between the two rabbis died down and their relationship improved. Some three and a half years after his arrival in Damascus, Alfandari restored Abulafia to his position as head of the rabbinic court.[24]

The new *ḥakham bashi* seems to have realized that, if he wished to attain any standing in the community, he would need to appease his great rival; otherwise, the long shadow of his predecessor would continue to fall over his own tenure of office. For several years from this point, with Abulafia once

21 The editor of Rabbi Alfandari's book chose to delete the name of the rabbi.

22 S. E. Alfandari, *Teshuvot hasava kadisha*, ii. 1–2.

23 AAIU, Syrie, XIX.E., Damas, 190*b*, Ouziel, 12 Feb. 1897.

24 Ben-Zvi, 'An Exchange of Letters' (Heb.), 94.

again at the head of the communal court, the two rabbis exchanged expressions of admiration and affection in their responsa. Rabbi Abulafia, grateful to the *ḥakham bashi* for the confidence he had shown in restoring him to his former position, in turn recognized Alfandari's authority, on more than one occasion even retracting his own decisions when the *ḥakham bashi* ruled differently. For his part, Alfandari came to show greater understanding of, and indeed admiration for, the decisions of his former rival.[25] However, this rapprochement was not to last indefinitely.

Meanwhile, Rabbi Alfandari's relations with the other Torah scholars, with the *gevirim* of the community, and with the Ottoman officials also quickly began to go downhill.[26] He advocated the imposition of the *gabilah* tax on meat, thereby disappointing those sages who had hoped that he would not take a controversial position on this matter, which had triggered the deposition of his predecessor, Rabbi Abulafia. He also imposed many additional taxes, including a high levy upon the baking of matzot and taxes on, among other things, marriage contracts (*ketubot*), on permits to travel away from Damascus, and on the buying and selling of homes. Rabbi Alfandari's control of the community's *kashrut* stamps, which were generally held by the *ḥakham bashi*, enabled him to impose his opinion upon other Torah scholars, and his deteriorating relations with them reached a nadir in the public shaming of scholars in the synagogue. The rabbi was then accused of informing on his opponents and turning them over to the authorities.[27]

Religious Conversion, Crime, and Sexual Licentiousness

These controversies, the harsh words uttered against the deposed *ḥakham bashi*, Yitshak Abulafia, and the rift between the rabbis and the new *ḥakham bashi*, Solomon Alfandari, ultimately damaged the authority of the Torah scholars in Damascus generally, and particularly that of the communal rabbinic court. The rabbis' authority was already waning at this time as the traditional partnership between the Torah scholars and the wealthy lay leaders of the community was replaced by growing tension between the two groups.[28]

[25] See e.g. S. E. Alfandari, *Teshuvot hasava kadisha*, iii, 'Even ha'ezer', 130, §23; also i, 'Yoreh de'ah', 87, §24; iii, 'Ḥoshen mishpat', 305, §5. See also Margaliot, *The Great Ones of Erets Yisra'el* (Heb.), 207.

[26] See e.g. Goldstein, *Travels in Jerusalem* (Heb.), 289–90; Ben-Ya'akov, 'Rabbi Solomon Alfandari *z"l* (Heb.), 7; AAIU, Syrie, XIX.E., Damas, 190*b*, Ouziel, 12 Feb. 1897, 9 Mar. 1898, 12 June 1898.

[27] ACRI, TR/Is/164*a*, people of Damascus to Rabbi Hayim Nahum, Damascus, 4 Elul 5668.

[28] See Ch. 7 above, in the section on 'Spiritual Decline and Religious Zealotry'.

The precarious economic situation, and the weakening of halakhic authority and of its spokesmen, exacerbated a number of negative trends already affecting the Damascus community. One of these was religious conversion, centred on Protestant missionary activity.

The Protestant mission worked energetically within the Jewish population, especially among young people: Jewish attendance at its educational institutions reached a peak in 1905, when 125 Jewish students were enrolled in the Protestant schools.[29] Missionary activity expanded greatly during Rabbi Alfandari's tenure to include other activities in addition to preaching and education. One of the means used to attract Jews to the Christian message was exploitation of the lack of a Jewish hospital in Damascus.[30] In 1895 a missionary-run infirmary was opened in the heart of the Jewish quarter, and in the following year 975 Jews turned to it for treatment. According to Dr Masterman, who worked there, most of those who came to the infirmary were women and children. This presented the missionaries with a problem in that the women were mostly uneducated, so that it was hard to involve them in even simple biblical study. The missionaries therefore resorted to hanging pictures and brief texts from the Holy Scriptures in Arabic and Hebrew in the waiting rooms and treatment rooms. They would also sometimes distribute such texts to patients who were calling out for help, as well as praying with them before taking them to see the doctor. The doctor himself would read a brief passage from the New Testament with his patients, in Arabic or Hebrew, and recite a brief prayer with them in Arabic, two or three times a week. This approach was carefully pitched, and by keeping communications at this elementary level the missionaries were able to conduct conversations with the women who knocked on the doors of the institution. Eventually, however, in 1898 the infirmary was closed due to lack of funds.[31]

The second phenomenon that characterized the end of the nineteenth century in Damascus was the growth of violent crime within Jewish society. From 1884 onwards, reports of arrests of Jewish men for violent behaviour began to appear in the newspapers.[32] As the teacher and writer Yitshak Shemi wrote at the end of 1910:

[29] On missionary activity during the preceding years, see ibid.; also Harel, 'Fighting Conversion to Christianity'.

[30] Although the Bikur Holim society was active in the community in the early 1890s, its resources were limited and served primarily to provide medicine and food for the indigent sick and to pay the doctors' salaries. See AAIU, Syrie, XIV.E., Damas, 133, Bikur Holim society to the Alliance, Damascus, 3 Heshvan 5650.

[31] Gidney, *The History of the London Society*, 560.

[32] In 1884, eight Jews were tried for crimes of violence. See *Ḥavatselet*, 30 (27 Sivan 5644), 238.

> In ordinary times, when most of the young Hebrews were in Damascus [i.e. before the mass emigration of young Jews from the city], no Christian or Arab dared set foot in the Jewish street. The young Hebrews knew how to use their fists and loved scandal, and even now not a single sabbath passes without disputes and outbreaks and fights and conflicts among the hooligans from all three sides, leading directly to imprisonment. And there is much weeping every Saturday night after the wine wears off.[33]

But the main crime-related problem that troubled the Damascus community, which also had a bearing on the rising number of violent incidents in the Jewish quarter, was the significant increase in the involvement of Jewish girls in prostitution within the Jewish quarter. It is well known that there were Jewish prostitutes in several communities, not only in the Middle East but also in Europe, and in North and South America.[34] Nevertheless, Damascus was unique both in the extent of the problem, and in the fact that it occurred in the heart of the Jewish quarter rather than at the margins of society. Various studies of Jewish prostitution in Damascus have offered a range of explanations and have attempted to identify mitigating circumstances. Blame was attached primarily to the poverty and economic hardship that were widespread in the community after the bankruptcies of 1875. But poverty and hardship in themselves do not provide an adequate explanation for the scope of this phenomenon, for many other Jewish communities throughout the world experienced difficult economic conditions without seeing public prostitution emerge on the same scale.[35] Other possible factors contributing to this development in Damascus included the customary behaviour of many Jewish women in the city, who from the sixteenth century onwards had had a reputation for sexual permissiveness, for a lack of seriousness regarding such matters, and for their revealing dress—which, of course, aroused the anger of the rabbis.[36]

Nevertheless, it is only after the bankruptcies of the mid-1870s that we begin to hear of Jewish prostitution in Damascus. The first reference to Jew-

[33] *Ha'aḥdut*, 7 (8 Kislev 5671), 10.

[34] The phenomenon was not a new one, having been observed in the ancient and medieval periods in both the Ashkenazi and Sephardi worlds. See e.g. Epstein, *Ways and Customs* (Heb.), 137–59; Assis, 'Sexual Behaviour', 44–5; Grossman, *Pious and Rebellious*, 133–47. On prostitution in Jerusalem, see Shilo, *Princess or Captive?* (Heb.), 230–5; ead., 'The Promiscuity of the Daughters of Jerusalem' (Heb.). On prostitution in Iraq, see Meir, *The Socio-cultural Development of Iraqi Jewry* (Heb.), 340–1; on the phenomenon in Yemen, see Harel, 'The Relations' (Heb.), 45; on the phenomenon in London, see Marks, 'Jewish Women and Jewish Prostitution'. For more recent work, see also Bernstein, *Women on the Margin* (Heb.); Avni, *Impure* (Heb.).

[35] On this, see H. Cohen, *The Jews in Middle Eastern Countries* (Heb.), 152.

[36] On this, see Harel, 'On the Jewish "Singing Women"' (Heb.).

ish girls being led into sexual immorality was made by Rabbi Yitshak Abulafia in 1878, some three years after the economic collapse. Jewish girls began to appear, provocatively dressed, as musicians and singers entertaining both Jews and non-Jews, and before long they were being paid to have sexual relations with some of the men who came to watch them. As a result, the terms 'singers', 'musicians', and 'players' began to be used as euphemisms for 'prostitutes'. Attempts by the rabbinic courts to prevent these women from appearing were unsuccessful, as Ottoman law did not give the rabbis the tools they needed to punish those who deviated from halakhically suitable behaviour and to force them to submit to their discipline. The situation became even more serious, when the girls and women were joined by male Jewish musicians, who appeared with them in coffee-houses, at parties, and at balls held by non-Jews. Rabbi Abulafia was outraged by this behaviour and prescribed severe penalties for anyone consorting with the performers:

> The wicked Egyptian Hebrew women play [musical instruments] before men, both Jews and non-Jews, for they are arrogant and we have no authority over them to prevent them doing this, because of the freedom given them, due to our great sins. However, we have imposed and declared a strong ban and edict of *naḥash—nidui, ḥerem, shamta* [i.e. excommunication]—that no person may go to make music with these impudent girls and women, to play with them or to assist them at all; and whoever violates this and goes with them is subject to *ḥerem* and *nidui*.[37]

The atmosphere of permissiveness was strengthened by the spirit of modernization—particularly among the children of the elite who had been educated in French and British institutions, both Jewish and non-Jewish—which weakened the authority of parents and their ability to impose their will upon their children. This led in turn to other manifestations of rebelliousness, including sexual licence, often initiated—at least according to the Damascus sages—by young betrothed women, who encouraged their fiancés to the point of engaging in sexual relations before marriage.[38]

This tendency grew even stronger once women—both young girls and married women, at all social levels in the community—started to work in factories en masse. The phenomenon of Jewish women working outside the home was unique to Damascus among the Middle Eastern communities. According to the prevailing ethos of acceptable gendered behaviour during the nineteenth and early twentieth centuries, both in Jewish communities and in the surrounding social milieu, paid work was detrimental to female purity. There were clear sexual connotations, conscious or unconscious, deriving from the very fact of the woman's exposure in public,[39] and the implications of

[37] Abulafia, *Penei yitsḥak*, ii, 76*b*. [38] Elyashar, *Yisa ish*, 'Even ha'ezer', 27*b*, §3.
[39] See Melman, 'Freedom behind the Veil' (Heb.), 237–8.

this situation were frequently borne out in reality. Jewish women, working unveiled alongside strange men, became involved in romantic connections, often displayed in public demonstrations of affection.[40]

During Alfandari's term of office as *ḥakham bashi*, social and sexual permissiveness led to an increase in the number of births outside marriage and the number of single-parent families. The distress and suffering of the unmarried mothers at times led them to engage in prostitution simply to support themselves and their offspring. Sometimes a woman would give up her daughter for adoption by one of the wealthy prostitutes, who agreed to care for the child in exchange for various kinds of services; once she matured, the girl was also employed in prostitution.[41]

The concentration of this activity in the Jewish quarter did not come about by accident. Until the first decade of the twentieth century, Jewish and non-Jewish prostitutes often lived and worked outside the Jewish quarter. However, at the end of that decade, the Muslim residents of Damascus asked the municipality to remove these women from their streets, claiming they had a bad moral influence upon other women. The authorities, who wished in any case to gain better control over prostitution, responded by removing all prostitutes to the Jewish quarter, thereby making it the centre of prostitution in Damascus. Even the non-Jewish prostitutes chose to live there, and many brothels were opened in its alleys. In 1911 the number of Jewish prostitutes in the quarter was estimated at between 150 and 200.[42] The 'Jewish Street' became a synonym for the 'red-light district'. The concentration of prostitution in the Jewish quarter is the strongest indication of the marginality of the area in the city's social consciousness. Moreover, as Muslims were prohibited from drinking alcohol, taverns were also concentrated in the Jewish quarter, and young people from all parts of Damascus came there to drink and to enjoy themselves, 'for the daughters of Israel sing and dance before the masses of lowly Gentiles who visit the taverns and coffee-houses, so that even respectable Gentiles are ashamed to go into the Jewish Street'.[43]

40 *Ha'aḥdut*, 6 (1 Kislev 5671), 12. On the custom of Damascus women wrapping themselves with a scarf, but not with a veil, when they went out in public, see Abulafia, *Penei yitsḥak*, vi. 12*b*, §6.

41 Tarab, *Sefer ezra*, 124[–5]*a*, §5.

42 Idelsohn, 'The Jewish Community in Damascus' (Heb.), 98; *Ha'aḥdut*, 7 (8 Kislev 5671), 11; *Haḥerut*, 143 (29 Aug. 1911), title page. The numbers given regarding the extent of prostitution are generally fragmentary, as prostitution by its very nature is conducted clandestinely. It nevertheless appears that in this case the numbers do reflect reality, as there is no attempt to hide the problem but on the contrary a deliberate intention to note its severity.

43 ACRI, TR/Is/63, Rabbi Jacob Danon to Rabbi Hayim Nahum, Damascus, 29 Heshvan 5671.

In contrast to other Jewish communities, in Damascus the problem of sexual promiscuity was not confined to the margins of society but affected the very heart of the community, both its everyday behaviour and its image in the eyes of the surrounding society. Moreover, whereas in other communities prostitution tended to develop in the wake of immigration, with most prostitutes themselves being immigrants, in Damascus the phenomenon was a local one and the women and girls working as prostitutes were almost all local.

Prostitution in the Jewish quarter led to an increase in other criminal activity, until the district was crawling with pimps, drunks, murderers, and hooligans. Life for the ordinary people of the community became almost unbearable, and the occasional steps taken against this trend, such as the arrest or expulsion of one or another prostitute, were quite inadequate in the face of the deteriorating situation.[44] The blame for this grim state of affairs was placed squarely upon the unsuccessful leadership of Rabbi Alfandari.

In 1898 Rabbi Alfandari asked the authorities to remove the prostitutes from the Jewish quarter, but this was never done, because the inhabitants of the Muslim and Christian quarters refused to allow prostitution in their own neighbourhoods. Within his own community, Alfandari's initiative aroused criticism because it did not confront the phenomenon as such, but simply attempted to remove it or hide it.[45] While the other rabbis, the spiritual shepherds of the community, preached publicly against the phenomenon, they too failed to take any concrete steps to eliminate it.[46]

The main action to counter prostitution was taken not by the community, but by private initiative. During the winter of 1898, at the end of a period of famine, cold, and terrible economic crisis that had continued for more than two years, the number of young Jewish girls converting to Islam, and the number of those who slid into prostitution, were increasing yet further. Both phenomena, indeed, became so common that they ceased to elicit any reaction, but were accepted in the community with a sense of inevitability. In response to this situation, that February a number of young people created an organization called Yismah Yisra'el (Israel Will Rejoice), whose purpose was to help poor girls without dowries to get married, thereby reducing the number of unmarried girls in the community and the temptation to change their religion or to take to the streets.[47] This represented an attempt not simply to quash the phenomenon itself, but to address its causes. The association's

44 AAIU, Syrie, I.B., 5, Damas, 20 May 1884.

45 Ibid., Syrie, XXI.E., Damas, 190*b*, Ouziel, 7 Aug. 1898.

46 See e.g. Maslaton, *Kol yehudah*, 123.

47 The sum required for a dowry was 100–150 French francs, an enormous sum for the vast majority of the Jews of Damascus. See AAIU, Syrie, XIX.E., Damas, 190b, Ouziel, 7 Aug. 1898.

income came from monthly subscriptions paid by its 130 members, from contributions from members of the community and, primarily, from money raised from wealthy Jews in Europe. Thus, for example, the fund established by Baron Morris de Hirsch contributed 1,000 francs per year to buy bridal clothing for the poor girls of Damascus.[48] Efforts by Rabbi Zadok Hakohen, chief rabbi of France, to whom members of the association appealed for help, later led to the involvement in Yismah Yisra'el's work of Baron Hirsch's widow, Clara, who gave an annual donation to the association in order to help poor and orphan girls to get married.[49] At the recommendation of Rabbi Hakohen, the AIU also became involved in the cause, donating 50 francs per year to the association. With support from these sources, Yismah Yisra'el succeeded in arranging marriages at its own expense for about fifteen girls a year.[50]

The association's work was, however, hindered by the difficult economic situation in Damascus. A particular blow came when, in 1901, the Alliance decided to reduce its annual donation by half, and thereafter to halt it completely. The leading figures in Yismah Yisra'el—Abraham Hazan, Ezra Daniel, Ya'ir Halevi, and Bekhor Abraham Daniel Halevi—again turned to Rabbi Hakohen with a desperate appeal that he use his influence with the leaders of the Alliance to persuade them to sustain their support.[51] Their pleas were evidently unsuccessful, for in 1901 the association was forced to disband.

Yismah Yisra'el, as a private initiative, could not solve the problem on its own. In the absence of backing from the chief rabbi or the institutions of communal leadership—institutions which in practice did not even exist—the association was doomed to failure. Moreover, even the serious problem it was attempting to address was pushed aside by the struggles surrounding the office of the rabbinate.

The Struggle against the Emissaries of the Alliance

The emissaries of the AIU in Damascus and their supporters in the community saw Rabbi Alfandari as their great enemy. It is striking that a large proportion of the Alliance's reports from the period of Rabbi Alfandari's term

48 *JC*, 11 Apr. 1902, p. 16*b*.

49 See AAIU, Syrie, XIX.E., Damas, 190*b*, Ouziel, 7 Aug. 1898; see further ibid., members of the society to Rabbi Zadok Hakohen, Rosh Hodesh Heshvan 5659.

50 See ibid., Syrie, I.B., 5, Damas, Yismah Yisra'el Society to Rabbi Zadok Hakohen in Paris, 2 Tevet 5661.

51 Ibid.; see further ibid., Syrie, XI.E., Damas, 100, Alhalel, 9 Feb. 1901, 20 Apr. 1902.

in office relate to his behaviour towards the institutions of the Alliance rather than to purely educational matters. Controversy focused on the issue of control over the *talmudei torah*. The Alliance sought to maintain the communal *talmudei torah* under its own supervision and to extend its support to the private schools as well. Rabbi Alfandari, by contrast, wished to remove the Alliance's influence over the *talmudei torah* so as to achieve control and supervision over both their administration and their curriculum. From the standpoint of the Alliance's emissaries, this would nullify the great revolution it had brought about in Jewish education in Damascus in concert with the previous *ḥakham bashi*, Yitshak Abulafia. In this context, it is worth remembering that the number of students in the *talmudei torah* was always greater than the number of students in the Alliance school. Representatives of the Alliance were afraid that, just as their work was beginning to bear fruit after years of running the *talmudei torah*, the schools would return to disorder and modern secular studies would be replaced by the study of Talmud and Zohar.[52] In fact, Rabbi Alfandari's entire term of office as *ḥakham bashi* was dominated by the struggle with the Alliance's representatives in Damascus, in whose eyes he was 'the great enemy of the light of progress'.[53] During his first years in office, it seemed to them that the *ḥakham bashi* brought in from Istanbul was trying to prove, through his attempts to dominate the *talmudei torah*, that those who had supported his appointment had not wasted their money.[54]

The emissaries of the Alliance took a stubborn and consistent stand against the *ḥakham bashi*'s attempts to wrest control of the *talmudei torah* from them. As more and more of Alfandari's supporters changed sides to support the Alliance, weakening the *ḥakham bashi*'s position, he cut off all contact with the Alliance's representatives and in effect allowed them to run the *talmudei torah*. At one stage it even looked as though the rabbi's surrender would allow the Alliance to gain control of even those *talmudei torah* that had not hitherto come under its supervision. In the end this did not happen, because the administration of the Alliance failed to allocate the additional funds needed. Nevertheless, representatives of the Alliance continued to complain to their superiors in Paris about the miserable situation of those *talmudei torah* that remained outside their supervision and to put pressure on them to enable them to take these schools under their sponsorship as well.[55]

52 Ibid., Syrie, XIX.E., Damas, 190*a*, Ouziel, 26 Nov. 1895. For a report on the sad state of the *talmudei torah*, see *JC*, 8 Apr. 1898, p. 16.

53 AAIU, Syrie, XI.E., Damas, 100, Alhalel, 4 June 1903.

54 Ibid. XIX.E., Damas, 190*a*, Ouziel, 26 Nov. 1895.

55 Ibid., Damas, 190*a*, Ouziel, 10 Mar. 1896, Rapport moral; ibid., XI.E. Damas, 110, Alhalel, 20 Apr. 1903.

A number of public events connected to the Alliance, its institutions, and its leaders provided Rabbi Alfandari and representatives of the organization with opportunities to make peace—or, alternatively, to deepen the enmity between them. For example, in 1896, after a long period of estrangement from the chief emissary of the Alliance, Rahamim Ouziel, the *ḥakham bashi* took advantage of the memorial service in honour of Baron Hirsch to attempt to heal relations. Not only did he attend the service in person, he also gave an impressive sermon in Hebrew. This seems to have brought about a reconciliation between the *ḥakham bashi* and Ouziel. For his part, Ouziel, whose negative opinion of Alfandari was already well established, craftily sought to appeal to the rabbi's *amour propre* in order to bring about an improvement in the situation of the *talmudei torah*. He sent a letter to the heads of the Alliance—in which he described the chief rabbi as an arrogant and contentious person—asking them to send Alfandari a letter of thanks for his assistance in organizing the memorial service, flattering him 'so that he will be satisfied to see that somebody in Paris thinks of him'.[56]

By contrast, the memorial service some two years later, in 1898, for the president of the Alliance, Salomon Goldschmidt, led to a deepening of the hostility between Alfandari and Ouziel. The rabbi claimed that the Alliance did not send him an official letter inviting him to deliver a sermon at the service, and as a result he boycotted it. According to Ouziel, this move on the part of the rabbi was generally condemned throughout the community. The public did not accept the rabbi's instruction to stay away, nor did they follow him in boycotting the memorial service; on the contrary, they attended en masse. Ouziel, as the representative of the Alliance, thought that advantage ought to be taken of this occasion as an opportunity for bringing about change in the community, as it had made the public aware that it was possible to act without the chief rabbi. In a letter to the president of the Alliance, Ouziel wrote:

> This is a great deal for a city like Damascus, that is still connected to the ancient tradition. The presence of these gentlemen [the lay leaders of the community] in the school, in opposition to the view of the chief rabbi, is a step that was taken in the direction of liberal ideas, a harsh initial blow to the destructive authority of our ignorant rabbis. These hesitant steps towards independence require a certain encouragement. It would be good if it was made known here that what has happened has been reported to you. For all these reasons, I think it necessary that you write a few of words of thanks to the honourable gentlemen.[57]

[56] AAIU, Syrie, XIX.E., Damas, 190*a*, Ouziel, 14 May 1896.
[57] Ibid. XIX.E.,190*b*, Ouziel, 27 Mar. 1898.

These words indicate the increasing involvement of several of the emissaries of the Alliance in the internal affairs of the community, to the extent of conducting a deliberate policy of 'divide and conquer' between the *ḥakham bashi* and the lay leadership.[58] This exacerbated Rabbi Alfandari's hostility to the Alliance representatives and to the values which they represented. On more than one occasion, the *ḥakham bashi* organized petitions calling on the leadership of the Alliance in Paris to replace Ouziel. The Alliance headquarters generally supported its representatives everywhere, although in cases where friction with the community and its leaders had become particularly severe, it would sometimes transfer an emissary to another city. In any event, the leadership of the Alliance was not going to take any step before hearing the arguments on both sides, particularly given that both parties had complained, on more than one occasion, that the other had resorted to falsification of signatures, lies, and deceit.[59]

During the course of the dispute between Rahamim Ouziel and Rabbi Alfandari, the *ḥakham bashi* was given the opportunity to present his complaints against the representative of the Alliance. If his opposition to secular studies, and particularly to the study of foreign languages, had already been formulated at that time, he did not give any expression to this in his letter, which was mainly concerned with the behaviour of the Alliance representative. His response to the request of the Alliance leadership that he give his version of the dispute was as follows:

I must reply out of respect, and it may be that things that come from the heart will enter into the heart . . . You know for sure that when M[onsieur] Ouziel first came to our city I told him that I wished to go to the school to supervise things from time to time, or to appoint certain people to do so, and he responded that even if I go myself it will change nothing of what, in his opinion, needs to be done, and therefore, if there will be no benefit to my going, why should I go? . . . For it is well known throughout the city that all of the people are very troubled by this improper behaviour, to the extent that many people in the city complain to me, asking how and why I can allow such an improper thing to persist for such a lengthy period of time without feeling it, until I was forced myself to give notice to the authorities that the schools are not under my supervision . . . And you should know faithfully that all the people of the city are concerned about the curtailment of Torah study, and the 'bad culture' affecting the children, apart from certain people who are very few in number. [And the people] always speak about the bad management of the school, but they are afraid that if they write to your honour perhaps the benefit that

[58] It is nevertheless worth noting that some emissaries exercised extraordinary caution and attempted not to become involved in the intra-communal dispute. See ibid. XI.E., Damas, 101*b*, Alhalel, 6 Oct. 1905.

[59] Ibid. XIX.E., Damas, 190*b*, Ouziel, 26 Oct. 1898.

comes from your side will no longer be available, and they are unable to make it up, and they said that I should write to you . . . and this man, Monsieur Ouziel . . . sent a letter to the synagogues saying that if the people of the city wish to supervise even the other schools without him, then the Alliance society will withhold all benefits, even the provision of food for the poor and orphans who are fed every day will no longer be made—and this is certainly not to the honour of Your Excellency to speak thus before all the people.[60]

The threat of withdrawal of the Alliance's support was a powerful weapon in the hands of the society's representatives, particularly in the light of the grave financial situation. Meanwhile, in their reports to their leadership, the emissaries in Damascus repeatedly emphasized that any concessions to the *ḥakham bashi* would nullify the work of the Alliance in the community.[61] For his part, Rabbi Alfandari tried to bypass the Alliance's control over the *talmudei torah* by setting up a new *talmud torah*.[62]

Throughout these struggles, both sides attempted to marshal support from the local authorities. The *ḥakham bashi* appealed to the *wali*, Nazem Pasha, to transfer into his hands, as head of the community, responsibility for the schools of the Alliance and the authority to determine their educational programme. In order to convince the *wali* that he was acting on patriotic motives, he stated that the Alliance invested all its efforts in teaching the French language and completely neglected the teaching of Hebrew, Arabic, and Turkish. But the *wali* was suspicious of the *ḥakham bashi*'s intentions and asked the supervisor of public education to begin an investigation. That investigation revealed Rabbi Alfandari's true intentions—namely, to dominate the *talmudei torah*, rather than to encourage the study of Arabic or Turkish. His request was rejected, officially on the grounds that the only body with authority to supervise the schools was the government, so that granting supervisory privileges to the *ḥakham bashi* would violate the authority of the director of public education. In the community the conflict continued, with the police being called on several occasions to intervene in the struggle between supporters of the chief rabbi and those of the directors of Alliance institutions in the city.[63]

The next two emissaries, Yom-Tov Tsemah and Aaron Alhalel, failed to establish any better relations with the *ḥakham bashi*. Following a major dispute with Alhalel, Rabbi Alfandari sent a complaint to the *wali* and to the director of public education—but again the authorities took the side of

[60] AAIU, Syrie, XI.E., Damas, 94, Alfandari to the Alliance, Damascus, 21 Heshvan 5659.

[61] Ibid. XIX.E., Damas, 190*b*, Ouziel, 10 Oct. 1898.

[62] Ibid. 190*a*, Ouziel, 2 Dec. 1895.

[63] Ibid. 190*b*, Ouziel, 26 Oct. 1898.

the Alliance emissary.[64] The anomalous situation of the private *talmudei torah*, particularly of the school for orphans, troubled Alhalel, who never ceased insisting that all the *talmudei torah* be transferred to Alliance sponsorship, proposing various ways of achieving this end.[65] Finally, after numerous struggles and discussions, an agreement was reached with the chief rabbi. Alhalel's first priority was to repair the building of the main *talmud torah*. The community elected a committee, ostensibly to assist Alhalel in his activity on behalf of the *talmudei torah*, but in practice also to supervise him. The members of this committee were Rabbis Jacob Maslaton, Jacob Na'em, Yitshak Harari, Abraham Atar, Aaron Yedid, and the son-in-law of Shemaiah Angel, Abraham Pinto.[66]

The establishment of this committee was of great significance, as it prompted Rabbi Alfandari to agree to change his centralized approach to running the community, in which he relied upon a limited circle of supporters and advisers, and to set up an official communal board. Alhalel, who had long sought to extend the patronage of the Alliance to all the *talmudei torah* in the community, used the opportunity to arrive at an agreement on this subject with the new committee. The matter was handled carefully, and the agreement of the *ḥakham bashi* was obtained. After many years of conflict, Rabbi Alfandari seems to have realized that, if he could not overpower his opponents, it would be better for him to co-operate with them and, within that co-operative framework, to try to keep to a minimum what he saw as harmful to the Jewish tradition.

On 31 January 1904 a party was held to mark the Alliance's taking the independent *talmudei torah* under its aegis. Rabbi Alfandari agreed to preside over the official celebration, and even gave a long speech.[67] By allowing all the *talmudei torah* in the city to be gathered under the wing of the Alliance, Alfandari made his peace, albeit reluctantly, perhaps even under duress, with the educational revolution begun by his predecessor as *ḥakham bashi*, Rabbi Yitshak Abulafia. From now on the Jewish children of Damascus, with the exception of those who studied in institutions run by the Christian missions, or who did not study at all, were educated in schools run by the Alliance. In the *talmudei torah*, the main change in the educational programme was in fact the introduction of the study of Arabic, with religious studies continuing to be the core of the curriculum.[68]

[64] Ibid. XI.E., Damas, 100, Alhalel, 24 July 1903. On Rabbi Alfandari's relation to Yom-Tov Tsemah, Alhalel's predecessor, see ibid., 29 Oct. 1899.

[65] Ibid., 20 Apr. 1903, 13 Aug. 1903, 11 Sept. 1903.

[66] Ibid., 22 Nov. 1903, 29 Nov. 1903, 11 Dec. 1903.

[67] Ibid. 101*b*, Alhalel, 8 Jan. 1904.

[68] On the *talmudei torah* until the revolution of the Young Turks, see *Bulletin*, 1904, p. 113;

Notwithstanding this apparent resolution of the educational question, tensions persisted between Rabbi Alfandari and the emissaries of the Alliance, and his relationships with the community elites and government authorities alike were also very poor.[69] In retrospect, the leaders of the Damascus community and its sages summarized the years of Rabbi Alfandari's leadership as follows: 'He did not have a good character—neither with the holy community nor with the people of the government.'[70]

Towards Revolution and Deposition

Rabbi Alfandari's main supporters during the first two years of his term as chief rabbi were the members of the Union Israélite association, who had been responsible for bringing him to Damascus. But not many people remained from that original group, most of whom had been either young graduates of the Alliance schools or traditional Torah scholars. Some of the young educated people had switched their allegiance to the representatives of the Alliance, while others, out of frustration, had abandoned community activity completely, in some cases emigrating overseas. Those who remained, and who formed the *ḥakham bashi*'s circle of advisers, belonged either to the middle class or to the group of traditional Torah scholars—the group described by the Alliance's representative Rahamim Ouziel as 'extremists and enemies of progress, who zealously defended their prejudices and made use of the weapon known as *ḥerem* [excommunication] against any deviation'.[71] Clearly, the relationship between the emissary of the Alliance and the members of the association had deteriorated markedly. The lack of any distinguished members of the community among the association's membership—a factor which in the past had been seen as a virtue in the eyes of the Alliance representatives—now became a drawback. Suddenly, questions began to be asked about the process by which members of the association were selected; supporters of the Alliance claimed that public apathy enabled the members of Union Israélite to accumulate power and influence which they exploited for their own personal benefit. The dominant element in the association was the group of Torah scholars, who had become religious extremists in the spirit of the *ḥakham bashi*—a position at odds with most members of the community.

1905, p. 131; 1906, p. 131; 1907, p. 120; 1908, p. 161; 1909, p. 129; see also AAIU, Syrie, XV.E., Damas, 142*a*, Farhi, 20 Jan. 1906. Cf. ibid., appeal for economic assistance by the instructors in the *talmud torah* to the Alliance, Damascus, 3 Elul 5669.

69 See e.g. AAIU, Syrie, XI.E., Damas, 101*b*, Alhalel, 5 June 1906.

70 ACRI, TR/Is/63, heads of the Damascus community and its rabbis to Rabbi Hayim Nahum, 12 Tevet 5670.

71 AAIU, Syrie, XIX.E., Damas, 190*a*, Ouziel, 5 Jan. 1896, Rapport moral.

The association also controlled the social welfare societies and, in practice, ran all the affairs of the community, unaccountable to anyone except the *ḥakham bashi* himself. A number of members of the association, indeed, were accused by emissaries of the Alliance of corruption and misuse of communal funds.[72] Just two years after Alfandari's arrival in Damascus, reports from Damascus along the following lines began to appear in the Hebrew press in Jerusalem:

> There is no unity at all in the city between the elders and the new generation: whatever the one destroys the others build up, and what these build up the others destroy. In general, nothing good comes out of such a situation. The elders have completely ceased to be involved with matters of education, and the young people, even if they are somewhat involved, act without any benefit to the advancement of the people.[73]

This state of affairs led the people of the Damascus community to regret having deposed Rabbi Abulafia and to seek his reinstatement as *ḥakham bashi*. But Alfandari's appointment with a firman from the sultan made it difficult to depose him in turn.[74] As the years passed, the number of Rabbi Alfandari's supporters within the community dwindled, the communal institutions were neglected, and in practice the communal administration was operated under central control, without any support or assistance from additional committees. Pushed into a corner, isolated in a strange and alien city, Rabbi Alfandari became more and more rigid and adhered even more stubbornly to his established positions. His responses to his opponents became more extreme and his behaviour more uncompromising as he attempted to buttress his shaky authority. In practice, this meant that the *ḥakham bashi* concentrated all the income of the community in his own hands and controlled all its expenditure, while his dictatorial behaviour alienated even those who might have been able to arrest the community's decline.

The question inevitably arises: how was it that the leading figures of the community saw what was going on and did not intervene to improve matters? The answer is that they were reluctant to take responsibility for the management of the community, for fear of how the Ottoman authorities might react. The old families of the hereditary and moneyed elites, which had formerly produced the community's leaders—such as the Lisbona, Harari, Farhi, and Stambuli families—had either lost their money or left Damascus. The new candidates for leadership, who came from the new middle class or the new educated elite, lacked the experience, abilities, and talents required to

[72] Ibid., Rapport moral, 2 Dec. 1895, 5 Jan. 1896.

[73] *Hatsevi*, 3 (9 Heshvan 5657), 12.

[74] AAIU, Syrie, XIX.E., Damas, 190*b*, Ouziel, 12 Feb. 1897.

take their place.[75] Aware of their shortcomings compared to their cosmopolitan predecessors, they were unwilling to take upon themselves the burden of public leadership. Above all, they feared that if they set up a new official administrative committee to run the community, the government would hold it accountable for the huge debt incurred by the community under the *ʿaskariyya* tax, and that if they were unable to deliver this money to the government they would be held personally responsible and either imprisoned or required to pay the money from their own pockets. Thus the only people who might have served as a new leadership for the community were deterred from offering a real alternative to that of the *ḥakham bashi*.[76]

Suffering from both the limitations of the *ḥakham bashi* and the lack of any alternative focus of leadership, the community's welfare institutions deteriorated gravely during Rabbi Alfandari's tenure of office.[77] The wider population of Syria benefited hardly at all under the institutions of Ottoman rule, which invested little in any social welfare infrastructure and required the various religious communities and congregations throughout the empire to set up on their own institutions of charitable and medical help for their own members. Given the lack of any effective community leadership while Alfandari was *ḥakham bashi*, the Damascus community relied on private initiative for its welfare provision.

In 1903 the Damascus Jewish community numbered something over 10,000 people. Of these, only about 300 families had an assured livelihood, while the rest endured lives of impoverishment or, at best, economic insecurity.[78] In an effort to meet their needs, a number of charitable societies were set up in Damascus at the end of the nineteenth century and the beginning of the twentieth. In 1897 the Ahi Ezer society was established by graduates of evening classes at the Alliance school to gather money and food for the needy. This society officially joined the Alliance and co-operated with its representatives in Damascus.[79] It did not enjoy the support of Rabbi Alfandari, who saw its activity as an attempt to interfere in the running of the community. After an intensely cold winter, economic conditions deteriorated further, rising inflation dramatically increasing the price of bread, which

75 See e.g. the list of 'Sages, rabbis and prominent and generous men of the noted city in Israel, Damascus' who signed a statement in Tamuz 5663 (1903) regarding contributions to the fund of Rabbi Me'ir Ba'al Hanes (cited in Alhadif, *Yatsev gevulot*, 39–40). Most of the names are new to the leadership. *Ḥakham bashi* Alfandari specifically did not sign this statement, which may suggest a certain break between him and the community.

76 AAIU, Syrie, XI.E., Damas, 100, Alhalel, 20 Apr. 1902.

77 Ibid. XIX.E., Damas, 190*b*, Ouziel, 9 Mar. 1898.

78 For an extensive description of poverty in this community, see ibid. XI.E., Damas, 100, Alhalel, 3 Mar. 1903.

79 On this association's joining the Alliance, see *Bulletin*, 1901, 223.

was almost the only food of the poor people. The situation became so dire that there were many instances of suicide. The community was particularly shocked by one dramatic case in which three brothers from a single family decided to put an end to their lives a few days before Passover, unable to bear starvation any longer: two of them hanged themselves in their rooms, while a third drowned himself in a well.[80] In March 1898 the Ahi Ezer society, with the assistance of the Alliance's emissary Rahamim Ouziel, planned to put on a theatrical performance as a benefit for the poor of the community. The *ḥakham bashi* seems to have seen in this attempt to raise money a criticism of his own incompetence, and he tried to prevent the performance by turning to the police station in the Jewish quarter. When this was unsuccessful, he ordered the parents of the actors, under threat of *ḥerem*, not to allow their sons to participate in it. In this way he prevented the staging of the play, and thus also prevented the gathering of contributions for the poor.[81] At the end of 1902 the association, seeing that it was unable to meet the goals it had set itself, disbanded.

Another charitable organization established in Damascus at this time was Agudat Hanashim (Association of Women), whose aim was to assist women during pregnancy and following childbirth. This group too seems to have operated for only a brief period at the beginning of the twentieth century.[82] There is also an isolated report concerning another women's society, known as Rodfot Tsedek (Seekers of Justice), whose members contributed a sum of money in 1896 for the Alliance girls' school.[83] The establishment of these societies seems indicative of an awakening among the educated women in the community, the vast majority of whom were graduates of the Alliance school, and a willingness to take part in the institutions of the community. However, the comprehensive failure of these attempts to organize indicates that Jewish society in Damascus was not yet prepared to allow women to become involved in communal activity.

In July 1897 an association was organized among the wealthy families who sent their daughters to the Alliance girls' school with the purpose of providing poorer students with clothing for Passover and Sukkot. It is possible that this organization was the basis for the Malbish Arumim society, set up around the turn of the century, which ran an annual clothing distribution for indigent students. The activity of Malbish Arumim was supported by contributions from the Baron Hirsch Fund, from Baron Edmond James de Rothschild, and from the Alliance. The distribution was performed at a widely

80 AAIU, Syrie, XIX.E., Damas, 190*b*, Ouziel, 12 June 1898.

81 Ibid., 9 Mar. 1898, 13 Mar. 1898.

82 Ibid. XI.E., Damas, 100, Alhalel, 7 Jan. 1900.

83 *Bulletin*, 1st–2nd sem., 1896, p. 89.

attended ceremony, to which the supervisor of public education in the city and the French consul were usually invited. This association too disbanded during the first decade of the twentieth century, owing to lack of funds. Even after its demise, however, the Alliance continued every year to provide clothing to destitute students.[84]

The oldest charitable society acting in Damascus was Bikur Holim (Visiting the Sick), established in 1882 with the goal of providing free medical care, medicines, and food to the indigent ill, so that they would not fall prey to the missionary groups.[85] This society was initially funded through monthly payments from its members, but its expenses were far greater than its income, and although it received some help from the Alliance from time to time, over the years its situation deteriorated until by 1895 it was run by a single individual, Rabbi Shhadé Maslaton, a member of the Union Israélite society. For about ten years, Rabbi Maslaton lived in a house that belonged to the society, which had originally been intended to serve as a hospital for the destitute.[86]

During the spring of 1902 a London Jewish philanthropist named A. D. Stern visited Damascus and became aware of the poverty and distress of the Jewish community in the city, and in particular of the absence of adequate medical care. Stern noted that many Jews in need of medical help were forced to turn to institutions that had been established by Protestant missionary groups with the intention of converting their patients to Christianity. He established a trust fund which earned interest of £150 a year—a tremendous sum in those days by any standard—and using the money thus generated he opened a pharmacy in the city that employed a doctor, a pharmacist, and an assistant. Medicines were given to patients free of charge, while the doctor received patients on the premises and also made house calls to poor patients. The remainder of the money was used to buy basic supplies for new mothers and destitute patients. The fund was administered from London, and the profits were transferred to Damascus through the Alliance. Responsibility for its administration was put in the hands of the headmaster of the local Alliance school—a decision of great significance, as control over money donated to help the poor gave him a position of power and influence in the community.[87]

[84] *JC*, 16 July 1897, p. 22.

[85] Before the Jewish infirmary was established in Damascus, the Jews of the city used to go for healing to the Cave of Elijah the Prophet in Jobar. See Idelsohn, 'The Jewish Community in Damascus' (Heb.), 102.

[86] AAIU, Syrie, XIV.E., Damascus, 133, Cohen, Ezra Hakohen Tarab, Shemuel Totakh, and Netanael Mahadib, heads of the Bikur Holim society, to the Alliance, 3 Heshvan 5650; XIX.E., Damas, 190*a*, Ouziel, 2 Dec. 1895.

[87] Almaleh, *The Jews in Damascus* (Heb.), 43–4.

The foundation of the pharmacy could hardly have been more timely. At the beginning of February 1903 a cholera epidemic broke out in Damascus, and many inhabitants of the Jewish quarter were affected—although most of them suffered less from the disease itself than as a result of the steps taken by the health authorities of the city to combat the epidemic. It must be remembered that most of the poor Jews in Damascus earned their livelihood by gathering and selling scraps. The authorities, in order to prevent infection and stop the epidemic spreading, ordered them to burn almost all of their wares. In many cases, even the beds of these pedlars were also burned, so that many people were literally left with nothing, having seen both their means of livelihood and their personal furniture destroyed. At one point it was even suggested that the pharmacy be closed for fear of contagion, but this idea was rejected so as not to withhold medical help from the poor. The pharmacy, indeed, became the main centre of help for all those suffering as a result of the epidemic, whether directly or indirectly.[88]

At the height of the epidemic a new charitable society was established, entitled Pikuah Nefashot (Saving Lives), which over the course of its existence exerted considerable influence on the leadership of the community. The society was headed by Shemaiah ben Eleazar Angel, the grandson of the banker and philanthropist Shemaiah Angel who had gained such notoriety in Damascus some decades earlier and was well connected in the elite circles of his time.[89] The appearance of another philanthropist in a later generation of the Angel family raised hopes for a renewal of community life as it had existed in former times.[90]

In practice, the establishment of this society represented a challenge to Rabbi Alfandari's sole control over communal funds and was seen by the *ḥakham bashi* and his circle as an attempt by one of the descendants of the old elite to reassert his family's former significant role in the community leadership. Members of the society established contact with the Cairo community—a significant number of whose members were emigrants from Damascus, including members of the old elite—in their quest for contributions on behalf of the needy people of Damascus.[91] A small number of contributions were also received from Jerusalem and Beirut. Backed by these donors, the association became an alternative to the official system of charity

[88] *JC*, 24 Apr. 1903, p. 15*a*.

[89] On the multifaceted character of Shemaiah Angel the grandfather, see Ch. 6 above.

[90] ACRI, TR/Is/164*a*, Rabbi Raphael Aaron ben Shimon to Shemaiah Angel, Cairo, 23 Sivan 5663.

[91] On the organization of fundraising in Egypt and the conditions placed by the donors upon the distribution of the money, see ibid., Rabbi Raphael Aaron ben Shimon to Aaron Yadid and Shemaiah Angel, Cairo, 18 Adar 5663.

in Damascus which, as noted above, was concentrated in the hands of a single person—the *ḥakham bashi*. As the immediate purpose of Pikuah Nefashot was to distribute basic food supplies to the needy, its members joined forces with Aaron Alhalel, the headmaster of the Alliance school, who controlled the funds received from London. Thus Alfandari was confronted by a united front of all his opponents, including both the headmaster of the Alliance school and the descendants of the old social elite, who together controlled all the external assistance given to the community and served as a focal point for all the needs of the poor. Disputes rapidly broke out between members of the Pikuah Nefashot association and the *ḥakham bashi*, who lost no time in complaining about them to the governor, Nazem Pasha.[92]

When the Pikuah Nefashot society was set up, it sought to take over the running of the old Bikur Holim society which, with the encouragement of the *ḥakham bashi*, was attempting to control the contributions sent from London by Stern. The issue of control over Bikur Holim became an additional point of contention between the *ḥakham bashi* and members of the new society. The position of power enjoyed by Pikuah Nefashot and the widespread public support it enjoyed—thanks to its record of success in caring for the poor and needy of the community during the cholera epidemic—prompted its members to demand the establishment of a new steering committee that would act alongside the *ḥakham bashi* in running the community. Under pressure of public opinion, Rabbi Alfandari agreed to allow the election of a new committee, whose first step was officially to hand over the running of Bikur Holim to Pikuah Nefashot and to transfer the small amount of money which belonged to the older society to the new one. This move aroused hopes that, after long years of anarchy, a new leadership would take shape that would set the community on the right path. Alhalel, the Alliance emissary, was placed at the head of Pikuah Nefashot, an appointment that made his already tense relationship with the *ḥakham bashi* even worse.[93] In practice, the Bikur Holim society continued to exist, used by Rabbi Alfandari in his attempts to control the welfare funds which came to the community from London via members of the Alliance. The society was finally dismantled only at the end of 1904.[94] The opposition to the *ḥakham bashi* grew stronger when, shortly thereafter, Nisim Farhi, headmaster of the Alliance school in Damascus, was appointed head of Pikuah Nefashot.[95]

92 Ibid., Rabbi Raphael Aaron ben Shimon to Shemaiah Angel, Cairo, 23 Sivan 5663.

93 Ibid., 4 June 1903; AAIU, Syrie, XI.E., 101*b*, Alhalel, 6 Oct. 1905.

94 AAIU, Syrie, XI.E., 101*b*, Alhalel, 27 Dec. 1904.

95 It would appear that Shemaiah Angel left Damascus with his father, Eleazar, and went to live in Istanbul. See Almaleh, *The Jews in Damascus* (Heb.), 15.

The pharmacy and clinic that had been established with Stern's contributions became the central charitable institution of the community. Foreign consuls and visitors from outside the country were brought to the clinic to see its work.[96] In April 1904, a Jewish physician by the name of Benjamin Alfandari was employed there on a regular basis.[97] The importance of this institution went beyond the medical help it provided; it became a symbol of opposition to Rabbi Alfandari and a focus of power for the new group seeking an alternative to his leadership. Indeed, following Rabbi Alfandari's deposition, a significant number of the members of Pikuah Nefashot were elected to the new community board in the elections organized by Rabbi Yitshak Abulafia. This indicates the strong political identity of this association, which over the course of time became the principal public support of the new *ḥakham bashi*, Jacob Danon.

This being so, the establishment of a philanthropic society was not only a means of helping the needy, but also an acceptable way for young people to attempt to put themselves forward as candidates for community leadership. In 1907 another such organization was established: Ozer Dalim Bedamasek (Succour for the Poor in Damascus), which set out to deal with what its members saw as the public scandal of Jews begging in the streets. Every week the society distributed bread and a certain sum of money to all the poor so that they would not need to beg for handouts. Anyone caught begging in the street lost his right to the support provided. Following the revolution of the Young Turks in 1908, the deposition of Rabbi Alfandari, and the reorganization brought about by Rabbi Abulafia, the resources of the association grew and it began to distribute flour and meat to families in distress. It seems from contemporary accounts that it had considerable success, significantly reducing the number of Jewish beggars.[98]

Towards the end of the nineteenth century, poverty, and rumours of the economic opportunities available both in nearby Beirut and overseas, led to greatly increased emigration from Damascus. What had begun as a small trickle during the mid-1880s became, by the end of the 1890s, a great stream. Dozens of young people, and at times even entire families, left Damascus every year in search of a new livelihood. These emigrants included many of the young people who, it was hoped, would help the community to progress towards a better future, thus exacerbating the plight of the struggling community.[99]

[96] AAIU, Syrie, XVIII.E., Damas, 182, Nahon, 4 May 1914.

[97] Ibid., XV.E., Damas, 142*a*, Farhi, 4 Nov. 1906, 13 July 1908. There is no evidence in the extant sources of any family relationship between the doctor and the *ḥakham bashi*.

[98] Almaleh, *The Jews in Damascus* (Heb.), 44–5.

[99] AAIU, Syrie, XIX.E., Damas, 190*b*, Ouziel, Rapport moral, 12 June 1898; for an extensive

As conditions for the population deteriorated, so the hostility between Rabbi Alfandari and members of the community increased, reaching fresh heights with every new episode of distress, as it appeared to the people that their chief rabbi did nothing to help them. Thus, for example, during the cholera epidemic of 1903, many people died due to lack of medical care, poor and starving people wandered the streets, community buildings were destroyed, and many children were denied an education. But the rabbi seemed entirely unable—and, according to the chief Alliance representative, even unwilling—to assist the community, seeming to regard its members merely as 'donkeys deserving of being exploited and beaten'.[100]

Rabbi Alfandari's relations with the government authorities, and particularly with the governor, were also very poor. He was mistrusted by the Ottoman officials, who perceived him as arrogant, haughty, and deficient in ability. The authorities rejected almost all of his complaints against the representatives of the Alliance and his rivals in the community, while he himself frequently refused to listen to the instructions of the governor.[101] There is extant testimony to this effect that reputedly came from Rabbi Alfandari himself. Even if this report is not accurate in terms of the historical facts, it is nevertheless revealing in respect of the state of relations between the *ḥakham bashi* and the authorities. According to this report, Rabbi Alfandari's prohibitions on women wearing wigs, sitting in coffee-houses in the company of strangers, and taking part in musical troupes aroused considerable opposition among people who did not share his strict outlook, and they approached the governor to request that he be removed from his office. Twice Nazem Pasha summoned the *ḥakham bashi* to come to him, and twice he failed to turn up for the meeting. Only the third time, when the summons was accompanied by threats, did the rabbi appear before the governor. In response to the warning that he was risking dismissal, Rabbi Alfandari replied that he could more easily bring about the dismissal of the *wali* than the latter could bring about his own. This incident—as described by Alfandari himself—not surprisingly soured relations with the governor even further.[102]

As noted above, during the summer of 1903 Rabbi Alfandari submitted to public pressure and agreed to the election of a new community board. The independent activity of this board inevitably led it into confrontation with

description of the motivations of the beginnings of the immigration to Argentina, see ibid. XI.E., Damas, 101*b*, Alhalel, 4 June 1905; and cf. Harel, *Syrian Jewry*, 250–3, 324–7.

[100] AAIU, Syrie, XI.E., Damas, 100, Alhalel, 3 Mar. 1903.

[101] Ibid. 101*b*, Alhalel, 5 Mar. 1906.

[102] See Ben-Ya'akov, 'Rabbi Solomon Alfandari *z"l*' (Heb.), 7.

the chief rabbi, who for years had concentrated the community's income and all of its other affairs in his own hands. At the end of 1905, the board submitted a formal complaint to the *wali* of Damascus requesting the dismissal of the chief rabbi. The governor, whose own relations with Rabbi Alfandari were not good, gave the board his backing, at which point all the rabbis of Damascus, along with another two hundred distinguished members and leaders of the community, added their names to the petition. The *wali* confirmed the claims set out in the petition and sent it on to the minister of justice in Istanbul. In an accompanying letter, he added that, in view of the lack of trust existing between the community and Alfandari, the administrative council of the region had stripped the chief rabbi of all his authority and prerogatives and transferred them to the communal board. The chief rabbi was thus left with the title of *ḥakham bashi*, but without any authority.[103] Rabbi Alfandari's relationship with his long-standing opponent—the spiritual head of the community and head of the rabbinic court, Rabbi Yitshak Abulafia—became even worse after the latter published, without any advance warning, his own halakhic ruling permitting women to wear wigs. So bad did the ill feeling between the *ḥakham bashi* and the other Torah scholars in the city become that the latter refused to attend any event at which Alfandari was present.[104]

From that point on, the opponents of the *ḥakham bashi* were led by Abulafia's son-in-law, Hayim Moses Laniado, who was the personal banker of the governor and was generally reputed to be the wealthiest person in the Jewish quarter. Rabbi Alfandari's supporters attempted to undermine Laniado's reliability in the eyes of the *wali*, but without success. They also tried to blacken the name of Aaron Yedid, the secretary of the communal board, by making allegations against him to the heads of the Beirut trade association, whom Yedid represented in Damascus, and similarly slandered other opponents of the *ḥakham bashi*. This intolerable situation led to the increasing involvement of the governor in the community's affairs. A few days before Passover 1907, he assembled the rival groups in his palace and defined the areas of responsibility of each. The chief rabbi's spiritual authority was restored, while community matters were declared to be the responsibility of the elected board.[105] But this intervention provided no lasting solution: the rift between the rabbi and the members of the community persisted, and the

[103] AAIU, Syrie, XI.E., Damas, 101*b*, Alhalel, 6 Oct. 1905.

[104] Ibid. XV.E., Damas, 142*a*; XI.E., Damas, 101*b*, Alhalel, 3 June 1906; Farhi, 10 Jan. 1907.

[105] This compromise made it possible for the community to prepare itself properly to receive the Sephardi rabbi of London, Rabbi Moses Gaster, in May 1907. On Rabbi Gaster's visit, see *JC*, 7 June 1907, p. 15.

decline in the status of the community continued, until the revolution of the Young Turks the following year.

The assumption of power by the Young Turks on 23–24 July 1908 led to a wave of dismissals and resignations, bringing about a wholesale change of personnel in the senior Ottoman civil service, both in the heart of the empire and in the provinces. The new regime replaced the *ḥakham bashi* in Istanbul, Rabbi Moses Halevi, with one of its own supporters, Rabbi Hayim Nahum. This led to a series of demands on the part of numerous communities right across the empire for the replacement of their own chief rabbis. The governors of Jerusalem, Damascus, and Saida informed the Sublime Porte of the 'rebellion' of the Jews in these cities against their chief rabbis—who, according to the Jews themselves, had been imposed upon the communities by the previous rulers—and sought instructions on how to deal with the tumultuous demonstrations of the Jews in the streets and restore public order.

In Damascus, these demonstrations were influenced by the public atmosphere which was sweeping through the city with the publication of the new constitution and the consequent replacement of senior officials.[106] The phenomenon of Jews taking to the streets demanding the deposition of their chief rabbi should be seen as a revolution in the full sense of the word. The appointment of the chief rabbi was no longer an internal matter for the community, but had become, at its request, a matter for the government. The street demonstrations were an expression of the Jews' active political participation: they hoped to change the order of government within their own community, in a manner parallel to the reorganization of the secular government. Moreover, their demand to replace their chief rabbi was based upon the fundamental ideas of the Ottoman constitution, now reinstated by the Young Turks after having been held in abeyance for some thirty years by Sultan ʿAbd al-Hamid II. Thus the community broke out of its narrow and limited world and began to see its own Jewish leadership as part of the general political system. The leaders of this campaign among the Jews of Damascus saw themselves as among those who had brought about the revolution and wanted to be among those who enjoyed its fruits.

Immediately following the revolution, the people of Damascus asked the new government in Istanbul to remove Rabbi Alfandari, who, they alleged, had behaved in a high-handed, tyrannical manner for thirteen years. Earlier

[106] FO 618/3, 'Public Feeling in Damascus as Regards the Constitution and Izzet Pasha', 3 Aug. 1908; 'State of Affairs in Damascus Relating to the New Regime', Damascus, 12 Aug. 1908; AAIU, Syrie, XV.E., Damas, 142*a*, Farhi, 16 Aug. 1908.

complaints, they said, had been ignored as he had enjoyed the protection of the previous government, which had appointed him. Now, following the revolution, they felt the new spirit of freedom that was emerging from the ideas of revolution:

> Now that word has spread of the statement of our king, blessed be his majesty, that every person should speak of what troubles him and not fear or be afraid, we rise up and are encouraged . . . And we have immediately sent a telegram to the honourable viceroy to the king . . . to the glorious city of Constantinople [Istanbul]—may God protect it—which is your royal city, and we only told a thousandth part of our trouble; and we have requested of his honour the viceroy that he should immediately save us by removing his [Alfandari's] hand from us.[107]

When this request did not elicit a prompt response from Istanbul, the leaders of the community turned to the governor of Damascus with a request for help in deposing Alfandari. The governor suggested that they submit a petition on the subject to him and promised to forward it, with his own recommendations, to the ministries of justice and of religion in Istanbul. After the submission of this petition and the passage thereafter of another two weeks without any answer, the heads of the community turned to Rabbi Hayim Nahum, who had just been appointed *ḥakham bashi* in Istanbul. Rabbi Nahum appealed in turn to the minister of justice, who, fearing the outbreak of riots in Jewish communities throughout the empire, asked Rabbi Nahum to instruct that Rabbi Alfandari be suspended from his position in Damascus, along with rabbis in various other communities, pending the conclusion of an investigation. This was consistent with the Young Turks' practice of deposing those officials and religious figures who were perceived as supporters of the *ancien régime*, without hesitation and without consultation. Nahum himself, meanwhile, decided to go beyond the removal of particular chief rabbis and to implement far-reaching steps to provide a general solution for such problems. His intention was to appoint in every community a board that would agree on the election of a chief rabbi. A delegation from Istanbul was sent to examine the complaints against the rabbis whose deposition had been requested and to supervise the elections for their replacements. In this manner Rabbi Nahum began to establish control over what was done in Jewish communities throughout the empire.[108]

In Damascus, Rabbi Nahum appointed Yitshak Abulafia to replace the *ḥakham bashi* until the investigating committee could determine whether or

[107] ACRI, TR/Is/164*a*, people of Damascus to Rabbi Hayim Nahum, Damascus, 4 Elul 5668.

[108] Ibid., Rabbi Yitshak Abulafia to Rabbi Hayim Nahum, Damascus, 8 Elul 5668; *JC*, 4 Sept. 1908, p. 9; *Hashkafah*, 103 (20 Elul 5668), 2. Cf. Benbassa, *Hayim Nahum* (Heb.), 149.

not there was any truth in the allegations against Alfandari.[109] The reappointment of Rabbi Abulafia, a figure from the old establishment, could hardly be seen as revolutionary—but neither did it represent a return to the old ways. Under the inspiration of the revolution, and with the encouragement of educated young people within the community, Rabbi Abulafia took steps to reform its administrative framework. He organized a process for the election of a communal board of ten members. Several of those elected had previously been members of the Pikuah Nefashot society, the most important charitable organization within the community. Moses Totah was elected president; the others chosen included Joseph Laniado, Mordecai (Murad) Moses Farhi, David Kamkhaji, Aaron Yedid-Halevi, Joseph Abadi, and the Alliance's representative in Damascus, Nisim Farhi.[110] It should not be inferred from the familiarity of some of these names that they represented a return to influence of the old elites. The Farhi family, for example, had lost all its money years earlier; now, it was left with nothing but its name. More significant are some of the new names—Totah, Abadi, Kamkhaji, and Yedid-Halevi. It would seem that opening up the selection of the community leadership to all sectors of the public was a revolutionary step symbolizing the total disappearance of the old moneyed elite. The inclusion on the new board of a representative of the Alliance was particularly significant in this respect.

But the storm was not yet over. The investigating committee from Istanbul failed to arrive, giving Rabbi Alfandari and his few supporters the opportunity to ignore the instructions of Rabbi Nahum regarding his removal. He approached the governor with complaints about the election of the new communal board and publicly declared that he was not required to obey the directives of Rabbi Nahum. He claimed that, as he had received an official writ of appointment from the sultan, the sultan alone could depose him. For their part, the Torah scholars, no longer feeling intimidated by Alfandari, recanted past agreements and even halakhic rulings in which they had accepted the opinion of the forceful *ḥakham bashi*. In response, one of Rabbi Alfandari's supporters published articles in the local press criticizing the entire group of Torah scholars, thereby taking an internal Jewish debate beyond the boundaries of the community into the realm of general public discourse in Damascus. Alfandari himself attempted to bolster his own position by refusing to allow Rabbi Abulafia or the new board to use money

[109] ACRI, TR/Is/164*a*, Abulafia to Hayim Nahum, Damascus, 17 Elul 5668; AAIU, Syrie, XV.E., Damas, 142*a*, Farhi, 3 Nov. 1908.

[110] AAIU, Syrie, XV.E., Damas, 142*b*, Farhi, 3 Nov. 1908; ACRI, TR/Is/164*a*, Abulafia to Hayim Nahum, Damascus, 22 Elul 5668.

from the *gabilah* or other sources to finance the needs of the community.[111] In response to this, and in order to prevent Alfandari from arrogating to himself control of communal funds, the young people of the community sought to close the synagogues and to gather up all the knives used for kosher slaughtering, but Rabbi Abulafia dissuaded them from taking such drastic steps.[112]

It soon became clear to everyone that Rabbi Yitshak Abulafia's term in office could only be temporary. Although the office of *ḥakham bashi* was formally occupied, throughout the months that followed the deposition of Rabbi Alfandari the Damascus community remained without a spiritual or political leader. The communal board, hampered by the obstacles Alfandari had put in its way, was unable to bring about any improvement in communal administration. The deposed Rabbi Alfandari himself remained in the city for three more years without any official position and continued to cause difficulties within the community.[113] Rabbi Abulafia was by now over 80 years old; his contemporaries described him as an old man with poor sight, whose legs were barely able to carry him. In November 1909, about a year after his return to the position of chief rabbi of Damascus, Rabbi Abulafia left the city, expressing a desire to end his life in the city of his forefathers, Tiberias, where he died shortly thereafter, on 15 Adar II 5670 (26 March 1910).[114]

This left a leadership vacuum in Damascus. What the community needed at this point was a leader of spiritual stature and political talents, in order to put it back on the right path—especially given that, in wake of the revolution, many changes had been made in the administrative, legal, and political system of the city. Sadly, none among the few learned rabbis who remained in Damascus was capable of redeeming the community from its miserable situation.

[111] AAIU, Syrie, XV.E., Damas, 142*b*, Farhi, 13 Dec. 1908. For an example of Torah scholars recanting their halakhic agreement with Rabbi Alfandari, see Maslaton, *She'erit yehudah*, 72–3.

[112] ACRI, TR/Is/164*a*, 'Speakers of Truth' to Rabbi Hayim Nahum, Damascus, 11 Elul 5668. Strikes of this type, intended to deprive the chief rabbinate of its main income, took place immediately after the revolution in the community of Istanbul. See Benbassa, *Ottoman Jewry* (Heb.), 35–7.

[113] In Adar 5669 (1909), Rabbi Alfandari was still in Damascus. Only in the autumn of 1911 was he appointed rabbi of the Sephardi community in Safed. See *Haḥerut*, 136 (16 Aug. 1911), 2; 138 (21 Aug. 1911), 3; 144 (30 Aug. 1911), 3.

[114] AAIU, Syrie, XV.E., Damas, 142*b*, Farhi, 7 Jan. 1910; ACRI, TR/Is/63, heads of the community in Damascus to Rabbi Hayim Nahum, Damascus, 12 Tevet 5670. *Haḥerut*, reported that Rabbi Yitshak Abulafia returned from Damascus to Tiberias in his old age, when he was 87, where he took up residence in the home of Rabbi Jacob Moses Toledano (*Haḥerut*, 34 (15 Dec. 1909), 2).

CHAPTER NINE

Jacob Danon's Appointment as Chief Rabbi of Damascus and its Consequences

> Rabbi Abba son of Kahana said: When the elders were appointed, all Israel lit candles and rejoiced in them. Miriam saw the candles burning and asked Zipporah: What is the meaning of these candles? She told her what it was about. Miriam said: Happy are the wives of these people, whose husbands have ascended to positions of honour. Zipporah replied to her: Woe to them!
>
> *Yalkut shimoni*, 'Beha'alotekha'

Rabbi Hayim Nahum's Visit to Damascus

During the spring of 1910, having consolidated his position as *ḥakham bashi* in Istanbul, Rabbi Nahum resumed in earnest his reorganization of the rabbinic leadership throughout the communities of the Ottoman empire, a task he had begun two years earlier. His aim was to appoint rabbis who would be amenable to the norms and demands of the new rule. He may also have wished to entrench his centralized control over the network of rabbis throughout the empire by appointing men who would owe their office to him, rather than to the *ancien régime*. Many communities within the empire had experienced struggles over the rabbinate; among them was Jerusalem, which over time had become progressively weaker as a political centre of Judaism, and to a certain extent also as a centre of excellence in Torah—a fact which enabled Rabbi Nahum to promote Istanbul as a strong alternative. He called upon those communities in which there had been difficulties surrounding appointments to rabbinic office to convene their institutions and to elect new rabbis of the type described in the contemporary press as enlightened, educated, and non-fanatical. This call was coupled with an open threat that any community failing to comply with this instruction would be isolated from other communities in the empire, and that it and its institutions would not be recognized by the authorities.[1]

Rabbi Nahum gave the leading members of the Damascus community a list of three candidates from among the rabbis of Jerusalem and asked them to choose the one they deemed most suitable to serve as their chief rabbi. So weak was the Damascus community at this point, and so unwilling were its members to take responsibility for their own destiny, that they had no local spiritual and political leader of any stature who could take such an office upon himself. This weakness and passivity were further demonstrated in the response to Rabbi Nahum's shortlist: the Damascus community asked that the *ḥakham bashi* choose a suitable rabbi on their behalf, as they were not acquainted with the candidates or their qualifications. Nothing could have indicated more strikingly the isolation of Damascus from Jerusalem, so close physically, but so distant spiritually, were the two communities.[2]

The priority for the people of Damascus in the selection of their new *ḥakham bashi* was that he should possess political talents and the ability to deal with the Ottoman officials; Torah erudition, they felt, was much less important. Moreover, the leaders and sages of the community were well aware of the need to limit the power and authority of the *ḥakham bashi* chosen. They wished to strengthen their own authority, so as to serve as a counterweight to the *ḥakham bashi* and to create an impression of strength in the eyes of the community as a whole—as well as in those of government officials. To this end, they urged Rabbi Nahum to obtain official recognition for the communal board in the form of an official firman for the organization.[3]

In the summer of 1910 Rabbi Nahum set out on a tour of the communities of the Middle East—among other reasons, in order to observe more closely the problems of leadership and discipline and, by the very fact of his presence, to help resolve them.[4] On Sunday 3 July, travelling from Haifa, Rabbi Nahum arrived at the railway station some four hours' travelling time distant from Damascus, where a reception was held for him and his entourage, in the presence of communal leaders and dignitaries, headed by Hayim Moses Laniado and Moses (Moussa) Totah, accompanied by the headmaster of the Alliance school, Nisim Farhi. When the *ḥakham bashi* reached Damascus itself, he was greeted as befitted a figure bearing the approbation of

[1] *JC*, 3 Sept. 1901, p. 8*b*. On Rabbi Nahum's push to increase centralization, see Benbassa, *Ottoman Jewry* (Heb.), 68–9.

[2] ACRI, TR/Is/63, heads of the Damascus community and its rabbis to Rabbi Hayim Nahum, Damascus, 12 Tevet 5670.

[3] Ibid.

[4] On the motivations of the journey, its course, and its results, see Benbassa, *Ottoman Jewry* (Heb.), 70–6; and cf. Harshoshanim-Breitbart, 'The Journey of the *Ḥakham Bashi*' (Heb.).

the new regime in Istanbul, with a further and more elaborate reception in his honour. Those present here included the governor, foreign consuls, leaders of other religious faiths, dignitaries of the city, representatives of the ruling Committee of Union and Progress, and heads of the educational institutions in the city, among others. Numerous speeches were delivered, and in his response the chief rabbi—speaking in Turkish—extravagantly praised the constitution introduced by the new regime, and elaborated upon the hopes vested in it for the future, both for the Jews and for the empire as a whole.[5]

Rabbi Nahum was shocked by the state of the Damascus community, particularly its problem of prostitution, and may even have feared its potential to taint the image of Jewry in the empire as a whole.[6] He therefore viewed the appointment at its head of a rabbi with strong leadership abilities as an overriding imperative. Rabbi Nahum's right-hand man at that time was Abraham Almaleh, editor of the Jerusalem newspaper *Ḥaḥerut* and son-in-law of one of the candidates for *ḥakham bashi* in Damascus—Rabbi Jacob Danon. Almaleh knew that his father-in-law was on Rabbi Nahum's shortlist, and certainly had the opportunity to promote his appointment. While we can never definitively know to what extent he was motivated by family considerations as well as the welfare of the Damascus community, it would appear that Almaleh believed with all sincerity that his father-in-law was the right person in the right place at the right time, and that he was the individual who would best be able to rebuild the Damascus community and to bring it closer to the Zionist project gradually taking shape in Palestine.

Rabbi Jacob Danon was born in Bosnia in 1855 and educated in various Sephardi yeshivas in Jerusalem. He was appointed a member of the rabbinic court of the Sephardi congregation, and for many years served as a rabbinic emissary throughout Africa and Asia. In 1891, for example, he was sent on behalf of the Ezrat Nidahim society to gather money to build a settlement for immigrants from Yemen in the Silwan village near Jerusalem.[7] In the middle of August 1910 he left Jerusalem for Damascus.[8] The Jews of the city, rendered cautious by their bitter experience of previous appointments, set various conditions for the new incumbent. First, he needed to ensure that the community could take advantage of the new opportunities for freedom and equality opened up to the Jews by the revolution. This required that he main-

[5] FO 618/3, 'General Report for June Quarter, Damascus', 12 July 1910; AAIU, XV.E., Damas, 142*b*, Farhi, 8 July 1910.

[6] On Rabbi Nahum's shock at this 'shame' in Damascus, as he put it, see the interview he gave to the press upon his return from his trip: *JC*, 9 Sept. 1910, p. 12*b*.

[7] See the entry on him in Gaon, *The Jews of the East* (Heb.), 212.

[8] ACRI, TR/Is/63, Rabbi Jacob Danon to Rabbi Hayim Nahum, Jerusalem, 7 Tamuz 5670.

tain close links with the government, which in turn meant he had to be fluent in the vernacular, in order to converse freely with government officials. Second, the president of the new community board, Moses Totah, asked Rabbi Nahum to clarify the legal position of the board and to have it formally recognized by the government. Simultaneously, he requested that Rabbi Jacob Danon himself be appointed only as acting *ḥakham bashi*.[9] Even after it became clear that Rabbi Danon met all the requirements of the community —making a great impression, for example, in his courtesy calls on the *wali*— the heads of the community made it clear that they would give him a trial period of two months, and only thereafter would the final decision be made whether or not to appoint him as permanent head of the community.[10]

Well aware of the parlous state of the Damascus community, Rabbi Danon set out his terms. He would give the community a trial period of three months, and only thereafter would he make his final decision whether or not to stay in Damascus. Upon Rabbi Danon's hearing of his selection as head of the Damascus community, he hastened to ask the *ḥakham bashi* in Istanbul to inform the governor of Damascus of his appointment and to ask the latter to provide him with assistance and support.[11] The rabbi arrived in Damascus by himself, without his family, and stayed there for three months. Throughout this time he was a guest in the home of Hayim Moses Laniado, one of the two senior leaders of the community, and from there he began to reorganize its institutions. It would appear that his choice of lodgings was consciously made. Laniado was the son-in-law of Rabbi Yitshak Abulafia; his willingness to host the man who was to succeed his father-in-law as chief rabbi amounted to a declaration of support for the new leader.[12] Indeed, Rabbi Danon rapidly endeared himself to the leaders of the community and won their trust. Once it became evident that he was already acting tirelessly to improve community life in all areas, the members of the board agreed to appoint him as *ḥakham bashi* for two years. Moses Totah, however, the president of the board, did not wait until the end of this trial period, but asked Rabbi Nahum to appoint Jacob Danon as permanent *ḥakham bashi* of Damascus.[13] The official firman of appointment was issued in December 1910, backdated to his arrival in

[9] Ibid., Moussa Totah to Rabbi Hayim Nahum, Damascus, 22 July 1910.

[10] *Ha'or*, 162 (14 Elul 5670), 2.

[11] ACRI, TR/Is/63, Rabbi Jacob Danon to Rabbi Hayim Nahum, [Jerusalem], 13 Av 5670.

[12] For a comprehensive description of how Rabbi Danon ran the affairs of the community from Laniado's house, see JMA, Yishuv Yashan, 63, Hayim Moses Laniado to Rabbi Raphael Aaron ben Shimon, rabbi of Cairo, Damascus, 24 Shevat 5671.

[13] ACRI, TR/Is/63, Moussa Totah to Rabbi Moses Hayim Nahum, Damascus, 29 Sept. 1910; *JC*, 21 Oct. 1910, p. 10*a*.

Damascus and accompanied by all the ceremonial trappings—the medal of honour, the robes of office, and a turban from the sultan.[14]

Rabbi Danon's official appointment, achieved through the agency of the *ḥakham bashi* in Istanbul, transformed Damascus from an isolated community to one that enjoyed ties with the wider Jewish world. For the first time, after centuries during which its closest links had been with Tiberias and Jerusalem, it was now connected primarily to the centre of Ottoman rule in Istanbul. In this respect, it contributed to Rabbi Nahum's overall goal of making the rabbinate in Istanbul the centre to which all the chief rabbis of other communities looked—which they did all the more assiduously, given that they were personally indebted to him for their appointments.[15] Until the First World War, connections with Erets Yisra'el and the reinvigorated Zionist settlement there were relatively weak, although they became somewhat stronger a year after Rabbi Danon's arrival in Damascus when his son-in-law, Abraham Almaleh, was appointed in the new position of secretary of the community and headmaster of the Hebrew National School in Damascus.

Initiative for a Moral Revolution

Rabbi Danon's appointment as chief rabbi of the Damascus community met with virtually universal approval. Exercising unchallenged authority, he succeeded in mediating and making peace among the various factions within the congregation. Finally, after so many years, it began to seem that it would be possible to concentrate upon the true problems of the community—first and foremost, that of prostitution.

The phenomenon of prostitution in the Jewish quarter and among Jewish girls amounted to a plague which cast its shadow over all aspects of Jewish life in the city. Solving this problem was a precondition for success in all the new chief rabbi's other goals—restoration of the institutional framework of the community, strengthening the community's political status in the eyes of the government, and improving the communal system of education.

Rabbi Danon understood that the prostitutes' way of life, which combined religious orthodoxy with relaxed sexual morals, offered him a means of applying pressure on them. He issued a broadsheet stating that anyone who engaged in prostitution would not be buried in a Jewish grave. This threat was even extended to include close relatives of prostitutes. That this was

[14] *Haḥerut*, 33 (6 Jan. 1911), 2; Almaleh, *The Jews in Damascus* (Heb.), 38. On Almaleh's involvement in obtaining the firman and the letters of honour, see JMA, Yishuv Yashan, 63, Jacob Danon to Abraham Almaleh, Damascus, 28 Kislev 5671.

[15] See e.g. ACRI, TR/Is/160*a*, Rabbi Jacob Danon to Rabbi Hayim Nahum, Damascus, 11 Adar 5672.

no empty threat was demonstrated when one of the wealthiest prostitutes in the city died: the *ḥakham bashi* refused to allow her burial in a Jewish grave despite the imprecations of members of her family and their promise to contribute large sums of money to the communal coffers. Not even the intervention of government ministers and senior officials could change the rabbi's mind; and so, according to the testimony of contemporaries, the prostitute was 'buried as the burial of a donkey'. The shame of this made a deep impression. More than a few prostitutes abandoned their degrading profession, while others left the city.[16] Rabbi Danon had withstood this first challenge to his authority and had at the same time proved his seriousness and determination to act for the recovery of the community.

Parallel to this, Rabbi Danon informed the communal board of his intention to impose the *ḥerem*, the rabbinic ban, upon those women who continued to work as prostitutes, as well as on those relatives who assisted them. The prostitutes were given two months' notice of the imminent ban, during which they could either abandon their profession or leave the Jewish quarter; then, on Thursday 24 November 1910, the *ḥerem* came into force. Relatives of the prostitutes, many of whom were also their employers, reacted with outrage, and the community was immediately plunged into uproar; but the number of 'singers' fell further.

Rabbi Danon's firmness of purpose, and his ability to withstand the numerous pressures applied to him, relied to a considerable extent upon the support of the governor, Isma'il Pasha. Without this, indeed, the rabbi's edicts would have been to no avail. As it was, the enlightened governor signed without hesitation every order sent to him for approval by the chief rabbi regarding the restriction of prostitution in the Jewish quarter, and government officials and the police were ordered to assist in executing these orders. Thus, for example, on the day that the *ḥerem* was declared, policemen were sent to protect the central synagogue.[17] Isma'il Pasha also issued a comprehensive directive to close all the brothels in the Jewish quarter and to remove the prostitutes from the district. In the wake of a petition submitted in January 1911 by the Jewish community, concerned that prostitution was turning the quarter into a dangerous area at night, an order was given to the police not to allow non-Jews to enter the quarter during the hours of darkness. Once Muslim and Christian customers ceased to visit the Jewish quarter, many more of the prostitutes left.

[16] ACRI, TR/Is/72*a*, Rabbi Jacob Danon to Rabbi Hayim Nahum, Damascus, 29 Av 5671; *Ḥaḥerut*, 33 (6 Jan. 1911), 2.

[17] ACRI, TR/Is/72*a*, Rabbi Jacob Danon to Rabbi Hayim Nahum, Damascus, 29 Heshvan 5671.

These steps were of great importance in improving the image and status of the Jewish quarter and its inhabitants. Rabbi Danon himself testified that his efforts to raise the moral level of the Jewish quarter were welcomed not only by the Jews themselves, but also by the surrounding society. According to him, there were senior officials in Damascus 'whose sons squandered their money in such evil ways, thereby making our holy nation an object of curses in their mouths, and now they acknowledge and bless us'.[18] He described the day on which the ban was declared upon the prostitutes and their supporters:

> A great and awesome day, when the name of Israel was sanctified in the eyes of all the nations—so much so that even the head of the Christian religion (the Patriarch) preached in his church that they could only envy the dignity of the Jewish people, who were advancing the honour of their people and their religion, so much so that one cannot describe in words or speech how great was our honour in the eyes of the nations.[19]

Nevertheless, Rabbi Danon's campaign to rid the community of prostitution encountered numerous obstacles, notwithstanding the governor's support. One of the main problems lay in the relations established over the years between the prostitutes and members of the city police, many of whom enjoyed the women's favours in exchange for turning a blind eye to their activities. The elimination of prostitution from the Jewish quarter would also mean significant financial loss to the police, who received payments from many of the participants in the quarrels and fights that were constantly breaking out in the taverns and brothels of the quarter in exchange for their silence. Muslim policemen and Jewish prostitutes thus joined forces against those who sought to remove the sex trade from the streets of the Jewish quarter. Prostitutes began to make false accusations against the dignitaries of the community, alleging that these men had hit and cursed them.

Fearing that the campaign against prostitution might eventually be defeated owing to this lack of co-operation, even active obstruction, on the part of the police, the *ḥakham bashi* and the communal committee turned to Rabbi Nahum, asking him to use his influence on the governor to urge continued support for their activities, and to ensure that letters were sent from the ministers of police and justice to the police commanders and judges in Damascus requiring them to assist in cleaning up the Jewish quarter.[20] Unfortunately, about six months after Rabbi Danon's arrival in Damascus, Isma'il Pasha was transferred to another province. His replacement as governor, Galib Pasha, is described by his contemporaries as an honest and upright man, but unlike his

[18] ACRI, TR/Is/72*a*, Rabbi Jacob Danon to Rabbi Hayim Nahum, Damascus, 29 Heshvan 5671. [19] Ibid. [20] Ibid.

predecessor he was lacking in initiative and in the drive to assist the Jewish leaders in uprooting the problem. Those senior officials in the imperial administration 'who had always been the central pillars upon which the "singers" and women of ill-fame relied',[21] resumed their attempts to undermine the steps taken against prostitution. The prohibition upon non-Jews entering the Jewish quarter at night was not properly enforced. The police knew that drunken and armed Muslims and Christians were in the habit of knocking upon the doors and windows of Jews at all hours of the night, looking for women and beating the men; at times they even broke into Jewish homes and assaulted the women inside. Some Jews who dared to protect themselves were accused by the prostitutes of attacking them, arrested and thrown into prison without trial. Others, including several members of the communal council, were falsely accused of assault by prostitutes and forced to flee Damascus out of fear of the police.[22] The gravity of the situation is clearly apparent from a letter Rabbi Danon wrote to the *ḥakham bashi* in Istanbul:

> During these days, the days of *seliḥot*, nearly all the synagogues are empty because the beadles do not go out at night to awaken the Jews, out of the fear that they may be beaten by the evil men and drunkards who fill all the streets at night after leaving the houses of the 'singers', so that nobody dare endanger his life to go out alone at night; and it is intolerable for such a situation to continue.[23]

In view of this situation, in October 1911, Rabbi Danon and the secretary of the community, Abraham Almaleh, arranged to meet the new governor of the district, Galib Pasha, in the latter's palace. The three men discussed at length the situation of the Jews in Damascus, focusing particularly on the issue of prostitution. Prior to the meeting a memorandum had been brought to the governor, signed by hundreds of members of the Jewish community, calling upon him to put an end to this scandalous phenomenon. Members of the community also committed themselves to buying the property of prostitutes who were expelled, so that they would no longer have any excuse for remaining in or returning to the Jewish quarter.

During their talks, it became clear to the chief rabbi and his secretary that their worst fears had been realized: the phenomenon of Jewish prostitution had indeed besmirched the reputation of the Jewish community as a whole. The *wali* noted the difference between modest Muslim women, who did not speak with strangers, and Jewish women, who freely admitted into their

[21] Ibid., Rabbi Jacob Danon to Rabbi Hayim Nahum, Damascus, 22 Av 5671.
[22] Ibid. TR/Is/160*a*, Rabbi Jacob Danon to Rabbi Hayim Nahum, Damascus, 9 Sept. 1911.
[23] Ibid. TR/Is/72*a*, Rabbi Jacob Danon to Rabbi Hayim Nahum, Damascus, 8 Elul 5671.

homes what he referred to as 'friends and companions'. Rabbi Danon was deeply insulted by the comparison, and wrote later to the chief rabbi of Istanbul that 'by this reply he evidently wished to imply that all the Jewish women in Damascus are prostitutes'.[24] In addition to this religious insult, there was also a national dimension to the issue, to which Almaleh, who had initiated Zionist activity in Damascus, was especially sensitive: he sought to remove the plague of prostitution in particular because it was inconsistent with the idea of national renewal and the building of an ideal moral society in Palestine.

Danon and Almaleh reiterated their demand that the governor act more firmly to remove the prostitutes from the Jewish quarter, hinting that the government officials subject to him were not carrying out his orders owing to their own personal connections with the prostitutes. Galib Pasha, in an attempt to prove that he had a firm hold on the reins of authority, ordered the head of police summoned to him immediately and, in the presence of Rabbi Danon, chastised him for his laxity in carrying out his orders.

Prostitutes nevertheless continued to work in the Jewish quarter without any interference on the part of the authorities; in fact, the governor himself was among the first to prevent any real action being taken against them. Almaleh records that Galib Pasha feared chaos would break out in Damascus were the Jewish prostitutes to be removed from the city. By contrast, Rabbi Danon suspected that the sudden change in the *wali*'s behaviour was the result of bribes he had received from the prostitutes.[25] Frustrated at the governor's failure to act effectively, the heads of the Damascus Jewish community decided to turn to every possible authority to protest against the situation that was being allowed to persist in their district. Petitions were accordingly sent to the interior ministry and the justice ministry, to the central government, to the grand vizier, and even to the sultan himself.[26]

During this same year, a report was published in the Istanbul newspaper *L'Aurore* concerning Jewish prostitution in Damascus, provoking a very strong response in both the Jewish and the non-Jewish public. Several Turkish newspapers protested against the failure of the local authorities to act more effectively to eliminate the phenomenon. Rabbi Nahum—who was well acquainted with the situation, not least from the many letters on the sub-

[24] ACRI, TR/Is/160*a*, Rabbi Jacob Danon to Rabbi Hayim Nahum, Damascus, 27 Oct. 1911.

[25] *Haḥerut*, 158 (19 Sept. 1911), title page; ACRI, TR/Is/160*a*, Rabbi Jacob Danon to Rabbi Hayim Nahum, Damascus, 4 Kislev 5672; *JC*, 15 Sept. 1911, p. 12*a*.

[26] ACRI, TR/Is/72*a*, Rabbi Jacob Danon to Rabbi Hayim Nahum, 15 Elul 5671; ibid., TR/Is/160*a*, Rabbi Jacob Danon to Rabbi Hayim Nahum, 4 Kislev 5672.

ject he had received from Rabbi Danon—and the steering committee of the Jewish community of Istanbul now turned to the government authorities, asking them to order the governor of Damascus to act. In response, the interior minister instructed Galib Pasha to remove the brothels from the Jewish quarter to some other venue.[27]

And yet, despite this directive, and despite the appeals to the minister of justice, prostitutes remained in the Jewish quarter, and the authorities did not lift a finger to remove them. The *wali* preferred to close his eyes to the reality of the situation, claiming that it was only possible to expel licensed prostitutes from the Jewish quarter, whereas most of the 'singing women' were not licensed. Moreover, in response to the directive from the minister of the interior, the prostitutes themselves turned to the local authorities with the claim that the law prohibited their moving from one place to another—a complaint that even enjoyed the backing of some Jews within the quarter.

What had seemed a united front in the battle against prostitution in the Jewish quarter had fractured. Matters reached a head when those opposed to the abolition of prostitution in the community questioned the leadership of Rabbi Danon and the official institutions of the community, and even attempted to create alternative institutions in order to take the sting out of the threat of *ḥerem*. Among other things, they established *beit midrashim*—small new study houses and synagogues. In one case, a Jewish procurer even attacked Rabbi Danon: 'And he cursed and maligned me within my own home while holding a pistol in his hand. And he also cursed and maligned the firman and the sultan who gave the firman—and all this in the presence of other people.'[28] Improbable as it may seem, the supporters of prostitution, like the prostitutes themselves, sought to draw a distinction between their religious faith, including the observance of commandments, and their support of this blatant breach of Jewish morality. It would seem that they viewed prostitution as at most a minor transgression. According to Almaleh, 'among these lowly creatures prayer was one thing and lust a separate one. They adhered to the rule: "Hold firm to this, and from that as well do not withhold your hand" [Eccles. 7: 18]'.[29]

The identity of those Jews who wanted to keep the prostitutes in the Jewish quarter is well known; many of them earned their livelihood from the trade. First and foremost were the relatives of the prostitutes who lived off their profits; then there were also the owners of kiosks selling drinks to the women's clients, and those who rented the women apartments and rooms,

[27] *Ha'or*, 3 (13 Tishrei 5672), 3.
[28] ACRI, TR/Is/72*a*, Rabbi Jacob Danon to Rabbi Hayim Nahum, Damascus, 30 Av 5671.
[29] Almaleh, *The Jews in Damascus* (Heb.), 28.

who also stood to lose out financially from the rule preventing non-Jews from entering the quarter. In response to Rabbi Danon's complaint about the activities of these people, Rabbi Nahum issued an official order that the new *beit midrashim* would not be recognized by the authorities until they agreed to submit to the local rabbinic court. Rabbi Danon himself took drastic steps against the Jewish men related to or working with the prostitutes: he prohibited the *mohalim* from circumcising their children; he prohibited the butchers from selling them kosher meat; and he declared that their dead would not be interred in Jewish graves. Those prostitutes who declared their intention of leaving their profession were required to lodge large sums of money with the rabbinate as a bond to guarantee that they would not return to their old ways.

The campaign undertaken by Rabbi Danon and his supporters against prostitution in the Jewish quarter, as a first step towards rehabilitating the community and undertaking its general reorganization, was partially successful, in that it did somewhat reduce the number of prostitutes in the quarter. But the phenomenon was not eliminated, and indeed after a fairly short time it had grown back to its previous dimensions. Just a year after taking up office as *ḥakham bashi* in Damascus, Jacob Danon was almost defeated by the problem of the 'singers' and its consequences, to the point that he threatened Rabbi Hayim Nahum with his resignation.[30]

Even when brothels were reopened on the periphery of the city during the summer of 1913, the Damascus authorities refused to remove the Jewish prostitutes from the Jewish quarter—despite explicit orders to do so from the government in Istanbul, and despite the fact that other prostitutes, who had worked in the Christian and Muslim quarters, were forced to move to the new location. The First World War, during which Damascus became a major military centre, only exacerbated the problem of prostitution, so that it continued to cast a shadow over the Jewish community of Damascus during the war years and thereafter.[31]

Prostitution may have been the most urgent problem facing Rabbi Danon, but it was far from the only one, albeit the most fundamental. He also needed to rebuild the institutional framework of the community, which had collapsed years before his arrival in Damascus.

[30] ACRI, TR/Is/72*a*, Rabbi Jacob Danon to Rabbi Hayim Nahum, Damascus, 22 Av 5671, 15 Elul 5671.

[31] On the continuation, and continued failure, of attempts to remove the 'singing women' from the Jewish quarter, see ibid., TR/Is/81*a*, Rabbi Jacob Danon to Rabbi Hayim Nahum, Damascus, 17 Elul 5673, 29 Tishrei 5674.

Establishing an Institutional Framework

As previous chapters of this book have described, the Jewish institutional framework in Damascus was marked by instability, much of it arising from power struggles between the various wealthy families and their supporters. Abraham Almaleh, comparing community life in Damascus to the Zionist renaissance in Palestine, describes it as follows:

There is not a single city in all of Syria and Erets Yisra'el in which mutual hatred by man of his fellow is as deeply rooted as it is among the Jews of Damascus. The attitude of negation and lack of fellowship are the two characteristics most typical of the Jews of Damascus. The members of Family A look from on high on the members of Family B, while those of Family B negate as the dust of the earth all the acts of Family A. And when someone comes along and establishes a new institution, Family X comes along and derides its value as if it were a worthless broken pot and dismisses its originators as 'negligible'. And the results of all this are jealousy, hatred, and each man eating the flesh of his neighbour . . . You can do great and wonderful things for the welfare of the community . . . and the entire people from one end to the other will thank you, and will heap upon you words of praise and honour—but do not touch their pocket, and do not ask for money for help. Hence, there is no orderly and properly organized Jewish congregation in Damascus, but rather a collection of people who live together without any connection among them, who are unable to stand up for themselves and for their honour. Therefore the [number of] poor people grows, and they drown in poverty and lack, and the community does not lift the smallest finger to raise the level of the people.[32]

Modern critics, of Abraham Almaleh's type frequently tend to exaggerate the gravity of the situation they describe in order to convince their readers of the importance of their project. But even with this caveat, our own knowledge of the Damascus community suggests that, on this occasion at least, Almaleh's bleak description was no exaggeration, and his sharp criticism not unwarranted. There was indeed no tradition of organized communal institutions or of the addressing of communal needs by elected boards in the Damascus community. When a communal board was set up following the economic crash of 1875, it did not last long, dissolving itself shortly after its establishment. Twenty years later, Rabbi Alfandari chose to run the community throughout his term as *ḥakham bashi* without sharing responsibility with the prominent laymen. This being the case, to describe Rabbi Danon's activity in this area as 'reconstruction' or 'rebuilding' is rather wide of the mark: it is more appropriate to talk of 'establishment', that is, building an entire system from ground level up.

[32] Almaleh, *The Jews in Damascus* (Heb.), 26.

Rabbi Jacob Danon both stood at the head of the communal hierarchy and represented the community before the government. It is important to remember that he arrived in Damascus as a kind of knight in shining armour, and thus enjoyed a special status from the very beginning. His prestige increased further once his position as *ḥakham bashi* received the recognition of the Ottoman authorities, and as it became evident to the elite that the rabbi who had just arrived from Jerusalem was possessed of just those talents required to bring about the sorely needed revolution within the community. The formal system of community administration had been established by the Jewish millet decree of 1864–5: the taxpayers elected a general assembly of seventy members, headed by the chief rabbi, and this group in turn chose from among its number a steering committee of nine members which sat for a fixed term of two years. Alongside the steering committee there was a spiritual committee, responsible for all the religious affairs of the community.[33] However, whereas in many communities the head of the spiritual committee also sat as head of the rabbinic court, in Damascus the rabbinic court was presided over by the chief rabbi—a practice that had its roots in the generally low level of Torah scholarship, and now seemed particularly apposite in view of the new incumbent's illustrious reputation in Torah. These arrangements, long in abeyance and existing on paper only, were now put into practical effect by the new *ḥakham bashi*. The fact that Rabbi Danon arrived crowned with the halo of a redeemer, coupled with the backing he enjoyed from the authorities, made it possible for him to concentrate the political, material, and spiritual leadership of the community in his hands.

These developments are of far-reaching significance. In the distant past, the authority and coercive power of both the spiritual and secular leadership had derived from the willingness of members of the community to submit themselves to it in accordance with Torah law, even if the leadership on occasion resorted to external means of enforcement through the imperial authorities. However, in the more recent past—that is, from the middle of the nineteenth century, when implementation of the Ottoman Jewish millet decree began—the Jewish authorities had come to depend on the government authorities as well as on communal recognition for their power. Now, under Rabbi Danon, a new situation took shape in which the government authorities were the *main* source of power. The new community structures were not sufficiently well established to serve as a source of support for the chief rabbi; thus, rather than the rabbi relying upon the community, the community relied upon the rabbi. When the *ḥakham bashi* encountered a viola-

[33] Almaleh, *The Jews in Damascus* (Heb.), 38.

tion of accepted communal norms, he did not hesitate to respond by calling on the government's means of coercion, such as the police, as in the fight against prostitution. After the revolution of the Young Turks and the promulgation of the constitution that sought to bring new order to the institutions of the empire, such an approach was no longer considered extraordinary. On the contrary: it was expected that the *ḥakham bashi*—who was a representative of, indeed an integral part of, the government—would implement the power he had derived from the government in the interests of the community. Nevertheless, as the community was essentially conservative, Rabbi Danon continued to use traditional means of enforcement as well, such as the threat of withholding religious services from those who violated community norms and regulations. This would suggest that, at the beginning of the second decade of the twentieth century, the Jews in Damascus did not have any alternative social framework. The reference group of the individual Jew continued to be the Jewish community alone, and consciousness of the religious identity of the individual and of the group was very high. Thus, in Damascus the phenomenon of secularization had not yet borne any ideological fruit.

By the time he had been in post about a year, during which he had become only too well aware of the complexities and problems of the Damascus community, particularly those stemming from prostitution, Rabbi Danon realized that it would be difficult for him to effect a significant transformation in the life of the community by himself. This being the case, with the encouragement of young people of Hebrew nationalist inclinations, he took a calculated political step and summoned his son-in-law, Abraham Almaleh, who at the time was headmaster of the Jewish day school in the Galata neighbourhood of Istanbul, to come to Damascus and serve alongside him as secretary of the community.[34] Almaleh—who was young, educated, talented, and an enthusiastic Zionist—took up his new position in August 1911 and set about assisting in the reconstruction of the Damascus community. His arrival gave a new momentum to the reorganization of the communal institutions.

For the first time in the history of the community, an annual budget was drawn up based on a calculation of estimated income against expenses. The income of the community derived from two main sources: the individual tax, imposed upon every Jew demonstrably capable of earning a living, and the meat tax (*gabilah*). After the bankruptcy of 1875 there was a sharp decrease in income from the individual tax. Were any further proof needed of Rabbi Danon's power and ability to change old arrangements and accepted traditions, it may be found in his decision that the individual tax would henceforth

[34] *Haḥerut*, 152 (14 Sept. 1911), title page.

apply also to those few foreign citizens who remained in Damascus, who until then had been exempt from community taxes. The steering committee set up an 'appraisal' (*arikha*) subcommittee to determine the amount of tax to be imposed upon each individual within the community. The tax itself was progressive, and was fixed at five levels to reflect the income and property holdings of taxpayers. To ensure that justice was both done and seen to be done, and to avoid errors in appraisal, Rabbi Danon decided that artisans and merchants would be appraised by their professional colleagues. Three appraisal committees were set up, each of which appraised all those who would have to pay the tax: the results of the three appraisals were then put together, and an average calculated. This was the amount that each person was required to pay. Those who refused to pay were threatened with religious sanctions: their sons would not be circumcised, the traditional marriage ceremony or *ḥupah* would not be conducted for their offspring, their dead would not be buried, and so on.[35] As in the past, Torah scholars and religious functionaries, those who worked in the rabbinic office, and those with no means of livelihood were exempt from the tax. After Danon's appraisals, about 40 per cent of the communal income derived from the personal tax.

The *gabilah* was imposed in Damascus by means of the authority granted by the government to every *ḥakham bashi* throughout the empire to impose such indirect taxation as he saw fit. This evidently derived from the difficulty in collecting direct taxes, to the great detriment of the community's coffers. The authorities gave the rabbi almost unlimited means of imposing the tax upon those who refused to pay it, thereby putting to an end the disputes and quarrels that had taken place in the community around the *gabilah* over the course of many years. The tax on meat also generated about 40 per cent of the community's income after the new appraisals. In addition, an indirect tax was imposed upon matzah, which was sold through a franchise granted exclusively to the Torah scholars.[36]

The community derived further income from annual payments levied on the eleven major synagogues of Damascus, as well as from fees charged for marriage contracts (*ketubot*), circumcisions, and permits for real estate transactions within the Jewish quarter.[37] All these indirect taxes were intended to make up the deficit in the community's income arising from the shortfall in income from the individual tax.

From these revenues, sums were drawn to pay the salaries of the *ḥakham*

[35] For criticism of the method of appraisal, see Tarab, *Milei de'ezra* (Heb.), 'Hashmatot yoreh de'ah', 86*b*, §2.

[36] ACRI, TR/Is/160*a*, Rabbi Jacob Danon to Rabbi Hayim Nahum, Damascus, 15 Tevet 5672.

[37] On this, see Almaleh, *The Jews in Damascus* (Heb.), 38–42.

bashi and the secretary of the community. The salaries of the *shoḥatim* were also paid from the communal treasury, a practice adopted in many communities of the Middle East in order to remove the temptation to pass off non-kosher meat as kosher. Further expenditure was necessary to support needy Torah scholars, to support the Hebrew day school, and to make contributions to emissaries from Erets Yisra'el.

The annual payment imposed upon the synagogues and study houses aroused discontent in certain sectors of the community. In protest, and in an attempt to avoid paying the tax, a number of private people opened new study houses in their own homes. This stratagem not only represented defiance of the communal board and the chief rabbi, but also led to a diminution in both the community's income and the numbers of worshippers in the synagogues. Rabbi Danon appealed to the governor to order the closing of these new study houses, but his appeal was rejected on the grounds that every citizen had the right to freedom of religion and ritual observance. The new study houses functioned for a number of months at the end of 1911 and the beginning of 1912 and served as a centre of opposition to the official leadership of the community.[38]

A number of charitable societies were created and dismantled in the Damascus community during the final decade of the nineteenth century and the opening years of the twentieth. The Pikuah Nefashot society, originally established to distribute basic foods to the needy, also undertook the task of helping needy Jews who arrived in Damascus en route to other destinations without means to continue their journey. This seems to have been intended to prevent increasing numbers of beggars becoming a burden on the public purse. However, since the society's own income derived primarily from the subscriptions paid by its membership, in the absence of other means of support it had to scale back its activities to the point where it ceased to function. By 1911 the number of Jewish street beggars was rising again. The situation became even worse the following year, after the great fire that raged in Damascus for two days on 26 and 27 April 1912, destroying large parts of the city: approximately 400 stores and warehouses and 200 homes were destroyed completely, and damage was estimated at over 50 million francs. The Jewish community was among the main victims of this catastrophe. Overnight, some forty families lost everything they owned and were reduced to penury. Those Jewish stores which were not destroyed were looted and completely emptied, while those households that escaped fire or robbery suffered from the general business collapse which occurred in Damascus in the wake

[38] ACRI, TR/Is/160*a*, Rabbi Jacob Danon to Rabbi Hayim Nahum, Damascus, 9 Sept. 1911, 27 Oct. 1911, 15 Tevet 5672.

of this disaster. At a stroke, the number of impoverished families and the need for charitable support to help them increased dramatically. Two days after the fire Rabbi Danon sent telegrams to Jews already known for their generosity in Europe and America, and to the charitable societies and main Jewish newspapers in Istanbul, Palestine, Egypt, and Europe, appealing for their assistance: 'A great cataclysm has destroyed Damascus. Many Hebrew families are left naked and lacking everything. There is need for urgent help to save people from starvation. Please help!'[39]

To meet this increased need for charitable support, and in the context of the newly reorganized community institutions, the Ozer Dalim society was reactivated, with new by-laws published in January 1913.[40] To its previous functions of distributing food and providing transport, the society now added the provision of accommodation in a guest-house—Hakhnasat Orhim—open to any needy Jew. Guests were allowed to stay here for three consecutive days, after which the society paid for them to travel on to their final destination. To fund its work, the society relied on weekly membership subscriptions, augmented by contributions from outside sources.

This relief society differed from its precursors in three ways. First, it was established on democratic principles. Second, the names of the twelve members of its steering committee—Shhadé Abadi, Elijah Ma'aravi, David Sasson, Murad Sa'adya, Mussa Balya, Mussa Kamkhaji, Abraham Zaituni, Joseph Dweck, Shhadé Mahadib, Yitshak Yatshé, Murad Luziya, and Shhadé Farakh—indicate that none of them belonged to the old elite. Rather, this was an initiative of young, educated people who wanted to see the community on the path towards renewal and modernization. Third, the by-laws of the society were formulated in the Hebrew language. It is worth noting here that, during the years leading up to the First World War, Arabic was overwhelmingly dominant among the Jews of Damascus, with social, economic, religious, and political life all conducted in that language.[41] The young people who re-established the Ozer Dalim society were evidently influenced by the

[39] *Haherut*, 113 (10 May 1912), title page. See also *JC*, 3 May 1912, p. 14*b*; ACRI, TR/Is/160*a*, Rabbi Jacob Danon to Rabbi Hayim Nahum, Damascus, 5 Sivan 5612. The fire broke out in the editorial offices of a newspaper located above a store run by an Italian Jew named Delmedigo. At the time, the store had been closed for a number of weeks, since the expulsion of Italian citizens from Damascus in the wake of the war between the Ottoman empire and Italy. Some thought that thieves had broken into the store and then set fire to it with the aim of covering their tracks; others thought the arson had been motivated by hatred of Italy. However, the British consul claimed that there was no doubt that the fire had broken out in the newspaper offices, and therefore rejected these theories. See further FO 78 618/3, British consul to Lowether, Damascus, 30 Dec. 1904.

[40] See *Hevrat Ozer Dalim Society in Damascus*.

[41] Almaleh, *The Jews in Damascus* (Heb.), 23.

renewed Zionist settlement in Erets Yisra'el, and therefore insisted that the by-laws of the society be formulated in Hebrew, and that the society be run on the same principles as guided similar societies in Erets Yisra'el. One indication of the influence of this resurgent nationalism may be seen in their appeal to the Ezra (Hilfsverein) society in Germany, with a request to open a Hebrew kindergarten and elementary school in Damascus.[42] It would seem that these young people wished to influence the leadership of the community, possibly even to gain control over it. Rabbi Danon, in his own quest for allies within the community, drew them into his own ambit, taking care to invite them to various events and meetings with important and influential people visiting in Damascus.[43]

Changes in the Political and Legal Status of the Jews

Up to the time of the Young Turk Revolution, the Jews of Damascus remained strikingly separate from any general political organization in the city. Two main factors contributed to the persistence of this separation. First, the Jewish sense of a connection to the community which could be severed only by renouncing the religious faith which defined it perpetuated attachment to the old frameworks. Second, the new national movements and frameworks that began to take shape in Syria at the end of the nineteenth century were not readily accessible to Jews: the Arabic–Muslim movement demanded religious identification, while the patriotic movement demanded secularism and Arab identity. Those external connections that were available—for example, with Jewish communities in Europe—and the establishment of the Alliance schools in Damascus tended to strengthen rather than diminish the individual's consciousness of his Jewish identity, on both a religious and a national basis, thereby militating against the development of either a local or a pan-Ottoman national identity. This separatist tendency, coupled with the decline in the weight and importance of Jews in the local economy, tended to marginalize the Jewish community in Damascus.[44]

The joy at the promulgation of the new constitution and the end of the tyrannical rule of Sultan ʿAbd al-Hamid II was expressed at the beginning of August 1908 with parades in the streets of Damascus, accompanied by gunfire and fireworks. In several places in Syria Muslims could even be seen embracing Christians and Jews in their great joy in the revolution.[45]

42 See Idelson, 'The Jewish Community in Damascus' (Heb.), 99.

43 AAIU, Syrie, XVIII.E., Damas, 182, Nahon, 9 Mar. 1914.

44 On the decline in the status of the Jews in the local economy, see Harel, *Syrian Jewry*, 53–7.

45 Jessup, *Fifty-Three Years in Syria*, ii. 786–7.

However, after the initial euphoria deep disappointment set in among the Muslim Arabs, who had expected the promised participation and equality within the imperial framework. The members of the Committee of Union and Progress who led the Young Turk Revolution rapidly abandoned their liberal ideas and the vision of a multinational Ottoman state in which religious and national minorities would enjoy certain autonomous rights. The 'Ottomanist' dream of freedom, equality, and peace among all nations and sects constituting the population of the empire—coupled with a shared loyalty to the Ottoman ruler—disappeared, and was replaced by a policy of oppressive centralization. The 'Turkification' of the empire, in which efforts were made to assimilate all the peoples of the empire within a dominant Turkish nationality, began in April 1909, following suppression of the attempt by supporters of the *ancien régime* to bring about a counter-revolution. The new government tried to impose the Turkish language on the Arab regions by declaring it the only language allowed in the courts and government offices; Arab civil servants were fired and Turks appointed in their place; Arab army officers were suspected of disloyalty and passed over for promotion.

As feelings of oppression began to spread among the Arabs, nationalist secret societies began to emerge.[46] The proliferation of these groups strengthened the new regime's suspicion of organized activity,[47] and the consequent stricter conditions on the issue of permits to establish new organizations excluded many societies of a nationalist character. This policy was given explicit legal force in a law promulgated on 23 August 1909, which prohibited the setting up of any political organization based upon ethnic or national origin, or bearing the name of a national or ethnic group.[48] One of the victims of this policy was the revitalized Jewish communal organization that had been set up in the Damascus community after Rabbi Hayim Nahum's visit to the city. Local authorities refused to recognize the new communal board as a *majlis jismani* (steering committee) or to accord formal backing to its decisions. This placed the committee in a dilemma, as it represented it to the community as lacking in all authority. One of the opponents of the new board, who was evidently one of the remaining supporters of Rabbi Alfandari, exploited this fact to attack the board in the local Arab press.[49]

Between the end of the Young Turk Revolution and the end of the First World War, the Jews of Damascus found themselves needing to choose

46 See Lewis, *The Emergence of Modern Turkey*, 209–33.
47 On this subject see Tauber, *Secret Societies* (Heb.). See also Kayali, *Arabs and Young Turks*.
48 Lewis, *The Emergence of Modern Turkey*, 212–14.
49 ACRI, TR/Is/63, Moussa Totah to Rabbi Hayim Nahum, Damascus, 5 Aug. 1910.

among three different circles of identity: a Jewish–Ottoman national identity, a Jewish–Arabic national identity, and a Jewish–Hebrew–Zionist national identity. The problem, as articulated by Abraham Almaleh, was that the Jews of Damascus did not act as a distinctive group—as members of a well-defined nation and religion, demanding its civil rights within the new framework of the post-revolutionary Ottoman state—but rather behaved as a collection of individuals. This fact troubled both Almaleh and his father-in-law, Rabbi Danon, in their attempts to represent the community before the authorities. As Almaleh wrote:

If they were at least more nationalistic, more aware of their own minds, more concerned for their own dignity, then their representatives could fight on their behalf and protect their rights; and if they knew how to make use of the political freedom and their rights as individuals and as a people, then they would be able, without restriction, to develop their national life and to preserve their national form, shoulder to shoulder with all the other nations that dwell in this city.[50]

Nevertheless, the revolution and the ideas behind it did strike a chord among a small group of young Jews in Damascus, who found in them an echo of their own desire to improve their civil standing in Ottoman society. These were educated young people who, like many others, might have chosen to emigrate to the West had they not dared to hope that the revolution's ideals of freedom and equality would open up new possibilities for them in the land of their birth. Moreover, these young people, who had been influenced by modern nationalist ideas, channelled these ideas in the direction of Hebrew nationalism. In the first decade of the twentieth century Zionist ideas had made little impression on the Jews in Damascus: according to Almaleh, the subject of Jewish nationalism was vague and unclear to them, and they saw Zionism as an 'Ashkenazi' concern, one that pertained to the Jews of Europe and had nothing to do with them.[51] The small group of young nationalist Jews in Damascus constituted a marked exception to this general indifference. Following the proclamation of the new constitution, they established a society in Damascus known as al-Nahda (The Revival). Although its goals at the time of its establishment are not known, the name chosen by its founder members, like those taken by contemporary Arab nationalist associations, indicates their desire for renewal in the wake of the revolution.

[50] Almaleh, *The Jews in Damascus* (Heb.), 26. Yitshak Shemi describes the same phenomenon in more colourful terms: 'Whereas the population [of Damascus] awakened shortly after the Turkish revolution, the Hebrew community was still self-encapsulated and enwrapped like a foetus in its mother's womb. I doubt whether it is possible to call the group of Jews here a community' (*Ha'aḥdut*, 5 (23 Heshvan 5671), 4).

[51] Almaleh, *The Jews in Damascus* (Heb.), 24–5.

During the first two years of its existence this association did not leave any particular mark upon the life of the Jews in Damascus, and its membership gradually dwindled in number, whether as a result of emigration or lack of interest. After Rabbi Nahum's visit to Damascus the association resumed its activity, this time as the Association of Ottoman Jews, with the stated aim of disseminating general education and enlightenment among the Jews of Damascus. Both the association's name and its declared goal indicate its intention of forging a national identification of the Jews with the new regime in Istanbul and promoting Jewish integration within the renewed Turkish state. However, closer examination of the words and deeds of its members reveals that this was not their only goal. In addition to spreading general education among the younger generation of Jews, members of the association also wanted to give them a knowledge of the Hebrew language. The study of Hebrew was of course inconsistent with the policy of Turkification, and suggests a possible attempt to introduce specifically Hebrew nationalist ideas to the Jews of Damascus. In a conversation with an unnamed interviewer, the founders of the association stated that the society was essentially nationalist, but it is not clear what they meant by the term in this context—that is, whether it referred to Ottoman nationalism or to Hebrew nationalism. They explained their main concern, to give young people a general education, by saying that the Jews of Damascus lacked any framework for understanding or accepting the nationalist idea, and that the society wanted to find a way to make it accessible to them.[52] Perhaps what they meant by this was that their first priority was to give the Jews of Damascus a way of understanding what it meant to be simultaneously citizens of a modern state and also members of another well-defined national group. To this end, by means of study of the Hebrew language, they wished to introduce the idea of Jewish national consciousness. The seed of Hebrew nationalism may already have been sown in the hearts of these young people in Beirut, where some of them had studied Hebrew at evening classes taught by the Zionist Asher Ehrlich.[53] It would thus seem that the original intention of the Association of Ottoman Jews was to strengthen the linguistic and historical Hebrew identity—as distinct from the cultural and religious Jewish identity—of the Jews of Damascus, within the mosaic of nations that comprised the Ottoman empire.

It is interesting that, unlike other Jewish groups founded in Ottoman lands after the revolution—which sought to spread knowledge of the Turkish language among the Jews in order to facilitate their acceptance within higher

[52] *Ha'or*, 162 (14 Elul 5670), 2; *JC*, 17 Feb. 1911, p. 10.
[53] On Asher Ehrlich, see Tidhar, *Encyclopedia*, ii. 947.

education institutions and ease their entry into the civil service—this group did not attempt to teach Turkish to the Jews of Damascus.[54] In order to attract both the Jewish masses, who spoke only Arabic, and the educated elite, who having studied at the Alliance schools also spoke French, the association established a reading room with Arabic and French newspapers. It did not, however, provide newspapers in Hebrew. The ostensible reason for this was that the small number of Hebrew readers within the community did not justify the cost of purchasing newspapers from Erets Yisra'el; but the real reason seems to have been fear of attracting unwelcome attention from the authorities and being closed down as an illegal Zionist political organization. And indeed, the association's activities were frowned on by some within the community leadership, who feared that they might light a 'spark of Zionism' that would endanger the community as a whole.

Discouraged by this internal opposition, the membership of the association dwindled until by early September 1910 it numbered only about twenty. However, this decline in numbers did not cause a decline in activity so much as a change of direction: it began to appeal specifically to the Arab population. Now it promoted integration within Arab society, and may have even indirectly alluded to identification with its national goals. One Saturday night the Damascus public, both Jewish and non-Jewish, was invited to participate in a musical and theatrical soirée in the auditorium of the Alliance school. The evening was conducted entirely in Arabic, and its musical portion included singers who sang from the best of the Arabic repertoire. The play was translated from French into Arabic, and young Jewish actors took part in it. The income from the event was intended to finance evening classes in Arabic.

It is worth noting the participation in this play of young Jewish girls, a precursor of the prominent involvement of women in later Zionist activity in Damascus. The appearance in public of these Jewish girls, who belonged to the social elite of graduates of the Alliance school, was all the more striking in view of the fact that the Arab audience that came to watch the play consisted entirely of men. According to a contemporary observer, the audience greatly enjoyed the entertainment, particularly the acting of the young girls. The entire event lasted for five hours, and its success led the young people of the association to present the play again two days later, before Muslim families, so that the Muslim women could also enjoy it.[55]

Thus it appears that the young Jews who had founded the association changed tack, both as a result of government suspicion and intra-communal

[54] On Jewish groups which encouraged Ottomanization following the revolution, see Benbassa, *Ottoman Jewry* (Heb.), 102–3.

[55] *Ha'or*, 162 (14 Elul 5670), 2.

discouragement and in response to the admiration of the Arab public for their cultural innovations. Having originally set out to strengthen the Hebrew national identity of the Jews among the multitude of national identities within the empire, without detriment to the cultivation of an Ottoman identity or political loyalty to the state framework, they now became more deeply involved in cultural activity identified with the surrounding milieu. Learning the Arabic language, which was initially seen as a tool for developing concepts of national identity among the Jewish community in Damascus, became a goal in its own right.

Abraham Almaleh arrived in Damascus at a time when this Arabic tendency within the association was growing, eclipsing the original goal of bringing about a Jewish national revival within the Arabic–Ottoman framework. Almaleh, with his Hebrew nationalist approach, was not impressed by what he saw as the excessively enthusiastic 'Arabization' of the members of the association and mocked their activities, describing them as 'filling their belly with Arabic literature, in which they find all of their spiritual food and satisfaction'.[56] Almaleh was particularly disturbed by the presence of anti-Zionist Arabic newspapers, such as *al-Muqtabas* and *al-Karmil*, in the association's reading room. It is impossible to say definitively whether this indicated that the association's leaders identified themselves with Arab national ambitions which were, in the final analysis, opposed to the Zionist movement developing in Erets Yisra'el. It is more likely, in fact, that these newspapers were placed in the reading room because they were the main platform for public discourse in Damascus, and it was impossible to ignore their existence.

The organization of young Jews in the framework of a 'literary club' was not accidental. During the years following the revolution of the Young Turks, such an organization could hold meetings and other activities openly while also serving as a cover for social activity or underground political activity of one sort or another. In any event, even if the association's underlying intention was to strengthen Hebrew national sentiment, externally it demonstrated total loyalty to the Ottoman rulers. Under the headline 'Jewish Patriotism in Damascus', the press reported that on 22 January 1911 the Jewish Literature Association in Damascus had presented to Sami Pasha, the commander of the Ottoman brigades in the Syrian district of Horan, an Ottoman flag decorated with a medal of recognition for his suppression of the rebellion that had broken out in the area and for restoring peace to the district. On the flag were embroidered the words: 'A faithful souvenir for

56 Almaleh, *The Jews in Damascus* (Heb.), 42–3. Following Almaleh, others also misunderstood the nature of this association: see e.g. Cohen, *The Jews in Middle Eastern Countries* (Heb.), 84; Landau and Maoz, 'Jews and Non-Jews' (Heb.), 12.

the heroic victor, Sami Pasha al-Faruqui, from the young Jews of Damascus'. Many young Jews were in the large crowd that awaited Sami Pasha at the police headquarters. When he arrived, the young people went out to greet him to the sound of a band playing accompanied by dances, and gave him the flag, and a bouquet of flowers, in an impressive public ceremony. The presentation seems to have been co-ordinated with the *ḥakham bashi*, Jacob Danon, who arrived at the head of an official delegation of the community to bless Sami Pasha. Members of the Jewish Literature Association, along with leaders of the community, delivered speeches in Turkish in honour of the commander and the Ottoman homeland; in return, Sami Pasha blessed the association for its patriotism and for the affection that the Jewish nation showed towards the state.[57] This event clearly testifies to the growing tendency towards the involvement of at least some sections of the Jewish community in public life and in what was happening in the empire. Conversely, there is no sign of even the first shoots of Zionist activity.

Also in 1911, Jewish patriotism was expressed in prayers held in the central synagogue for the success of the Ottoman army in its war with Italy on the Libyan front. The uniqueness of this ceremony lay in the presence of all the government leaders of Damascus. ʿAbduh Farhi, a member of the Jewish community and a senior official in the government, delivered a fiery, patriotic speech in Arabic. He was followed by Abraham Almaleh, secretary of the community—who spoke in Hebrew, though he was also fluent in Turkish, evidently wishing to express his Jewish loyalty by speaking specifically in the language unique to the Jews. Thereafter Rabbi Danon recited the prayer for the government, 'Hanoten teshuah lamelahim', and the cantor chanted a special prayer composed for the occasion.[58]

The same patriotism was on display during the Balkan war that broke out in October 1912, when young Jews expressed their support for the empire and their hopes for Ottoman victory. Some of them even participated in mass demonstrations of support for the Turkish army held in Damascus. This was not mere lip-service to keep on the right side of the authorities; even reports to the Hebrew press in Palestine were filled with enthusiastic admiration for the government. Thus, for example, Abraham Almaleh, using the pseudonym 'Ben-Zion Raful, an educated young Jew from Damascus', noted that the Ottoman information agencies did not give the Hebrew press all the information they had about the course of the war in the Balkans, whereas the Arabic press in Damascus reported the campaigns in minute detail. He therefore gave a full account of the war for his readers in Palestine, as it was

57 *JC*, 17 Feb. 1911, p. 10.

58 *Ha'or*, 24 (18 Heshvan 5672), 2.

reported in the Arabic press, and concluded by saying: 'With all our hearts, so too we Ottoman Jews, whose attachment to our homeland is well known, hope that in the great, decisive battle, our forces will emerge crowned with glory and victory.'[59]

All these declarations of loyalty to the Ottoman regime on the part of Damascus Jews were doubtless made in sincere belief in the government's promises of equality and freedom, and in the desire to improve the civil status of the Jews in the city. However, as time passed, such belief gave way to disappointment. The public atmosphere in Damascus was not yet ripe for the granting of full equality to the Jews—a consequence of both the zealous Muslim character of the population and the fact that, since the economic collapse of 1875, the Jewish community had ceased to have any significant influence on public life in the city. The gradual shrinking of the community as a result of emigration, the closing in on themselves of those who remained in the Jewish quarter, and the fact that almost all of them were more concerned with problems of livelihood and simple survival than with the great issues of the time—all these factors contributed to push the Jewish community to the margins of public life in Damascus. Jewish connections with the authorities were no longer as strong as they had been in the past; nor were their connections with the Jews of western Europe, who had in the past exercised their considerable influence to promote the legal and civil status of the Jews of Syria.[60] About three years after the revolution, Rabbi Danon complained that the local government looked at the Jewish community of Damascus 'as at something negligible, almost null due to its smallness', as a result of which life was not worth living for its members.[61] To explain the situation and to ask for his intervention on behalf of the Jews of Damascus, Rabbi Danon wrote to the *ḥakham bashi* in Istanbul, choosing a telling example to illustrate his case:

> In order to show to Your Honour how the local government considers the Jews, I shall relate to him that all over the city there are electric wires to light up the courtyards at night, and only the Jewish street does not enjoy this; yet at the same time they are required to pay the taxes for street lighting, even though their own streets are covered at night in darkness and gloom.[62]

The difference between backwardness and decline on the one hand and progress and modernization on the other was comparable to the difference

[59] *Haḥerut*, 48 (17 Nov. 1912), 2.

[60] On relations between Jews and Muslims in Damascus and their connections with Jews in Europe during the second half of the 19th century, see Harel, *Syrian Jewry*, 151–68, 235–50.

[61] ACRI, TR/Is/72*a*, Rabbi Jacob Danon to Rabbi Hayim Nahum, Damascus, 22 Av 5671.

[62] Ibid., Rabbi Jacob Danon to Rabbi Hayim Nahum, Damascus, 30 Av 5671.

between the darkness which covered the Jewish quarter and the light which shone upon the other quarters of Damascus. There was also the practical point that the darkness in the Jewish quarter facilitated crime and personal and public immorality.

The small number of Jews and their general lack of involvement in public life in Damascus was reflected in the fact that only three Jews held positions in the city administration: Moses Totah, who was a member of the *majlis idara* of the district; Joseph Abadi, a member of the merchants' council; and 'Abduh Farhi, a senior official in the district treasury department. There was no Jewish representation in the Damascus municipality—which no doubt was at least part of the reason why the Jewish quarter was so neglected in comparison with the Muslim and Christian quarters of the city.[63]

The transfer of the red-light district of Damascus to the Jewish quarter, which took place, as noted above, in the wake of a complaint by the Muslim men that Jewish women exerted a negative influence on the morals of their wives and daughters, was perceived by Rabbi Danon as yet another expression of the prevailing contempt felt towards the Jews. He commented with bitter irony: 'Indeed, is this not a proper judgement? But who will incline his ear to listen to the just protests of the Jews . . . for to him [the government official] a single "singer" with whom he can enjoy many nights is equal to many thousands of Jews.'[64]

The connections between certain prostitutes and the most senior officials of the Ottoman administration in Damascus led to another assault on the legal rights of Jews, as well as to intervention by the governor in the internal affairs of the Jewish community. When several prostitutes wished to sell their homes to others, Rabbi Danon instructed the *mukhtar* of the Jewish quarter—whose job was to manage the list of male inhabitants, and to record movements and transfers of ownership of real property—not to approve these sales, but to inform the vendors that the community was willing to buy their houses at any price. The prostitutes complained to the governor, explaining that they were not selling their homes permanently, but only for a period of five years, during which, they said, they intended to travel to America, and after which they would wish to buy back the houses upon their return to Damascus. Rabbi Danon informed the governor that the community was prepared to buy the houses even under such conditions, and to sell the houses back to the prostitutes upon their return. However, the governor brushed his protest aside and insisted that the *mukhtar* approve the sale against his will.

63 Almaleh, *The Jews in Damascus* (Heb.), 48.

64 ACRI, TR/Is/72*a*, Rabbi Jacob Danon to Rabbi Hayim Nahum, Damascus, 22 Av 5671.

The governor also instructed Rabbi Danon to dismiss the *mukhtar* and to appoint another in his place. The *ḥakham bashi* argued that the appointment or dismissal of the *mukhtar* was a matter for the community, not for the governor, and that the community did not want a different *mukhtar*. At this point the governor made an unprecedented intervention, himself dismissing the *mukhtar* and demanding that another be appointed in his place. In order not to aggravate the tension, the community chose an alternative *mukhtar*; but the new appointee resigned a few days later for fear of becoming embroiled in confrontation with the government authorities. The community was thus left without a *mukhtar*, and all real estate transactions in the Jewish quarter came to a halt—with the exception of those involving the prostitutes, which the governor waved through himself.

This involvement on the part of the governor was completely opposed to the spirit of the new constitution as well as to the traditional pattern of relations between the Ottoman authorities and the Jewish community. The leadership of the Jewish community found itself exposed to the public in all its weakness, with everyone able to see how the prostitutes had succeeded in drawing the systems of administration, law, and justice over to their side in their struggle against the leaders of their own community.

As mentioned earlier, Rabbi Jacob Danon's uncompromising campaign against prostitution in the Jewish quarter aroused the particular fury of one of the Jewish pimps, who cursed and reviled the rabbi in his own home, and even threatened him with a pistol. The rabbi lodged a complaint with the authorities, who imprisoned his assailant and laid criminal charges against him; but the pimp succeeded in 'mysteriously' fleeing the city before the beginning of his trial. He returned to Damascus a few days later, publicly bragging that no harm had come to him thanks to his connections with a senior official in the judiciary. He boasted even more when this friend reduced the charge from a criminal one to a civil one.[65] This episode dealt a harsh blow to the authority and status of the chief rabbi, who was revealed before both the Jewish and the Arab public as a weak figure, unable to obtain justice even for himself.

The opposition to Rabbi Danon and to the new arrangements that he attempted to introduce enjoyed the passive support of the government. The governor did not help the *ḥakham bashi* to impose his full authority, for example failing to order the closing of alternative institutions of worship set up by those protecting the prostitutes or the imprisonment of those who evaded payment of communal taxes. In public, the governor justified his inaction in respect of the new religious institutions in terms of the provisions of the new

[65] ACRI, TR/Is/72*a*, Rabbi Jacob Danon to Rabbi Hayim Nahum, Damascus, 30 Av 5671.

constitution, which gave every individual the right to worship his God as he chose, but Rabbi Danon strongly suspected that the real reason lay in the connections of the governor and his officials with the Jewish prostitutes.[66]

Life for the Jews of Damascus became almost unbearable. They were subjected to repeated insults and humiliation by Arabs, which those charged with enforcing the law did nothing to stop. It became apparent that Jews could not even rely on the judicial system for justice. In May 1911 Muslims accused a young Jewish man of cursing the Muslim religion. A Muslim mob beat the young man almost to death, and he was then thrown into gaol for three months. During his imprisonment he became gravely ill but, despite the advice of the doctors and the pleas of Rabbi Danon, the authorities refused to move him to a hospital. In the end he died in gaol, totally innocent and without even a trial. Rabbi Danon wrote bitterly to the *ḥakham bashi* in Istanbul: 'As I stated, the attitude of the local government officials towards us is like that of a master to his slaves . . . The protests of the Jews here are of no value in the eyes of the local government because, as we said, they think that there is nobody to fight on behalf of the Jews.'[67]

A few days after the death of this young Jew in prison, the newspaper *al-Muqtabas*, which consistently took an anti-Jewish line, published a blood libel against the Jews of Istanbul which it followed up with almost daily inflammatory reports attacking the Jews. Anti-Jewish feeling in Damascus mounted to the extent that violent street fights began to break out between Muslims and Jews.[68]

Paradoxically, it was precisely after the Young Turk Revolution that the Arabic press in Damascus took on an increasingly anti-Jewish tone. Before that, the newspapers could not publish anything explicitly against the Jews as the authorities, particularly during the reign of ʿAbd al-Hamid II, forbade any racially hostile comment.[69] In any case, there was very little interest in the Jews—both because of the traditional disregard of Muslim writers for the Jewish community, and because the community had been marginalized by the bankruptcy of 1875 and its subsequent reduction to a small and uninfluential element in the public life of Damascus.

All this changed with the removal of ʿAbd al-Hamid II and the beginning of both practical and political Zionist activity in Palestine. In the wake of the Young Turk Revolution, the empire was flooded with new periodicals and newspapers, many of which reflected ideas and approaches that had hitherto

[66] ACRI, TR/Is/160*a*, Rabbi Jacob Danon to Rabbi Hayim Nahum, Damascus, 9 Sept. 1911, 27 Oct. 1911.

[67] ACRI, TR/Is/72*a*, Rabbi Jacob Danon to Rabbi Hayim Nahum, Damascus, 22 Av 5671.

[68] *JC*, 15 Sept. 1911, p. 12*a*.

[69] See Cioeta, 'Ottoman Censorship'.

been banned. At the same time, the Zionist movement was gradually becoming a permanent feature of the Palestinian scene, demanding some sort of response on the part of the Arabic press in Syria. The Syrian papers were divided almost evenly between those that were apathetic on the subject of Zionism and those that were violently antagonistic to it.[70] The first resident of Damascus to raise the subject of the 'Zionist danger' in Palestine publicly was Shukri al-ʿAsali, a young Arab in the parliament in Istanbul, whose attacks on the Zionist enterprise paved the way for the Damascus press to come out against what it saw as the hateful domination of Palestine by the Zionists.[71] During this period such newspapers as *al-Muqtabas* began to blur the distinction between Zionists and Jews, and press attacks on Zionism broadened on more than one occasion into general attacks on the Jews as a people. This approach presented a real danger to the Jews living in Damascus, for while it did not always reflect the opinion of the newspaper-reading public in the city, it certainly attempted to shape it.

Once it had become clear that *al-Muqtabas* was deliberately inciting hostility towards the Jews, a significant number of its readers protested against this inflammatory tone. Muslim dignitaries and religious leaders in Damascus sent a memorandum to the prime minister in which they expressed their disgust at the paper's line and declared that its statements had no value and bore no relation to public opinion in Syria.[72] This initiative on the part of prominent Muslims may well have been made in response to appeals from leaders of the Jewish community: Rabbi Danon repeatedly turned to the leaders of other religions when attacks were made upon Jews, with the aim of creating a united front in the defence of all religious minorities. Whatever prompted them, these protests from leaders of the Muslim community in Damascus are clear evidence of their concern for the well-being of the Jewish community—a concern that seems to have derived more from the traditional Muslim view of the Jews as a protected group (*dhimmi*) than from modern ideas of equality and brotherhood. The violation of that old pact by the Jews would have immediately made them vulnerable to harm.

In September 1913, a Muslim accused a Jew who had got into an argument with him in the Jewish quarter of cursing the Muslim religion. Other Muslims nearby fell upon the Jew and attacked him violently. As had

[70] Malul, 'The Arabic Press' (Heb.), 445, 449.

[71] On Shukri al-ʿAsali, his activity on behalf of the Arab interest in the Ottoman state, and his view that Zionism presented a danger to the Arabs, see Kurd Ali, *Description of Syria* (Heb.), iii. 130–3. On his activity prior to the separation of Syria from the Ottoman state and its annexation to Egypt, see al-Sayyid, *The Story of my Life* (Arab.), 137; Tauber, *Secret Societies* (Heb.), 16–17; Beska, 'Shukri al-ʿAsali'.

[72] *JC*, 24 Nov. 1911, p. 12*b*.

happened in other such cases since before the revolution, once the police eventually arrived blame for the violation of public order was placed upon the Jew, who was thrown into prison, while none of his attackers were arrested. But unlike similar cases in the past, in which the Jewish community would not dare to make public demands for the release of a Jew from prison but would work secretly, behind the scenes, usually through the intervention of one of the foreign consuls, this time the Jews protested openly. The younger and more educated elements in the Jewish community were aware of the values espoused by the revolutionaries and of the promises of equality held out by the new constitution. They were also familiar with the new tools of public protest, such as public demonstrations, as well as the time-honoured procedures such as submitting petitions. On this occasion their protests were not addressed to the government authorities but to the *ḥakham bashi* Jacob Danon, leaving him in no doubt about their expectations of him. Demonstrators outside the chief rabbi's home demanded that he confront the governor and insisted that he take action to release the imprisoned Jew. A newspaper reported their outrage in the following terms:

> For they are unable to understand how it is, in a time of freedom and liberty, that a Jewish man can be beaten without any wrongdoing, be imprisoned without a trial, and languish in gaol, while dozens of Jews are insulted and do not insult others, hear their shame and do not respond. Their religion is cursed dozens of times daily, and nobody defends it against shame.[73]

Rabbi Danon turned to the governor, who claimed that he was unable to help in the matter because it was under the authority of the general investigator. 'Ben-Zion Raful' (alias Abraham Almaleh) explained the cause of the authorities' attitude as follows: 'We never demanded our rights by law; we never asked that we be taken into consideration as a living people, which works and acts as an important part of the Ottoman nation.'[74]

In these circumstances, the activity of the al-Nahda association had little influence on the involvement of Jews in the public life of Damascus. Most Jews remained unaware of their rights under the constitution and were in no position to insist on their observance—either in times of trouble, or in everyday life.

Rabbi Jacob Danon's approach to resolving the problem represented a return to the pattern of pre-revolutionary days. He turned in the first instance to the traditional channel of Jewish influence, informing the *ḥakham bashi* in Istanbul about the situation of the Jews in Damascus, and asking him

[73] *Haḥerut*, 310 (30 Sept. 1913), 2. [74] Ibid.

to act on their behalf with the government. That is, as in so many other cases, the struggle shifted from the local civil context to the hidden arena of behind-the-scenes influence (*shetadlanut*).

Second, Rabbi Danon turned in another direction: to the leaders of the Christian churches, hoping to draw them with him into a united front of all religious minorities that would struggle together for their legal and civil rights. This attempt by a senior rabbi to make common cause with Christian priests for mutual benefit was almost unprecedented. The only other occasion on which a similar attempt had been made to set up a united front of non-Muslim minorities against what was perceived as the injustice of the government had been some fifty years earlier. At that time, the leaders of the Christian religion arranged a meeting with the chief rabbi of the Damascus community, Rabbi Jacob Perets, with the aim of mounting a joint protest against the *bedel-i ʿaskeri or ʿaskariyya* (military commutation) tax. This initiative failed owing to the Jews' fears of Muslim anger.[75] At the time Rabbi Danon made his appeal, the Christians in Damascus, like the Jews, found themselves in an increasingly hostile atmosphere and on the receiving end of repressive policies introduced by the Young Turks. The revolutionaries seem to have felt anger, bitterness, and disappointment towards the Christians, whom they saw as acting aggressively and treacherously in response to promises of freedom and equality. In fact, notwithstanding the new constitution, the population at large was not yet ready to accept non-Muslims within Turkish Ottoman society.[76] Rabbi Danon sought to present the arrest and mistreatment of an innocent Jew as an event relevant to all non-Muslim minorities, and to use it as an impetus for joint activity to advance their standing in Ottoman society. He suggested that the Christian leaders join him in an approach to the minister of justice to demand that, in every future case in which a Muslim accused a minority member of cursing Islam, a serious investigation be undertaken before the accused was arrested. Thus, argued Rabbi Danon, 'there will be one law for all religions, and there will not be a double standard'.[77] In the end, on the eve of the Jewish new year 5674 (1913/14), the Jewish prisoner at the centre of the controversy was released after another Jew, Baruch Pais, and his Muslim business partner, Subhi Bey Urfali, provided surety that he would be returned to prison should he be found guilty under the law.[78] Overtaken by events, the initiative for a united

[75] See Harel, *Syrian Jewry*, 162.

[76] This situation continued for many years, even during the republic of Kemal. See Lewis, *The Emergence of Modern Turkey*, 350–1.

[77] *Haḥerut*, 310 (30 Sept. 1913), 2.

[78] *Haḥerut*, 3 (5 Oct. 1913), 2. Rabbi Jacob Danon claimed that the prisoner was freed as a result of his discussions with the state attorney, and made no mention of the intervention of

front of the non-Muslim minorities, the only one of its kind in Damascus during the course of the twentieth century, faded away.

It is nevertheless worth mentioning that as *ḥakham bashi* Danon did achieve a respected position among the leaders of the various religions in Damascus. While he did so by virtue of his own personality, his status elevated that of the community as a whole. Following a lengthy estrangement between Jews and members of other religions during the period of Rabbi Alfandari, interreligious relations were renewed during Rabbi Danon's time. As was customary in the Middle East, on festive days and special occasions mutual visits took place between the heads of the Jewish community and the heads of the government, the foreign consuls, and the leaders of the Muslim community and the Christian churches.[79]

Another factor that led to tension between Chief Rabbi Danon and the government authorities, and particularly the military, related to the conscription of young Jews into the army and respect for their religious rights during their period of service. The obligation to serve in the army was one of the main factors leading young people from the community to emigrate, resulting in a contraction of the community.

Rabbi Danon not only acted to bring about the exemption of many young Damascus Jews from service in the army, but was also asked to intervene on behalf of young Jews in Jerusalem who had declared the study of Torah to be their occupation, and claimed exemption on this ground. The *mufattish*, the general supervisor of the army, sat at the regional headquarters in Damascus, as did the head of the military staff. The personal relations formed by Rabbi Danon with these military functionaries were of great importance in obtaining the release of young Jews from military service. His relations with Nuri Bey, head of the military staff in Damascus until the spring of 1913, were excellent. When Nuri Bey left Damascus to return to Istanbul after a dispute between himself and the governor of Beirut, Danon wrote to the *ḥakham bashi* in Istanbul:

> This man is a true lover of Israel, and in every matter pertaining to Jews and to military people from among our brethren where I turned to him, he never turned me away empty-handed. He always helped our brethren in every matter that depended upon him. His departure from Damascus will certainly cause much damage, particularly regarding military matters, and particularly to us Jews . . . His departure left a miserable feeling in all circles. For that reason, many letters were written this

these two men. See ACRI, TR/Is/81*a*, Rabbi Jacob Danon to Rabbi Hayim Nahum, Damascus, 29 Tishrei 5674.

[79] See e.g. *Haḥerut*, 189 (9 May 1913), 2.

week to Constantinople—from the *mushir* [head of the army], from the general supervisor, from the heads of all the various religions, requesting the minister of war to return Nuri Bey to Damascus . . . I too fulfil my obligation to this man, who has done so many good things for our Jewish brethren, and turn to your honour with the request that, if he can speak either directly or indirectly on behalf of that man, he would do a great kindness to the Jews of Damascus. Also, we wish Nuri Bey himself to know that we are not ungrateful for all the favours he did for the Jews.[80]

These words reflect the great caution exercised by Danon—himself a senior Ottoman official—to avoid any clumsily direct intervention in internal Ottoman political affairs. He did not join in the appeal made by the heads of other religious groups to the war ministry to return Nuri Bey to Damascus; instead, he took a more subtle, indirect approach, addressing the most senior Jewish official in the empire, the *ḥakham bashi* in Istanbul. In doing so, he was also giving due recognition to the position and instructions of Rabbi Nahum, who had appointed him.

In any event, the appeal was unsuccessful, and after Nuri Bey left, relations between Rabbi Danon and the military authorities became less affable, with Nuri's replacement taking little heed of the needs of the Jewish community in Damascus and in its environs.[81]

The verbal attacks upon the Jews as a nation, as well as the physical violence against individuals, the problem of prostitution and its effects on everyday communal life, and the attacks by the juridical institutions upon the Jews—all these led Rabbi Danon at an early stage in his term as chief rabbi to express disappointment in the new government, and even to threaten his own resignation. In 1911 he wrote to Rabbi Nahum in Istanbul:

May his honour believe me that my life is unbearable here. There are people who come in the middle of the night, knocking on the door of my house, crying out: Get up, save us! Evil men have attacked us, beat us and injured us! While they are still speaking, another one comes along and says: Such-and-such a prostitute has arrested five innocent Jews! And so on. Had I known that the situation was thus in Damascus, I would never under any circumstances have accepted this office—not, Heaven forbid, because I want to live an easy life. To the contrary: I want to work for the welfare and benefit of my brethren and for my people. I would like to make this community grow and flourish, to strengthen its institutions and to increase societies dedicated to charity, kindness and education—and indeed, there is much to be done here. Peace and tranquillity reign in our city, thank God. I am happy with my flock, and all of them, both great and small, are happy. But the great stumbling block that stands in our way and that embitters our life is: the 'singers'. Now if

[80] ACRI, TR/Is/81*a*, Rabbi Jacob Danon to Rabbi Hayim Nahum, Damascus, 2 Iyar 5673.

[81] AAIU, Syrie, XVIII.E., Damas, 182, Nahon, 15 Dec. 1913.

your honour, the Rabbi, together with the honourable members of the steering *majlis*, succeed in removing them from us, then our community will be one of the most flourishing communities in all of Turkey. But if, Heaven forbid, we do not succeed in doing so, I will need, to my great sorrow, to resign my office, for I cannot see the evil that befalls my people; I cannot bear, in an age of freedom and equality, to see my brethren and the members of my flock swept up and placed in prison by a shameful, lowly harlot. My warm heart cannot be apathetic to all these sights without rising up against the tyranny being done to my brethren, the children of Israel, in these days of a new political regime.[82]

The Jews of Damascus and the Elections of 1912

There was nevertheless one area in which the Jews were not ignored; indeed, there were even signs of their being courted. The free elections introduced in the Ottoman empire in the wake of the revolution encouraged Jews to become more involved in questions pertaining to the leadership of the state. Although they were a small minority in Damascus, the votes of the Jews were of great importance in the political struggle that took place in the city in the winter of 1911–12 prior to the Turkish parliamentary elections in April that year.

After the Young Turk Revolution, Abraham Almaleh championed the approach taken by leaders of the Zionist movement, who had high hopes of the new regime. Their policy was to show the government that there was no contradiction between being a Zionist Jew and being an Ottoman patriot. The Zionists believed that, within the framework of the new regime—which demanded loyalty to the idea of the Ottoman state, but promised to respect the national and cultural characteristics of each group within it—the Zionist interest needed to be represented as not contradicting the Ottoman interest; indeed, as consistent with it. The Zionists wished to disabuse the government of any suspicion that the Jews had any desire for separation from the empire. Their goal was, first and foremost, to persuade the Ottoman rulers to allow the Jews within their territories to emigrate without restriction to Erets Yisra'el in order to set up their cultural centre there.[83]

The hopes pinned by the Zionists upon the Young Turks were reflected in their support for the official political party of the revolutionaries, the Committee of Union and Progress. Also contributing to this support was the fact that the opposition party, Ahrar (Liberal Union), was composed of a coalition of Armenians, Greeks, and Arabs. The Armenians and the Greeks

82 ACRI, TR/Is/72*a*, Rabbi Jacob Danon to Rabbi Hayim Nahum, 22 Av 5671.

83 See Benbassa, *Ottoman Jewry* (Heb.), 77–8; and cf. Weiker, *Ottomans, Turks and the Jewish Polity*, 234–7.

had been considered enemies of the Jews from time immemorial, while Arab hostility towards Jews had been growing against the background of Zionist activity in Palestine. The attacks upon the Jews in the local Arab press further strengthened the tendency of Damascus Jews to support the Committee of Union and Progress, as its principles were opposed to those of the Arab parties and organizations associated with the pan-Arabic approach opposed to Zionism and indeed increasingly to Jews as a whole.

It is quite possible that Jacob Danon—whose power and authority as *ḥakham bashi* derived from his connections with Rabbi Hayim Nahum, a key ally of the Committee of Union and Progress—took vigorous action to enlist the support of Damascus Jewry for the revolutionaries' party. The stronger the party was, the stronger would Rabbi Nahum's position be—and, by implication, that of Rabbi Danon.[84]

The Jews' opportunity to prove their loyalty to the Committee of Union and Progress came about when the party began to organize itself for the parliamentary elections of April 1912. During the course of the campaign, party members sought to win the support of various groups within the population, and as part of this effort a high-level delegation arrived in Damascus to create a counterweight to Arab nationalist propaganda. This delegation was received by the *ḥakham bashi* Jacob Danon, the secretary of the community Abraham Almaleh, and by various other communal dignitaries. The visit was a source of great joy and pride among the inhabitants of the Jewish quarter, who were not used to being paid this kind of attention, particularly as the party delegation was accompanied by twenty leading figures from the local government, including the *qadi*, the *mufti*, and the head of the Ottoman Bank.

As is usual in election campaigns, the reception opened with words of friendship towards the Jews on the part of their guests. Less predictable was the eloquent speech given in response by Abraham Almaleh, which created the mistaken impression of a community that was deeply involved in Ottoman politics and expert in the details of its constitution. In his speech, Almaleh noted the equality granted by Turkish law to the Jews and extolled the friendship shown by the Muslim empire to the Jews, as opposed to the hatred felt for them by the Christians. He criticized the activity of the opposition party in Turkey, which made use in its propaganda of anti-Zionist expressions that at times glided over into antisemitism and encouraged hatred of the Jews.[85] Almaleh likewise exploited the occasion to assuage the

[84] On the attitude of the Jews to the Committee of Union and Progress throughout the empire and the role played by Rabbi Nahum in these elections, see Benbassa, *Ottoman Jewry* (Heb.), 165–74.

[85] On the anti-Zionist and antisemitic activity of the opposition in the Ottoman parliament,

fears of those present concerning the growing wave of migration of Jews to Palestine. As he presented it, this *aliyah* was intended to strengthen Turkey rather than to weaken it. In essence, his explicitly Zionist speech was intended to make it unequivocally clear to the members of the delegation that it was not the intention of the Zionist Jews to undermine Turkey's integrity through their Zionism. Echoing the line taken by Zionist propaganda in Istanbul, Almaleh sought to emphasize the economic benefit that would accrue to Palestine as a result of Jewish immigration and settlement—telling his audience, indeed, that many places in Erets Yisra'el had already become a veritable 'Garden of Eden'—and to downplay the political intentions of Zionism. Almaleh concluded his speech by wishing Turkey success on behalf of all the nations of its empire, including that which in his view was the most loyal of all—the Jews. His words seem to have made a deep impression upon the members of the delegation, who promised to report what they had heard to the policy-makers in Istanbul.[86]

Almaleh did not speak as a representative of the Jews of Damascus. He did not describe their difficulties to this delegation of the ruling party, nor did he present demands for improvements in their condition and status in Damascus. Rather, he spoke as a representative of the Zionist movement, and as such connected the Jews of Damascus, in the eyes of the delegation from the Committee of Union and Progress, to an enterprise in which they as yet had no real part. While the Damascus community was indeed losing members through emigration, at this stage hardly any of those leaving were heading for Palestine. The few who did go there were for the most part, as in the past, elderly people who wished to die and be buried in the Holy Land, not to make their lives there—people at the end of their path rather than at the beginning, and certainly not people wishing to make *aliyah* for Zionist reasons. But from Almaleh's viewpoint, strengthening the involvement of Damascus Jewry in the Ottoman political system was inextricably connected with his primary goal of strengthening Jewish national identity among members of the community and drawing them close to the Zionist project in Erets Yisra'el. It may be that Almaleh was also prompted to deliver such a speech by anti-Zionist articles and anti-Jewish incitement in the local press, which

see Kayali, 'Jewish Representation', 513–15; Benbassa, *Ottoman Jewry* (Heb.), 84, 124; id., *Hayim Nahum* (Heb.), 25.

[86] *Haḥerut*, 94 (22 Mar. 1912), title page and p. 2. On the attitude towards Zionism of the Young Turks at the beginning of the 20th century, see Hanioglu, 'Jews in the Young Turk Movement', 524. On their attitude towards Zionism during the period between the revolution and the outbreak of the First World War, see Ortayli, 'Ottomanism and Zionism'.

supported the Arab candidates standing against the Committee of Union and Progress.

The parliamentary elections of April 1912 were the only ones in the history of Damascus under Ottoman rule in which Jews played a significant role, both ceremonial and practical—perhaps even a decisive one. Before the ballot boxes were opened the heads of all the religious groups, including *ḥakham bashi* Jacob Danon, were invited to say a prayer on behalf of Sultan Mehmed V Reshad. Once the boxes were opened and the votes were counted, it became clear that all four of the representatives elected in Damascus were members of the Committee of Union and Progress, who had been identified by 'Ben-Zion Raful' (Almaleh) as friends of the Jews.[87] The opposition party and its leader in Damascus, Shukri al-ʿAsali, suffered a crushing defeat within an Arab city which had been its primary stronghold and the source of its strength. After all the votes had been counted, the religious leaders, including Rabbi Jacob Danon, signed off on the results, and they were sent to the parliament.

This was not the end of the Jews' involvement in these elections. They were well aware that candidates only too often made extravagant promises before elections and forgot to honour them once elected. To try to avoid the same thing happening on this occasion, a delegation on behalf of the Jewish community—consisting of Rabbi Danon, Almaleh, and the two bankers who sat on the community board, Hayim Laniado and Moses Totah—went to visit the newly elected delegates before they left to participate in the parliamentary sessions in Istanbul. Rabbi Danon's words to the Damascus delegates, who had been elected in part by Jewish votes, were reported as follows: 'The chief rabbi told each of the delegates that the homeland had high hopes from them, and that the Ottoman Jews in particular were certain of their love for them and hope that they will protect them whenever one of their enemies attempts to attack them.'[88]

The rabbi spoke from two points of view, and this too was a significant innovation: first as a citizen and as an official of the Ottoman state, and only second as spokesman for the Jewish minority in Damascus. This approach reflected Rabbi Nahum's policy in appointing chief rabbis to communities throughout the empire. Rabbi Danon thereby performed everything that was expected of him in relation to the elections. He behaved as an enlightened Torah scholar, enjoying authority conferred on him by the state, who by virtue of his office was involved in the general life of his district and not only in that of the Jewish community. In their response to the rabbi's words, the

[87] *Haḥerut*, 104 (19 Apr. 1912), 2. [88] Ibid.

delegates promised to fulfil their obligation to the Jews, 'as they know that the Jewish people have always been loyal to their country and to their homeland'.[89]

Although the results of the poll were perceived as a political success for the Jews, it must be noted that the Jews of Damascus participated in the elections as voters alone, not as candidates. Whether from lack of capacity or lack of foresight, the Damascus community never put forward a Jewish candidate for the parliament in Istanbul. Unlike the communities in Baghdad, Salonica, İzmir, and Istanbul, the Jews of Damascus were never active participants in pan-Ottoman political life, nor were any of them either members of or activists in the Committee of Union and Progress.

The elections of 1912 were the last to be held under Ottoman rule. In 1913, safely returned to power, the Committee of Union and Progress established an authoritarian regime that suppressed all opposition so that, in practice, it remained the only political party until the ceasefire of 1918.

Epilogue

As the end of his initial two-year contract with the Damascus community approached, Rabbi Jacob Danon was already hoping to leave the city, wishing to take up a position in Baghdad. He was dissatisfied with his salary, and difficulties in administering the community were growing progressively worse: the steering committee had ceased to function almost completely, so that the entire burden of running the community fell on the shoulders of the chief rabbi. Then in September 1913 his son-in-law, Abraham Almaleh, who had served as the secretary of the community and his right-hand man, left the city, owing to disputes with elements of the community that opposed his modern Zionist educational activity.[90] With increasing frequency Rabbi Danon wrote to the *ḥakham bashi* in Istanbul requesting that he be transferred away from Damascus to serve in another community.[91] But long months passed without bringing any response to his pleas; and so Rabbi Danon continued to serve in the Damascus community against his will. Then, in August 1914, the First World War broke out, and Rabbi Danon was forced to remain as chief rabbi of Damascus through its most testing times.[92]

[89] Ibid.

[90] See Harel, *Zionism in Damascus*.

[91] See e.g. ACRI, TR/Is/81*a*, Rabbi Jacob Danon to Rabbi Hayim Nahum, Damascus, 17 Elul 5673, 29 Tishrei 5674.

[92] On this period of office and the period following it, see Harel, 'From the Ruins of Jaffa' (Heb.); id., '"Great Progress"' (Heb.).

CHAPTER TEN

Hezekiah Shabetai's Struggle against Deposition in Aleppo

'And you shall take them to the Tent of Meeting' [Num. 11: 16]. He [God] said to him [Moses]: Take them [i.e. persuade them] with words. First tell them words of praise: Happy are you that you have been appointed. Then go and tell them about their faults: You should know that they [the sons of Israel] are troublesome and stubborn people; you take [this task] upon yourselves [knowing] the condition, that they will curse you and stone you.

Sifrei bamidbar, 'Beha'alotekha'

The Beginnings of Modernization

For the Jews of Aleppo, the seeds of transition from the old world to the new were sown during the early decades of the eighteenth century, as a result of the first prolonged encounter of local Jewry with European Jewish merchants who settled in their city, coming to be known as the 'Francos'.[1] The decision of European Jews to settle in Syria and to establish commercial bases there derived from a complex mixture of economic and political considerations. They saw that a window of business opportunity had opened in Syria—particularly in Aleppo, which for centuries had served as a bridge in the international trade between East and West.[2] France was the most important European commercial presence in the area at the time, French economic involvement in the Middle East having grown through the establishment of the French Levant Company, the capitulation agreements signed with the Ottoman empire in 1673, and the special status granted to the port of Marseilles in 1699.[3] The French trade led in turn to an increase in the number of Italian Jewish merchants in Aleppo, who enjoyed the protection of France for

[1] On the Francos, see Ch. 2 above.

[2] On the political circumstances of the period, see Le Calloc'h, 'La Dynastie consulaire', 137.

[3] AECCC, Alep, vol. 30, Deval, 25 Feb. 1838; Marcus, *The Middle East*, 148–9. On France's economic interests in Syria, see Rayyan, 'France's Economic Interests' (Arab.).

the purposes of their dealings with the Ottoman empire.[4] Thus the Italian Jewish colony in Aleppo grew in both number and prosperity. At its head was the Picciotto family, whose members also enjoyed the protection of the French consul.[5]

The expansion of the Franco colony in Aleppo laid the foundations for the modernization of the Jewish communities of Syria. The changes associated with this process during the eighteenth and nineteenth centuries took several forms:

(*a*) change in the social composition of the community, which led in turn to social unrest, reshaping of the communal institutions, movement of population from the villages to the cities, and, finally, to increasing emigration overseas;

(*b*) the involvement of many local Jews in the Francos' international commercial transactions, leading to an expansion in credit transactions and the entry of Jews into new economic areas;

(*c*) the penetration of modern education in its European form, and in its wake a transformation of the students' world-view;

(*d*) a polarization in the relationships between Jews and Christians, with a concomitant establishment of relative amity between Jews and Muslims;

(*e*) a turning towards the West, with the acquisition of consular protection by western powers and a reliance upon Jewish communities in the West;

(*f*) improvement in the legal status of Jews in the wake of the Ottoman reforms of the mid-nineteenth century.

The Francos, who enjoyed foreign citizenship and far-reaching commercial privileges, remained apart from the Jewish community of Aleppo, but did not establish a separate community of their own, with its own institutions; their separate identity derived entirely from their unique economic and social status. Even when the commercial status of the city declined, the Francos retained their special position and, though diminished in number, continued to function as a separate body, not subject to the community or to its arrangements, until the end of the nineteenth century. Contemporary accounts even divide Aleppo Jewry in 1869 into two groups: the locals and the Europeans.[6]

[4] Rozen, *In the Paths of the Mediterranean* (Heb.), 54. On the place of Aleppo in trade with the West until the mid-18th century, see Masters, *The Origins of Western Economic Dominance in the Middle East*.

[5] See Rozen, 'The Archives' (Heb.); Schwarzfuchs, 'La "Nazione Ebrea"', 711–12; Philipp, 'French Merchants and Jews', 318.

[6] AAIU, Syrie, III.E., Alep, 21, Behar, 13 Nov. 1869.

The question arises: what caused the Francos to continue to maintain their distinction from the local Jewish community even after some 200 years of living in the Middle East, and what made it possible for them to do so? If, in the past, their economic and commercial connections with Europe had given them a special status, by the latter half of the nineteenth century they no longer had a monopoly on those connections: on the one hand, the circle of Jews who enjoyed special commercial privileges had greatly expanded, while on the other hand Aleppo, along with the rest of Syria, had lost much of its former significance in international commerce. The answer to this question lies in fact in the special consular status of the Francos, and particularly of the Picciotto family. So long as members of this family continued to hold numerous consular offices and to serve as the official representatives of European states in Aleppo, the Francos, however long they had been established there, were able to maintain the uniquely European characteristics that set them apart from the local Jews. By contrast, in Damascus and other cities of the Middle East where the Francos did not enjoy the special consular status they did in Aleppo, the Francos lost their uniqueness more quickly and were assimilated earlier within the local Jewish communities. In Aleppo too the Francos, after many years of living in the Middle East, inevitably combined European and Oriental characteristics; nevertheless they remained distinct from the local population, as the western connection was uppermost in their own consciousness. They remained a 'bridge' to the West, their extensive consular employment and their connections with family members who remained in Europe investing them with a role as 'carriers of western culture'—with all the values, ideas, and transformations implied therein—among their coreligionists in the Middle East.

The record tells us that members of the Picciotto family served between 1840 and 1880 as consular representatives of Russia and Prussia (Raphael Picciotto), Austria–Hungary and Tuscany (Elijah Picciotto, and after his death his son Moses), the Netherlands (Daniel Picciotto), Belgium (Hillel Picciotto), Persia (Joseph Picciotto), Denmark (Moses Picciotto—as general consul, with his son Daniel as vice consul), Sweden (Joseph Picciotto), the United States (Hillel Picciotto), and Norway (Joseph Picciotto).[7] This unusual phenomenon, in which Jewish consuls were appointed as the official representatives of European Christian countries in the Muslim Middle East, was a source of astonishment to many European Christian travellers.

[7] For the sources of this information, see Harel, *Syrian Jewry*, 226; AECADN, Consulat de France à Alep, Cote 15, 29 Dec. 1854.

It may be that during the nineteenth century the Francos felt that their special status was under threat, and in response became even more conscious of a need to preserve their position as a social elite. One of the main areas in which this new vigour found expression was that of education, specifically the activity of the Alliance Israélite Universelle in Aleppo. It was the Francos who in the 1860s initiated the first links with the Alliance, with the goal of persuading it to open an elite school in Aleppo for their own children and for those of the upper class within the Jewish community. This elitist approach aroused opposition, both within the community and in the Alliance itself, and ironically contributed to a decline in both their prestige and their image in the eyes of the Jewish community.[8]

The Francos began to become integrated within the communal frameworks only at the beginning of the 1880s, when they no longer held any consular functions, with the exception of the representation of Austria–Hungary by Moses de Picciotto. By the first decade of the twentieth century it began to look as if they would become completely assimilated within the local community and lose the unique status and identity they had hitherto maintained throughout the history of the Jews in Aleppo.

The process that symbolizes the beginning of the end for the Francos' separation from the Aleppo community began before the invitation to Hezekiah Shabetai, until then *ḥakham bashi* in the city of Tripoli in Libya, to serve the Aleppo community as *ḥakham bashi*. It is worth reiterating that, right from the time they began to settle in Aleppo, the Francos had firmly and consistently resisted any attempt to bring them under the authority of the local chief rabbi. For example, at the end of the eighteenth century the Francos struggled uncompromisingly against the attempt to force them to submit to the authority of the chief rabbi Raphael Solomon Laniado and to the regulations of the community.[9] Likewise in 1895, at the time of the controversy that led to the deposition of the *ḥakham bashi* Abraham Dweck Hakohen, the Francos declared that they did not belong to the community and did not have any part in its institutions or its leadership—and yet they openly supported the deposition of the rabbi and were involved in bringing it about.[10] After this incident the Francos became increasingly involved in the community's affairs and in its institutions—an involvement that over time would lead to the assimilation they had long resisted.

[8] See Harel, *Syrian Jewry*, 83–8. For an evaluation of the role of the Francos in introducing western education to the Jewish communities in the centre of the Ottoman empire, see Rodrigue, *French Jews*, 39.

[9] See Ch. 2 above.

[10] See Ch. 5 above.

Rabbi Jacob Saul Dweck Hakohen

Following the deposition of Abraham Dweck Hakohen, Rabbi Solomon Safdeyé, an outstanding Torah scholar who had previously served on the teaching staff of the Alliance school in Aleppo, was appointed in his place. This appointment of Rabbi Safdeyé, who served also as the head of the community's spiritual committee, did not enjoy the official recognition of the Sublime Porte, so that he was formally only acting *ḥakham bashi*. Notwithstanding this lack of official endorsement, which detracted from the status of both the office and the individual holding it, Rabbi Safdeyé seems to have been able to perform his duties adequately and to exercise authority over the community. Several accounts indicate that the rabbi was also respected by the Arab population of Aleppo.[11]

When Rabbi Safdeyé died on 29 Av 5664 (10 August 1904), the community found itself in a quandary. The doubts and struggles that ensued over the question of who should succeed him reflected the weakness of the Torah leadership in the city, several of the notable sages qualified to take on the office having left Aleppo and emigrated to Jerusalem. Finally, after several months without a chief rabbi, a compromise candidate was chosen: Rabbi Jacob Saul Dweck Hakohen, a native of Aleppo who at the time was serving as rabbi of the neighbouring community of Kilis. Rabbi Dweck Hakohen had studied under Rabbi Mordecai Abadi, one of the outstanding sages in Aleppo,[12] and as a young man had earned his living teaching Talmud to the sons of several wealthy families in the city.[13] His return now, at a relatively mature age, to head the community indicates the weakness of the local rabbinic sages, who were unable to unite around the candidacy of one of their number. Like his predecessor, Rabbi Dweck Hakohen was appointed as acting *ḥakham bashi*, lacking the firman that would give him official endorsement.

The period of Jacob Saul Dweck Hakohen's service as chief rabbi was characterized by repeated attempts on his part to establish control over a community many of whose members, particularly the children of the elite, had become less punctilious in their religious observance. In summer 1906 he promulgated an edict imposing severe penalties upon those who violated the sabbath or ate forbidden foods—two phenomena which became widespread during his term of office. Realizing that the authority of the local sages had

[11] See Laniado, *For the Sake of the Holy Ones* (Heb.), 160–1.

[12] On Rabbi Mordecai Abadi, see ibid. 123–5.

[13] On Jacob Saul Dweck Hakohen, see ibid. 19–20; J. S. Dweck Hakohen, *Derekh emunah*, author's introduction, 9–12; id., *She'erit ya'akov*, introduction by the author's son, Abraham.

weakened, he added weight to his decree by gaining the support of the sages of Tiberias and Hebron, of the Aleppo sages living in Jerusalem, of members of the rabbinic court in Jerusalem, and of the *rishon letsiyon*, Rabbi Jacob Me'ir.[14] He also launched an all-out war against various manifestations of what he saw as social laxity: specifically, women going out with their hair uncovered, and young men and women mixing in public, whether dancing together at parties in hotels and coffee-houses, participating in theatrical performances, or playing games of chance in casinos and private homes. The rabbi also opposed the growing phenomenon of Jewish women working as singers in coffee-houses and theatres.[15]

Rabbi Dweck Hakohen identified the root of these phenomena in general education and modernization—the very processes encouraged and promoted by the economic and educational elites of the community. His criticism was not directed primarily against the perpetrators of these indiscretions, such as the young girls and women who sang in the coffee-houses, but rather against the wealthy members of the community who not only failed to protest against these departures from established customs, but even organized theatre evenings and dancing parties in their own homes.[16] Rabbi Dweck Hakohen likewise opposed the sending of Jewish children to mission schools and the tendency of many members of the community to seek medical help in clinics run by the missionaries. To Rabbi Zadok Hakohen, the chief rabbi of France, he wrote:

> For some time now the Protestant mission has been active in our city . . . And they opened a large medical clinic to treat every sick person among our brethren, the children of Israel, for free. Every day, masses of our brethren flock there to seek healing for their illness and unwittingly listen to and nod their heads to all the drivel and words of heresy that the Protestants speak in their sermons . . . Moreover, the Protestants have become further strengthened in our land and opened another large school for the boys and girls of our Jewish brethren for free, without payment, and nearly one hundred and fifty girls of the children of the Hebrews have gone to them and begun to learn the laws of their religion and their prayers . . . Therefore our rabbis see that, if an attempt is not made to create a school for the daughters of the poor [where they may learn] for free, this matter will not be corrected.[17]

In an attempt to address the pressing problem of poor Jewish children going to Protestant schools, Rabbi Dweck Hakohen asked Rabbi Zadok

[14] See J. S. Dweck Hakohen, *Derekh emunah*, 120*b*–121*a*; also ibid. 105*b*–106*a*.

[15] J. S. Dweck Hakohen, *She'erit ya'akov*, 53*a*–54*a*.

[16] Ibid. 53*a*–*b*.

[17] AAIU, Syrie, I.C., Alep, 3, Rabbi Jacob Saul Dweck Hakohen to Rabbi Zadok Hakohen, Aleppo, 42nd day of the Omer, 5665.

Hakohen to try to persuade the leadership of the Alliance in Paris to fund the education of the daughters of the poor, so that they could study in Jewish schools without incurring tuition fees. This suggests that he viewed the Alliance's work in his community in a positive light. In fact, he made a clear distinction between the Alliance's activity among the girls and among the boys. He was severely critical of the Alliance's educational work with boys and young men, expressing the disappointment of the Aleppo sages generally at its failure to honour promises made in the past and the nature of its work in the present. It should be noted, to Rabbi Dweck Hakohen's credit, that his objections to the Alliance's activities were not based on mere prejudice: he visited the society's school in person precisely to see its educational programme in action for himself. After his visit, the rabbi wrote a harshly critical letter in which he demanded that the directors of the Alliance change the programme of study in the school.[18] He was particularly disturbed by what he saw as the imbalance between religious and sacred studies. His campaign against 'the education of boys in the schools of the French Jewish society' was long remembered in Aleppo, and from this point on, the city's sages were predominantly hostile towards the representatives of the Alliance.[19] The rabbi also attacked those members of the elite who joined the Freemasons. He claimed that the rituals and ceremonies involved in this group's secret activities were actually idolatrous, involving the incorporation of another religion within the service of the Creator.[20] Overall, he saw the 'Enlightenment' and modernizers as the enemy within and was severe in his criticism of them—especially as, in his opinion, 'they led the youth astray'.[21]

Notwithstanding his strictures on modern education, in other areas Rabbi Dweck Hakohen seems to have been surprisingly tolerant—specifically towards missionary activity being conducted in the great synagogue of Aleppo. Joseph Segall, a Jewish apostate who had become a Protestant missionary, was sent to Aleppo by the London Society for Promoting Christianity amongst the Jews. In his account of his mission he notes that in 1907 the great synagogue in Aleppo was his principal meeting place for talking to Jews who wished to learn about Christianity. According to Segall, the synagogue beadle, upon seeing the large number of Jews who were coming to see

[18] AAIU, Syrie, I.E., Alep, 1, Rabbi Jacob Saul Dweck Hakohen to Rabbi Zadok Hakohen, Aleppo, Elul 5665.

[19] Laniado, *For the Sake of the Holy Ones* (Heb.), 19. The aim of the new edition of this book in English (D. Sutton, *Aleppo*) is to show that the sages of Aleppo were opposed to the institutions of the Alliance from the day they were introduced in the city; however, this is not consistent with the findings that emerge from the extant documentation. On the development of the relations between the sages of Aleppo and the Alliance, see Harel, 'From Openness to Closedness' (Heb.), 1–3.

[20] J. S. Dweck Hakohen, *She'erit ya'akov*, 6*b*–8*b*.

[21] Ibid. 33*a*.

the missionary, opened the synagogue to him and even allowed Segall and his assistant Boutros to present the books of the New Testament there. The missionaries, of course, snapped up this opportunity to preach Christianity in the most sacred place for Aleppo Jews. Segall himself noted that the sight of numerous Jews coming to the synagogue every morning to study Christian literature and discuss it with him was a strange one in a place of Jewish worship.[22] Reports of this activity reached the ears of the chief rabbi, and one morning he came to see with his own eyes what was going on there. Joseph Segall describes this visit as follows:

> Suddenly [the chief rabbi] appeared on the scene with his silver-headed staff of office, and accompanied by his kavass [guard] and secretary. I must confess that I felt somewhat anxious when, in the middle of one of my addresses, my attention was drawn to his sudden appearance. In approaching me, he had to pass by the bookstall first; and Boutros innocently offered him a New Testament and some tracts which, I noticed, he carefully stowed away in the folds of his inner garment. As may be supposed, he did not quite relish our doings in the synagogue; but he was of a gentle disposition, and too well-bred and courteous to cause an open disturbance. He took me aside and began gently to remonstrate with me.[23]

There was a surprising conclusion to this visit, which also proves that the missionary was speaking the truth: once the rabbi realized that Segall was equipped with a camera, he asked him to photograph him with his guard and secretary. The reason for this was that, a few days earlier, the rabbi had received a letter from the editor of a Jewish newspaper in the United States asking for a photograph of himself and the great synagogue for publication in the paper. Segall did as he was asked, and from that time on—by his own account—Rabbi Dweck Hakohen became very friendly towards him. Segall visited the chief rabbi a number of times in his home and, according to him, took the opportunity provided by these visits to teach the gospel to the chief rabbi and to the many other Jews who gathered at his home. The rabbi even allowed Segall to photograph the greatest treasure of the community, the famous Bible manuscript known in English as the Aleppo Codex and in Hebrew as the Keter Aram Zovah. This precious text was most carefully preserved and was kept under lock and key; even members of the community were only allowed to view it on rare occasions, so its display to a stranger was a notable event.[24]

[22] Segall, *Travels*, 97.

[23] Ibid.

[24] On Keter Aram Zovah, the famous Bible manuscript in Aleppo, see Shamosh, *The Keter* (Heb.). Segall's words seem suspect, but they are backed by photographs of the sages of Aleppo, including Rabbi Dweck Hakohen, as well as by photographs of the Keter Aram Zovah reproduced in his book.

Rabbi Dweck Hakohen's direct attacks upon two powerful sectors within the community—the moneyed class and the intelligentsia—prompted them to begin questioning his leadership. These elites were also uneasy at the political weakness of the community's spiritual leadership, particularly of the *ḥakham bashi* himself. They felt that the lack of official recognition of their chief rabbi left a gulf between him and the institutions of government, placing the community in an inferior position vis-à-vis the other Jewish communities and the other religious groups, and even damaging it, by preventing it from receiving what it was entitled to by law.[25] These elite groups—including the Francos—wanted to bring in a new *ḥakham bashi* of greater stature from outside Aleppo, not holding the local rabbinic sages in great esteem. This lack of regard reflects the declining level of scholarship in the community, which was losing many of its young rabbis to Erets Yisra'el or to Aleppan communities throughout the world.[26] This dwindling in the number and reputation of the city's sages, along with the numerous disputes that arose among those who remained, had led to a situation in which, for the first time in its history, Aleppo, formerly known as 'a city of scholars and scribes', was unable to find a chief rabbi from among its own people.

Thus two opposing forces emerged within the community. On the one side were ranged the economic and educated elites, who seem to have had the support of the weaker classes and most of the rabbinic scholars. For some time there had been a sense of uneasiness among the poorer groups in the community owing to what they perceived as an unfair distribution of the tax burden, particularly that of the *'askariyya*, and many of them hoped that the appointment of a new, strong *ḥakham bashi* from outside Aleppo, officially recognized by the government, would both redress this imbalance and also restore the community's standing within the wider society. On the other side were the supporters of the interim *ḥakham bashi*, Rabbi Dweck Hakohen. This group included the chief rabbi's extended family and close associates, and possibly some of his rabbinic colleagues, but these amounted—at least according to the testimony of his opponents, which must of course be taken with a pinch of salt—to only a small number of people.[27]

The Appointment of Rabbi Hezekiah Shabetai

To arrange the replacement of Rabbi Dweck Hakohen by a new *ḥakham bashi* from outside Aleppo, the community appointed a special committee headed

[25] *Hashkafah*, 50 (8 Adar II 5668), 2. For a description of Rabbi Dweck Hakohen's passivity as community leader, see also AAIU, Syrie, II.E., Alep, 14, Aranias, 12 Apr. 1908.

[26] See e.g. Harel, 'The First Jews', 199.

[27] *Hashkafah*, 50 (8 Adar II 5668), 2; AAIU, Syrie, II.E., Alep, 14, Aranias, 12 Apr. 1908.

by David Hillel Silvera, a member of a prominent Franco family.[28] It is worth noting that this was not the first time that one of the Francos had headed a communal committee: in 1902, during a period of drought and famine that led to suffering in many parts of the community, Yitshak Ancona was placed at the head of a relief committee set up by the chief rabbi at the time, Solomon Safdeyé.[29] In their search for a new *ḥakham bashi*, members of the committee turned to the sages of Jerusalem and the *ḥakham bashi* in Istanbul, Rabbi Moses Halevi, for assistance in finding an appropriate candidate. In the end they chose Rabbi Hezekiah Shabetai, who at the time was serving as *ḥakham bashi* in Tripoli in Libya.[30] A letter, signed by David Silvera, was sent inviting Rabbi Shabetai to serve as *ḥakham bashi* in Aleppo.[31] The invitation was accepted with alacrity; some accounts suggest that Rabbi Shabetai was only too willing to leave Tripoli owing to its great distance from the spiritual and cultural centre of Jerusalem.[32] His move to Aleppo was rapidly arranged, and in parallel an effort was made to persuade the Ottoman ministries of law and religion to confer official recognition on the new *ḥakham bashi*. This effort evidently required the disbursement of a great deal of money, which was sent in the first instance to the *ḥakham bashi* in Istanbul, for forwarding to the appropriate authorities. Such an outlay could only have been undertaken by members of the community's economic elite, motivated by their desire to ensure that their new *ḥakham bashi* would enjoy full status and authority.[33]

Rabbi Hezekiah Shabetai, son of Rabbi Shabetai Gabriel and his wife Rachel, was born in Salonica in 1862. When he was 6 years old his family moved to Jerusalem, where he was educated in the Sephardi yeshivas of that city. Later, he was sent on fundraising missions on behalf of the Sephardi communities in Jerusalem and Hebron. In 1900, at the recommendation of the *rishon letsiyon* Rabbi Jacob Saul Elyashar, he was appointed vice *ḥakham bashi* in Jaffa, where he served until 1904. In that year he was invited to serve as *ḥakham bashi* in Tripoli, where he remained until his invitation to Aleppo.[34]

On 12 March 1908, Rabbi Hezekiah Shabetai arrived in Istanbul to receive the official firman from the sultan appointing him *ḥakham bashi* of Aleppo. The reception that awaited him was elaborate and dignified by any standard: when he disembarked from the ship, he was received by the sage

[28] On David Silvera, see Harel, 'In the Wake of the Dreyfus Affair'.

[29] AAIU, Syrie, I.C., Alep, 3, Solomon Safdeyé to the Alliance, Aleppo, 25 Adar I 5662.

[30] *JC*, 3 Apr. 1908, p. 14*a*; AAIU, Syrie, II.E., Alep, 14, Aranias, 12 Apr. 1908.

[31] *Hashkafah*, 44 (17 Adar 5668), 2.

[32] Ibid.

[33] AAIU, Syrie, II.E., Alep, 14, Aranias, 12 Apr. 1908.

[34] For more biographical information, see Gaon, *The Jews of the East* (Heb.), 661–2; cf. Shabetai, *Divrei yeḥizkiyahu* (1921), author's introduction.

Hezekiah Hatim, secretary of the chief rabbinate, and by Murad Bey Dweck, son of the former *ḥakham bashi* of Aleppo Rabbi Abraham Dweck Hakohen, attended by two kavasses. Rabbi Shabetai was invited to stay as a guest at the home of Rabbi Moses Halevi, who accompanied him to the ceremony at which he received his official appointment.[35] The firman granted extensive authority to the new *ḥakham bashi*. He was authorized to issue rulings banishing from the city anyone found guilty by the rabbinic court, without any involvement of the judiciary or executive branches of the district government. Likewise, all marriages and divorces of Jews within the district required his approval, and he had the right to deny burial in the Jewish cemetery to anyone breaking the laws of the community. The local police were required to make officers available to the *ḥakham bashi* to enforce his authority in the event of opposition. He also had an exclusive writ empowering him to determine whether food in the community complied with *kashrut* and to determine a *gabilah* tax, intended among other things to fund the activity of the rabbinic office that he headed. All these prerogatives and many other clauses in the firman gave the strongest government backing to the new *ḥakham bashi*.[36]

At the end of March Rabbi Hezekiah Shabetai arrived in Aleppo. The committee that had arranged his appointment organized an elaborate reception in his honour, in order to make a significant public event—in the eyes of the whole city, not just the Jewish community—of the arrival of a *ḥakham bashi* equipped with a firman from the sultan. The governor, the commander of the army, the director of the Aleppo branch of the Ottoman Bank, and all the foreign consuls were invited. At the railway station, where the hall had been decorated in honour of the illustrious newcomer, more than 10,000 people were said to have crowded together for the occasion, including students from the schools wearing their sabbath finery. Although the most senior government officials did not attend personally, they sent their sons to pay their respects to the rabbi on their behalf; the foreign consuls sent their personal translators to perform the same courtesy. Notwithstanding these absences, the central goal of those who had organized the event, and the appointment it celebrated, was accomplished: in a single step, the Jewish community had moved from the margins of Aleppo society to the centre of the stage, and was once more a sector of the city that had to be taken into account—if only because its head enjoyed the standing of a senior Ottoman official. Muslim dignitaries expressed their admiration for the new *ḥakham*

35 *Hashkafah*, 55 (24 Adar II 5668), 2.

36 The original official firman, bearing the sultan's signature, is preserved to this day in the Ben-Mordechai Collection. The full Hebrew text of the firman is cited by Beck, *From Hidden Things* (Heb.), 55–6.

bashi, and one of them even sent an elaborate chariot accompanied by four soldiers to take the rabbi to the dignitary's home. The reception continued with visits of the city's chief personalities to the rabbi's home. One member of the community stated that this was the first time that such a great honour had been bestowed upon a Jewish religious leader in Aleppo.[37] On the following days further ceremonies were held, all intended to establish the public status of the new *ḥakham bashi* and to raise the status and image of the Jewish community in the eyes of the Aleppo public. A description of the Shabat Hagadol sermon delivered by the rabbi shortly after his arrival in Aleppo includes a record by one of those present of the public's reaction:

When he spoke it was as if he breathed sparks of light into the hearts of the entire community, and one could see on their faces signs of the spirit of life, the spirit of turning from slavery to freedom, a spirit of the self-recognition that they were a blessed and precious community. Hence all of them looked upon their rabbi as a redeeming angel sent by Supernal Providence.[38]

Rabbi Shabetai was invited to the home of the governor of the Aleppo district for the traditional ceremony of publicly presenting his firman from the sultan. Thousands of people, both Jews and non-Jews, crowded the streets in order to see a sight whose like had not been seen in Aleppo since the appointment of Abraham Dweck Hakohen in the 1880s—the appearance of an official *ḥakham bashi*.[39] The rabbi, dressed in his robes of office, was received with all due honour by the governor and by the members of the *majlis idara*. Over the following days he visited the home of the Ottoman army commander and also the homes of the foreign consuls, who in turn made the customary reciprocal visits. The British consul even stated in public that, from now on, he would allow the Jewish chief rabbi to adjudicate in legal matters pertaining to those Jews who were English subjects. During the course of the Passover festival the rabbi made further courtesy calls on the governor of Aleppo and the consuls at their homes. The members of the community felt that their new chief rabbi had restored their dignity in the eyes of the other inhabitants of Aleppo, and showed their appreciation by forming long queues on the eve of the Passover festival in order to kiss his hand and receive his blessing.[40]

There are two particular points worth noting in relation to the events surrounding Rabbi Shabetai's arrival in Aleppo. First, throughout the course

37 *Hashkafah*, 63 (26 Nisan 5668), 4.

38 Description of the Shabat Hagadol sermon of Rabbi Hezekiah Shabetai upon his arrival in Aleppo, Ben-Mordechai Collection.

39 The sultanic firman received by Rabbi Shabetai ignores the periods of service of Rabbis Safdeyé and Saul Dweck Hakohen, describing him as the replacement of Rabbi Abraham Dweck Hakohen.

40 *Hashkafah*, 70 (21 Iyar 5668), 2–3.

of the reception ceremonies Rabbi Shabetai was accompanied by dignitaries from the community, headed by members of the Franco families. Thus, for example, the only person to accompany him to the home of the Muslim dignitary was a Franco, Solomon Picciotto. Second, during his visit to the homes of the foreign consuls, he was accompanied by Michael Aranias, the director of the Alliance school in Aleppo.[41] The latter observation suggests that a new chapter had been opened in relations between the rabbinate and the modern school; the former that the Francos had abandoned their conscious separation from the Aleppo community, and that from this point on, having dominated the community from within and even determined who would stand at its head, they would become members of the community like any others. In fact, after only a brief period, this apparent trend was abruptly reversed and an unprecedented attempt was made by the Francos to establish an independent community.

New Arrangements and Political Involvement

David Silvera evidently expected the new *ḥakham bashi* to demonstrate his gratitude to those responsible for his appointment, and thus to serve as a tool in their hands. However, from the time of his arrival, possibly as a result of the great honour shown him, Rabbi Shabetai recognized the importance of his office and sought to rearrange the distribution of power in the community. He lost no time in beginning this process, starting in the days immediately after Passover by appointing on his own authority a new steering committee, composed of 'distinguished and God-fearing people', with Yom-Tov Shamma as its president.[42] In this way, control of the community leadership passed out of the hands of the Francos back into those of the old elite families. Shamma and the *ḥakham bashi* completely reorganized the community's charitable provision. In addition to the venerable Tsedakah Umarpeh society—founded in 1898 to provide medical assistance to Jewish patients so that they would not need go to Christian missionary institutions—a number of new societies were established with the aim of providing support to the less well-off.[43] Among them was Neshei Hayil (Women of Valour), a society headed by Shamma's wife. One of its main activities was to monitor the cost of clothing: the women of the society established a maximum price for each item, in order to prevent overcharging. They also helped poor mothers to fund the maintenance of a housemaid and other expenses after childbirth. The establishing of Neshei Hayil was not a trivial matter: it was an unprece-

[41] AAIU, Syrie, II.E., Alep, 14, Aranias, 12 Apr. 1908.

[42] *Hashkafah*, 70 (21 Iyar 5668), 3.

[43] On the founding of the Tsedakah Umarpeh society, see *Ḥevrat tsedakah umarpe* (Heb.).

dented initiative on the part of women, which could not have taken place had they not been prepared for such a role by the girls' school run by the Alliance over the preceding years. Another new society was Hakhnasat Orehim, set up to build a suitable hostel for poor Jewish immigrant families from Persia, Iraq, Bukhara, Afghanistan, and India who passed through Aleppo during their travels and had nowhere to stay. New arrangements were also introduced in the burial society (*ḥevrah kadisha*) and in administering the income of the great synagogue, new boards being appointed for each institution. More generally, in response to complaints from the poorer majority within the community, the *ḥakham bashi* began to examine in depth the financial affairs of the community, including its system of tax collection, as the most frequent complaints related to the inequitable division of the burden of the *ʿaskariyya* tax.[44]

Rabbi Hezekiah Shabetai acted decisively to move his community towards modernization. For example, he prohibited the elderly local midwives from continuing to deliver children, owing to the risks to women in childbirth associated with their practices. Instead, he facilitated the move to Aleppo of a Jewish midwife who had been trained in Switzerland, allotting her a salary from the communal coffer, so that she might care, primarily, for poor women during their labour.[45]

In July 1908, at the height of these transformations in the community, the Young Turk Revolution broke out. In its wake, new arrangements were introduced both in government circles and in the conduct of the non-Muslim minority communities. Elections were organized in each city for the leadership of associations which supported the Committee of Union and Progress, the political party of the Young Turks. This activity bore a new and fresh message of democracy, which evidently influenced the conduct of Rabbi Shabetai, who became increasingly deeply involved in politics. His personality and energy made him a figure it was impossible to ignore. Senior representatives of the Committee of Union and Progress, who came from Salonica to supervise the Aleppo branch of the party, requested a meeting with the rabbi, asking him whether there were any rights or privileges that the government was denying the Jews. He responded that it would be appropriate for the government to require by law that all administrative councils, at local and regional level, appoint one Jew to their membership, there being at present hardly any Jewish representation in the country's courts or administration. Party representatives promised to act to correct this injustice.[46]

The community leadership also made an effort to raise the public status of the *ḥakham bashi* to that of the heads of the Christian churches. One way of

[44] *Hashkafah*, 98 (1 Elul 5668), 2. [45] *Hatsevi*, 40 (1 Kislev 5669), 3. [46] Ibid.

doing this was to arrange the granting of a medal of honour from the sultan to the *ḥakham bashi*. The community council had already spent a great deal of money to this end during the period of the *ancien régime*, all of which was lost at the revolution. After the revolution, once the institutions of the empire had been reorganized, the leaders of the community turned once again to Istanbul and to the new *ḥakham bashi*, Hayim Nahum, with a request that he arrange for a medal of honour, similar to that given to the Christian patriarch, to be conferred on their chief rabbi.[47]

Hezekiah Shabetai had a highly developed political consciousness, and the revolution of the Young Turks provided him, as a senior government official, with the opportunity to apply it in practice. Sweeping the community along with him, he brought the political involvement of the Jews in Aleppo to a peak. Thus, for example, in April 1909, following the removal of Sultan ʿAbd al-Hamid II, the *ḥakham bashi* organized a special event in the Jewish community to mark the coronation of the new sultan, Mehmed V Reshad.[48] This event took place in the great synagogue, and all the leading government figures in Aleppo were invited: the governor, the commanders of the military and of the police, leaders of the Committee of Union and Progress, and the heads of the district judicial system. The synagogue was decorated with flowers and with flags of the empire, and twelve of its Torah scrolls were adorned with colourful cloths. Jews, both men and women, filled the synagogue and received with enthusiastic applause the senior officials who had come, for the first time in the community's history, to the synagogue, the centre of Jewish life in the city. Rabbi Shabetai delivered a prayer in Hebrew for the welfare of the new sultan and then addressed the assembly in Turkish. The commander of the reserve units of the Ottoman army responded with a speech in which he spoke warmly of the Jewish people, saying that they had shown mankind the proper path in many areas. He praised their wisdom and knowledge, and noted in particular their patriotism. Going beyond mere words, he embraced and kissed the *ḥakham bashi*, and then addressed the audience and said that in embracing the most honourable personage of the community, 'whom I appreciate very highly, I have embraced all the Jewish community of Aleppo'. Every time the sultan or the Committee of Union and Progress was mentioned in one of the speeches, the audience broke out in renewed applause.[49]

Political and cultural events became a common feature of the Aleppo community. In this respect the lead was taken by the boys' school run by the

[47] ACRI, TR/Is/57*a*, Joseph Elijah Shamma to Hayim Nahum, Aleppo, 27 Elul 5669.

[48] On the deposition of one sultan and the appointment of the other, see Lewis, *The Emergence of Modern Turkey*, 212.

[49] *JC*, 11 June 1909, p. 10*a*.

Alliance. This institution served as the vanguard of European culture in the city, promoting the values of freedom, equality, and brotherhood upon which the Ottoman revolution had also been based; its social events became a magnet, not only for Jews but also for non-Jews who wished to enjoy a taste of European culture. Thus, for example, at the end of the summer of 1909 a ball was held at which the governor of the district, the army commanders, the senior officials, the European consuls, the heads of the Committee of Union and Progress, and the mayor were all present. The evening was accompanied by music from the army band; the students sang a 'Song of Freedom', specially composed in honour of the new Ottoman constitution, as well as national songs in Turkish and Arabic. Jewish Ottoman patriotism was also expressed in the presentation of theatrical scenes about the leaders of the Young Turks, Anwar Bey and Ahmad Niazi.[50] French culture and Jewish national pride were also represented: the youths sang in French and Hebrew, and presented the play *Hannah and Her Seven Sons* in Hebrew and Molière's *The Physician* in French. Nor were the Arab dignitaries in the audience deprived, as there was also a satirical play in Arabic.[51] There is no doubt that an event of this type, with all the political and cultural gestures it incorporated, honed the political consciousness of the Jewish community in Aleppo and moved it from the margins of the city's life to its centre. It became a factor that needed to be taken into account in political calculations relating to the Aleppo region. From now on, the *ḥakham bashi*, the city's most senior Jewish official under the system of Ottoman rule, was invited to every political event organized by the Committee of Union and Progress.[52]

The new democratic spirit in the air encouraged Rabbi Hezekiah Shabetai to attempt to establish a democratic basis for the communal institutions. He introduced internal elections, an unprecedented innovation in Aleppo—with the exception of the poll conducted thirteen years earlier, following the deposition of the *ḥakham bashi* Abraham Dweck Hakohen in 1895. Up to that point the hereditary and moneyed elites of the community had apportioned positions of leadership in the community among themselves. It was only after the deposition of Rabbi Abraham Dweck Hakohen that a communal leadership was appointed for the first time on the basis of lots drawn rather than through appointment by an oligarchy. Thereafter the leaders of the community returned to the old system—until Rabbi Shabetai introduced the use of the secret ballot in elections for the steering committee. These elections were held in the autumn of 1908. Rabbi Shabetai adopted the

[50] For more on these two individuals, see Lewis, *The Emergence of Modern Turkey*, 204 ff.

[51] *Hatsevi*, 3 (7 Tishrei 5670), 2.

[52] See e.g. *Hatsevi*, 20 (7 Heshvan 5670), 2.

procedure followed in Istanbul, as stipulated in the Jewish millet decree promulgated some fifty years earlier.[53] In contrast to the past, the process was formally announced and transparent to the public. Half of the 120 candidates for election would be chosen by the *ḥakham bashi* himself, half by the *mukhtars*, the heads of each street. The list of 120 names was then to be posted on the walls of the synagogue, and an announcement distributed on behalf of the *ḥakham bashi* stating that each member of the community must choose sixty people from the list to serve on the general board of the community. In order to ensure freedom of choice, the voters were also allowed to nominate (among the sixty they could choose) candidates who did not appear on the list. Polling continued for four days, during which members of the community went to the chief rabbi's home to cast their ballots. At the end of the voting period, the ballots were counted; to the sixty people who enjoyed the largest number of votes were added another twenty rabbis, selected by Shabetai. The resulting eighty members of the general board in turn chose nine people from among their number to serve on the steering committee, headed by Joseph Elijah Shamma. The process was completed with the confirmation of the final list by the authorities, thereby granting official approval to the activity of the elected board and steering committee.[54] The alliance created between the new heads of the community and the *ḥakham bashi* was cemented by marital connections, with Joseph Elijah Shamma's son being married to Rabbi Shabetai's daughter.[55]

The *ḥakham bashi* also acted to promote both Jewish and general education in the community. In 1909 a government teacher training institution was opened in Aleppo. Students received a monthly wage, and at the end of their studies the government helped them to attain positions in Aleppo and its environs, with a guaranteed salary. Initially Jews were not admitted, but Rabbi Shabetai demanded that those responsible for education in the district open the college to all students regardless of religion or race, as required by the new Ottoman constitution. The ministry of education in Istanbul responded to the *ḥakham bashi*'s demand and six young Jews were accepted for training. Moreover, the official responsible for education gave the rabbi funds from the ministry of education in Istanbul in order to finance studies in the Turkish

[53] Davison, *Reform in the Ottoman Empire*, 129–31.

[54] *Hatsevi*, 40 (1 Kislev 5669), 3. Shabetai (*Divrei yeḥizkiyahu* (1935), 50, §9) describes the electoral process in the following years, with particular attention to the withdrawal from the democratic approach in the empire generally and in the Jewish communities in particular. It is worth remembering that Rabbi Shabetai first wrote this account in 1926, without direct reference to the elections conducted in 1908.

[55] ACRI, TR/Is/72*a*, Saul David Sutton to Hayim Nahum, Aleppo, 23 Sivan 5671.

language and general studies in the Jewish educational institutions. Rabbi Shabetai used this money to open a new educational institution, called Yesod Hahokhmah (The Foundation of Wisdom), in which thirty to forty students from among the poorer classes studied without charge. Its daily curriculum included two and a half hours of Talmud, one and a half hours of Hebrew, one and a half hours of Turkish, and one hour of Arabic.[56]

The new *ḥakham bashi* also tackled the problem of sexual laxity in the community with characteristic efficiency. An area known for the activity of Jewish prostitutes had begun to take shape in the Jewish quarter, near the great synagogue, attracting people of dubious character from all parts of the city. Rabbi Shabetai took serious steps to remove these girls from the emerging red-light district and return them to a respectable life. His success in removing this scourge from the Jewish quarter added to both his own prestige and that of the community, which had been tainted by this phenomenon.[57]

The status of *ḥakham bashi* Hezekiah Shabetai became progressively stronger, both within the community and within the Ottoman administration. Rabbis Jacob Saul Dweck Hakohen and Elijah Hamawi, both members of the rabbinic court, wrote to the *ḥakham bashi* in Istanbul that on the very day of Rabbi Shabetai's arrival in the city, 'we went out to greet him and gave him great honour, and we also went to his house and met him with joy and a good heart, and we blessed him with the blessing that God had sent a redeemer to Israel'.[58] Even these veteran sages of Aleppo, who notwithstanding these warm words accepted the authority of this chief rabbi from outside the city only begrudgingly, seem to have had the good sense at least to attempt to coexist in harmony with their new head. A division of labour was established, according to which the *ḥakham bashi* exercised authority in the political and organizational affairs of the community, while the rabbinic court dealt with spiritual questions and matters governed by religious law. The new rabbi's senior political status, in the eyes of both the *ḥakham bashi* in Istanbul and government ministers, was reflected in his being selected to go

[56] AAIU, Syrie, II.E., Alep, 19*b*, Bassan, 20 Jan. 1910. On the regulations of the Yesod Hahokhmah society, which had been established previously, see *Maḥberet ḥevrat yesod haḥokhmah*. Later on the name of the association was changed to Reshit Hokhmah. For more on the activity of this school and its Hebrew-nationalist orientation, see *Haḥerut*, 68 (24 Mar. 1911), 3; 154 (18 Sept. 1911), 2.

[57] See the report of Rabbis Raphael David Saban and Yitshak Shaki as presented to Rabbi Hayim Nahum, Aleppo, 25 Heshvan 5672, Ben-Mordechai Collection.

[58] ACRI, TR/Is/57*a*, Jacob Saul Dweck Hakohen and Elijah Hamawi to Hayim Nahum, Aleppo, 28 Kislev 5669; cf. *Hashkafah*, 92 (10 Av 5668), 2.

to Jerusalem towards the end of 1908, representing the Ottoman ministers of justice and religion, to supervise the elections for the steering committee and the spiritual committee in the community there, so that these bodies might elect a permanent *ḥakham bashi* for the city.[59] Further evidence of Rabbi Shabetai's high public standing appears in the fact that, from the time of his arrival in Aleppo, his full title—like that of Hayim Nahum in the imperial capital—was *ḥakham bashi efendi.*

The Aleppo community seemed to have achieved at least one of the goals it had set for itself with the election of a new *ḥakham bashi*: it had a leader who guided the community with a sure hand and was accepted both throughout the Jewish community and by the imperial authorities. The rabbi's success in revitalizing the communal institutions aroused the hope that, within five years, the period of employment fixed in his contract, the community of Aleppo might be restored to the condition of its golden age. In view of these hopes, the people of Aleppo were rather anxious about Rabbi Shabetai's departure for Jerusalem, lest he be offered the position of *ḥakham bashi* there and never return to Aleppo. So great was the concern, indeed, that mass demonstrations were mounted, some in attempts to prevent his departure, others at least to ensure his return by appealing to Rabbi Nahum that he guarantee that Rabbi Shabetai would return to Aleppo at the conclusion of his mission.[60]

The outline given above paints a uniformly positive picture of Rabbi Shabetai's first months in Aleppo. However, in their letters to Istanbul while the chief rabbi was on his mission to Jerusalem, the leaders of the community expressed their fear that, during his absence, 'harsh controversy will break out within the community'.[61] What they were referring to was a dispute that had broken out between the *ḥakham bashi* Hezekiah Shabetai and the two members of the rabbinic court who had written so fulsomely of their new chief on his appointment, Jacob Saul Dweck Hakohen and Elijah Hamawi. The two rabbis exploited Rabbi Shabetai's absence to write to the *ḥakham bashi* in Istanbul asking him to take their side in the struggle against the *ḥakham bashi* in their own city. In these letters, they describe strained relations across a variety of issues, including Rabbi Shabetai's attempt to trespass upon their realm in placing younger rabbis, who would be subject to his authority, in the communal rabbinic court. According to Rabbis Dweck Hakohen

[59] See *Ḥavatselet*, 30 (20 Kislev 5669), 157. On the 'war of the rabbis' in the Jerusalem community, see Hayim, *Particularity and Integration* (Heb.), 12–15.

[60] ACRI, TR/Is/57*a*, Rabbi Hezekiah Shabetai to Rabbi Hayim Nahum, Aleppo, 29 Heshvan 5669.

[61] Ibid., Joseph Elijah Shamma to Rabbi Hayim Nahum, Aleppo, 13 Kislev 5669.

and Hamawi, Rabbi Shabetai and his supporters adopted an insulting attitude towards them; moreover, the chief rabbi had even asked the government authorities to prohibit them from serving on the rabbinic court. They claimed that, shortly after his arrival in Aleppo, the *ḥakham bashi* had attempted to depose the pair of elderly judges; he tore up a ruling they had written, and even sent his beadle to take the court seal away from them. According to their account, they succeeded in convincing him that their deposition was prohibited by Jewish law, and even got the other sages of Aleppo to sign a petition stating that they did not want any other judges. They further alleged that this attempt to remove them from office and deprive them of their salaries was mere personal vindictiveness, because they had supposedly insulted his dignity. They also made it clear that they feared him by asking that the content of their letters not be revealed to him.[62] Aware of the great power that the sultan's firman gave to the *ḥakham bashi*, they explicitly asked Rabbi Hayim Nahum to acquire for them an official appointment recognizing them as the spiritual committee of the community, and thereby giving them an authority equivalent to that of the *ḥakham bashi*.

The judges' understanding of the division of authority between the *ḥakham bashi* and the rabbinic court, which in their opinion Rabbi Shabetai had violated, was based upon long-standing tradition going back to the earliest times of the community in Aleppo. According to this tradition, the court's function was to rule on interpersonal and marital disputes; the *ḥakham bashi* was to assist the rabbinic court in imposing its rulings upon those who refused to obey its orders, and was also responsible for collecting taxes and conducting the community's relations with the authorities. Rabbis Dweck Hakohen and Hamawi argued that whereas in the past the *ḥakham bashi* and the judges had worked in harmony and co-operation, the new incumbent, Rabbi Shabetai, now wished to dominate the rabbinic court.[63] Whether or not the judges' account exaggerated matters, it is certainly possible that Shabetai, who had both a wealth of knowledge of Torah and a sharp analytical mind, wished to extend his authority into spiritual matters.

Shabetai was away for about two months. It may be that his stay in Jerusalem, and his experience of the disputes among the rabbis there, may have caused him to reconsider his attempt to dismiss the two judges from the

[62] ACRI, TR/Is/57*a*, Jacob Saul Dweck Hakohen and Elijah Hamawi to Hayim Nahum, 28 Kislev 5669; TR/Is/62, Jacob Saul Dweck Hakohen and Elijah Hamawi to Hayim Nahum, 17 Kislev 5670.

[63] ACRI, TR/Is/57*a*, Jacob Saul Dweck Hakohen and Elijah Hamawi to Hayim Nahum, 28 Kislev 5669.

rabbinic court, or it may be that the rabbis agreed to forgo some of their own authority in favour of the *ḥakham bashi*. In either event, it would appear that the struggle between the chief rabbi and the local rabbinic scholars died down, though an element of tension persisted.

Activity for Equal Rights

Upon his return to Aleppo, Rabbi Shabetai continued to engage in the struggle for Jewish legal rights, and also his efforts to promote his own status and that of his community within Aleppo society. Under Ottoman law, the *ḥakham bashi* was supposed to be included among the members of the *majlis idara*, the provincial council. In practice, this privilege had been withheld for many years. In other councils, too, there had been no representation of Jews since the beginning of the twentieth century, their places having been taken by Christians.[64] Hezekiah Shabetai tirelessly petitioned both the authorities in Istanbul and the district governor to correct this injustice, writing to Rabbi Nahum: 'For in truth, my jealousy concerning this matter eats at me. Why have we been made different, even in these times, from the other nations? . . . Permit me to say that in the *idara* and in all the *majalis* others have a place, but not us.'[65] He claimed that, notwithstanding the revolution and the new constitution, the old prejudices and discrimination still held sway in Aleppo. Under law, any community that numbered fewer than 400 people was not allowed to participate in the elections for the various councils. By this token, the Jewish and the Catholic communities, as the largest minority groups, should have enjoyed corresponding representation on the councils. However, in reality small Christian groups were allowed to take part, while the Jews remained unrepresented. In the end, with the support of the governor, Rabbi Shabetai succeeded in introducing a representative of the Jewish community, named Abraham Ades, into the lower court of the first instance.[66]

The rabbi's greatest success in this field came about when the district governor established a council of twenty-five members, some of whom were Ottoman citizens and some of whom were foreigners, with the task of finding ways of augmenting the municipality's income, supervising the activities of the municipality, and planning the future development of the Aleppo region. As initially drawn up, its membership comprised thirteen Muslims, eleven Christians, and only one Jew. The *ḥakham bashi* complained to the district

[64] ACRI, TR/Is/57*a*, Rabbi Hezekiah Shabetai to Rabbi Hayim Nahum, 19 Iyar 5669.

[65] Ibid., emphasis in original.

[66] Ibid., Rabbi Hezekiah Shabetai to Rabbi Hayim Nahum, Aleppo, 3 Av 5669, 27 Elul 5669.

governor that the Jewish community, which numbered 10,000 people, and whose members were no less well educated than the rest of the population, deserved greater representation. In response, the number of Jewish representatives on the council was increased to five.[67]

Not all of the Ottoman officials welcomed improvements in the status of the Jewish community and of its leader; there were those who wished to continue to discriminate against Jews, and sometimes against Christians as well. One of the sensitive matters with which the *ḥakham bashi* had to deal was that of conscription of young Jewish men into the army. Just before the conscription law was enacted in August 1909, the official responsible for tax collection in the Aleppo district demanded urgent repayment from the *ḥakham bashi* of the balance of the Jewish community's debt in respect of the *'askariyya* tax. The *ḥakham bashi* objected to this demand for two reasons: one, under the new conscription law, Jews were liable for military service like all other citizens, and were no longer obliged to pay this tax as the price of exemption; two, if the tax were still to be paid, then the same demand ought to have been made of the Christian community. The response of the tax collector was harsh and uncompromising, including the arbitrary and illegal imprisonment of wealthy Jews. The *ḥakham bashi* complained vociferously but composedly: basing his case on the approach he had followed consistently since the revolution, he asked not for mercy or clemency, but for justice under the law: his claims against the official responsible were based upon the Ottoman constitution and his criticism was directed at the 'evil deeds which they are doing with the Jews, and only with the Jews, whose like had not been done even in the days of tyranny'.[68] Following his usual practice, Hezekiah Shabetai wrote both to the ministry of justice and the treasury in Istanbul, and simultaneously to the *ḥakham bashi* in Istanbul—who succeeded in cancelling the remainder of the Jews' debt.

On 25 September 1909, the call-up of non-Muslims for military service began in Aleppo. Young men born in 1883 and 1884 were summoned to appear before a conscription board, which would determine who would be exempt from service owing to family obligations or other reasons. Anyone seeking release from military conscription had to pay 50 Turkish pounds. The first conscription quota included 2,000 Christians and 500 Jews. The Christian patriarch published a patriotic appeal in which he called upon young Christians to fulfil their obligation to the country; the *ḥakham bashi*, by contrast, did not.[69] Shabetai, like many other rabbis throughout the communities

67 *Haḥerut*, 39 (27 Dec. 1909), 2.
68 ACRI, TR/Is/57*a*, Hezekiah Shabetai to Hayim Nahum, 27 Elul 5669.
69 AENS, Turquie (Syrie–Liban), vol. 112, pp. 191–2, Laronce, Alep, 3 Oct. 1909.

of the empire, seems to have been worried that Jewish conscripts might be forced to violate the sabbath and Jewish holidays, and to eat non-kosher food, during the period of their military service.[70] In any event, he co-operated with the leaders of the Christian communities in protesting to the authorities in Istanbul about the manner in which the conscription board in Aleppo was run. According to them, the board failed to take into consideration the notes that had been sent them about the ages of the conscripts.[71]

The new conscription law swelled yet further the stream of young Christians and Jews leaving Aleppo, displacing economic factors as the main motive for emigration.[72] Among those who remained, the conscription of young Jews into the army plunged many families into severe economic hardship. In response to this new need, the community leaders and the *ḥakham bashi* established a charitable organization called Ma'oz La'evyon (Bastion for the Poor), whose purpose was to assist the conscripts and their families, as well as Jewish émigrés passing through Aleppo. During the winter of 1910–11 this association distributed flour and coal to the poor, and in practice became the most active and effective welfare organization in Aleppo. Hezekiah Shabetai saw the society as his own creation, and assisted a great deal in its development and funding.[73]

The Issue of Taxation

Another area demanding fundamental reorganization was the economic framework of the community. Since the opening of the Suez Canal in 1869 and the migration of many of the wealthier members, the income of the Aleppo community had declined sharply. At the same time, its expenses had greatly increased, with growing demands for assistance to poor people, to families without a breadwinner, to the *talmudei torah* and other schools, and to the various charitable institutions. As *ḥakham bashi*, Shabetai succeeded in obtaining the agreement of both the steering committee and the rabbinic sages for the imposition of an indirect tax or *gabilah* on various goods and services in order to raise more income for the community. This tax was duly levied on, among other things, cheese, marriage documents (*ketubot*), circumcisions, the sale of houses, burials, and various documents and permissions

70 ACRI, TR/Is/57*a*, Hezekiah Shabetai to Hayim Nahum, Aleppo, 8 Av 5669.

71 *Haḥerut*, 19 (5 Dec. 1910), 3.

72 On the beginnings of this emigration, see Harel, *Syrian Jewry*, 250–3.

73 ACRI, TR/Is/72*a*, Hezekiah Shabetai to Hayim Nahum, Aleppo, 4 Sivan 5671; *Haḥerut*, 14 (25 Nov. 1910), 2. On the Jewish soldiers from Aleppo in the Ottoman army, see e.g. *Haḥerut*, 35 (11 Jan. 1911), 2.

issued by the communal institutions.[74] It is nevertheless worth noting that, unlike many other communities of the Ottoman empire, the Aleppo community did not impose the *gabilah* on meat.

These steps were revolutionary as until that time the income of the community had come entirely from taxes levied by *arikha* (appraisal). Moreover, whereas previously only the wealthier had been assessed for taxation while the poor were exempt, the new taxes, being indirect levies, were imposed on all, both rich and poor. They had the desired effect in that the community's income increased appreciably; however, this led to centralization and ultimately the domination of the office of the chief rabbi over all the religious activities of the community. Thus, for example, no rabbi or learned person was permitted to perform a circumcision or to conduct a wedding ceremony without the permission of the *ḥakham bashi*. Moreover, Rabbi Shabetai brought in from Jerusalem new machines for baking matzot, possibly in order to generate greater profits from their sale.[75]

The *Maskilim* and the *Ḥakham Bashi*

From the end of the nineteenth century onwards, the status of the rabbinic court in the Syrian communities progressively declined, as did the standing of Torah scholars and their world-view.[76] The protests against the sages and their authority to impose their decisions upon the broad public originated in widely shared public feeling, even though it was the *maskilim*, the advocates of the Jewish Enlightenment or Haskalah, who provided them with an ideological basis. Thus, for example, in a letter addressed to the *ḥakham bashi* in Istanbul, Rabbi Hayim Nahum, one of the *maskilim*, described the case of a member of the community who had performed a marriage despite the objections of the *ḥakham bashi* and the rabbinic court, who wished the wedding to be postponed. After the person who had performed the marriage publicly declared that he was not interested in the opinion of the sages or of the court, the members of the rabbinic court and the chief rabbi decided to impose the *ḥerem* (ban) upon him. Secularist *maskilim* among the Francos, headed by Abraham Ancona, wrote to the *ḥakham bashi* in Istanbul, Hayim Nahum, asking him to declare the *ḥerem* null and void and to prohibit further use of this sanction, on the grounds that it was unsuitable to modern times and had no practical force. According to them, the *ḥakham bashi* Shabetai had responded

[74] ACRI, TR/Is/62, announcement; also steering committee to Hayim Nahum, 9 Elul 5670. On how regulations regarding taxation were formulated, see Shabetai, *Divrei yeḥizkiyahu*, i, 'Ḥelek hateshuvot', p. 40, §9.

[75] *Haḥerut*, 34 (9 Jan. 1911), 4.

[76] See Harel, *Syrian Jewry*, 91–4.

to their request by declaring that henceforth the sanction of *ḥerem* was abolished, to be replaced by imprisonment of offenders.[77]

It would appear that the *maskilim*—who wished Rabbi Nahum to publish an order prohibiting the use of the *ḥerem*, and even spread a rumour in Aleppo that they had a written promise to that effect—heard what they wished to hear and did not fully understand what Rabbi Shabetai was saying. The *ḥakham bashi*'s own account of the group of *maskilim* and their goals gives a completely different picture. The terms and tone of his letter to Rabbi Hayim Nahum on the subject reflect the duality of his position as, on the one hand, an enlightened person in a changing world and, on the other, a rabbi loyal to the tradition:

> Abraham Ancona is one of those people who are complete freethinkers. This man takes pride in the fact that he has visited Your Honour and that you promised him, regarding this matter of bans, that within one or two weeks a royal edict would be issued to abolish it. And I am greatly puzzled as to whether, Heaven forbid, such a thing really came out of the mouth of His Honour. True, the present time does not tolerate such things, and Heaven forbid that we should actually make use of such tools; but even so they are useful for frightening people, and particularly in this place, where they still hold fast to Judaism, more so than in other places . . . in such a manner that this destructive tool is of great assistance at certain times. And how can it be that we would throw into the sea a weapon which is in our hands?[78]

These 'freethinkers' also opposed the *ḥakham bashi* in his struggle to replace the headmaster of the Alliance boys' school, Yitshak (Jacques) Bassan. In Bassan's favour was the increased number of students attending the school since his arrival in Aleppo in 1910;[79] to his detriment were the many complaints made against him and against his wife Rebecca, the headmistress of the girls' school. Most of these complaints related primarily to Bassan's negligence in fulfilling his duties, and his wastefulness and mishandling of money matters; but it was also asserted that he taught the children scepticism and heresy, that he set a bad example through his own behaviour, and that he displayed contempt for the leaders of the community.[80] The community found itself in a quandary, as there was no alternative, modern, Jewish public school, and Rabbi Shabetai was immovable in his insistence that parents should not send their children to Christian schools. Some defied him in this, and continued to send their sons to Christian schools, while others sent their children away to a secular French school in Beirut. Eventually, members of the rabbinic court in Aleppo demanded that the Alliance remove Bassan from

77 ACRI, TR/Is/57*a*, [unidentified signature] to Hayim Nahum, Aleppo, 19 Sept. 1909.

78 Ibid., Hezekiah Shabetai to Hayim Nahum, Aleppo, 8 Av 5669.

79 *Haḥerut*, 19 (5 Dec. 1910), 3.

80 *Haḥerut*, 125 (26 July 1911), 2.

his position. The *ḥakham bashi* included with this request a personal letter to the management of the society, in which he wrote:

Certainly, Your Honours know that in all the places I have been, I have always supported the schools of the Alliance, and here too, since my arrival I have given great support to the school and to its students. But now Mr and Mrs Bassan have crossed the line and it is impossible for our congregation to tolerate their acts and behaviour. And one should not pay heed to the writings of certain individuals who, because of their own interests which are not deserving of mention, offer them support.[81]

These 'certain individuals', or 'assimilationists', as the supporters of the *ḥakham bashi* called them, sent their own letters to the headquarters of the Alliance in Paris, praising Bassan's activity in the community.[82]

This united front of the opponents of Rabbi Shabetai and the headmaster of the Alliance school in Aleppo had not come about by chance. The establishment by the *ḥakham bashi* of the Yesod Hahokhmah school was interpreted by the Francos and the *maskilim* as an attempt to put himself on a par with the Silvera and Picciotto families, who had owned their own private school for many years. For his part, Bassan was furious with the *ḥakham bashi* for using monies he had received from the authorities to establish a new school, rather than dividing that sum among the existing educational institutions, and complained about this to the local authorities. Rabbi Shabetai's responses to the enquiries addressed to him by the authorities on this matter further incensed Bassan, for the *ḥakham bashi* claimed that the Alliance schools were not Ottoman institutions but French ones, and therefore not entitled to the support of the local authorities. Bassan in turn obtained official recognition by the authorities that the Alliance school was indeed an Ottoman institution in every respect. Hezekiah Shabetai retaliated by claiming that the Alliance institutions had no need of government support, since they were funded entirely from Paris. Bassan did not find it difficult to prove to the supervisor of public education that the school he ran was in fact running a constant deficit, and in recognition of this the authorities gave the Alliance school a separate funding allocation to encourage the study of

[81] AAIU, Syrie, II.E., Alep, 19*b*, Rabbi Hezekiah Shabetai to the Alliance, Aleppo, 20 Tamuz 5671. Cf. ibid. I.E., Alep, 1, members of the rabbinic court of Aleppo to the Alliance, Aleppo, 28 Av 5671. Rabbi Hezekiah Shabetai did not hesitate to express in public his warm, positive attitude towards the Alliance and his views regarding the merits of secular studies. He took an active part in the celebrations conducted in Aleppo to mark the jubilee of the founding of the Alliance, and in his public lecture he praised its activity and extolled the study of foreign languages and sciences. See ibid. II.E., Alep, 19*b*, Bassan, 28 May 1910.

[82] *Haḥerut*, 130 (7 Aug. 1911), 3.

the Turkish language. These funds did not pass through the hands of the *ḥakham bashi*, who presumably saw this bypassing of himself as an insult to his position.[83]

Rabbi Shabetai evidently felt that it would not be easy to preserve his status as head of the Aleppo community, and that he could expect significant power struggles in the future. Perhaps it was for this reason that, as early as the intermediate days of Sukkot in 1909, he submitted to the *ḥakham bashi* in Istanbul his candidacy for the chief rabbinate in İzmir.[84] While he explained his desire to leave Aleppo with reference to the low salary that he was paid there, it seems reasonable to suppose that in fact he wished to escape from the conflicts and controversies in which he was constantly embroiled.

From Beloved to Enemy

David Silvera, who had been responsible for bringing Rabbi Hezekiah Shabetai to Aleppo, also encouraged him to get rid of the older rabbinic judges. While the new *ḥakham bashi* initially accepted his advice, after a certain period of time he changed his mind. Silvera—whom the supporters of the *ḥakham bashi* described as 'one of the wealthy members of our community who behaves in a violent and tyrannical manner against all those who oppose his views'—had not expected such independence and forcefulness on the part of a man whose appointment he had promoted, and in consequence turned from being a key supporter of the *ḥakham bashi* into his main opponent.[85] Rabbi Shabetai portrayed the situation as follows:

> A certain Italian man, named David Silvera, who was among those who acted to bring the *ḥakham bashi* to Aram Zova—may God protect it and establish it—and to institute the above-mentioned *gabilah* tax, had a private dispute with the honourable rabbis of the rabbinic court. He therefore attempted to convince the Holy Community—may the Rock preserve it and give it life—to remove them from their office. And when he saw that these things were not accepted by the Holy Community, nor by myself, he left our domain and began to make efforts to destroy the organization of the Holy Community. He attempted to stir up the old conflict between certain people among the Francos and the Holy Community (but now, praise to Almighty God, may He be blessed, peace prevails between us).[86]

Silvera, along with six others who were not Francos, and who had been oppressed by the old Torah elite of the city, sought to exploit the appointment

83 AAIU, Syrie, II.E., Alep, 19*b*, Bassan, 20 Jan. 1910.

84 ACRI, TR/Is/62, Hezekiah Shabetai to Hayim Nahum, Aleppo, 19 Tishrei 5670.

85 *Haḥerut*, 57 (9 Jan. 1912), 1.

86 ACRI, TR/Is/72*a*, Hezekiah Shabetai to Hayim Nahum, Aleppo, 4 Sivan 5671.

of a *ḥakham bashi* from outside the city in order to reassert what they considered their rightful place in the community. Silvera, as an Italian citizen, worked behind the scenes, whereas the overt opposition to the rabbi was conducted by Ottoman Jews.[87] The outstanding figure among these was Rabbi Saul David Sutton, a *shoḥet* with leadership abilities and ambitions, who had been one of the main players in the dispute that had led to the deposition of Rabbi Abraham Dweck Hakohen from the office of *ḥakham bashi* some fifteen years earlier. In the wake of that incident, Sutton had been forced into exile in the community of ʿAyntab, north of Aleppo, where he served for many years as a teacher in the *talmud torah*. Some time later he returned to Aleppo, where his participation in the opposition to Rabbi Hezekiah Shabetai was intertwined with his personal struggle to restore his status as a *shoḥet* and a respected Torah scholar within the community.[88]

Rabbi Shabetai's opponents accused him of imposing taxes to suit his whim, of imposing high tariffs for various religious services, of threatening those who refused to pay with *ḥerem* or *nidui*, of generally behaving in a high-handed manner, and of throwing his opponents in prison. He was further accused of siphoning off money from the taxes that he collected into his own pocket rather than devoting the funds to the needs of the community. It was also alleged that he had overstepped the bounds of the authority given him by law, that he sought to rule as a dictator, that he was opposed to the Ottoman constitution and the principles of freedom, and that he undermined the basis of Muslim rule.[89] These accusations were not made only within the community; on the contrary, the rabbi's opponents sent numerous complaints to the offices of both local and central government, thereby involving external bodies in the community's internal affairs. At the end of an announcement distributed to members of the community by his opponents, containing a detailed list of the taxes imposed by Rabbi Shabetai, there appeared the following statement:

> The above-mentioned tariffs were established by the *ḥakham bashi* against our holy Torah and against the custom of the kingdom, and it is forbidden for any Jew to pay them, because they constitute theft from the public. And most of the community

[87] See e.g. Rabbi Hezekiah Shabetai's complaint regarding Rabbi Ezra Shamosh, ibid., Hezekiah Shabetai to Hayim Nahum, Aleppo, 16 Tamuz 5671, in which he argued that Shamosh wrote letters of complaint to the ministry of justice 'according to what David Silvera put in his mouth'.

[88] See Ch. 5 above. On the departure of Sutton Dabah to ʿAyntab, see JNUL, DMA, Arc. 4to, 1271/622, Safdeyé to Elyashar, 27 Nisan 5657.

[89] ACRI, TR/Is/62, Hezekiah Shabetai to Hayim Nahum, Aleppo, 11 Elul [5669].

has already agreed to do whatever is necessary at the rabbinic court of Jerusalem—may it speedily be rebuilt in our days, Amen—or with the government, to destroy and nullify the yoke which has been imposed upon us, and you shall eradicate the evil from amongst you, and we will go out from slavery to freedom.[90]

One of the specific accusations directed against the *ḥakham bashi* was that the Ma'oz La'evyon charitable society which he had established was in effect created simply as a means of enforcing and extending his own authority. The rabbi was accused of employing violent people in order to impose his rule in general, and to collect taxes in particular, and of compelling the judges to rule in accordance with his opinion—in particular, to approve the imposition of the *gabilah* against their will. He was likewise accused of insulting Torah scholars, of making selective use of the *ḥerem* to punish his opponents while not using it against those who publicly violated the sabbath, of causing a split with the Francos, of harming the livelihood of his opponents, and of using the judicial authorities of the state against them. He was further accused of easing the tax burden on the wealthy, upon whom he was dependent for his position, of cajoling witnesses to give false testimony, and even of plotting to kill Saul David Sutton.[91]

In the face of this welter of accusations, Rabbi Shabetai's supporters did not sit idly by. They sent their own opposing letters to the minister of justice and to the *ḥakham bashi* in Istanbul, Hayim Nahum, asking them to give official authorization to the tariffs that had been imposed by Rabbi Shabetai and to prohibit his opponents from acting against him. Shabetai himself denied that he had put a single penny of public funds into his own pocket and asserted that all the monies raised through the *gabilah* were used to finance the community's charitable institutions. Moreover, he asserted that he had not departed from the authority granted him by the sultanic firman, and that he had fixed the *gabilah* on the basis of the firman and on authorization from the district governor, backed by special permission from Istanbul and with the agreement of the community. He accused his opponents, led by David Silvera, of deliberately having marriages conducted by ignorant and unqualified people and of challenging accepted communal arrangements, particularly those surrounding the collection of taxes. Shabetai also accused them of denouncing him to the authorities in order to blacken his name and those of the community's leaders, and of falsifying the signatures of members of the community on the letters of complaint directed against him.[92]

[90] ACRI, TR/Is/62, announcement.

[91] ACRI, TR/Is/72*a*, Saul David Sutton, Aleppo, 3 Sivan 5671, 23 Sivan 5671.

[92] Ibid. TR/Is/62, members of the steering committee in Aleppo to Nahum, 9 Elul 5670; TR/Is/72*a*, Hezekiah Shabetai to Hayim Nahum, 4 Sivan 5671, 16 Tamuz 5671.

However, at a time when the district governor was absent from the city, opponents of the *ḥakham bashi* succeeded in convincing the *qadi*, who was serving as acting governor, that Rabbi Shabetai had indeed departed from the prerogatives granted him by law. The *qadi* ordered the *ḥakham bashi* to appear before a legal inquiry and stand trial within one day of the bringing of the suit.

This development reignited an old conflict between the *ḥakham bashi* and the Muslim *qadi*, which at the time it first arose caused controversy across the entire city. A Jew, who had not received permission from Rabbi Shabetai to take a second wife, or alternatively to divorce his wife without paying her the sum stipulated in the *ketubah*, decided to convert to Islam. The *qadi*, who welcomed this new Muslim with open arms, was astonished to discover that the *ḥakham bashi* was refusing to recognize the conversion and indeed ruling that the Jew was required to compensate his wife in accordance with Jewish law before becoming a Muslim. The *qadi*, wishing to demonstrate that his power was superior to that of the *ḥakham bashi*, refused to nullify the Jew's conversion to Islam. Moreover, he even attempted to forcibly convert his wife to Islam by imprisoning her. The *ḥakham bashi* asked the district governor to intervene, and the latter ordered the woman released. Rabbi Shabetai then ruled that the man must pay his wife the money stipulated in the *ketubah* and divorce her in accordance with Jewish law. Emissaries whom the rabbi sent to the apostate succeeded in persuading him to act in accordance with these instructions. The *qadi*, seeing his own authority flouted, ordered the apostate to divorce his wife according to Muslim law as well. While this order was also carried out, he continued to bear a grudge against the rabbi. Thus, when the *qadi* received the new complaints about the *ḥakham bashi*, he quickly ordered a police investigation and had the rabbi summoned to investigation and trial. Moreover, he even encouraged the opponents of the *ḥakham bashi* to complain against him to the authorities in Istanbul. For their part, Hezekiah Shabetai and his supporters argued that his opponents had bribed senior government officials to act against the *ḥakham bashi* and demanded that they be punished by law.[93] In the end, the local courts decided that the *ḥakham bashi* was in the right, but the incident further harmed both his standing in the community and the community's standing in the city as a whole.[94]

The scandal worsened when reports on the conflict within the community began to appear in the local press, in the Jerusalem press, and in that of the capital city of Istanbul. The rabbi's supporters were extremely sensitive to

[93] *Haḥerut* 36 (1 Dec. 1911), 3; ACRI, TR/Is/62, Hezekiah Shabetai to Hayim Nahum, Aleppo, 11 Elul [5669]; TR/Is/72*a*, Shabetai to Nahum, Aleppo, 9 Tishrei 5671.

[94] ACRI, TR/Is/72*a*, Joseph Elijah Shamma to Hayim Nahum, 2 Sivan 5671.

the wording of these reports, which were full of stories of the deposition of rabbis and disputes over their activities. They tried to point out that those opposed to Rabbi Shabetai were a small but vocal minority, consisting of fifteen people in all, and that the vast majority of the community supported him. The head of the steering committee, Joseph Elijah Shamma, sent a complaint to *ḥakham bashi* Hayim Nahum concerning reports in the newspapers *L'Aurore* and *El telegrafo* in Istanbul, according to which the community was divided. His complaint read as follows:

One cannot deny that there are always some thistles in the vineyard of the people, and every rabbi who is greater than others and does more on behalf of justice and righteousness and order within his community will find himself with more enemies and jealous rumour-mongers whose strength is only in their mouths, who think they may build themselves up from the destruction of the community. But who pays attention to them at all? To the contrary, we show our rabbi even greater honour and glory. For in truth, our rabbi knows how to wisely unite all the parties and to bring the hearts closer together and to arrange all matters of the community with wonderful skill—nevertheless, it is impossible to bring close those who are distant from the outset . . . But now, when we read the reports mentioned in the newspapers, our hearts were greatly distressed. Therefore we immediately sent a telegram protesting at this false report to the ʿAdliyya [ministry of justice] and to his Excellency, the Honour of his Torah. And we hereby officially deny this report, for in truth there is no basis to it whatsoever, and throughout the community there is peace and tranquillity, no conflict or dispute at all. And there is no need to send a special person to punish these ignorant malcontents, nor should they be judged in Constantinople; on the contrary, the courts here suffice to judge them properly.[95]

In response, Rabbi Hayim Nahum asked the *ḥakham bashi* of Damascus to visit Aleppo to examine the roots of this dispute. Rabbi Shabetai's opponents asked that the investigating committee to be sent by Rabbi Nahum also include representatives of the executive council and the judicial council of the district—the reason being that the Jewish investigator was not expert in the laws of the state and would therefore examine only those matters pertaining to religion, while the other two would examine matters in the light of Ottoman law.[96] Meanwhile, they continued to declare publicly that they did not consider themselves subject to the edicts of the *ḥakham bashi* Hezekiah Shabetai—particularly by having weddings conducted by Rabbi Saul David Sutton, without the celebrants paying the tax imposed upon them to the office of the rabbinate.[97] The *ḥakham bashi* retaliated by banning his opponents from the synagogues.

[95] ACRI, TR/Is/72*a*, Joseph Elijah Shamma to Hayim Nahum, 2 Sivan 5671.

[96] Ibid., Saul David Sutton to Hayim Nahum, Aleppo, 3 Sivan 5671.

[97] Ibid. TR/Is/160*a*, Hezekiah Shabetai to Hayim Nahum, Aleppo, 13 Tishrei 5672.

The Francos' Attempts at Separation

In January 1910, after the rift between himself and the *ḥakham bashi*, David Silvera attempted to avoid subjugation to the edicts and decisions of Hezekiah Shabetai by persuading the Franco families to cut themselves off from the community definitively and to establish an independent community. From that point on, members of the Picciotto family led the opponents of Rabbi Shabetai and took all the steps necessary to organize a separate community.[98] They appointed Rabbi Reuben Ancona, an Italian citizen, who had until that point earned his living from ritual slaughtering and from writing Torah scrolls and *mezuzot*, as their rabbi.[99] This was an unprecedented step in Aleppo: hitherto, while maintaining their separate status, the Francos had always acted alongside the official community without establishing a community of their own. Now the Franco families, who had previously supported the charity and welfare institutions of the community, withdrew from all communal activity. These families—who had been the first to create a connection with the Alliance Israélite Universelle, and had encouraged it to open educational institutions in Aleppo—were conspicuously absent from the festivities conducted to mark the jubilee of the founding of that organization. They even sought to open a separate school to operate under the patronage of the Alliance, but had to abandon this idea owing to opposition from the central committee of the Alliance in Paris.[100]

The establishment of an alternative community headed by Rabbi Ancona implied the granting of authority to a foreign citizen to conduct marriages and divorces without the approval of the *ḥakham bashi*. This not only undermined the exclusive authority of the chief rabbi—a prerogative expressed in his sultanic firman—but was also greatly damaging to the communal coffers. Moreover, by establishing a community of foreign citizens, Silvera sought to cut himself and the other Francos off, not only from the Aleppo rabbinate, but also from the chief rabbinate in Istanbul, in such a way that neither he nor his supporters would have any need of halakhic or political authority reliant on the approval of the Ottoman government.

Members of the steering committee of the Aleppo community, alarmed about the repercussions of this split in the Jewish community, turned to the *ḥakham bashi* in Istanbul to ask that he nullify this act of separation. They wrote:

98 AAIU, Syrie, II.E., Alep, 19*b*, Bassan, 20 Jan. 1910.

99 Rabbi Ancona died on 1 July 1917. On him, see Laniado, *For the Sake of the Holy Ones* (Heb.), 7.

100 AAIU, Syrie, II.E., Alep, 19*b*, Bassan, 28 May 1910.

Behold, there have risen up within our community citizens of the kingdom of Italy and Namsa [Austria], who number no more than ten families who had previously been counted within our community. Now they have left the collectivity to build a 'high place' [*bamah*] for themselves. And they sought a certain person, an Italian citizen, a man of quarrel and controversy, who refers to himself with the title of *ḥakham*, and they gave him the title of Grand Rabbin, the likes of which has never been heard of in our city since the day it was established. And he wishes to involve himself in all matters of the members of the Ottoman community in order to destroy and to confuse the regulations of the community and its institutions. He divorces and marries people who are Ottoman subjects, delivers sermons in the synagogues, and so forth. And all this is done against the will of our great rabbi and that of the rabbinic court and the community board. And if we do not act to counter this evil thing, there is a great concern lest the scourge spread and destroy all the regulations of the community.[101]

In addition to the complaints sent to the *ḥakham bashi* Hayim Nahum and to the district officials, Rabbi Hezekiah Shabetai also complained to the Italian consul concerning Rabbi Ancona, arguing that he had departed from the prerogatives granted him under Jewish law. Rabbi Ancona responded to this complaint on an official letterhead bearing the words: 'Grand rabbinate de la communauté israélite européenne d'Alep'—a tangible indication of the seriousness of the Francos' intentions to organize themselves in a separate body. According to Ancona, all of Rabbi Shabetai's complaints were arbitrary and were themselves opposed to Jewish law. He argued that Rabbi Shabetai could not prohibit him from preaching words of Torah, and that his standing as rabbi of the community of European Jews was equivalent to that of Rabbi Shabetai in that community. If Rabbi Shabetai was not happy with the new developments, added Rabbi Ancona, he was entitled to appeal to a higher rabbinic court (that is, in Jerusalem) that was authorized to deal with such questions.[102]

The unity of the community suffered another blow when a dispute arose concerning those Jews who were British subjects. The *ḥakham bashi* and the sages of the rabbinic court disagreed among themselves regarding questions relating to the sale of the courtyard of a Jewish woman who was a British subject. The British consul, angered at the attitude shown towards his compatriot, instructed all those Jews who were British subjects to give the community no further donations.[103]

[101] ACRI, TR/Is/62, members of the steering committee in Aleppo to Nahum, 15 Adar 5670.

[102] Ibid., Ancona à Beauregard, Alep, 24 Feb. 1910.

[103] ACRI, TR/Is/72*a*, Hezekiah Shabetai to Hayim Nahum, Aleppo, 17 Sivan 5671.

At the height of this controversy Rabbi Hezekiah Shabetai suffered a double personal blow: in January 1910 his eldest daughter suddenly died in Jerusalem, and a few months later his elder brother, Rabbi Gabriel Shabetai, whom he had much admired, also died.[104]

Meanwhile, the opponents of the *ḥakham bashi* continued to seek opportunities to blacken his name in the eyes of the authorities, particularly those of the Muslim clergy. Such an opportunity fell into their hands when a female Jewish musician from Damascus who played with a Muslim band was kidnapped by the leader of the band, raped by him, and in effect made into his sex slave. The girl sent a secret message to the *ḥakham bashi* about her plight, indicating that she wished to repent and no longer to play in public. In response, Rabbi Shabetai, in concert with the governor, took steps to obtain her release. However, the local *mufti* issued a counter-ruling, stating that the girl was no longer Jewish but Muslim. Policemen removed her in the night from the house of the Jew where she had been staying, 'and she cried out bitterly: "I am a Jewish woman, I do not wish the Ishmaelite religion", but they did not listen to her'. She was then returned to the Muslim who had kidnapped her, after the latter took a false oath that he had converted her to Islam and married her in accordance with Muslim law. The *ḥakham bashi* did not give up, writing a letter of complaint to the ministries of justice and of religion in Istanbul. They responded that, according to the constitution, the girl herself must be asked what she wished, and if she did not wish to be a Muslim she should be freed.

Rabbi Shabetai's championing of the girl's cause exacerbated the *mufti*'s hostility towards the *ḥakham bashi*. The rabbi's supporters accused his opponents of bribing the Muslim kidnapper to make sensational allegations in the Arab press—and indeed, the local newspaper had quoted the kidnapper as saying that the *ḥakham bashi* had promised his servants 300 pounds if they would murder him, for which reason he had issued a complaint against him. These reports had a highly inflammatory effect on the mood within the Muslim population.[105]

On another front, David Silvera sent a letter of complaint to *ḥakham bashi* Hayim Nahum concerning the taxes that Rabbi Shabetai had imposed upon his arrival in Aleppo. According to him, the rabbi's taxation policy was a source of ongoing controversy within the community. Knowing that Rabbi Nahum was close to the people of the Alliance and that his views on human rights were similar to those of the French revolutionaries, Silvera wrote as

[104] See *Haḥerut*, 64 (23 Feb. 1910), 2; 19 (5 Dec. 1910), 2–3. On Rabbi Gabriel Shabetai, see Gaon, *The Jews of the East*, ii. 661.

[105] ACRI, TR/Is/72*a*, Hezekiah Shabetai to Hayim Nahum, Aleppo, 17 Sivan 5671.

follows:

I think that this is the time to intervene so as to put an end to this state of things. We see you as the protector of human freedom and the enemy of the unceasing inquisitorial activities performed by fanatical rabbis in order to establish their shaky authority, and it is not only the community of Constantinople that should enjoy your light. It is very important that you extend your kindness also over our unfortunate city.[106]

At the beginning of 1911 Silvera and his supporters publicized a rumour that the Ottoman government in Istanbul had decided to depose Rabbi Shabetai from his position, and that the *ḥakham bashi* in Istanbul, Hayim Nahum, was expected to give his consent to the move. They added that if Rabbi Nahum failed to remove Rabbi Shabetai from office, they would initiate a campaign to do so themselves.[107] When these complaints were conveyed by the local governor to the ministry of justice, Rabbi Nahum was called upon to investigate whether there was indeed cause to depose Rabbi Shabetai. In November 1911 he sent an investigating committee to Aleppo, consisting of Rabbis Yitshak Shaki and Raphael David Saban,[108] who called upon both the supporters and the opponents of Rabbi Shabetai to present their testimony. Initially, Silvera and his supporters were reluctant to acknowledge the investigating committee, 'saying that they had no portion or inheritance in the chief rabbinate of Turkey, neither have we inheritance in its Jewish supervisors',[109] but in the end they agreed to appear. Most of the testimonies given to the investigators by members of the community and its rabbinic sages supported Rabbi Shabetai, though the three rabbinic judges—Jacob Saul Dweck Hakohen, Elijah Hamawi, and Ezra Hamawi—exploited the opportunity to attack the *ḥakham bashi* for restricting their own authority, and particularly for imposing the *gabilah* in the face of their opposition.

In presenting their report, Rabbis Shaki and Saban described their impressions of the Aleppo community:

It is true that, unfortunately, we found and saw that which we did not expect, that three distinguished judges, pillars of the *erets* [i.e. Aleppo] who sit in judgement, two of whom are elderly people of advanced age, opposed the chief rabbi and are not pleased with his actions. In particular, they cannot speak well of him because he introduced and established the *gabilah* tax . . . and although we were convinced with clear knowledge that all the complaints of the judges concerning the honourable

106 ACRI, TR/Is/72*a*, David Silvera to Hayim Nahum, Aleppo, 4 April 1911.

107 Ibid. TR/Is/160*a*, Moses Menasheh Sutton to Hayim Nahum, Aleppo, 13 Tishrei 5672.

108 See Gaon, *The Jews of the East*, ii. 737.

109 *Haḥerut*, 34 (29 Nov. 1911), 2. See 2 Sam. 20: 1.

rabbi have no sound foundation, and all the things are inconsequential, Heaven forbid that the removal from office of the honourable rabbi *gaon* even be considered, yet in order to make peace in the land, we have girded ourselves with strength and might to speak to the hearts of both sides, that they might be lenient to one another in halakhah. But despite all our efforts and trouble to find the path of peace, we were unable to calm the tumultuous spirit of the judges, whose heart is like a stormy sea, and they are in agreement that they cannot dwell in the land, and that the *erets* cannot bear their dwelling together, with no reason for their words at all.[110]

The investigators concluded that all the complaints against *ḥakham bashi* Hezekiah Shabetai were lies, promulgated primarily by two people, David Silvera and Saul David Sutton. They advised that the chief rabbi be left in his position without any challenge, and even agreed to authorize him to appoint and to remove rabbinic judges as he saw fit. They further recommended that those who stirred up the controversy against the *ḥakham bashi* be severely punished, and indeed be removed from the community until they repented of their evil deeds.[111]

Despite the determination of Rabbi Shabetai's opponents, the separatist European community established by David Silvera did not last long. During the presentation of testimony to the investigating committee, Rabbi Reuben Ancona recanted his position, and indeed led the group of rabbinic sages in Aleppo who expressed their support for the incumbent *ḥakham bashi*.[112] The investigators' report and the subsequent official reassertion of Shabetai's authority led to the final breakdown of the new framework, which had in any event been built upon shaky foundations with only a handful of key participants. In the elections to the steering committee that had been held in January 1911 all those elected were Ottoman subjects, although the foreign residents elected their own delegate, Raphael Daniel Halevi, to represent them at meetings of the board.[113] When a relief committee was set up during the winter of 1910–11, which was a very harsh one, two of its six members—Aaron Silvera and Saul Ancona—were Francos, holding foreign citizenship.[114] The existence of the Francos as a separate body in Aleppo finally shrivelled upon the outbreak of the First World War, when their foreign citizenship, which had in the past been a source of special privilege, became a

110 'Ḥikur din' by Rabbis Raphael Saban and Yitshak Shaki as presented to Rabbi Hayim Nahum, Aleppo, 25 Heshvan 5672, Ben-Mordechai Collection; see further *Haḥerut*, 57 (9 Jan. 1912), 2–3.

111 'Ḥikur din' by Rabbis Raphael Saban and Yitshak Shaki as presented to Rabbi Hayim Nahum, Aleppo, 25 Heshvan 5672, Ben-Mordechai Collection.

112 ACRI, TR/Is/160*a*, testimony of Torah scholars of Aleppo before the committee, Aleppo, 14 Heshvan 5672

113 *Haḥerut*, 35 (11 Jan. 1911), 2.

114 *Haḥerut*, 68 (24 Mar. 1911), 2.

drawback. From this point on they were viewed as enemy subjects in the eyes of the Ottoman authorities, and many of them went into exile overseas.

Notwithstanding his victory in this episode and the apparent strengthening of his position with its outcome, Rabbi Shabetai felt that it had damaged the institutions of the rabbinate in the community, especially the rabbinic court. One indication of this weakness was the emergence of opposition on the part of rabbis in the satellite communities, such as Kilis, to the Aleppo court's insistence that every legal case be brought before it rather than before the local sage.[115] This challenge reflected a clear loss of authority by the Aleppo Torah centre and of the figure at its head—a weakness further reflected in its declining size: in 1912 the number of Torah scholars recorded as living in Aleppo was under twenty.[116] Hezekiah Shabetai's own relations with the judges of the city remained extremely tense, and the ill feeling generated by the episode persisted among all concerned. The Aleppo judges were both offended by the criticism of the two rabbis from Istanbul and obdurate in their position: after the investigators had left, they published a 'Great Statement' of their own in which they reasserted their claim that the *ḥakham bashi* Hezekiah Shabetai was not fit to serve in that office. As a result of this the judges were temporarily suspended from their duties and *ḥakham bashi* Hayim Nahum referred the matter to the ministry of justice.[117] As for Shabetai himself, he knew that as long as his opponents continued to be active within the community he would be unable to carry out his functions peacefully; hence, he continued to demand that they be either imprisoned or banished from the city,[118] while also pleading for Rabbi Nahum's assistance in finding a position in another city, 'for I can no longer bear it here'.[119] But no such assistance was forthcoming, and Hezekiah Shabetai continued to serve as the head of the Aleppo community until 1926.

115 See e.g. D. Sutton, *Ya'aleh hadas*, 107, §8.

116 See ACRI, TR/Is/160*a*, testimony of the sages and rabbis of Aleppo before the investigative committee, Aleppo, 14 Heshvan 5672. The testimony is signed by only twelve scholars. If we add to these the three judges the number reaches fifteen.

117 See *Haḥerut*, 57 (9 Jan. 1912), 2.

118 Version of the findings of Rabbis Raphael David Saban and Yitshak Shaki presented to Rabbi Hayim Nahum, Aleppo, 25 Heshvan 5672, Ben-Mordechai Collection. For the continuation of the complaints against him, see e.g. ACRI, TR/Is/160*a*, A. Ancona to Hayim Nahum, Aleppo, 11 Dec. 1911. See ibid., Hezekiah Shabetai to Hayim Nahum, Aleppo, 21 Kislev 5672, 28 Tevet 5672, 23 Adar 5672.

119 ACRI, TR/Is/160*a*, Hezekiah Shabetai to Hayim Nahum, Aleppo, 21 Kislev 5672, 28 Heshvan 5672.

CHAPTER ELEVEN

The Removal of the *Ḥakham Bashi* of Baghdad, David Pappo, by the Young Turks

Rabban Gamaliel son of Rabbi Judah the President said: Be careful about the governing authorities, for they only draw close to a person for their own needs. They appear to be your friend when it is to their benefit, but they do not stand by a person's side at the time of his trouble.

Mishnah *Pirkei avot* 2: 3

Taxes and Anarchy

At the beginning of the twentieth century, the Baghdad community did not yet have an organized system of direct taxation. Rather, the community's main income came from the indirect tax levied upon the sale of meat—the *gabilah*.[1] This funded everything: the salaries of the chief rabbi, the rabbinic judges, and the ritual slaughterers; payment of several Torah scholars; the philanthropic societies such as *bikur ḥolim*; and the meals fed to the students in the *talmudei torah*. In the absence of other income, in order to cover all these expenses the *gabilah* had to be set at a very high level, and in practice control of the *gabilah* ensured almost total control over the communal budget. This being so, disputes were prone to break out regarding the level of the *gabilah* and the proper allocation of the sums it generated. In view of shortcomings in the system of leadership and governance within the community, and the recurrent internal disputes that characterized it, on 24 January 1905 the ruling council of the Baghdad district ordered the abolition of the *gabilah*. This step placed the survival of the community, whose income was very low and whose institutions were fragile, in real danger. This section of the chapter will review the developments that led up to the council's decision.

[1] Hayim, *Rav pe'alim*, 'Yoreh de'ah', iv, §1, 413; see also Ben-Ya'akov, *Babylonian Jewry from the End of the Geonic Period* (Heb.), 268–9, 274, 277, 284, 366–7.

At the time, the chief rabbi of the Baghdad community was Rabbi Yitshak Abraham Solomon, who had served in this position for some twelve years and was known by the nickname Almujalid ('the Binder'). Born in 1835 and educated in the rabbinic school Midrash Beit Zilkhah, he was a weak, rather colourless person, hesitant and lacking in both the energy and the wisdom needed to lead the community through the transformations to come with the change of century. His own education was exclusively religious. He was not fluent in Turkish, and so was unable to cultivate direct relations with government officials. His status in the Ottoman hierarchy was in any case quite low, as his appointment had not received official approval from the Sublime Porte, so he was formally only an acting *ḥakham bashi*.[2] The leadership vacuum created by Rabbi Solomon's lack of charisma and ability was exploited by his son, whom his opponents described as a brash young man undeserving of trust, a corrupt schemer with no respect for the law. The younger man in effect took over the running of both the financial and the spiritual matters of the community, making use of his father's official seal to exercise a virtual monopoly on decisions relating to community affairs.[3]

The underlying problem that enabled one individual to claim so much power was the lack of institutions to supervise or check the activities of the *ḥakham bashi* or anyone exercising his authority, a situation that the Jewish millet decree promulgated decades earlier in the mid-1860s was meant to prevent. There had been no steering committee in the community for several years, as a result of which it had sunk into complete anarchy, with disputes and arguments over issues of control and leadership constantly breaking out. The situation in Baghdad seems to have been similar to that in Damascus after the economic collapse of 1875. The wealthy were unwilling to assume responsibility for leadership of the community lest the government hold them responsible for defraying its debts—and, should they fail to hand over the sums demanded, force them to pay the money from their own pockets on pain of imprisonment. This prospect inhibited those who ought to have provided the secular leadership of the community from coming forward to suggest a more effective alternative to the leadership of the incumbent *ḥakham bashi*.

The main grievance of those within the community opposed to the *ḥakham bashi*, Rabbi Solomon, was that his son was behaving in a dictatorial fashion and acting only for his own personal benefit. Among other things, he concentrated the administration of the funds generated by the *gabilah*, which

[2] On the writings of Rabbi Yitshak Abraham Solomon, see Ben-Ya'akov, *Babylonian Jewry from the End of the Geonic Period* (Heb.), 169. He died on 1 Elul 5680 (15 August 1920).

[3] AAIU, Irak, I.C., 4, Bagdad, Rapport sur la Gabella, 30 Jan. 1905.

amounted to some 69,000 francs every year, in his own hands. About half that sum went on paying the *ʿaskariyya* tax and financing the community's educational institutions, including the yeshivas. The remainder—so the rabbi's opponents claimed—found its way into his own and his son's pockets, and into those of several other well-connected individuals.[4] At the same time, too, a number of members of the Hayim family were involved in an intracommunal dispute—just as others had been some years earlier at the time of the campaign against Rabbi Sason Elijah Halevi (Samoha).[5] Contemporaries pointed the finger at Nisim ben Elijah Hayim, brother of Rabbi Joseph Hayim, as a key figure in these machinations: according to them, he exploited his brother's fame as a holy man to dominate the communal dignitaries and wealthy men, and also exploited the weakness of the *ḥakham bashi*, making common cause with his son.[6] In this manner the moneyed elite and the rabbinic elite formed a behind-the-scenes alliance to their mutual benefit. This situation aroused a great deal of anger in the community against the *ḥakham bashi*, which was given expression in the curses that were constantly uttered against him. Some years later, Rabbi Solomon himself recalled these attacks when he wrote:

> I too, the smallest one in my clan, Yitshak Abraham Solomon, who was acting as *ḥakham bashi* in the glorious city of Baghdad—may the Almighty establish it, Amen—every night forgive whoever may curse or malign me, be it man or woman, great or small, wealthy or poor, sage or ignoramus—it is forgiven him and excused him. And anyone of whom I knew that he cursed me during the day, at night I forgive him.[7]

For years, members of the lower classes in the community believed that the income from the *gabilah* was primarily used to pay the *ʿaskariyya* tax owed to the government, and did not imagine that systematic and widespread embezzlement of these funds was taking place. The truth of the matter began to emerge only after an imperial order of October 1902 led to a review of the *ʿaskariyya*, thenceforth requiring every person, both rich and poor, to pay this tax. In other words, the *ʿaskariyya* would no longer be collected as a lump sum from the community as a whole, but would be a personal levy, collected from each individual. This meant that it would no longer have to be paid from the *gabilah*, so that the money gathered from the *gabilah* could be devoted exclusively to financing the needs of the community. Following this order a com-

[4] The extant sources do not make clear whether the son of the chief rabbi leased the *gabilah* according to the accepted system in the communities of the centre of the empire. See Levi, 'Changes in the Leadership' (Heb.), 243–4.

[5] See Ch. 4 above.

[6] AAIU, Irak, II.E., Bagdad, 8*a*, Albala, 15 Feb. 1905.

[7] Solomon, *Akim et yitsḥak*, 111*b*.

mittee was set up, consisting of three dignitaries, to compile a new list of all those liable to pay the *ʿaskariyya*, along with the amount each was to pay, from 50 piastres up to 300 piastres. There is no doubt that this new division of the tax burden was strongly skewed in favour of the wealthy. The poorer members of the community, on whom the new system would weigh most heavily, protested angrily, threatening the members of the committee to the extent that they were forced to shut themselves up in their homes for weeks. When the new law was finally approved, many poor people, who were unable to pay the sums demanded of them, were beaten by the soldiers charged with collecting the tax; a number of them were even gaoled for lengthy periods and forced to sell their personal property in order to pay the tax. Once they were freed, they lost no time in taking their revenge upon the wealthy members of the community, whom they held responsible for the sufferings they had undergone. Violent brawls broke out in the community, one of which ended in a stabbing.[8] Eventually the situation calmed down, and the leading members of the community realized that, in order to prevent further unrest, they needed to reorganize the handling of income from the *gabilah*.

The community was also burdened by debts arising from unpaid *ʿaskariyya* from previous years. It arrived at an agreement with the district treasury whereby the debt was distributed over eight annual payments, to be paid using income from the *gabilah*. What remained after these dues were paid would have to finance the salaries of the *ḥakham bashi*, of the judges, and of the rabbis who taught in the yeshiva, as well as supporting the *beit midrash*, the *talmudei torah*, the communal pharmacy, and the welfare of about forty blind people who studied at the grave of Yitshak Gaon.[9] A special secretary was appointed to examine the income generated by the *gabilah* as against the expenses it was required to meet.

The broader public resented the joint control of the communal finances assumed by the moneyed and the rabbinic elites. The poor, who realized that they would not gain any benefit from the *gabilah*, argued that, now that they were required to pay their shares of the *ʿaskariyya* directly to the government, there was no longer any need for the *gabilah* and it ought to be abolished completely. The question of the *gabilah* thus divided the community and became a flashpoint of conflict between the classes: on the one hand, the poor people wished to abolish the tax; on the other hand, the moneyed class and the rabbis wished to leave it intact as far as possible, so that they would not be

[8] AAIU, Irak, II.E., Bagdad, 8*a*, Albala, 15 Feb. 1905.

[9] Ibid. Regarding the grave of Yitshak Gaon, known among the Jews of Baghdad as 'Sheikh Yitshak', see D. Sassoon, *Journey to Babylonia* (Heb.), 182; Ben-Ya'akov, *Holy Graves* (Heb.), 218–24.

required to finance the religious institutions of the community from their own pockets.

This emerging class consciousness on the part of the poor, their awareness of their rights and their duties, and their demand for real, practical involvement in managing the community's financial affairs were all new phenomena in the Baghdad community. The large majority of its members understood its potential power. Finally driven beyond endurance by the traditional manner in which the community was run by the wealthy laymen and the Torah scholars around the *ḥakham bashi*, the poor people lodged a direct complaint with the *wali*. It was this that led to the decision mentioned at the beginning of this chapter, whereby the regional administrative council resolved almost unanimously at its meeting on 24 January 1905 to accept the complaints of the poor Jews and to order the abolition of the *gabilah*. The only opponent to this was the Jewish representative on the council, who presumably represented the wealthy members of the community. That very day an order was sent to the *ḥakham bashi* ordering him to execute the decision without delay.

But while the poor people had won this battle, the community now faced empty coffers. In practice, all of the community institutions—the yeshivas, the *talmudei torah*, the infirmary, and the rabbinic court—were facing closure owing to lack of funds. The ritual slaughterers, the rabbinic judges, and the teachers in the *talmudei torah* were no longer being paid;[10] the chief rabbi was about to be dismissed because it was impossible to pay his salary. Meanwhile, the community found itself without a supply of fresh meat. The wealthier members of the community quarrelled among themselves and were unable to agree upon a course of action to save the community from total collapse. The *ḥakham bashi*, Rabbi Solomon, the greatest loser from the abolition of the *gabilah*, protested to the *wali*, objecting that the abolition of the *gabilah* was an arbitrary move opposed to the imperial firman granting the *ḥakham bashi* the right to impose the meat tax in all communities of the Ottoman empire.[11] The rabbi also turned to the emissary of the Alliance, Nisim Albala, whose school was among the institutions suffering from the cessation of communal support, in an attempt to persuade the central committee of the Alliance to put pressure on the Jewish leaders in Istanbul, so that they might in turn persuade the minister of the interior to nullify the order of the administrative council of Baghdad abolishing the *gabilah*. The *ḥakham bashi* promised the heads of the Alliance that, if they were to abolish the order, he would

[10] AAIU, Irak, I.C., 4, Bagdad, Rapport sur la Gabella, 30 Jan. 1905; ibid., II.E., Baghdad, 8*a*, Albala, 16 Mar. 1905.

[11] Ibid.

make sure that the funds gathered through the *gabilah* were properly supervised and used only for the welfare of the community and its institutions.[12] Albala saw in this approach an opportunity to entrench his position within the community and to gain influence over its conduct.

Reorganization of the Community

Nisim Albala, headmaster of the main Alliance school in Baghdad, reported these events not only to the central committee of the society in Paris, but also to the chairman of the Alliance committee in Istanbul, Yitshak Fernandez. Fernandez, who had connections with senior figures in the government, succeeded in persuading the grand vizier to send an order to Baghdad permitting the restoration of the *gabilah*. This accomplishment added to the Alliance's prestige in the eyes of the Baghdad public, and Albala set out to use this popularity to combat what he saw as the destructive influence on the community of the *ḥakham bashi* and those who surrounded him. In particular, he was determined to stop the misuse of public funds by the chief rabbi and his circle for their own ends. With the help of those wealthy laymen who stood outside the *ḥakham bashi*'s circle, he embarked on a propaganda campaign intended to convince the public of the need to set up an administrative board which would take the community's financial affairs out of the hands of the few Torah scholars who were close to the *ḥakham bashi*. It is worth mentioning here that one of the explicit goals of the Alliance emissaries was to gain positions of influence in the communities where they lived and worked in order to promote the organization's key agenda—introducing modern western values of freedom and equality, restoring justice, honesty, and fairness in law, advancing women and their education, and modernizing the social structure of the community, among other things.[13] Albala hoped that a committee of the type he proposed would be more open and responsive to the needs of Alliance institutions in the city.

This propaganda initiative naturally aroused the hostility of the Torah scholars against whom it was aimed, and once again led to unrest and controversy within the community. Albala gathered together the dignitaries and sages—including Rabbi Joseph Hayim and his brother Nisim, the chief opponents of any reform within the community—to read Fernandez's formal message that the government had given permission for the restoration of the

[12] AAIU, Irak, I.C., 4, Bagdad, Rapport sur la Gabella, 30 Jan. 1905

[13] On cultural missions in the communities as understood by the emissaries of the Alliance, see Rodrigue, *French Jews*, 181–3.

gabilah. At this meeting the rabbis declared that they could not approve the creation of the new committee until those who had accused them of misuse of public funds had been properly punished. Albala, who had been expecting this, delivered the response he had planned in advance: he turned to the rabbis and, in a conciliatory tone, told them that their position required them to forgive those who insulted them and that, moreover, as they were meant to set an example of moral behaviour, they needed to conduct themselves in a peaceful and fraternal manner. He added that Yitshak Fernandez and the leadership of the Alliance, who had made so great a contribution to the welfare of the community by restoring its ability to benefit from the *gabilah*, would not be impressed by their stubborn refusal of its proposals. The laymen who supported Albala reinforced his position, explaining to the rabbis that if they chose to perpetuate disorder and anarchy, then even the *gevirim* who had hitherto supported them would lose patience and they would have the entire community ranged against them. According to Albala's account, these declarations had their effect. The rabbis were forced to retreat from their position and to give their approval to the decision that, once the order enabling them to resume collection of the *gabilah* tax had been passed, a committee would be set up to conduct all the financial affairs of the community. Albala's success was registered in the stipulation that he would be one of the members of the committee. It was further decided that the committee would prepare a budget that would include, first and foremost, the funding of the community's educational institutions, including those of the Alliance.[14]

Albala saw this as a great victory over what he called the 'routine laziness, deceit, and pursuit of wealth by the rabbis'. The taste of victory was all the sweeter given that it was not long since an attempt by Albala to mediate between two rival groups had been presented to the *wali* as the interference of a foreign citizen in internal Ottoman affairs. At that time he had been forced to abandon overt involvement in communal matters for a while and to commit himself to a neutral position.[15] But Albala knew that the victory was not yet complete. He needed to ensure that the members of the committee to be chosen would support the Alliance and its ideas and would not serve, as he put it, as 'puppets of the rabbis'.[16] Albala understood that organizational change without a change in thinking would not lead to a true transformation in the conduct of the Baghdad community, so he made use of this period of disorder and confusion to attempt to change the attitude of the Baghdad sages towards

[14] AAIU, Irak, II.E., Bagdad, 8*a*, Albala, 16 Mar. 1905. At this time the Alliance ran three schools for boys and one for girls in Baghdad.

[15] Ibid., 3 Apr. 1905.

[16] Ibid., 16 Mar. 1905.

the Alliance's project within the community. Thus, with the aim of encouraging the flow of funds from the community to the educational institutions run by the Alliance, and thereby enabling the expansion of Alliance activity among the youth of the community, he sought to draw the rabbis closer to the Alliance schools.

Even so, Albala's opinion of the local rabbis remained extremely negative. In his view, they were fanatics, ignoramuses, and enemies of progress. He claimed that the rabbis had, in the past, slandered the Alliance by making false accusations, the main one being that Hebrew was not taught at all in its institutions. Albala sought to prove to the public that these accusations were baseless, while also challenging the critics by increasing the number of hours of instruction in the French language. Soon enough the rabbis protested; even Rabbi Joseph Hayim—whom Albala admired, stating that, unlike the other rabbis, he was 'an enlightened man, whose influence extends over all of Iraq'—sent a letter on this matter to Albala, who then met Rabbi Hayim and explained to him personally the importance of studying French. He also invited him, together with the other rabbis, to visit the school and examine the students' knowledge of Hebrew. He even promised them that, in accordance with the results of this examination, he would be prepared to re-evaluate the question of the role of French instruction in the school. Rabbi Hayim took up the challenge, arriving at the school to examine the students accompanied by several judges from the rabbinic court. The results astonished him: the children knew how to read from the Bible and the Talmud, and were even able to explain what they read. He was impressed by the pupils' Hebrew notebooks, and particularly by the clarity of their writing. According to Albala, Rabbi Hayim turned to his fellow rabbis and pointed out the error of their notion of what was happening within the walls of the Alliance institutions. He praised their level of Hebrew studies as well as speaking favourably of the study of foreign languages as a tool that would be useful to the children in their lives.[17] He apologized to Albala for having listened to malicious rumours about the school, and assured him that he would support the Alliance's request to grant communal funding to the institution. Reflecting this new rapprochement, Rabbi Hayim was appointed honorary president of the new local committee of the Alliance. Alongside him stood the wealthy layman Me'ir Elijah (Elias), who was appointed chairman of the committee.[18] Albala and his supporters hoped that, under the leadership of a new *ḥakham*

[17] AAIU, Irak, II.E., Bagdad, 8*a*, Albala, 20 July 1905.

[18] On Me'ir ben Eliyahu Shlomo David, see Ben-Ya'akov, *Babylonian Jewry from the End of the Geonic Period* (Heb.), 185–6. For a list of the members of the AIU committee, see AAIU, Irak, II.E., Bagdad, 8*a*, Albala, 20 July 1905.

bashi who would enjoy the moral support of Rabbi Joseph Hayim, the community would move forward towards modernization and enlightenment.

However, the biggest obstacle to reorganization of the community was Rabbi Joseph Hayim's own brother, Nisim Hayim. He feared that the new committee set up to run the community's financial affairs would strip him of the power and influence he had hitherto enjoyed during Rabbi Solomon's tenure as *ḥakham bashi*, and did everything possible to undermine its activity. His opponents described Nisim Hayim as a man lacking in any inhibitions, who had a finger in every pie and intimidated everyone in the community. As he had a wide network of family connections, many of the prominent laymen in the community being his relatives, he wielded great influence.[19] Thus a situation arose in which the majority of the people supported the new committee, proper management of the community's financial matters, and division of the budget according to new criteria, whereas the minority—which included a smattering of rabbis and dignitaries of considerable financial weight, headed by Nisim Hayim—were opposed to any change in the running of the community. The eventual success of this minority in imposing its will upon the majority is attributable largely to the influence of Nisim Hayim's group upon the head of the new committee, the *gevir* Me'ir Elijah, the richest man in the community.[20]

The Arrival of Rabbi David Pappo

According to one Baghdad tradition, during the course of the events described above Rabbi Moses ben Reuben Sedaka was appointed *ḥakham bashi* in place of Rabbi Solomon. The same tradition claims that Sedaka, wishing to raise the status of the Baghdad community, asked the *ḥakham bashi* in Istanbul, Rabbi Moses Halevi, to send to the city a new *ḥakham bashi* who was fluent in Turkish and French and familiar with the government system and the laws of the state—and that it was in response to this request that Rabbi David Pappo was sent to Baghdad.[21] Another Baghdad tradition states that Rabbi Solomon wished to resign from his office, and was replaced by a *ḥakham bashi* from outside the community, appointed by sultanic firman, as the result of an initiative by the wealthy men of the community.[22] Other documents—such as the reports of the Alliance emissary and the letters from Baghdad addressed to the *ḥakham bashi*—make no mention of the appointment of Rabbi Sedaka or of any appeal to *ḥakham bashi* Moses Halevi; nor is

19 AAIU, Irak, II.E., Bagdad, 8*a*, Albala, 10 Aug. 1905.

20 Ibid., 14 Sept. 1905, 28 Sept. 1905.

21 Ben-Zvi Institute, MS 3750.

22 Twena, *Exiled and Redeemed* (Heb.), 20.

there any mention in these sources of any initiative on the part of the communal dignitaries to bring in a *ḥakham bashi* from another community. Furthermore, it seems rather unlikely that a Baghdad rabbi serving as interim or substitute *ḥakham bashi* would turn to Istanbul with a request to give up his own position to a stranger.

It seems more plausible that the individual who lobbied the Ottoman authorities to replace Rabbi Solomon as *ḥakham bashi* in Istanbul was in fact Yitshak Fernandez, chairman of the Alliance committee in Istanbul, and that he did so in response to a request from Albala. While we have no record of such an explicit request from Albala, we know that he made repeated requests to the president of the Alliance in Paris to put pressure on Fernandez to take the necessary steps using his connections in Istanbul, which may indicate that the president also intervened in this matter. Certainly, the replacement of Rabbi Solomon with a new and better-qualified *ḥakham bashi* would be likely to assist him in his project of bringing about the changes he wanted to see in the Baghdad community. Albala did not particularly respect or admire Solomon, whom he viewed as lacking in the character and ability to protect the interests of the community. In his view, the best proof of Solomon's helplessness was the fact that even after numerous telegrams had arrived reporting the instructions from the Sublime Porte ordering the *wali* to nullify the decision of the administrative council abolishing the *gabilah*, the *wali* denied that he had ever received such instructions. Albala conjectured that the governor expected to receive *baqshish* (a bribe) from the community before reinstating the legal status of the *gabilah*. Albala was likewise disappointed at the apathy shown by the leading members of the community, who failed to put pressure on the *wali*, according to him, out of cowardice and egotism. In letters addressed to the head of the Alliance, Albala harshly criticizes the members of the community who, he claims, were quite ready to condemn the *ḥakham bashi*'s weakness, but took no practical steps to replace him.[23]

Rumours began to be heard in Baghdad that their new *ḥakham bashi* was to be Rabbi David Pappo, who had previously served as *ḥakham bashi* in the cities of Tripoli in Libya, Bursa in Turkey, and Monastir in Macedonia. Born in Istanbul on 26 May 1848 and educated in the yeshivas of Jerusalem, Pappo had later returned to the Turkish capital, where for many years he lived off his inheritance from his father, until he lost all his property in a fire and was forced to make his own way in the world. For some time he travelled as a rabbinic emissary, during the course of which he served, in 1892–4, as acting *ḥakham bashi* in Tripoli.[24] During his stay in Istanbul, Pappo became

[23] AAIU, Irak, II.E., Bagdad, 8*a*, Albala, 3 Apr. 1905.

acquainted with the *ḥakham bashi* Moses Halevi, who appointed him *ḥakham bashi* and head of the rabbinic court in the community of Bursa. Thereafter he moved on to serve in the community of Monastir.[25]

For the director of the Alliance institutions in Baghdad, Pappo was a long-standing but not particularly pleasant acquaintance: Albala had been Alliance emissary in Bursa during Rabbi Pappo's service there and by his own account their relationship had not been a smooth one. Pappo had opposed the merging of the communal *talmud torah* with the Alliance school —the very issue, indeed, that had forced his departure from Bursa and move to Monastir. In view of this history, from Albala's perspective the arrival in Baghdad of this former adversary as the new head of the community was not a promising sign. He took some small comfort in the fact that Pappo's secretary, Joseph Hai Panigel, was a graduate of the Alliance's rabbinic seminary in the Hasköy quarter of Istanbul.[26] Another point that gave Albala some hope that his relations with Rabbi Pappo would be better this time around was the selection of the rabbi's son, Me'ir Pappo, by the headmaster of the Alliance school in Monastir, and accepted by the Alliance headquarters, as a candidate to study in the teachers' seminar run by the society in Paris (École Normale Israélite Universelle). Rabbi Pappo's agreement to his son's studying in Europe, Albala surmised, might indicate a change in attitude towards the Alliance enterprise.[27]

Rabbi David Pappo took up his new post in Baghdad armed with an official firman from the sultan—the first *ḥakham bashi* of the city to be so recognized since Rabbi Elisha Dangoor over twenty years earlier. The arrival of this new leader, adorned with official trappings of honour from the Sublime Porte, seems to have given the new communal board an influx of confidence and energy.[28] Its financial matters were put on a sound footing, and relations with institutions of the Alliance improved. The committee even took upon itself the cost of feeding the 450 students in the Alliance schools, notwithstanding the additional expense entailed in paying the salaries of Rabbi Pappo and his secretary.[29] Even the issue of the curriculum in the community's educational institutions seemed to be on the path to resolution, with the *ḥakham*

[24] See his comments in Pappo, *Penei david*, 5*a*, §2. According to M. Hakohen, his appointment in Tripoli was in 1891 (Hakohen, *Higid mordekhai*, 147).

[25] See the entry on Pappo in Gaon, *The Jews of the East*, ii. 535–6; also Grayevski, *In Memory* (Heb.), 167–70.

[26] AAIU, Irak, II.E., Bagdad, 8*a*, Albala, 14 Sept. 1905; on Panigel, see Gaon, *The Jews of the East*, ii. 530–3.

[27] AAIU, Irak, II.E., Bagdad, 8*a*, Albala, 26 Oct. 1905.

[28] For the sermon Pappo delivered in Baghdad at the time of his appointment as *ḥakham bashi*, see Pappo, *Beni me'ir*, 48*b*–51*a*.

[29] AAIU, Irak, II.E., Bagdad, 8*a*, Albala, 28 Sept. 1905.

bashi declaring his willingness to discuss the implementation of educational reform, even in the *talmudei torah*, with the headmaster of the Alliance institutions. However, this question led to renewed opposition from the other Torah scholars in the city, who feared that the Alliance intended to 'Frenchify' the *talmudei torah*. Albala reassured them that there was no requirement to teach French, but pointed out that it was necessary to teach the language of the state, and that this obligation fell first and foremost upon the community; but the rabbis remained obdurate, refusing to allow any change in the curriculum of these institutions. Nevertheless, the chief rabbi did succeeded in gaining acceptance of a decision concerning the construction of a new building that would solve the problem of inadequate study space. Rabbi Joseph Hayim, who had great influence in the community and whose support for the Alliance institutions was already well established, joined forces with the new *ḥakham bashi*, and the two of them were in turn joined by Me'ir Elijah, chairman of the new committee set up to administer the community's finances.[30] Under the sponsorship of these three figures, an appeal for funds was conducted among the members of the community, during which a sum of about 1,000 Turkish pounds was collected, probably to finance the new school building. This achievement weakened the case of those rabbis who were opposed to the Alliance and strengthened those who supported its greater involvement in the *talmudei torah*. Albala was greatly heartened by Rabbi Pappo's conduct in this matter, writing confidently: 'The rabbis protested, but whatever they may do, they cannot stop progress. In Baghdad, as in the other large cities of Turkey, the community will in the final analysis place the *talmudei torah* under the sponsorship of the Alliance.'[31]

But this encouraging momentum quickly died away. The committee's activity gradually declined and community matters once more fell into neglect. In practice, all decisions were taken alone by the head of the committee, Me'ir Elijah, without any discussion. Rabbi Joseph Hayim's brother, Nisim, who for a time had withdrawn from all communal affairs, now began to threaten the new *ḥakham bashi*. First he borrowed large sums of money from the new chief rabbi and his secretary and did not repay them. Thereafter he introduced a series of rabbinic rulings against aspects of how the Alliance's institutions were run—particularly the employment of male teachers in workshops set up by the Alliance to teach poor girls carpet-weaving. The

[30] Rabbi Joseph Hayim publicly expressed his admiration for the Alliance and for its project in the eulogy he delivered for Rabbi Zadok Hakohen—the chief rabbi of France, who was a member of the central committee of the Alliance—at a memorial service organized in his honour by Albala in Baghdad's central synagogue. See ibid., 1 Feb. 1906.

[31] Ibid., 14 Dec. 1905.

chief rabbi was unable to intervene; indeed, he admitted to Nisim Albala that the final decision in this matter rested with Rabbi Joseph Hayim.[32] In reality, David Pappo's title as *ḥakham bashi* was almost completely devoid of meaning. In spiritual matters, the Baghdad community turned to Rabbi Hayim as its exclusive halakhic authority, whereas material matters were run by a small cadre of wealthy men.[33] From this point onwards relations between the *ḥakham bashi* and Rabbi Hayim progressively deteriorated, albeit not to the point of a complete rift.[34] The *ḥakham bashi*, who had been expected to guide the community towards progress and modernization, remained virtually a stranger to the community, on the margins of its life. Thus the community began to slip back into anarchy, to the great disappointment of all the hopes that had been attached to Rabbi Pappo. Albala was not sparing in his criticism:

As a foreigner in Baghdad, had Chief Rabbi Pappo been graced with a broad and enlightened soul, he would have been able to overcome the plots and intrigues and exert a positive influence upon the community, which had grown more prosperous economically from year to year. But his own egotism, pride, and concern for the personal interest of the wealthy men, and the zealotry and pursuit of profit by the rabbis, perpetuated the disorder and anarchy. Unfortunately, the chief rabbi is a closed and small-minded person with narrow thinking. Only one thing concerns him: to become wealthy. He earns a good living and is able to live a comfortable life. He receives nearly 500 francs per month, but his way of life and his behaviour are directed towards glorifying his honour and status.[35]

Albala was not alone in his disillusionment. Aaron David Shohet, who served as a translator in the British consulate in Baghdad, wrote in his report for February 1910 that the title 'chief rabbi' borne by David Pappo was, in practice, devoid of content. The *ḥakham bashi*, he said, lacked any influence

[32] AAIU, Irak, II.E., Bagdad, 8*a*, Albala, 11 Feb. 1906. On this incident, see the documentation published by Zvi Yehudah in 'Babylonian Jewry and Cultural Changes' (Heb.), 56–8).

[33] Even though Pappo's book *Penei david* was published close to his departure from Baghdad, it contains hardly any halakhic questions from the period of his service there as chief rabbi. In the absence of any manuscript sources indicating otherwise, it would appear that Rabbi David Pappo was not considered an important halakhic authority in Baghdad.

[34] See AAIU, Irak, I.B., 7, Bagdad, Rabbi Pappo to the president of the Alliance, 25 Adar 5667; also Irak, II.E., Bagdad, 8*a*, Albala, 29 Apr. 1907. Rabbi Pappo did not attend the funeral of Rabbi Joseph Hayim. He argued in his defence that he thought the funeral was to take place on the following day; however, his absence angered the late rabbi's disciples and students, who attributed it to his laziness (see Agassi, *Imrei shimon*, 243). See also Pappo,, Sermon §3, pp. 56*a*–59*b*. On the circumstances of Rabbi Joseph Hayim's death on 30 August 1909, see Ben-Ya'akov, *Babylonian Jewry from the End of the Geonic Period* (Heb.), 197.

[35] AAIU, Irak, II.E., Bagdad, 8*a*, Albala, 29 Apr. 1907.

upon either the Ottoman authorities or the members of the community, and communal matters were conducted by a small group of wealthy men on the one hand, and by the spiritual council composed of local rabbis on the other.[36]

The Young Turk Revolution and the Community

Echoes of the Young Turk Revolution quickly reached Baghdad. Whereas in Damascus, Beirut, and Jerusalem the communities were hostile towards those rabbis who were identified with the old and oppressive system, in Baghdad members of the community did not demand the deposition of the *ḥakham bashi* David Pappo. This may have been for no more positive reason than that his rather colourless and nondescript personality was too weak to arouse any hostility. In any event, as he had virtually no control over any area of community life, his removal would not have changed anything. Moreover, a year after the revolution, Rabbi Joseph Hayim had died, leaving no rabbinic authority of any stature to replace him, and the perpetuation of such a vacuum made it easier for the *gevirim* to retain their firm hold on the reins of communal leadership. This may have been the reason why they preferred that Rabbi Pappo, who was entirely under their thumb, should continue to serve in the position of *ḥakham bashi*. Also, at this point the interest of the *gevirim* in Baghdad was primarily directed outwards, towards the wider politics of Baghdad, and not inwards on the affairs of the Jewish community. One person who did describe Rabbi Pappo as unsympathetic to the new regime was Albala. While he did not call for the removal of the *ḥakham bashi*, in his letters to the new *ḥakham bashi* in Istanbul, Hayim Nahum, an ally of the revolutionary regime, he described Rabbi Pappo as a man belonging to the past, a figure of the *ancien régime*.[37]

In Baghdad, as in other central cities of the Ottoman empire, the Jews took to the streets, together with the rest of the population, to celebrate the revolution, with its promise of equality and freedom, justice and liberty.[38]

[36] For the report in full, see Meir, *The Socio-cultural Development of Iraqi Jewry* (Heb.), 508–12; also Kedourie, 'The Jews of Baghdad'. On Rabbi David Pappo's function in examining students in the *talmud torah*, see Moshe, *End of the Days* (Heb.), 44.

[37] ACRI, TR/Is/57*a*, Albala to Nahum, Baghdad, 29 Aug. 1909. Nevertheless it is worth mentioning that later relations between Rabbi Pappo and the Alliance and its representatives changed. See e.g. AAIU, Irak, I.B., 7, Pappo to the president of the Alliance, 27 July 1910; Pappo to the committee of the Alliance, 12 Jan. 1911; Pappo to the president of the Alliance, 22 May 1911.

[38] AAIU, Irak, I.C., 4, Bagdad, Franco, 28 May 1909. See also Kazaz, 'The Political Activity of Iraqi Jews' (Heb.), 40–1; CHBJ, No. 7308, al-Kabir, *My Communal Life*, 88; Ghanima, *The Delight* (Arab.), 179–80.

About 100 young Jewish people joined the revolutionary political party, the Committee of Union and Progress, and, along with their Muslim and Christian compatriots, sought to remove senior local officials who belonged to the old regime.[39] Nevertheless, most of the Jewish community watched with concern, perhaps even anxiety, the changes taking place and the fluctuating fortunes in the struggle between the revolutionaries and defendants of the sultanic monarchy. For the Jews of Baghdad, the victory of those who supported freedom, equality, and progress was not merely a matter of ideological significance, but a matter of life and death, knowing that their destiny depended upon the outcome of this struggle. The new regime would save them—so it seemed—from the arbitrary whims of the old rulers and, in particular, would protect them from Muslim zealotry. Following the revolution, the Muslims lost the official backing they had enjoyed in fomenting disturbances and attacks upon the Jews.[40] The implications of the revolution were clear to the Muslim population: equality of non-Muslims before the law and a prohibition against harassing or attacking members of minorities or inciting hatred against them. However, many Muslims found it difficult to accept 'heretics' as equal to themselves, and in consequence not only opposed the revolution and its values, but saw a clear connection between the revolutionaries and the Jews and Christians—a connection which, in their view, constituted a threat to Islam and to its world-view. Muslim scholars began to whip up popular feeling against the Jews, claiming that the Jews were the real rulers of the country and that the new constitution had been written and promulgated under their inspiration.[41]

This feeling became even stronger when a Jew, Sason Ezekiel Efendi, was elected as one of the representatives of Baghdad in the newly constituted representative assembly in Istanbul. He was an educated man, fluent in Turkish and European languages, and was a member of the local committee of the Alliance. He was also the chief translator both for the governorship and for the director of the French shipping company La Compagnie de Navigation de la Liste Civile. Sasson Ezekiel stood for election not as a representative of the Jewish community, but as a delegate of the Committee of Union and

39 *Ḥavatselet*, 25 (8 Kislev 5669), 131.

40 On the low social status of the Jews in Baghdad and the provocations offered by the rulers to the Jewish community during the last decades of Ottoman rule, see Ben-Ya'akov, *Babylonian Jewry from the End of the Geonic Period* (Heb.), 147, 154–6, 226; Kazaz, 'The Political Activity of Iraqi Jews' (Heb.), 38–9.

41 AAIU, Irak, I.C., 4, Bagdad, Franco, 28 May 1909. Bernard Lewis has already noted the unique circumstances that gave rise to the wide dissemination through the empire of an account of the revolution attributing it to Jewish–Masonic (Freemason) activity (Lewis, *The Emergence of Modern Turkey*, 207, n. 4; and cf. Kedourie, 'Young Turks').

Progress, the party which supported the revolution and whose members included those who had brought it about. He was opposed by a Muslim candidate who represented the forces of reaction, an opponent of the revolution and of its ideas. While the Muslim supporters of the *ancien régime* conducted a widespread and intense campaign against the election of Sason Ezekiel, the supporters of Union and Progress conducted a vigorous campaign on his behalf. While in Baghdad itself the Jewish candidate was defeated, he was elected with the votes of those in the district as a whole, Jews and Muslims alike. That is, his election was made possible by virtue of the supporters of Union and Progress who, through their votes, put into effect their principles of equality and brotherhood.[42]

As noted above, the egalitarian approach of the Committee of Union and Progress was frowned upon in conservative Muslim circles. Even those Muslim dignitaries who joined the party and ostensibly supported the ideas of the revolution did not entirely internalize its values, and many of them were reluctant to sit alongside Jews on the party committee. When in October 1908 representatives of the party central committee from Salonica visited Baghdad, opponents of the Jews in the city took the opportunity to demand that Jews be removed from membership of the party committee. When this demand was rejected, they joined those who were inciting ill feeling against the Jews.

The results of this incitement were not slow to come. During the festival of Sukkot in 1908, Jewish members of the Committee of Union and Progress marched with their comrades in the streets of Baghdad, carrying flags and accompanied by a military band, in honour of the arrival of the party representatives. This public parade offended the opponents of the constitution and, during the course of the festival, on 15 October 1908, riots broke out during which Muslims attacked Jews. According to contemporary accounts, it was as if life itself stopped on that day: stores were closed, homes were locked up, and those few people who dared to walk in the streets were robbed. One account states that the Jews did not resist the bandits, who contented themselves with taking their money and watches, and thereby avoided bloodshed. Others, however, assert that an active Jewish opposition was organized and that, by the end of the riots, more than forty people on both sides had been injured. Afterwards, the Jews claimed that the attacks had continued for hours because the authorities ignored them, despite calls for help on the part of the community. The government, of course, rejected these accusations. In any event, it was only on the next day that the authorities sent in subsidiary

[42] AAIU, Irak, I.C., 4, Bagdad, Albala, 4 Jan. 1909; CHBJ, No. 7308, al-Kabir, *My Governmental Life*, 1.

forces, who easily overcame the rioters.[43] Thirty of the rioters were arrested, but were released at the order of the governor under pressure from conservative Muslim elements. The *wali*'s weakness outraged supporters of the constitution, who turned to Istanbul to demand his removal. The central government responded to this request and the *wali*, himself a man of the *ancien régime*, was immediately removed from office.[44]

It is worth noting that the behaviour of some of those Jews and Christians who supported the revolution and joined the Committee of Union and Progress undoubtedly contributed to the eruption of Muslim anger. Emboldened by the promise of equality and the right of self-defence offered by the revolution, they displayed open contempt for the religious sensibilities of Muslims: for example, they gathered in the mosques on Fridays when sermons were being preached, forcibly removed the imams from the pulpit, and preached the principles of the revolution to the outraged worshippers. This provocative behaviour led a group of Muslim clergy to establish a party known as al-Hizb al-Ahli, the Nationalist Party, in opposition to the Committee for Union and Progress.[45] The new party embarked on a propaganda campaign to rouse the Muslim population in Baghdad, and as a result attacks against Jews became more common. Tension reached a peak in April 1909 when rumours broke out about a counter-revolution initiated by the opponents of Union and Progress in the capital city.[46] Fear of attacks and acts of vengeance by opponents of the revolution in Baghdad increased under the influence of the reactionary spirit emanating from Istanbul, with calls to nullify the constitution. However, the decisive victory of the Committee of Union and Progress, as expressed in the removal of the sultan, ʿAbd al-Hamid II, in 1909 weakened opponents of the revolution even in Baghdad.[47]

The loyalty of the young educated Jews of Baghdad to the ideas of equality and liberty was strikingly expressed in their overwhelming willingness to serve in the Ottoman army as part of their civil obligations. In August 1909, upon the publication of the order requiring young people of all religions to perform full military service, hundreds of young Jews turned out to apply for places in the officer training school.[48]

43 AAIU, Irak, I.C., 4, Bagdad, Franco, 28 May 1909; Ghanima, *The Delight* (Arab.), 180. Cf. *Ha'olam*, 3 (17 Adar 5669), 11–12; Kedourie, 'The Jews of Baghdad', 355–61; id., *Arabic Political Memoirs*, 140–2; Safwat, *Iraq in the Memoir* (Arab.), 77.

44 *Ḥavatselet*, 25 (8 Kislev 5669), 131. For more on the weakness of the *wali*, see Kazaz, 'The Political Activity of Iraqi Jews' (Heb.), 44–5.

45 See Kazaz, 'The Political Activity of Iraqi Jews' (Heb.).

46 On the attempt at a counter-revolution see Lewis, *The Emergence of Modern Turkey*, 210–12.

47 AAIU, Irak, I.C., 4, Bagdad, Franco, 28 May 1909.

48 See Ben-Ya'akov, *Babylonian Jewry from the End of the Geonic Period* (Heb.), 148, and

The Activity of Nazem Pasha

The years following the revolution were marked by increasing rivalry among various factions both within and outside the Committee of Union and Progress. A parliamentary opposition began to take shape in the first elected assembly following the introduction of the constitution. Tensions ran high for both personal and political reasons, and disputes broke out both between members of the ruling group and between the rival factions. As early as July 1910 a reactionary conspiracy led by a senior police officer was uncovered; at the beginning of the following year the ruling party itself split in the wake of increasingly widespread dissatisfaction with the conduct of the regime. A group was set up, calling itself the New Party, which voiced severe criticism of the political and social line taken by the Committee of Union and Progress. At the heart of these criticisms was a demand for greater attention to democratic and constitutional processes. In response, members of Union and Progress took illegal steps to remove the legitimate opposition from parliament. Matters reached a head in January 1912 with the dissolution of the parliament and the calling of new elections, in which the Committee of Union and Progress hoped to prevent its opponents being elected.[49]

These events form the crucial background to the removal from office of the governor of the Baghdad district, Nazem Pasha, which ultimately led to the deposition of the *ḥakham bashi*, Rabbi David Pappo. Nazem Pasha arrived in Baghdad in the spring of 1910. His appointment gave him extremely wide powers as, apart from being the governor of Baghdad, he was also the commander of the Sixth Turkish Army, which was at the time stationed in Baghdad.[50] Nazem Pasha possessed outstanding organizational abilities and proceeded to apply them in his new post. He began to execute far-reaching changes in the regional administration, in accordance with the spirit of the revolution and indeed of those who had shaped the earlier reformist policy of the Ottoman empire—such as Midhat Pasha, who had been governor of Baghdad forty years earlier. According to contemporary accounts, during the ten months he was in Baghdad Nazem Pasha achieved things that had eluded all of his predecessors since the days of Midhat Pasha. He revitalized the weak

sources cited there. This phenomenon was unusual in view of the fear felt by Jews in many other communities, such as Jerusalem, Damascus, and Aleppo, when the military conscription law was introduced. For more on the co-operation of young educated Jews with representatives of the Committee of Union and Progress and their activities in Baghdad, see Meir, *The Socio-cultural Development of Iraqi Jewry* (Heb.), 402–6.

[49] Lewis, *The Emergence of Modern Turkey*, 215–17.

[50] For the firman he received from the sultan, see Ben-Ya'akov, 'A Firman' (Heb.).

military force by ordering a new round of conscription for both the regular army and the reserve army and by introducing excellent military training and exercises, and even set up army camps at the gates of the city. This energetic approach, and its results, impressed both the local population and even the foreigners living in Baghdad, who were used to seeing sophisticated European armies. The people of Baghdad were also struck by the honesty of the new officers and the great improvements overall in the behaviour of the soldiers towards the civilian population.

Nazem Pasha also created an efficient administrative system in the government offices, with the help of a staff of Turkish officials whom he had brought with him from Istanbul with the goal of improving the quality of the civil service and thereby the general appearance of the region. Baghdad had been notorious for the filth and refuse that filled its narrow streets. In many quarters of the city, particularly the poorer ones, the houses were so close to one another that no fresh air, let alone sunlight, could penetrate, and sewage flowed in the alleys. The population's ignorance of public hygiene turned the city, in the words of one contemporary, into one big garbage dump. Nazem Pasha launched a project of cleaning and purifying Baghdad. In addition, he had two enormous dams built either side of the city in order to protect it from flooding, and widened the main arterial roads and paved them with asphalt. He also set about creating the infrastructure for electric trolley lines in Baghdad, and for an automobile transport service between Baghdad and Syria.[51] In addition, Nazem Pasha began the transformation of the Euphrates river into a properly navigable commercial waterway, with the intention of setting up a waterborne service that would shorten the journey time between Baghdad and Aleppo from twenty days to just seven. Tenders were issued for the cleaning of the waterways, and ships were ordered.

Over and above all these ambitious public works, the crowning glory of Nazem Pasha's tenure of office in Baghdad was the sense of complete security he succeeded in instilling throughout the district. According to contemporary accounts, he eliminated most of the violent criminal gangs, making it possible to walk the streets of Baghdad without fear until midnight, and even to leave the door of one's home open after dark. His prestige was so great that even the leaders of the rebellious tribes in surrounding areas were afraid of him. Many even took the trouble to come to Baghdad in order to express their loyalty to him in person.[52]

[51] AENS, Turquie, 152, Wiet à son excellence monsieur le ministre des affaires étrangères à Paris, Bagdad, 17 Feb. 1911, 2 June 1911. Cf. AAIU, Irak, I.C., 4, Bagdad, Albala, 22 Mar. 1911.

[52] AENS, Turquie, 152, Wiet à son excellence monsieur le ministre des affaires étrangères à Paris, Bagdad, 17 Feb. 1911, 2 June 1911.

The Jewish community also benefited from the expansive and confident tone of Nazem Pasha's term of office. With the encouragement of the governor, the *gevir* Me'ir Elijah built a new hospital outside the city at his own expense. The governor himself, along with senior civil and military officials of the district, was present at the opening celebrations of what was at this time the third largest hospital in Baghdad. While it was open to patients of all religions, it was the only one in which Jews could be sure of receiving kosher food and of being cared for in an atmosphere suitable to their way of life and customs.[53]

The Ousting of Nazem Pasha

While most of Baghdad's inhabitants benefited from Nazem Pasha's energy and purposefulness, in the course of his activities he also made numerous enemies. For example, he appropriated many areas of private property for public purposes, and as he did not have readily to hand the sums required to compensate the owners, he became subject to lawsuits. His opponents exploited these claims against him as the basis for a campaign to oust him from office, in the course of which they were prepared to use any means available to persuade the authorities in Istanbul to remove him. Over time, a loose alliance of varied interests banded together against their reformist governor. Anonymous articles attacking him were sent to the newspapers and to government officials in Istanbul.[54] According to accounts given later by people who had lived through this period, rumours arose that the British objected to both the administrative reforms and the development and infrastructural work carried out by Nazem Pasha, wishing to build up their own importance by contrasting their efficiency with the 'weakness' of the Ottomans as part of their overall plan to dominate the oil-rich region; hence they put pressure on the authorities in Istanbul to have him removed.[55] It is clear from the reports of the French consul in Baghdad, that as the months passed Nazem Pasha found himself in severe conflict with the consuls of Britain, the United States, Italy, Austria, and Germany.[56] It also seems that the leaders of the Committee

[53] Ibid. 151, Le gerant du consulat de France à Bagdad à son excellence monsieur le ministre des affaires étrangères à Paris, Bagdad, 21 Aug. 1910, 15 Sept. 1910.

[54] Ibid. 152, Wiet à son excellence monsieur le ministre des affaires étrangères à Paris, Bagdad, 17 Feb. 1911.

[55] Ben-Ya'akov, *Babylonian Jewry in Recent Times* (Heb.), 93–4.

[56] On disputes with the consuls, see AENS, Turquie, 151, Le gerant du consulat de France à Bagdad à son excellence monsieur le ministre des affaires étrangères à Paris, Bagdad, 19 July 1910, 6 Aug. 1910, 9 Aug. 1910, 10 Aug. 1910, 23 Sept. 1910, 18 Oct. 1910, 2 Feb. 1911 (among others).

of Union and Progress, who at this time were engaged in their own struggle against the liberal opposition, were troubled by Nazem Pasha's great popularity and the accumulation of what they viewed as excessive power in his hands; the greater the demonstrations of public support for him, the greater their fears of this charismatic figure.[57] They too wished to be rid of him.

The Jews were among those who benefited from Pasha's activities, whereas until his arrival they had seen more of the costs of the revolution. Specifically, after the support they had given to the Committee of Union and Progress, they were particularly disappointed at the failure to implement the provisions of the constitution in full. As noted above, conservative Muslims saw the ideas of equality and liberty as a blow against the status of Muslims in the empire, and were hostile to the very idea of granting these rights to Jews. For their part, the Jews had been accustomed to behaving submissively towards the Muslims, absorbing insults and worse from the zealots in the population surrounding them, and subject to the arbitrary whims of Ottoman officialdom, so they were pleasantly surprised by Nazem Pasha's approach to his task and the style of his governorship. Here was the first Ottoman official who sought to realize the principles of the new constitution in practice. For the Jews, the promise of freedom granted in the constitution began to be realized upon Nazem Pasha's arrival in Baghdad. The list of accomplishments during his term included the restoration to the community's possession of a grave site attributed to Joshua the high priest, which had been under Muslim control following a struggle over the burial place of Rabbi Abdallah Somekh in 1889.[58] Nisim Albala described the Jews' feelings vividly: 'Once they began to feel in practice their equality with the Muslims, they began to walk about with uplifted heads; they enjoyed full recognition of their status as human beings and as citizens.'[59]

It is not surprising, therefore, that when news of the campaign to have Nazem Pasha removed from office reached the Jews, they took a leading role in the public campaign for his retention. They participated in mass demonstrations, and even initiated demonstrations of their own in which they called for the governor to be confirmed in post. Telegrams were sent to Istanbul in the name of the Jewish community, protesting against his removal. For about a week, the whole city was transformed into a protest zone, with business suspended and demonstrators marching through the streets, cheering Nazem Pasha and protesting against his removal.

[57] AAIU, Irak, I.C., 4, Bagdad, Albala; 22 Mar. 1911; and cf. Twena, *Exiled and Redeemed* (Heb.), 21.

[58] On this incident, see Dumont, 'Jews, Muslims and Cholera'.

[59] AAIU, Irak, I.C., 4, Bagdad, Albala, 22 Mar. 1911; and see further ibid., 5 June 1911.

The Jews' intervention on behalf of Nazem Pasha should not be seen merely as a spontaneous expression of admiration for a popular governor.[60] By this time, young educated people in the Baghdad Jewish community had a fairly well-developed political consciousness—both because they were educated in the values of the French Revolution at the schools of the Alliance Israélite Universelle and because the ideas of the Young Turk Revolution had filtered down to students throughout the Jewish communities of the empire. This growing political consciousness was further deepened through the widespread support for the Committee of Union and Progress, participation in demonstrations to celebrate the news of the renewed implementation of the constitution, and the effort to bring about the election of Sason Ezekiel to the parliament in Istanbul. Thus when it came to the struggle on behalf of Nazem Pasha and against his removal from office, the Jews of Baghdad were expressing their own political inclinations in support of liberal forces and the full implementation of the doctrines of the revolution, and their willingness to fight on behalf of its ideas. These young people demonstrated, not only as Jews or on behalf of the Jewish community, but as equal citizens and on behalf of the Baghdad district as a whole. Nisim Albala, delighted to see how deeply the ideas that underpinned the Alliance's work had penetrated the hearts of his students, described the political involvement of the young people of the community as 'a new act, deserving of mention, that testifies to the longing for the values of freedom and progress that burns in the heart of Jewish youth in Baghdad'.[61]

There are several descriptions of the young Jews' admiration for Nazem Pasha, and of the ways they found to express their unusually fervent regard for the reforming governor. One account describes an occasion on which he was riding in his coach when a number of young Jews approached it, released the reins of the two horses attached to it, and began to draw the coach in their place.[62] Demonstrations of this type certainly made a deep impression on the *wali*.

But all the letters and protests and demonstrations were to no avail, and Nazem Pasha was removed from his position. Even at the point of his departure, the Jews helped him all they could. Before leaving Baghdad, Nazem Pasha wanted to sell his possessions; at public auction they were given

[60] See Kazaz, 'The Political Activity of Iraqi Jews' (Heb.), 47.

[61] AAIU, Irak, I.C., 4, Bagdad, Albala, 22 Mar. 1911.

[62] Ben-Ya'akov, *Babylonian Jewry in Recent Times*, 94. On Nazem Pasha's removal from office and the subsequent agitation in the city, see also AENS, Turquie, 152, Wiet à son excellence monsieur le ministre des affaires étrangères à Paris, Bagdad, 21 Mar. 1911.

a very low valuation, but thanks to the intervention of the Jews the items were sold at ten times their quoted price.[63]

The Dismissal of the *Ḥakham Bashi*

By this time the Ottoman government of the Committee of Union and Progress feared for its future in power; consequently, not content with removing Nazem Pasha himself, it now set about suppressing his supporters so as to prevent further agitation. His chief supporters were arrested, and an investigating committee headed by a senior official was sent to Baghdad. The investigators recommended removing the *ḥakham bashi*, Rabbi David Pappo, whose signature appeared at the head of a telegram from the Jewish community demanding that the governor be retained in his position. They accordingly suspected Rabbi Pappo of being a subversive personality, and when the investigators reported on their mission the regime in Istanbul decided he should be removed from office and put on trial. In keeping with the centralizing policy of the Union and Progress government, the minister of the interior approached the *ḥakham bashi* in Istanbul, Hayim Nahum, and demanded that he depose Rabbi Pappo. Rabbi Nahum pointed to a clause in the law stating that a *ḥakham bashi* could only be removed from office after being convicted in a court of law, adding that he would summon Rabbi Pappo to be tried in Istanbul.[64]

Rumours began to circulate in Baghdad about the intention to depose the *ḥakham bashi*, prompting Albala to write about him and Nazem Pasha in starkly contrasting terms:

> It is said that the chief rabbi will be removed from his office (which will not be a great loss to the community). [On the other hand,] the loss of Nazem Pasha is an irreparable loss to Iraq. For members of our religion, there is definitely cause for sorrow . . . In Nazem Pasha, our schools have lost a protector and a friend.[65]

The question arises whether the views of Nisim Albala, an outside Jewish observer with his own interests, reflect those of the community as a whole. As we have seen, Rabbi Pappo's influence over the behaviour of the community was not significant, nor was he held in generally high regard. Indeed, for several of the local sages his very appointment was an insult to themselves and the community, his presence in the city implying that there were no

[63] See Kazaz, 'The Political Activity of Iraqi Jews' (Heb.), 46; Ghanima, *The Delight* (Arab.), 180.

[64] *Hamevaser*, 10 (24 Adar 5671), 119; *Ha'or*, 134 (5 Nisan 5671), 309.

[65] AAIU, Irak, I.C., 4, Bagdad, Albala, 22 Mar. 1911.

Torah scholars in Baghdad deserving of the position of *ḥakham bashi*; as a result, several of the local scholars viewed him with contempt, or with only grudging acceptance. Rabbi Shimon Agasi, a disciple of Rabbi Joseph Hayim, clearly had no great opinion of his Jewish scholarship:

I have heard from one trustworthy person that, at the time that the members of our congregation needed to bring as *ḥakham bashi* the *ḥakham* Rabbi David Pappo—may God give him life and protect him—from the city of Constantinople—may God protect it—he was asked by one of the distinguished ministers of the government: Was not the city of Baghdad previously known as a great city of scholars and of scribes? I am astonished as to how it has declined so much, that you need to bring a *ḥakham bashi* from afar. And I am greatly pained by this, for it is a shame that there be such a thing under our government, such a great city lacking in wisdom and knowledge. And the man responded to him: Sir, take it easy and be calm, for thank God we have great sages and people learned in our law, far greater than the sage who was brought. For it is not his wisdom that we need, but that he knows how to speak Turkish and to negotiate in communal matters before the government ministers.[66]

In the end, Rabbi Nahum submitted to pressure from the Ottoman government and removed David Pappo from office—possibly realizing that it was preferable that the rabbi be withdrawn without having to stand trial. In any event, the government did not insist on pursuing charges of subversion against him.[67] On 30 August 1911, Rabbi David Pappo returned to the city where he had been raised, Jerusalem, where he was appointed head of a rabbinic court.[68]

But this was not the end of his troubles. Shortly after his departure from Baghdad, Rabbi Pappo was informed that his son Me'ir—a graduate of the Alliance's teachers' seminary in Paris and a representative of the society in Iraq—had suddenly died at the age of 22. Rabbi Pappo's first book, published in Jerusalem in 1914, was named after him: *Beni me'ir* (My Son Me'ir).

Rabbi David Pappo died in Jerusalem in April 1927. Although he served only a short term as *ḥakham bashi* in Baghdad and was ultimately removed from the post, and although he had previously served in a number of communities throughout the Ottoman empire and subsequently served as head of a rabbinic court in Jerusalem, he viewed his term of service in Baghdad as the pinnacle of his career. This feeling was expressed in the terms he used to

66 Agassi, *Imrei shimon*, 181; and see also what his son, Rabbi Elijah Agassi, wrote: ibid. 11.

67 *Moriyah*, 27 Nisan 5671, p. 3.

68 In the account of the episode given by S. N. Gottlieb, Rabbi Pappo took an oath that if he were exempted from standing trial, he would move to Jerusalem and decline any further political or rabbinic office (Gottlieb, *Ohalei shem*, 496).

sign the introductions to his books: 'The young one in Israel David Pappo, previously chief rabbi in a number of cities, and in the celebrated city in Israel Baghdad—may the Almighty establish it, Amen, on behalf of the king, may his glory be exalted.'[69]

[69] For the eulogy given by Rabbi Ezra Dangoor—chief rabbi and head of the rabbinic court in Baghdad—when the news of Rabbi Pappo's death arrived in the city, see Batzri (ed.), *Siaḥ shoshanim*, 31–2.

Epilogue

> Rabbi Judah said: Three things shorten a person's days and years: One who is given a Torah scroll to read from and does not read therein; [who is given] a cup of blessing and does not bless over it; and one who places himself in the rabbinate.
>
> BT *Berakhot* 55*a*

THE OFFICE OF *ḥakham bashi* was created on the cusp of an extended period of profound crisis in the Jewish communities of the Ottoman empire. This atmosphere of crisis permeates the history of many of those communities during the second half of the nineteenth century, decades characterized by bitter disputes and controversies around issues of leadership. Confrontations and polemics of various sorts were of course endemic to premodern Jewish society as well, but it appears that, as in eighteenth-century Europe, so in the nineteenth-century Middle East the rise of individualism and the increasing variety of cultural options available led to widespread and often dramatic conflicts entailing complex and difficult personal and public choices. These controversies, which began with a realignment of forces within the community and continued with demands on the part of various social groups for a share of power, more than once ended with the removal of the incumbent *ḥakham bashi*.

The legal changes gradually introduced by the Ottoman authorities over the course of the nineteenth century accelerated and brought to the surface social tensions in the Jewish communities at the centre of the empire. The Jewish millet decree of 1864–5 defined the rules for electing the *ḥakham bashi* and the spiritual and steering committees of the community, with the intention of creating a balance among the three foci of power—the *ḥakham bashi*, the rabbinic scholars, and the wealthy laymen (*gevirim*)—within the communities. Almost all the disputes over the office of *ḥakham bashi* derived from tensions which developed in the wake of these reforms. But the confrontations and power struggles within the communities were also motivated by factors rooted in human nature—jealousy, hatred, and rivalry—which further exacerbated the tension between the *ḥakham bashi* and his rivals.

Very few chief rabbis during these decades served out their full term of office, and even those who did rarely escaped embroilment in conflict with one or another group in the communities they served. These confrontations, moreover, unlike those of earlier times, were not confined to mere polemics, attacks carried out with whiplash tongue and acid-dipped pen. Developments during the second half of the eighteenth century presaged great upheavals that in the following century plunged the Jewish communities into instability and turmoil. During the period discussed in this study, the 'silent masses' underwent a process of transformation in which they came to recognize the significance of their status as the majority element in the population. This awareness found practical expression in large public gatherings and demonstrations outside the homes of rabbis, in throwing them out of the synagogues, in cursing them and hitting them, in cutting off contact with them, even in denouncing them to the authorities—and in many cases, demanding the removal of the incumbent *ḥakham bashi*.

Given that the authority of the *ḥakham bashi* derived not only from his selection by the community but also from his recognition by the authorities, on more than one occasion we find those who occupied this position, upon confronting militant opposition in their communities, appealing to the authorities to assist them and to punish their opponents. At times the sanctions applied involved corporal punishment, imprisonment, or banishment from the city. These measures gave explicit expression to the fact that the *ḥakham bashi* was a chief rabbi characterized not necessarily by 'leadership' so much as by 'rulership'.[1] Obedience to the *ḥakham bashi* was required by virtue of his official authority; if he also had charisma, that merely strengthened his ability to win over the public. Hence almost all those rabbis chosen for the office of *ḥakham bashi* adopted the external trappings of rulership, such as bodyguards, impressive robes of office, and various titles and medals of honour conferred by the sultan.

Notwithstanding the new ideas that gradually penetrated the Jewish communities during the final decades of the nineteenth century, the appointment and removal of rabbis came about not as the result of a modern, enlightened revolution of ideas, but primarily as the outcome of coalitions and struggles between and within different social classes over control of the communal institutions and their funds. In this respect, Avner Levi has portrayed the nineteenth century as a period of transition in the communities at the centre of the Ottoman empire. According to him, during the first two-thirds of the century, during which the leadership of the community was still the

[1] See Popper, *Charismatic Leadership* (Heb.), 112.

prerogative of the traditional elite groups—the wealthy laymen and the chief rabbinate—members of the ruling class grossly exploited their position in order to further their own interests, oppressing the public in a manner which was often tantamount to violent robbery in broad daylight.[2] Controversies over the methods used for collecting taxes, and particularly the distribution of the burden of the *ʿaskariyya* and *gabilah*, were at the centre of many intra-communal disputes, and the most explicit expression of the crisis in relations between the classes. It was only during the last third of the nineteenth century that the traditional partnership between the economic elite and the chief rabbinate was broken. In some cases this was the result of the accumulation of excessive power in the hands of the *ḥakham bashi*, who by virtue of his authority dominated both the tools of coercion and the economic resources of the community. Violation of the tacit pact between the wealthy laymen and the chief rabbi, and growing consciousness of power on the part of the masses, were the main factors behind the tumult that surrounded the office of *ḥakham bashi* throughout the communities of the empire. The desire by the elites to weaken the official rabbinate did not derive from a modern impulse to reduce the role of religion and the clergy in private and public life. For that reason, the disputes of this period cannot be described as a struggle between the 'powers of light' and the 'powers of darkness'. These struggles began as class struggles, but as they developed there was invariably a cynical and constant changing of sides by people of all classes and social groups. Alliances were created and broken overnight on the basis of the immediate interests of those involved. Control over the institutions and resources of the community, such as the system of collecting taxes, was understood as a means of accumulating wealth and creating connections with the authorities and with important economic agents both within and outside the region. Thus, up to the last decade of the nineteenth century, the leadership that came to dominate the communal institutions after each act of deposition cannot be described as a 'modern leadership', but is better characterized as an 'interested oligarchy'.

The years between the promulgation of the Jewish millet decree in 1864–5 and the Young Turk Revolution of 1908 were ones during which the revolution in the status of the chief rabbinate and the understanding of its role and function developed. The succession of upheavals and controversies surrounding the office of *ḥakham bashi* in the communities examined in the preceding chapters did not itself constitute that revolution; nevertheless, it is in the disputes over the issue of the chief rabbinate on the eve of the twentieth

[2] Levi, 'Changes in the Leadership' (Heb.), 268.

century that one can discern the seeds of the transition from intrigue to revolution—if not in the explicit motivations for the act of deposition, at least in its results. That is, even when the act of removing a chief rabbi did not derive from revolutionary ideological motivations, in retrospect its results were at times somewhat revolutionary. This phenomenon can be seen in, among other things, the participation of new social elements in the community leadership and in the strengthening of the 'secular' elements as opposed to the rabbis.

Matters came to a head in the demonstrations conducted in various communities in the wake of the Young Turk Revolution, in which the masses demanded that the rabbis of the old generation, whom they described as 'tyrannical' or 'exploitative', be replaced by enlightened and progressive rabbis who would act according to the principles of the revolution. Thus, in the wake of the revolution there developed within these Jewish communities not only a turning inward or self-examination, but also a turning outward. The Jewish public provided a fruitful soil for absorbing the ideas of the revolution. Many young Jewish men and women had been raised on the values of the French Revolution—*liberté, égalité, fraternité*—thanks to their education in modern institutions, such as the schools of the Alliance Israélite Universelle or the Christian missions. The involvement of representatives of the Alliance in the internal matters of the community, already substantial during the second half of the nineteenth century, became even deeper after the revolution. The Alliance schools moved from the margin to the centre of the community, serving as a hothouse within which the enlightened class forced the growth of modern ideas of equality, secularism, and public accountability; the students took their lessons to heart, and applied them without hesitation even to the rabbis who headed their communities.

In the first decade of the twentieth century there was a feeling of change in the air. The revolution further weakened both Jewish autonomy within the empire and, along with growing secularization, the official recognition and legal authority hitherto accorded to the law of the Torah and to the religious leadership. As had happened more than a century earlier in Europe, the consensus around social, political, and ideological-religious questions began to crack. In the controversies that broke out after the Young Turk Revolution, the call to remove the rabbis in a number of communities drew on revolutionary, reformist, and Enlightenment arguments, including the idea of free expression. Struggles over power in the community began to assume the character of a confrontation between those who were defined—by themselves or by others—as enlightened liberals, and their opponents, who were seen as benighted conservatives.

But it would seem that these descriptions were rather exaggerated. In fact, one may reasonably say that the Ottoman Jews absorbed modernization or even surrendered to it. Jewish society in Syria, for example, struggled neither for nor against modernization—not least because there were not enough people to do battle on either side, given the numbers emigrating, both from the enlightened and westernizing class on the one hand, and from the traditional Torah scholars on the other. Many young people from Damascus and Aleppo left for the new satellite communities being created overseas, while Baghdad lost the best of its youth to the daughter communities which sprang up in the Far East and in Europe. In addition to the quest for new economic opportunities, one of the main reasons for this massive outflow was fear of conscription into the Ottoman military, which after the revolution was compulsory for members of all religious communities.

The need to grapple with these issues, which were a direct result of the revolution, pushed the rabbis who led the communities into new areas of activity and into closer contact with representatives of the new governing regime. Most of these chief rabbis had been appointed by Rabbi Hayim Nahum, and so tended to be sympathetic to his views, loyal to him personally, and alive to the possibilities inherent in the new constitution. Unlike their predecessors, these rabbis were not solely engaged in the internal politics of Jewish society, but were also imbued with political consciousness and, when necessary, ready to involve themselves in explicitly Ottoman political issues, such as general elections for parliament and public support of governors and military officers. Their involvement in Ottoman politics placed those who headed the empire's Jewish communities, for the first time, in danger of confrontation with the imperial regime, which in its new, post-revolutionary form acted strongly against those it suspected of subversion or opposition.

Overall, the 'secularization of the rabbinate'—that is, the involvement of the *ḥakham bashi* in political matters and his role as a government official fulfilling explicitly administrative functions—led to a 'cheapening of the rabbinate'. Whereas in the past the Jewish public had related to the rabbi on the basis of his halakhic, ethical, and spiritual status, over the course of time this perception began to change and to be replaced by an attitude formed more by political considerations.

Modernization, and especially the expansion of education, disseminated ideas of secularism and individualism, and facilitated the emergence of new kinds of leader.[3] During the first decade of the twentieth century, patterns of leadership that had been accepted in the Ottoman empire for generations,

[3] On the types of leadership that flourished as a result of modernity, see Lindholm, *Charisma*.

including the placing of a religious figure at the head of the community, were increasingly perceived as outdated. Ultimately, this transformation in outlook led to the impulse to detach the chief rabbi from the political and material leadership and instead to place communal leadership in the hands of the financial and educational elites. The emergence of a new educated elite, graduates of the institutes of the Alliance or of the missionary schools who were involved in the state establishment, and the coming into existence of new reference groups both created and fostered a desire for change. Whereas in the past intracommunal struggles had generally pitted the *gevirim*—that is, the elites of pedigree and wealth—against the *ḥakham bashi*, by the beginning of the twentieth century the struggle was primarily between the rabbis on the one hand and on the other the educated class, who wished to restrict the rabbis' activities to the realm of halakhah. From this point on, the rabbis were marginalized politically; in many cases the *ḥakham bashi* became a puppet manipulated by the old and new elites.

Among the clear signs of weakness of any particular community was the appointment of a chief rabbi from outside. A recurrent figure in the earlier period discussed in this book is that of the 'nomadic rabbi' who moves from one community to another. These nomadic rabbis were the reservoir from which the weaker communities chose their leaders. From time immemorial, Torah scholars had belonged to a broader framework of cultural identity—the 'mother group' of Torah scholars throughout the Jewish world—within which they enjoyed almost unlimited freedom of movement and cultural mobility. The phenomenon of autonomous rabbinic mobility is perhaps most strikingly represented by the figure of Rabbi Raphael Kassin, who at his own initiative set out to travel the world, taking up service in a variety of locations. Another such was Rabbi Aaron Jacob Benjamin, who moved from Baghdad to Damascus to serve as head of the spiritual committee. There was also another type of 'nomadic rabbi' with a long pedigree: these were the rabbinic emissaries who did not travel on their own initiative but were sent abroad by their communities to raise money. These individuals often took up appointment as rabbis in one or other of the communities they visited, where they then remained. Thus, for example, Rabbi Obadiah Halevi, who was born in Damascus and became an emissary for the Sephardi community of Jerusalem, assumed rabbinic office in Baghdad. These scholars, usually setting out from Jerusalem, enjoyed a certain reflected aura of holiness from the city of their origin; however, they rarely lived up to expectations, at least not in respect of organizational ability. Indeed, 'nomadic rabbis' of both types were not generally very successful as leaders of their adopted communities. Lacking either a local power base or official government endorsement to back up their authority, they were entirely dependent upon the elites which brought about their appointment. Moreover, Torah erudition, however outstanding, did not necessarily go with organizational and leadership ability. On the other hand, those who did project charismatic authority often aroused hostility on the part of local elites, who feared such leaders were attempting to displace them from traditional positions of power within the community.

From the last decade of the nineteenth century on we encounter a new type of rabbi, which we may call the 'recommended rabbi'. These rabbis also moved from place to place, but they did so after being appointed to the position of *ḥakham bashi* in a community at the behest of the *ḥakham bashi* in Istanbul. Occasionally the 'recommended rabbi' moved from one community to another. Thus, for example, Rabbi David Pappo served in Tripoli, Bursa, and Monastir before arriving in Baghdad. Rabbi Moses Halevi, the *ḥakham bashi* in Istanbul from 1872 to 1908, began to use the appointment of chief rabbis in the cities of the empire as a tool to strengthen his own authority in the peripheral communities.[4] Rabbi Hayim Nahum, who was appointed as *ḥakham bashi* in Istanbul following the deposition of Rabbi Moses Halevi, perfected this system. He took pains to ensure the removal of rabbis who were identified as loyal to his predecessor, a man of the *ancien régime*, and their replacement by new rabbis who were personally beholden to him for their office. The fact that the 'recommended rabbi' was preferred by the *ḥakham bashi* in Istanbul did not, however, necessarily strengthen his position in the community. A *ḥakham bashi* of this type was without a local power base, and was thus just as dependent as the 'nomadic rabbi' upon the local elites, both for his own livelihood and for his ability to function within the communal organizational framework.

Yet another kind of *ḥakham bashi* was the 'imported rabbi'—the rabbi brought in by the community itself to stand at its head. Thus, Rabbi Hezekiah Shabetai of Jerusalem was invited, while serving in Tripoli, to serve as *ḥakham bashi* of the Aleppo community.

In a few cases, the *ḥakham bashi* was chosen by the Ottoman governor: Ephraim Mercado Alkalai, for example, was appointed chief rabbi of Damascus by Midhat Pasha. It is nevertheless worth noting that all appointments were made with the agreement of the community, or at least with that of the elite that claimed to represent it. The *ḥakham bashi* was never initially imposed upon any community, whether by the *ḥakham bashi* in Istanbul or by the Ottoman governor.

4 An example would be the dispatch of Rabbi Yitshak Shaul to serve in the office of *ḥakham bashi* in San'a, analysed in Harel, 'The Relations' (Heb.).

If the choice of a local rabbi as *ḥakham bashi* was a sign of the organizational and scholarly strength of the community, then only Aleppo can be described as a strong community right from the mid-eighteenth century up to the 1890s. Damascus succeeded in appointing a local *ḥakham bashi*, Rabbi Jacob Perets, in the early 1850s, but not after the great crises of the 1870s; in Baghdad, while a number of local rabbis were appointed *ḥakham bashi*, all of them struggled to exercise authority in the shadow of the great sages of Baghdad, Abdallah Somekh and Joseph Hayim. It was not easy for a *ḥakham bashi* to function in the presence of a rabbi of the old type, who was revered because of his greatness in Torah, his prominent family lineage, or his personal charisma; the rabbinic judge who headed the spiritual committee usually enjoyed greater respect, because his leadership was based upon tradition and served as a symbol of stability and continuity. In any event, immediately before and after the Young Turk Revolution, none of the communities discussed here had a local rabbi serving as *ḥakham bashi*; all the incumbents were either 'recommended' or 'imported'.

How much support the foreign *ḥakham bashi* enjoyed in his adopted community depended considerably upon his world-view, his talents, and his ability to meet the community's expectations. First and foremost, the *ḥakham bashi* needed to have organizational abilities commensurate with the westernizing and modernizing tendencies of the Ottoman authorities. He also needed to be open to new trends in education and employment—and, indeed, we find that a good number of those who served in the office of *ḥakham bashi* had some kind of secular education, even if it was acquired as an autodidact and not through a modern educational institution. Thus, for example, Rabbis Hezekiah Shabetai and Jacob Danon were fluent in Turkish and Arabic, making it easier for them to communicate with the government authorities. Rabbis Yitshak Abulafia and Abraham Dweck Hakohen, even if not themselves fluent in foreign languages, supported the expansion of knowledge among the Jewish public and therefore encouraged the activities of the Alliance in their communities.

Nevertheless, it is worth emphasizing that it is premature to speak of an 'enlightened rabbi' in these communities. On the contrary, the sympathetic attitude towards secular studies evinced by these rabbis did not reflect a revolution in thought or ideology so much as an adherence to—or arguably a return to—values that had always been accepted among the sages of the Near East and the Sephardi world.[5] They acknowledged the importance of increased education as a value in itself, and also thought that, in a changing

[5] See Harel, 'From Openness to Closedness' (Heb.), 1–39.

world, there was room to respond to the challenges of modernization, so long as this did not entail any violation of religious principles. These rabbis adhered faithfully to the tradition, and their general knowledge was fragmentary and superficial. However, there were some among them, such as Hezekiah Shabetai and Jacob Danon, who had a genuine vision of the future and understood the significance of the transformation brought about by the Young Turks—an understanding enhanced in no small measure by the people surrounding them. Thus, for example, during the first years of his tenure of office in Damascus Rabbi Jacob Danon operated under the strong influence of his son-in-law, Abraham Almaleh, an educated young man with a well-defined Zionist nationalist orientation. The degree of openness to such trends and influences of those holding the office of *ḥakham bashi* was likewise influenced by their perception of the needs of the community, as well as by a feeling of responsibility for its future. After all, the most senior Jewish official in the government system, even if he was an explicitly religious figure, had to cultivate an overall vision, not one based solely upon the halakhah and the tradition.[6]

It only remains to examine the long-term contribution to their communities of those who served in the office of *ḥakham bashi* during the period examined here. In fact, they seem to have left little impression upon the functioning and development of the communities they headed. They did not have the wisdom or foresight to build new systems or new institutions. Generally speaking, they were involved in managing everyday life, in making peace between rivals, and in conducting their own personal feuds. Their leadership was oriented towards the short term, and they did not develop new tools for advancing the community. Though some—such as Yitshak Abulafia and Abraham Dweck Hakohen—did support the educational institutions of the Alliance, they did not encourage the graduates to apply their new knowledge and skills to create new communal mechanisms or bases of authority independent of themselves. A possible exception was Rabbi Jacob Danon in Damascus, but it is worth remembering that his activity in this area lasted only as long as his son-in-law, Abraham Almaleh, was by his side. Once Almaleh left Damascus, Rabbi Danon's activity ceased completely.[7]

It is also worth remembering that the *ḥakham bashi*'s primary source of authority, the imperial Ottoman regime, was itself in the midst of a long

[6] See Zohar, *Tradition and Change* (Heb.).

[7] Abraham Almaleh merits a separate study. I analyse his activity within the community at length in a new book, *Zionism in Damascus: Ideology and Activity in the Jewish Community at the Beginning of the Twentieth Century* (London: I. B. Tauris, 2015).

process of decline during the period under discussion. The rebellions which were constantly breaking out throughout the empire, the filth and corruption, the bankruptcies, the political unrest, the stalled attempts at constitutional reform, and finally the First World War—all these weakened the Ottoman establishment, and thereby undermined the authority of the *ḥakham bashi*. Moreover, the breakdown of the Ottoman empire after the war isolated the communities from the centre in Istanbul and from the administrative system that had created the office of *ḥakham bashi*. Although a number of communities continued to grant their chief rabbi the honorific of *ḥakham bashi* during the following years, in the course of time all that remained were the external signs of the robe and the turban, worn to this day by the Sephardi chief rabbis of the State of Israel and the chief rabbi of the Jews of Turkey in their public appearances.

Glossary

ʿAdliyya (Arab.) Ministry of justice

Agudat Ahim (Heb.) An Anglo-Jewish association, founded in Britain in 1871 with the aim of raising the level of education and ethics among the Jews and improving their position within society; generally acted in co-operation with the *Alliance Israélite Universelle

Ahrar (Arab.) 'Liberal Unity': the opposition party in the Ottoman parliament

al-Hizb al-Ahli (Arab.) Party established in Baghdad in opposition to the Committee of Union and Progress

al-Nahda (Arab.) 'The Revival': a society of young Jews founded in Damascus after the *Young Turk Revolution

Alliance Israélite Universelle A Jewish organization established in Paris in 1860 with the goal of furthering Jewish rights throughout the world and improving their economic and cultural situation

Aram Zova (Heb.) Hebrew name for Aleppo

arikha (Heb.) Appraisal (for tax purposes)

ʿaskariyya (Arab.) See *bedel-i ʿaskeri*

baqshish (Arab.) Bribe, tip

batei ishkolas See *iskola*

Bavel (Heb.) Lit. 'Babylonia'. Refers to Baghdad

bedel-i ʿaskeri (Turk.) ***ʿaskariyya*** (Arab.) Military service commutation tax

beit din Rabbinic court

beit midrash (Heb.) Study house

berat*, *beyrat (Turk.) Order, document, certificate, certificate of concession

bey (Turk.) Mr: term of respect

beyrat See *berat*

bikur ḥolim (Heb.) Jewish communal health fund

capitulation Contract between the Ottoman empire and any of a number of European powers granting these countries and their citizens special commercial and legal rights and privileges in respect of residence in and trade with Ottoman dominions

Capuchins Catholic monastic order, an offshoot of the Franciscans, whose members wear a cowl

çilibi (Turk.) Term of respect

Committee of Union and Progress Ruling party in the Ottoman empire following the *Young Turk Revolution

daftar ʿaskari (Arab.) Communal registry in which payment of the **bedel-i ʿaskeri* tax was recorded

dayan (pl. *dayanim*) (Heb.) Rabbi qualified to serve as a judge on a rabbinic court

dhimmi (Arab.) Member of Jewish or Christian minority, allowed to live under Muslim authority with some degree of communal and religious autonomy in return for payment of the poll tax (**jizya*) and other measures reinforcing subordinate status

dina de-malkhuta dina (Heb.) 'The law of the land is the law'; the principle that Jews are obliged to obey the laws of the non-Jewish rulers of the countries in which they live

efendi (Turk.) Sir, Mr: term of respect

exilarch See *resh galuta*

Fertile Crescent The fertile region of the Middle East, shaped like a crescent or bow, extending from the valley of the Euphrates and Tigris rivers in modern-day Iraq through what are now Syria, Jordan, and Palestine to Egypt

firman (Turk.) Edict of the Ottoman sultan

Franciscans Members of a monastic order, named after St Francis of Assisi, who take vows of poverty

Francos Jews of Italian origin who settled in Syria

Freemasons Members of a worldwide fraternal order that originated in the Middle Ages with the aim of cultivating the ethical virtues; owing to persecution by the Catholic Church and other authorities, its meetings are held in secret and involve solemn and mysterious ceremonies

gabilah (Heb.) Indirect Jewish communal tax on the sale of meat, wine, and other commodities and services

gaon (pl. *ge'onim*) One of the rabbis who headed the yeshivas in Babylonia between the seventh and eleventh centuries

gemilut ḥasadim (Heb.) Jewish charitable fund

gevir (pl. *gevirim*) (Heb.) Wealthy householder, often influential in the lay leadership of the community

great/grand vizier Head of the Ottoman government

ḥakham bashi Chief rabbi, officially appointed by the sultan; the term is a combination of the Hebrew *ḥakham* (sage), and the Turkish *basi* (chief, head, first)

halakhah (Heb.) The legal code of Judaism

Hatt-i Hümayun (Turk.) The second stage of the *Ottoman reforms, initiated in 1856

Hatt-i şerif of Gülhane (Turk.) The first stage of the *Ottoman reforms, initiated in 1839

hekdesh (pl. *hekdeshot*) (Heb.) Endowment in the Jewish community, created by the dedication of property for a charitable public cause

ḥerem (Heb.) Excommunication; see also *nidui*

ḥevrah kadisha (Heb.) Lit. 'holy society'; Jewish burial society

'Ḥoshen mishpat' (Heb.) The section of *Shulḥan arukh*, a widely accepted code of Jewish law, dealing with torts and other aspects of civil law

ḥupah (Heb.) Marriage ceremony, so called after the canopy used in that ceremony

hushma (Heb.) Hebrew abbreviation for the Ottoman constitution

imam (Arab.) Muslim prayer leader

intisab (Arab.) Patronage

iskola*, *ishkola (pl. *ishkolas*, *ishkolos*) School

istibdad (Arab.) Tyranny

Jesuits Members of an order of Catholic monks called the Society of Jesus, founded in 1534 by Ignatius Loyola in order to strengthen and propagate the Catholic faith; played an important role in countering Protestant influence during the Counter-Reformation

Jewish millet decree A law promulgated by the *Sublime Porte in 1864 and coming into force in 1865, prescribing the manner of election to the institutions of the Jewish *millet and defining its functions and manner of operation

jizya (Arab.) Poll tax imposed by the Muslim authorities on the **dhimmi* in return for a degree of autonomy

kafis Coffee-houses

kashrut (Heb.) Jewish dietary laws

kavass (Turk.) A guard of important individuals in the countries of the eastern Mediterranean

ketubah (pl. *ketubot*) (Heb.) Jewish marriage contract

khan (pl. *khans*) (Turk.) Inn or resting place for travellers

kohen (Heb.) Member of the Jewish hereditary priestly class, used also as family name

kolel (pl. *kolelim*) communal organization of Jewish immigrants to Jerusalem

kuttab (Arab.) Elementary school; see also *talmud torah*

Lazarists Monks belonging to the order of St Lazarus

madbata (Arab.) Legal ruling, verdict; petition

Maghrib (Arab.) Lit. 'the West'; term used to refer to the regions located to the west of the Middle East, i.e. North Africa

mahakim al-ʿadliyya (Arab.) Mixed courts, including Muslim, Jewish, and Christian judges

mahkamat bidayat al-juzʾ (Arab.) Lower court of first instance

majidi (Turk.) Turkish coin bearing the image of the sultan ʿAbd al-Majid; also a medal awarded by the sultan

majlis (pl. *majalis*) (Arab.) Administrative council, court

majlis idara (Arab.) Provincial council

majlis jismani (Arab.) *See* steering committee

Mamelukes Military caste composed of slaves of Turkish, Circassian, and Mongolian origin, usually kidnapped from their parents in childhood and educated as Muslim soldiers, and providing many of the Ottoman empire's officers and officials

maskil (pl. *maskilim*) (Heb.) Follower of the Haskalah or Jewish Enlightenment, usually western-educated

matzah (pl. matzot) (Heb.) Unleavened bread eaten on the Passover holiday

melamed (pl. *melamedim*) (Heb.) Teacher, usually of young children

menagnot (Heb.) Lit. 'female musicians'; euphemism for prostitutes

merannot (Heb.) Lit. 'female singers'. See *menagnot*

meshorerot (Heb.) Lit. 'singers'. See *menagnot*

mezuzah (pl. *mezuzot*) (Heb.) A piece of parchment inscribed on one side with Deut. 6: 4–9 and 11: 13–21 and on the other with the name *shadai*, rolled up in a scroll and placed in a case or tube affixed to the doorpost of the Jewish home as a reminder of faith in God

millet (Turk.) In the Ottoman empire, a religious community organized under a religious head of its own who also exercises significant civil authority

mohel (pl. *mohalim*) (Heb.) Person who carries out the circumcision of male infants

mufattish (Arab.) Supervisor

mufti (Arab.) Chief arbiter in Muslim religious law

mukhtar (Arab.) Local dignitary representing the interests of the neighbourhood's inhabitants to the authorities

mukhtariyya (Arab.) Committee responsible for collecting taxes in the Aleppo community

mushir (Arab.) Officer of senior rank; field marshal

musta'ribun (Arab.) Lit. 'Arabized'. Term used for the oldest Jewish families in the Middle East who had lived there for many generations, pre-dating the expulsion of the Jews from Spain

nagid (Heb.) Community leader; synonym for *nasi*

nasi (pl. *nesi'im*) (Heb.) Lay head or 'president' of the Jewish community. See also *nagid*

nidui (Heb.) Ban or sanction placed on an individual, less severe than *ḥerem*

Namsa (Arab.) Austria

nishan (Turk.) Decoration; medal of honour

nishtwan (Per.) Royal certificate or diploma

Ottoman reforms A series of orders promulgated by the imperial authorities between 1839 and 1876 which brought about many changes in Ottoman law, particularly in the areas of equality, military service, and tax collection

parnas (pl. *parnasim*) (Heb.) One of a group of lay leaders of the community, often prominent and wealthy individuals

pasha (Turk.) Term of honour, usually given to regional rulers or governors

piastre Small metal coin in the imperial Ottoman currency

pilpul (Heb.) Talmudic dialectic

piyut (pl. *piyutim*) (Heb.) Liturgical poem

posek (pl. *posekim*) (Heb.) Decisor, authority in halakhic matters

qadi (Arab.) Muslim judge

qayimaqam ḥakham bashi (Turk.) Acting or temporary chief rabbi; chief rabbi without an official appointment from the sultan by *firman

qirsh sagh (Arab.) See *piastre*

ra'is arkan harb (Arab.) Chief of staff

resh galuta (Heb.) 'Head of the exiles': leader of all Jewish communities in the Middle East; an office going back to the Geonic period (beginning late sixth or early seventh century)

rishon letsiyon (Heb.) Lit. 'first in Zion': rabbi, head of the Jewish community in the Land of Israel (term used today to refer to the chief Sephardi rabbi in Jerusalem)

rosh harabanim (Heb.) See *rosh haruḥaniyim*

rosh haruḥaniyim (Heb.) Spiritual head of the community

saray (Turk.) Building housing government offices

sarraf (Arab.) Money changer

sarraf bashi (Arab.) Chief banker of the governor

seliḥot (Heb.) Pre-dawn penitential prayers recited before the High Holy Days

seniores Francos *See* Francos

Shabat Hagadol (Heb.) 'The Great Sabbath': the sabbath before Passover, when the rabbi of the community would exercise the important prerogative of delivering a major sermon/lecture related to the coming festival

Shabat Shuvah (Heb.) 'The Sabbath of Repentance': the sabbath between Rosh Hashanah and Yom Kippur, when the rabbi of the community would exercise the important prerogative of delivering a major sermon/lecture. *See also* Shabbat Hagadol

shada'r sheliha de-rabanan (Heb.) A Torah scholar who served as the general emissary of his city to collect contributions to support Jewish settlement in the Land of Israel

shah The ruler of Persia

shari'a (Arab.) Islamic law

shoḥet (pl. *shoḥatim*) (Heb.) Ritual slaughterer: a crucial religious functionary in traditional Jewish communities, as the compliance of all meat consumed therein with the dietary laws depended upon his piety, skill, halakhic knowledge, and integrity

spiritual committee A committee composed of seven Torah scholars, charged under the *Jewish millet decree with running the religious affairs of the Jewish community

steering committee A committee of nine members charged under the *Jewish millet decree, with running the secular affairs of the Jewish community

Sublime Porte The central Ottoman government under the sultan

sufi Member of a mystical and ascetic Muslim sect

sultan The Ottoman ruler

tabu (Turk.) Registration of ownership of real property in the books of the imperial registry

takanot (Heb.) Regulations governing the internal life of Jewish communities and congregations

talmud torah (pl. *talmudei torah*) (Heb.) Jewish elementary schools, also known as *kuttabs*

Tanzimat (Arab.) *See* Ottoman reforms

tefilin (Heb.) Small black leather boxes containing strips of parchment inscribed with verses of Torah

tikun (Heb.) Mystical act of theurgy or atonement

tsitsit (Heb.) Ritual fringes worn by religious Jews on an undergarment

Tugarma (Heb.) Turkey

tuvei ha'ir (Heb.) 'The good ones of the city': talmudic term used for the lay leaders of a Jewish community, often seven in number

wakil ḥakham bashi See *qayimaqam ḥakham bashi*

wali (Arab.) Governor; ruler of a district or major city within the Ottoman empire

wilaya (Arab.) District, region

yeshiva (pl. yeshivas) (Heb.) Traditional Jewish academy devoted primarily to the study of the Talmud and rabbinic literature

Young Turks Terms used for a group of Ottoman officers who in 1908 led a constitutional revolution and deposed Sultan Abd al-Hamadi II

Young Turk Revolution *See* Young Turks

Bibliography

Archival Sources

Government Archives

Affaires Etrangères, Centre des Archives Diplomatiques de Nantes (AECADN)
- Constantinople, Correspondance avec les Echelles, Damas, 1846–53
- Constantinople, Correspondance avec les Echelles, Damas, 807 (1890–1), Carton 15
- Consulat de France à Alep, Cotes 15, 21

Archives du Ministère des Affaires Etrangères, Paris
- Correspondance Consulaire et Commerciale (AECCC), Alep, vols. 30, 32
- Correspondance Consulaire et Commerciale (AECCC), Damas, vol. 7
- Correspondance Politique du Consul (AECPC), Turquie, Damas, vols. 11, 15–17
- Correspondance Politique et Commerciale, Nouvelle Série (AECPC, NS), Turquie, vols. 151, 152
- Nouvelle Série (AENS), Turquie (Syrie–Liban), vol. 112

Jerusalem, Municipal Archives (JMA)
- File: Yishuv Yashan, 63

National Archives, Foreign Office Archives, London (FO)
- FO 78, vols. 618/3, 1689, 2242, 4290
- FO 195, vols. 1113, 1154, 1514, 1765
- FO 371, vol. 6455

Österreichisches Staatsarchiv, Haus-, Hof-, und Staatsarchiv, Vienna (HHSTA)
- Administrative Registratur (Adm. Reg.): F4, 258; F8, 6, 38
- Türkei: II, 129

Other Archives and Libraries

Archives de l'Alliance Israélite Universelle, Paris (AAIU)
- Irak, I.B., 3, Bagdad
- Irak, I.B., 7, Bagdad (1867–1931)
- Irak, I.C., 2, Bagdad
- Irak, I.C., 4, Bagdad
- Irak, II.E., Bagdad, 8*a*, Albala
- Irak, III.E., Bagdad
- Irak, VII.E., Bagdad, 75*a*, Louria
- Syrie, I.B., Alep, 1, Comités locaux et communautés (1868–1913)
- Syrie, I.B., 5, Damas, Comités locaux et communautés (1862–1938)
- Syrie, I.C., Alep, 3, Situation intérieure générale des Juifs (1888–1940)
- Syrie, I.C., Damas, 5, Situation générale des Juifs

Syrie, I.E., Alep, 1, Divers concernant les écoles (1870–1934)
Syrie, II.E., Alep, 11, Altaras
Syrie, II.E., Alep, 14, Aranias
Syrie, II.E., Alep, 19b, Bassan
Syrie, III.E., Alep, 21, Behar
Syrie, III.E., Alep, 23, Behor
Syrie, IX.E., Alep, 70b, Raffoul
Syrie, X.E., Alep, 83, Somekh
Syrie, XI.E., Damas, 94, Divers concernant les écoles
Syrie, XI.E., Damas, 96, Aboulafia
Syrie, XI.E., Damas, 100, Alhalel
Syrie, XI.E., Damas, 101b, Alhalel
Syrie, XII.E., Damas, 106b, Astruc
Syrie, XIV.E., Damas, 133, Cohen
Syrie, XV.E., 142*a*, Farhi
Syrie, XV.E., Damas, 142*b*, Farhi
Syrie, XV.E., Damas, 146, Fresco
Syrie, XVII.E., Damas, 160, Heymann
Syrie, XVIII.E., Damas, 175, Lizbona
Syrie, XVIII.E., Damas, 182, Nahon
Syrie, XIX.E., Damas, 190*a*, Ouziel
Syrie, XIX.E., Damas, 190*b*, Ouziel
Syrie, XXI.E., Damas, 213*a*, Somekh

Archive of the Chief Rabbinate, Istanbul (ACRI)
TR/Is, 57*a*, 62, 63, 72*a*, 81*a*, 160*a*, 162*a*, 162*b*, 164*a*

Ben-Mordechai Collection, Gederah
Various uncatalogued documents from the estate of Rabbi Hezekiah Shabetai

Ben-Zvi Institute, Jerusalem (BZI)
MS 3724, *Pinkas rabi mosheh sutton* [Record Book of Rabbi Moses Sutton]
MS 3750, Aharon Sasson, *Sefer zikaron leḥayim* [Book of Remembrances of Life: History of Great Rabbis and Figures of Babylonian Jewry in Recent Generations]

Center for the Heritage of Babylonian Jewry, Jerusalem (CHBJ)
No. 7308, I. al-Kabir, *My Communal Life, or Death of a Community*
No. 7308, I. al-Kabir, *My Governmental Life or Story of a Dream*

Central Zionist Archive, Jerusalem (CZA)
J-41, Mikveh Israel Archive: 83

Jewish National and University Library, Department of Manuscripts and Archives, Jerusalem (JNUL, DMA)
Arc. 4to, 1271, Rabbi Jacob Saul Elyashar papers: 24, 44, 48, 133, 606, 607, 610–14, 617, 618, 620–3
Arc. 4to, 1512, Miscellaneous Historical Documents: 269

8vo 196, Abraham b. Solomon Sutton, *Leket hashikhehah*—[Forgetfulness gleaning]

8vo 5655, *She'elot uteshuvot umafte'ah aharon ya'akov* [Responsa and Index of Aharon Ya'akov]

V-736, Rabbi Abraham Hayim Gagin papers: 28, 50, 51, 77, 88, 99, 101, 145, 218, 219, 221, 224, 242, 248, 252, 261

Metropolitan Archives, London

Board of Deputies of British Jews (BofD): Minute Book ACC/3121/C11A/001

Newspapers and Journals

Bulletin de l'Alliance Israélite Universelle
Ha'ahdut, Jerusalem
Haherut, Jerusalem
Halevanon, Jerusalem, Paris, Mainz
Hamagid, Lyck, Berlin, Kraków
Hamevaser, Istanbul
Ha'olam, Cologne
Ha'or, Jerusalem
Hashkafah, Jerusalem
Hatsevi, Jerusalem
Ḥavatselet, Jerusalem
Jewish Chronicle, London
The Missionary Herald at Home and Abroad, Boston
Moriyah, Jerusalem
Peraḥ, Calcutta

Printed Primary Sources

ABADI, MORDECAI, *Divrei mordekhai* [hymns] (Aleppo, 1873).
—— *Ma'ayan ganim* [responsa], vol. i (repr. Jerusalem, 1986).
—— *Melits na'im* [ethical literature] (Jerusalem, 1927).
—— *Mikra kodesh* [hymns] (Aleppo, 1873).
—— *Vikuaḥ na'im* [polemic] (Jerusalem, 1927).
ABULAFIA, YITSHAK BEN MOSES, *Lev nishbar* [responsa] (İzmir, 1879).
—— *Penei yitsḥak* [responsa and sermons], 7 vols. (Aleppo, Leghorn, İzmir, and Jerusalem, 1886–1908).
AGASSI, SHIMON, *Imrei shimon* [sermons] (Jerusalem, 1968).
ALFANDARI, SOLOMON ELI'EZER, *Teshuvot hasaba kadisha* [responsa], 3 vols. (Jerusalem, 1973–4).
ALFANDARI, JOSEPH, *Porat yosef* [responsa] (İzmir, 1828).
ALHADIF, HAYIM, *Yatsev gevulot* [responsa] (Tiberias, 1904).

ANTEBI, ABRAHAM, *Ḥokhmah umusar* [ethical literature] (Leghorn, 1850).
—— *Mor ve'aholot* [responsa] (Leghorn, 1843).
—— *Ohel yesharim* [ethical literature and liturgical poems] (Jerusalem, 1981).
ATTIAH, HAYIM, *Arshot haḥayim* [responsa] (Jerusalem, 1986).
ATTIAH, ISAIAH, *Bigdei yesha* [responsa] (Leghorn, 1827).
AZRIEL, AARON, *Kapei aharon* [responsa], 2 vols. (Jerusalem, 1874–5).
BATZRI, MOSHE (ed.), *Siaḥ shoshanim* (Jerusalem, 2006).
BENJAMIN, ISRAEL, *Travels of Israel* [Masei yisra'el] (Lyck, 1859).
BOST, JEAN AUGUSTIN, *Souvenirs d'orient* (Paris, 1875).
DANGOOR, ELISHA, *Gedulot elisha* [responsa] (Jerusalem, 1976).
—— *Ma'aseh beit din* [responsa] (Jerusalem, 1988).
DAYAN, ABRAHAM BEN ISAIAH, *Holekh tamim* [ethical literature] (Leghorn, 1850).
—— *Tuv ta'am* [commentary and ethical literature] (Leghorn, 1864; repr. Jerusalem, 1985).
—— *Vayosef avraham* [responsa] (Leghorn, 1864).
—— *Zikaron lanefesh* [ethical literature] (Leghorn, 1842; repr. Jerusalem, 1985).
DAYAN, MOSHE, *Yashir mosheh* [commentary] (Leghorn, 1879).
DAYAN, YESHAYAHU, *Imrei no'am* [responsa] (Aleppo, 1898).
DWECK HAKOHEN, ELIJAH, *Birkat eliyahu* [responsa and sermons] (Leghorn, 1893).
DWECK HAKOHEN, JACOB SAUL, *Derekh emunah* [ethical literature] (Aleppo, 1914).
—— *She'erit ya'akov* [sermons] (Aleppo, 1925).
DWECK HAKOHEN, SAUL, *Emet me'erets* [responsa] (Jerusalem, 1910).
ELYASHAR, JACOB SAUL, *Ma'aseh ish* [responsa] (Jerusalem, 1892).
—— *Yisa ish* [responsa] (Jerusalem, 1896).
FRANCO, RAHAMIM JOSEPH, *Sha'arei raḥamim* [responsa], 2 vols. (Jerusalem, 1881).
GAGIN, SHALOM MOSES HAI, *Yismaḥ lev* [responsa] (Jerusalem, 1878).
GALANTE, MORDECAI, *Divrei mordekhai* [responsa] (Leghorn, 1860).
GOLDSTEIN, MOSHE, *Travels in Jerusalem* [Masot yerushalayim] (Jerusalem, 1963).
GOTTLIEB, SAMUEL NOAH, *Ohalei shem* [biographies of rabbis] (Pinsk, 1912).
HAKOHEN, MORDECAI, *Higid mordekhai—korot luv viyehudeiha, yishuveihem uminhageihem* (Jerusalem, 1982).
HAYIM, JOSEPH, *Rav pe'alim* [responsa] (Jerusalem, 1994).
HAZAN, ELIYAHU BEKHOR, *Ta'alumot lev* [responsa], 4 vols. (Leghorn, 1879).
—— *Zikhron yerushalayim* (Leghorn, 1874).
HAZZAN, HAYIM DAVID, *Nediv lev: ḥelek even ha'ezer veḥoshen mishpat* [responsa] (Jerusalem, 1866).
Hevrat Ozer Dalim Society in Damascus (Beirut [1913]).
Ḥevrat tsedakah umarpe: mif'alah, hityasdutah, vetahalukhoteiha (Aleppo, 1898).
HOUSSIN, SADKAH, *Tsedakah umishpat* [responsa] (Jerusalem, 1926).
IRGAS, JOSEPH, *Divrei yosef* (Leghorn, 1742).
JESSUP, HENRY HARRIS, *Fifty-Three Years in Syria*, 2 vols. (New York, 1910).

KASSIN, JACOB, *Peri ets hagan* [ethical literature] (Jerusalem, 1931).
KASSIN, RAPHAEL, *Derekh haḥayim* [polemical literature] (Istanbul, 1848).
—— *Likutei amarim* [polemical literature] (İzmir, 1855).
KASSIN, YEHUDAH, *Maḥaneh yehudah* [responsa] (Leghorn, 1803).
—— EPHRAIM LANIADO, and RAPHAEL SOLOMON LANIADO, *Ro'ei yisra'el* [responsa] (Jerusalem, 1904).
KOVO, RAPHAEL ASHER, *Sha'ar asher* [responsa], vol. ii (Salonica, 1879).
LABATON, MORDECAI, *Nokhaḥ hashulḥan* [sermons] (İzmir, 1868).
LANIADO, EPHRAIM, *Degel maḥaneh efrayim* [responsa] (Jerusalem, 1902).
LANIADO, RAPHAEL SOLOMON, *Beit dino shel shelomoh* [responsa] (Istanbul, 1775: repr. Jerusalem, 1982).
—— *Hama'alot lishelomoh* [sermons] (Istanbul, 1775).
—— *Kise shelomoh* [responsa] (Jerusalem [1901]).
—— *She'elot uteshuvot maharash laniado heḥadashot* [responsa] (Jerusalem, 1997).
LANIADO, SAMUEL, *Keli ḥemdah* [commentary] (Venice, 1596).
—— *Keli paz* [commentary] (Venice, 1657).
—— *Keli yakar* [commentary] (Venice, 1603).
LOEWE, LOUIS, *Diaries of Sir Moses and Lady Montefiore*, 2 vols. (London, 1890).
MADOX, JOHN, *Excursions in the Holy Land, Egypt, Nubia, Syria...*, 2 vols. (London, 1834).
Maḥberet ḥevrat yesod haḥokhmah (Aleppo, 1900).
MASLATON, YEHUDAH HAYIM HACOHEN, *Kol yehudah* [sermons] (Cairo, 1937).
—— *She'erit yehudah* [responsa] (Cairo, 1938).
NAVON, BENJAMIN, and JACOB SAUL ELYASHAR, *The Sons of Benjamin and the Things a Man Hides in His Heart* [Benei binyamin verkerev ish] (Jerusalem, 1876).
NEIMARK, EPHRAIM, *Journey in an Ancient Land* [Masa be'erets hakedem] (Jerusalem, 1947).
PALAGI, HAYIM BEN JACOB, *Ḥayim veshalom* [responsa] (İzmir, 1857).
—— *Ḥikekei lev* [responsa], 2 vols. (Salonica, 1848).
—— *Ḥukot haḥayim* [responsa] (İzmir, 1873).
—— *Tsava'ah meḥayim* [ethical literature] (Jerusalem, 1997).
PAPPO, DAVID, *Beni me'ir* [sermons] (Jerusalem, 1914).
—— *Penei david* [responsa] (Jerusalem, 1924).
PINTO, JOSIAH, *Nivḥar mikesef* [responsa] (Aleppo, 1869).
SASSOON, DAVID, *Journey to Babylonia* [Masa bavel] (Jerusalem, 1955).
SASSOON, DAVID SOLOMON, *Come Yemen* [Bo'i teiman] (Budapest, 1924).
SASSOON, YISRAEL, *Keneset yisra'el* [responsa], vol. i (Leghorn, 1856).
SCHNEOUR, Z., *Zikhron yerushalayim* [Travels] (Jerusalem, 1876).
SEGALL, JOSEPH, *Travels through Northern Syria* (London, 1910).
SHABETAI, HIZKIYAH, *Divrei yeḥizkiyahu* [responsa, sermons] (Jerusalem, 1935).
—— *Divrei yeḥizkiyahu* [sermons, ethical literature], vol. i (Aleppo, 1921).
SHOR, WOLF, *The Plays of Life* [Maḥazot heḥayim] (Vienna, 1884).
SHREM, YITSHAK, *Hadar ezer* [commentaries] (İzmir, 1865).

SOLOMON, YITSHAK AVRAHAM, *Akim et yitsḥak* [sermons, responsa] (Baghdad, 1910).
SUCARI, JACOB, *Vayeḥi ya'akov* [commentary] (Leghorn, 1901).
—— *Vayikra ya'akov* [sermons] (Leghorn, 1880).
—— *Yoru mishpateikha leya'akov* [ethical literature] (Calcutta, 1882).
SUCARI, SOLOMON, *Ateret shelomoh* [sermons] (Jerusalem, 1902).
SUTTON, DAVID, *Ya'aleh hadas* [responsa, sermons] (Jerusalem, 1974).
SUTTON, MENASHEH, *Maḥberet pirḥei shoshanim* [ethical literature] (Aleppo, 1910).
SUTTON, SAUL, *Diber sha'ul* [responsa] (Jerusalem, 1928).
SUTTON, JOSEPH, *Vayelaket yosef* [laws] and *Birkat shamayim* [responsa], 2 vols. in 1 (Aleppo, 1915).
TARAB, EZRA BEN ELIJAH, *Milei de'ezra* [responsa] (Jerusalem, 1924).
—— *Sefer ezra* [sermons] (Jerusalem, 1907).
—— *Sha'arei ezra* [responsa] (Jerusalem, 1906).
TOLEDANO, JACOB MOSES, *Otsar genazim* [history] (Jerusalem, 1960).
WELD, AGNES G., *Sacred Palmlands; or, The Journal of a Spring Tour* (London, 1881).
WILSON, JOHN, *The Lands of the Bible*, 2 vols. (Edinburgh, 1847).
WOODCOCK, WILLIAM J., *Scripture Lands* (London, 1849).
YADID HALEVI, ELIEZER RAHAMIM BEN YOM TOV, *Shivḥei moharam* [accounts of Rabbi Mordecai Labaton] (Jerusalem, 1932).
YADID HALEVI, YOSEF, *A Ruling Regarding the Removal of a Chief Rabbi from His Office* [Pesak be'inyan hasarat rav rashi mimisrato] (Jerusalem, 1993).
—— *Yemei yosef* [responsa] (Jerusalem, 1913).

Secondary Sources

ABU ʿIZZ AL-DIN, SULAYMAN, *Ibrahim Basha in Syria* [Ibrahim basha fi suriya] (Beirut, 1929).
ADLER, ELKAN NATHAN, *Jews in Many Lands* (Philadelphia, 1905).
ALHALEL, AARON, 'An Important Original Document Concerning the Damascus Blood Libel' (Heb.), *Mizraḥ uma'arav*, 3 (1929), 34–49.
ALMALEH, ABRAHAM, *The Jews in Damascus and Their Economic and Cultural Situation* [Hayehudim bedamasek umatsavam hakalkali vehatarbuti] (Jaffa, 1912).
ARIELI, Y., 'The Role of the Leadership Personality in the History of the Modern Period' (Heb.), in A. Malkin and Z. Tsahor (eds.), *Leader and Leadership* [Manhig vehanhagah] (Jerusalem, 1980), 11–42.
ASSIS, YOM-TOV, 'Sexual Behaviour in Mediaeval Hispano-Jewish Society', in Ada Rapoport-Albert and Steven J. Zipperstein (eds.), *Jewish History: Essays in Honour of Chimen Abramsky* (Bristol, 1988), 25–59.
ASULIN, PIERRE, *The Last of the House of Kamondo* [Aḥaron leveit kamondo] (Jerusalem, 2004).
AVNI, HAYIM, *Impure: Trafficking in Women in Argentina and Israel* [Teme'im: sakhar benashim be'argentina uveyisra'el] (Tel Aviv, 2009).

BACON, GERSHON, 'The New Jewish Politics and the Rabbinate in Poland: New Directions in the Interwar Period', in J. Wertheimer (ed.), *Jewish Religious Leadership: Image and Reality*, vol. ii (New York, 2004), 447–77.

BARNAI, JACOB, 'The Jews in the Ottoman Empire (1650–1830)' (Heb.), in Shmuel Ettinger (ed.), *History of the Jews in Muslim Lands* [Toledot hayehudim be'artsot ha'islam], pt. 1 (Jerusalem, 1986), 73–118.

—— 'The Jews in the Ottoman Empire' (Heb.), in Shmuel Ettinger (ed.), *History of the Jews in Muslim Lands* [Toledot hayehudim be'artsot ha'islam], pt. 2: *From the Middle of the Nineteenth to the Middle of the Twentieth Century—Sources* [Me'emtsa hame'ah hatesha-esreh ad emtsa hame'ah ha'esrim—mekorot] (Jerusalem, 1986), 181–297.

BATATU, HANNA, *The Old Social Classes and the Revolutionary Movements of Iraq* (Princeton, 1978).

BECK, YITSHAK (ed.), *From Hidden Things of Old* [Miginzei kedem] (Jerusalem, 1977).

BENAYAHU, MEIR, *Books Composed in Babylonia and Books Printed There* [Sefarim shenitḥabru bebavel usefarim shene'etku bah] (Jerusalem, 1993).

—— *Preacher of Torah: His Prerogatives, Functions and Roles in Communal Institutions in Spain, Turkey, and the Near East* [Marbits torah: samkhuyotav, tafkidav veḥelko bemosdot hakehilah besefarad beturkiyah uve'aratsot hamizraḥ] (Jerusalem, 1953).

—— 'The Rabbinic Emissary R. Joseph ben Veniste' (Heb.), *Yerushalayim*, 1 (1948), 180–93.

—— 'Sources for the History of Babylonian Jewry and Its Interrelations with Kurdistan and Persian Jewry' (Heb.), in Y. Avishur (ed.), *Studies in the History of Iraqi Jewry and Its Culture* [Meḥkarim betoledot yehudei irak uvetarbutam] (Or Yehudah, 1982), 1–82.

BENBASSA, ESTHER, *Hayim Nahum: A Political Chief Rabbi, 1892–1923* [Ḥayim naḥum, rav rashi bepolitikah, 1892–1923] (Jerusalem, 1999).

—— *Ottoman Jewry: Between Westernization and Zionism, 1908–1920* [Hayahadut ha'otomanit bein hitma'arvut latsiyonut, 1908–1920] (Jerusalem, 1996).

BEN-NAEH, YARON, 'The Organization of the Jewish Community and Its Leadership in the Ottoman Empire During the Seventeenth to Nineteenth Centuries' (Heb.), in A. Grossman and J. Kaplan (eds.), *Community of Israel: Jewish Self-Government Throughout the Generations* [Kehal yisra'el: hashilton ha'atsmi hayehudi ledorotav], vol. ii (Jerusalem, 2004), 341–67.

BEN-YA'AKOV, AVRAHAM, *Babylonian Jewry in the Diaspora* [Yehudei bavel batefutsot] (Jerusalem, 1985).

—— *Babylonian Jewry from the End of the Geonic Period to the Present Day* [Yahadut bavel misof tekufat hage'onim ad yameinu] (Jerusalem, 1979).

—— *Babylonian Jewry in Recent Times* [Yehudei bavel batekufot ha'aḥaronot] (Jerusalem, 1980).

—— *A Biography of Rabbi Abdallah Somekh* [Toledot harav abdalah somekh] (Jerusalem, 1949).

BEN-YA'AKOV, AVRAHAM, 'Documents from Jerusalem: Concerning the Activities of R. Abdallah b. Moshe Hayyim of Baghdad' (Heb.), *Asufot*, 4 (1990), 389–414.

—— 'Emissaries from the Land of Israel in Babylonia, Kurdistan, India and China' (Heb.), *Yerushalayim*, 5 (1955), 257–86.

—— 'A Firman of the Wali Natcham Pasha' (Heb.), *Pe'amim*, 71 (1997), 83–5.

—— *Holy Graves in Babylonia* [Kevarim kedoshim bebavel] (Jerusalem, 1974).

—— 'A New Source for the Life of R. Elijah b. Moshe Hayim of Baghdad' (Heb.), *Yahadut bavel*, 2 (1998), 161–2.

—— 'R. Solomon Alfandari *z"l*' (Heb.), *Hed hamizraḥ*, 6 (22 June 1945).

—— *Rabbi Sassoon b. Mordechai Shandukh* [Harav sason b. mordekhai shandukh] (Jerusalem, 1994).

—— *Rabbi Joseph Hayim* [Harav yosef ḥayim] (Jerusalem, 1972).

—— 'Rabbi Joseph Hayim: A Renaissance Man' (Heb.), in Z. Yehuda (ed.), *Rabbi Joseph Hayim: Studies and Reflections Marking Ninety Years Since His Death* [Harav yosef ḥayim: pirkei meḥkar ve'iyun] (Or Yehudah, 1999), 31–4.

BEN-ZVI, YITZHAK, 'An Exchange of Letters between the *Rishon letsiyon* Rabbi Jacob Shaul Elyashar and the Chief Rabbi in Constantinople R. Moshe Halevi' (Heb.), in id., *Ketavim* [Writings], vol. iii (Jerusalem, 1969), 91–5.

BERNSTEIN, DEBORAH, *Women on the Margin: Gender and Nationalism in Mandatory Tel Aviv* [Nashim bashulayim: migdar ule'umiyut be-tel aviv] (Tel Aviv, 2008).

BESKA, EMANUEL, 'Shukri al-ʿAsali, an Extraordinary Anti-Zionist Activist', *Asian and African Studies*, 19/2 (2010), 237–54.

BORNSTEIN, LEAH, 'Leadership of Jewish Communities in the Near East from the Late Sixteenth Century to the End of the Eighteenth Century' (Heb.), Ph.D. diss., Bar-Ilan University (Ramat Gan, 1978).

BORNSTEIN-MAKOVATZKI, LEAH, 'The Activity of the American Mission Among the Jews in Istanbul, İzmir, and Salonica During the Nineteenth Century' (Heb.), in M. Rosen (ed.), *Days of the Crescent* [Yemei hasahar] (Jerusalem, 1996), 273–310.

BRAWER, ABRAHAM J., 'The Jews of Damascus after the Blood Libel of 1840' (Heb., Eng. abstract), *Tsiyon*, 11 (1945/6), 83–108.

—— 'New Material on the Damascus Libel' (Heb.), in *Jubilee Volume for Professor Shmuel Krauss* [Sefer yovel leprofesor shemuel kraus] (Jerusalem, 1937), 260–302.

BROWN, BINYAMIN, '"European" Modernization: Orthodox Responses and the Environmental Context' (Heb.), *Akdamut*, 10 (2001), 153–60.

—— 'Sages of the East and Religious Zealotry: Points Towards a New Examination' (Heb.), *Akdamut*, 10 (2001), 289–324.

CIOETA, DONALD J., 'Ottoman Censorship in Lebanon and Syria 1876–1908', *International Journal of Middle East Studies*, 10 (1979), 167–86.

COHEN, HAYIM J., *The Jews in Middle Eastern Countries in Our Day* [Hayehudim be'artsot hamizraḥ hatikhon beyameinu] (Tel Aviv, 1973).

COHEN-TAWIL, AVRAHAM, *Aleppo Jewry in the Perspective of the Generations* [Yahadut ḥalab bire'i hadorot] (Tel Aviv, 1993).

—— 'The Francos in Aleppo' (Heb.), *Shevet ve'am*, 2nd ser., 10 (1984), 129–35.

CUNNINGHAM, ALLAN, '"Dragomania": The Dragomans of the British Embassy in Turkey', *St Antony's Papers*, 2 (1961), 81–100.

DAVISON, RODERIC H., *Reform in the Ottoman Empire 1856–1876* (Princeton, 1963).

DESHEN, SHLOMO, 'Baghdad Jewry in Late Ottoman Times: The Emergence of Social Classes and of Secularization', in S. Deshen and W. P. Zenner (eds.), *Jews among Muslims: Communities in the Precolonial Middle East* (London, 1996), 187–96.

—— 'The Jews of Baghdad in the Nineteenth Century: The Growth of Class and Cultural Diversity' (Heb.), *Zemanim*, 73 (2000–1), 30–44.

DON-YEHIYA, ELIEZER, 'Religious Leadership and Political Leadership' (Heb.), in A. Belfer (ed.), *Spiritual Leadership in Israel* [Manhigut ruḥanit beyisra'el] (Jerusalem, 1982), 104–34.

DUMONT, PAUL, 'Jewish Communities in Turkey During the Last Decades of the Nineteenth Century in the Light of the Archives of the Alliance Israélite Universelle', in B. Braude and B. Lewis (eds.), *Christians and Jews in the Ottoman Empire*, vol. i (New York, 1982), 209–42.

—— 'Jews, Muslims, and Cholera: Intercommunal Relations in Baghdad at the End of the Nineteenth Century', in A. Levi (ed.), *The Jews of the Ottoman Empire* (Princeton, 1994), 353–72.

ELIAV, MORDECAI, *Under the Aegis of the Austrian Empire, 1849–1917* [Beḥasut mamlekhet ostriyah, 1849–1917] (Jerusalem, 1986).

EPSTEIN, ARYEH LEIB, *Ways and Customs of Marriage* [Darkei ishut uminhageiha] (Tel Aviv, 1959).

FRANCO, MOISE, *Essai sur l'histoire des Israélites de l'Empire Ottoman depuis les origines jusqu'à nos jours* (1st pub. 1897; repr. New York, 1973).

FRANKEL, JONATHAN, *The Damascus Affair: 'Ritual Murder', Politics, and the Jews in 1840* (New York, 1997).

FRANKEL, LUDWIG AUGUST, *To Jerusalem* [Yerushalaimah] (Vienna, 1858).

FRIEDMAN, MENAHEM, 'Basic Problems in the Structure of the Communal Rabbinate in Modern Society' (Heb.), in A. Belfer (ed.), *Spiritual Leadership in Israel* [Manhigut ruḥanit beyisra'el] (Jerusalem, 1982), 135–55.

—— 'Religious Zealotry in Israeli Society', in S. Poll and E. Krausz (eds.), *On Ethnic and Religious Diversity in Israel* (Ramat Gan, 1975), 91–112.

—— *Society and Religion: Non-Zionist Orthodoxy in Palestine, 1918–1936* [Ḥevrah vadat: ha'orthodoksya halo tsiyonit be'erets yisra'el, 1918–1936] (Jerusalem, 1988).

FRUMKIN, ARYEH LEIB, *A History of the Sages of Jerusalem* [Toledot ḥakhmei yerushalayim], vol. iii (Tel Aviv, 1969).

GABBAI, NILI, 'Education of Girls in the Jewish Community of Baghdad (1894–1951)' (Heb.), *Pe'amim*, 82 (2000), 94–118.

GALANTE, ABRAHAM, *Histoire des juifs de Turquie*, vol. iv (Istanbul, n.d.).

GAON, MOSES DAVID, *The Jews of the East in the Land of Israel* [Yehudei hamizraḥ be'erets yisra'el], 2 vols. (Jerusalem, 1938).

GERBER, HAYIM, 'Jews and Moneylending in the Ottoman Empire' (Heb.), in N. Gross (ed.), *Yehudim bekalkalah* [Jews in Economics] (Jerusalem, 1985), 169–72.

GHANIMA, Y. RIZQ ALLAH, *The Delight of Him Who Desires to Know the History of the Jews of Iraq* [Nuzhat al-mushtaq fi ta'rikh yahud al-ʿirak] (Baghdad, 1924).

GIDNEY, WILLIAM T., *The History of the London Society for Promoting Christianity amongst the Jews (from 1809 to 1908)* (London, 1908).

GRAYEVSKY, PINHAS, *In Memory of the Early Ḥovevei Zion* [Zikaron leḥovevim rishonim], vol. ii (Jerusalem, 1994).

GROSSMAN, AVRAHAM, 'From Father to Son: The Inheritance of the Spiritual Leadership of the Jewish Communities in the Early Middle Ages' (Heb., Eng. abstract), *Tsiyon*, 50 (1985), 189–220.

—— *Pious and Rebellious: Jewish Women in Europe in the Middle Ages* (Cambridge, Mass., 2004); 1st published in Hebrew as *Ḥasidot umoredot* (Jerusalem, 2001).

HACKER, JOSEPH, 'Community Organization in Communities of the Ottoman Empire' (Heb.), in A. Grossman and J. Kaplan (eds.), *The Congregation of Israel: Jewish Self-Rule throughout History* [Kehal yisra'el: hashilton ha'atsmi hayehudi ledoratav], vol. ii (Jerusalem, 2004), 287–309.

HANIOGLU, M. ŞÜKRÜ, 'Jews in the Young Turk Movement to the 1908 Revolution', in A. Levi (ed.), *The Jews of the Ottoman Empire* (Princeton, 1994), 519–26.

HAREL, YARON, *The Books of Aleppo: The Rabbinic Literature of the Scholars of Aleppo* [Sifrei erets: hasifrut hatoranit shel ḥakhmei aram tsovah] (Jerusalem, 1997).

—— 'The Citizenship of the Algerian-Jewish Immigrants in Damascus', *Maghreb Review*, 28 (2003), 294–305.

—— 'Controversy and Agreement: Sephardim and *Musta'aravim* in Aleppo' (Heb.), in Y. Dishon and S. Raphael (eds.), *Ladinar: Collected Studies in Literature, Music and History of Ladino Speakers* [Ladinar: kovets meḥkarim] (Tel Aviv, 1998), 119–38.

—— 'The Controversy over Rabbi Ephraim Laniado's Inheritance of the Rabbinate in Aleppo', *Jewish History*, 13/1 (1999), 83–101.

—— 'The Damascus Community and Its Leaders in the Lists of Eli'ezer Rivlin' (Heb.), *Pe'amim*, 74 (1998), 131–55.

—— 'The Edict to Destroy *Em LaMikra*—Aleppo 1865' (Heb.), *HUCA*, 64 (1993), 27–36.

—— 'Fighting Conversion to Christianity: The Syrian Case', *Jewish Studies Quarterly*, 17 (2010), 29–43.

—— 'The First Jews from Aleppo in Manchester: New Evidence', *AJS Review*, 23/2 (1998), 191–202.

—— 'From Openness to Closedness: The Motivation for Change in the Attitude of the Middle Eastern Torah Elite to the Values of Modernity' (Heb.), *AJS Review*, 26 (2002), 1–58.

—— 'From the Ruins of Jaffa Damascus was Built: The Encounter between Exiles from the Land of Israel and the Damascus Community, and Its Results' (Heb.), *Tsiyon*, 61/2 (1996), 183–207.

—— '"Great Progress"—The Committee of Deputies and the Damascus Community' (Heb.), *Pe'amim*, 67 (1996), 57–95.

—— 'The Impact of the Books *Penei yitsḥak*, *Yismaḥ lev*, and *Lev nishbar* on the Struggle for the Rabbinate in Damascus, 1873–1883' (Heb.), *Asufot*, 11 (1998), 211–43.

—— 'The Importance of the Archive of the *Ḥakham Bashi* in Istanbul for the History of Ottoman Jewry', in C. Imber, K. Kiyotaki, and R. Murphey (eds.), *Frontiers of Ottoman Studies: State, Province and the West*, vol. i (London, 2005), 251–64.

—— 'In the Wake of the Dreyfus Affair: An Alexandrian Jewish Intellectual Reconsiders His Admiration for France', *Revue des études juives*, 166 (2007), 473–91.

—— '"Likutei Amarim en Ladino": On the Polemical Literature of Rabbi Raphael Kassin' (Heb.), in D. Bunis et al. (eds.), *The Languages and Literature of the Sephardim and Oriental Jews* (Jerusalem, 2009), 106–19.

—— 'Midhat Pasha and the Jewish Community of Damascus: Two New Documents', *Turcica*, 28 (1996), 339–45.

—— 'On the Jewish "Singing Women" in Damascus' (Heb.), in T. Cohen and S. Regev (eds.), *Ishah bamizraḥ—ishah mimizraḥ* (Jerusalem, 2005), 109–28.

—— 'The Overthrow of the Last Aleppan Chief Rabbi' (Heb.), *Pe'amim*, 44 (1990), 110–31.

—— 'The Relations between the Jewish Community of San'a and the Sephardi *Ḥakham Bashi* Yitshak Shaul' (Heb.), *East and Maghreb*, 7 (2003), 41–71.

—— 'A Spiritual Agitation in the East: The Foundation of a Reform Community in Aleppo in 1862' (Heb.), *HUCA*, 63 (1992), 19–35.

—— 'The Status and Image of the Picciotto Family in the Eyes of the French Colony in Aleppo, 1784–1850' (Heb.), *Mikha'el*, 14 (1997), 171–86.

—— *Syrian Jewry in Transition 1840–1880* (Oxford, 2010).

—— *Zionism in Damascus: Ideology and Activity in the Jewish Community at the Beginning of the Twentieth Century* (London, 2015)

HARSHOSHANIM-BREITBART, TAL, 'The Journey of the *Ḥakham Bashi* Hayim Nahum from Istanbul to Jerusalem, Spring 1910: Success or Failure?' [Masa heḥakham bashi ḥayim naḥum me'istanbul liyerushalayim aviv 1910: hatslakha o kishalon?] (Heb.), MA diss., Bar-Ilan University (Ramat Gan, 2006).

HASAN, MUHAMMAD SALMAN, *Economic Development in Iraq 1958–1964* [Al-tatawwur al-iqtisadi fi al-ʿiraq] (Sidon and Beirut, 1965).

HAYYIM, AVRAHAM, *Particularity and Integration* [Yiḥud vehishtalvut] (Jerusalem, 2000).

HYAMSON, ALBERT M. (ed.), *The British Consulate in Jerusalem in Relation to the Jews of Palestine, 1838–1914*, 2 vols. (London, 1939, 1941).

IDELSOHN, ABRAHAM ZVI, 'The Jewish Community in Damascus' (Heb.), *Luaḥ erets yisra'el* (5671 [1911]), 87–106.

KARPAT, KEMAL H., 'Ottoman Population Records and the Census of 1881/2–1893', *IJMES*, 9 (1978), 237–74.

KATZ, JACOB, 'On the History of the Rabbinate in the Late Middle Ages' (Heb.), in E. Z. Melamed (ed.), *Benjamin de-Freis Memorial Volume* [Sefer zikaron lebinyamin de-freis] (Jerusalem, 1969), 196–201.

KATZ, JACOB, *Tradition and Crisis* [Masoret umashber] (Jerusalem, 1978).

KAYALI, HASAN, *Arabs and Young Turks: Ottomanism, Arabism, and Islamism in the Ottoman Empire, 1908–1918* (Berkeley, 1997).

KAYALI, HASAN, 'Jewish Representation in the Ottoman Parliaments', in A. Levi (ed.), *The Jews of the Ottoman Empire* (Princeton, 1994), 507–17.

KAZAZ, NISSIM, *The Jews in Iraq in the Twentieth Century* [Hayehudim be'irak bame'ah ha'esrim] (Jerusalem, 1991).

—— 'The Political Activity of Iraqi Jews at the End of Ottoman Rule' (Heb.), *Pe'amim*, 36 (1988), 35–51.

KEDOURIE, ELIE, *Arabic Political Memoirs and Other Studies* (London, 1974).

—— 'The Jews of Baghdad in 1910', *Middle Eastern Studies*, 7 (1971), 355–61.

—— 'Young Turks, Freemasons and Jews', *Middle Eastern Studies*, 7 (1971), 89–104.

KURD ʿALI, MUHAMMAD, *Kit b Khiṭaṭ al-Shām* [Description of Syria], 6 vols. (Damascus, 1925).

KUSHNER, DAVID, 'A Firman from the Ottoman Sultan that Confuted Anti-Jewish Blood Libels' (Heb.), *Pe'amim*, 20 (1984), 37–45.

—— *I Was a Governor in Jerusalem: The City and the District as Seen by Eli Akhrim Bey, 1906–1908* [Moshel hayiti biyerushalayim] (Jerusalem, 1995).

LANDAU, JACOB M., and MOSHE MAOZ, 'Jews and Non-Jews in Egypt and Syria in the Nineteenth Century' (Heb.), *Pe'amim*, 9 (1981), 4–13.

LANIADO, DAVID-SION, *For the Sake of the Holy Ones of Aleppo* [Likdoshim asher ba'arets] (Jerusalem, 1952; Eng. trans. Jerusalem, 1980).

LE CALLOC'H, B., 'La Dynastie consulaire des Piccioto (1784–1894)', *Revue d'histoire diplomatique*, 1–2 (1991), 35–172.

LEVI, AVNER, 'Changes in the Leadership of the Main Sephardi Communities in the Ottoman Empire During the Nineteenth Century' (Heb.), in M. Rosen (ed.), *The Days of the Crescent: Chapters in the History of Jewry in the Ottoman Empire* [Yemei hasahar: perakim betoledot hayehudim ba'imperiyah ha'otmanit] (Jerusalem, 1996), 237–71.

LEVY, AVIGDOR, 'The Founding of the Institution of the *Ḥakham Bashi* in the Ottoman Empire and Its Development, 1835–1865' (Heb.), *Pe'amim*, 55 (1993), 38–56.

LEWIS, BERNARD, *The Emergence of Modern Turkey* (London, 1966).

—— *The Jews of Islam* (Princeton, 1984).

LINDHOLM, CHARLES, *Charisma* (London, 1990).

LLOYD, SETON, *Twin Rivers: A Brief History of Iraq from the Earliest Times to the Present Day* (Bombay, 1961).

LONGRIGG, STEPHEN HEMSLEY, *Four Centuries of Modern Iraq* (1st pub. 1925; Oxford, 1968).

LUTZKY, AVRAHAM, 'The Francos in Aleppo and the Impact of the Capitulations on Its Jewish Inhabitants (1673 to the French Revolution)' (Heb., Eng. abstract), *Tsiyon*, 6 (1940–1), 46–76.

MALACHI, ELIEZER R., 'The Yishuv's Struggle against the Reform Movement' (Heb.), in id., *Chapters in the History of the Old Jewish Community in Palestine* [Perakim betoledot hayishuv hayashan] (Tel Aviv, 1971), 336–45.

MALKIN, IRAD, and ZE'EV ZAHOR (eds.), *Leader and Leadership* (Heb.) [Manhig vehanhagah] (Jerusalem, 1980).

MALUL, NISSIM, 'The Arab Press' (Heb.), *Ha-Shilo'aḥ*, 31 (1914–15), 364–74, 439–50.

MAOZ, MOSHE, 'Transformations in the Status of the Jews in the Ottoman Empire' (Heb.), in *From East and West* [Mikedem umiyam], 1 (1981), 11–28.

MARCUS, ABRAHAM, *The Middle East on the Eve of Modernity: Aleppo in the Eighteenth Century* (New York, 1989).

MARGALIOT, SHLOMO ELIEZER (ed.), *The Great Ones of the Land of Israel* [Gedolei erets yisra'el] (Jerusalem, 1969).

MARKS, LARA, 'Jewish Women and Jewish Prostitution in the East End of London', *Jewish Quarterly*, 34/2 (1987), 6–10.

MASTERS, BRUCE A., *The Origins of Western Economic Dominance in the Middle East: Mercantilism and the Islamic Economy in Aleppo, 1600–1750* (New York, 1988).

MEIR, YOSEF, *The Socio-cultural Development of Iraqi Jewry from 1830 until Our Day* [Hitpatḥut ḥevratit-tarbutit shel yehudei irak me'az 1830 ad yameinu] (Tel Aviv, 1989).

MELMAN, BILLIE, 'Freedom behind the Veil: An Examination of the "Other" in the Eighteenth and Nineteenth Centuries' (Heb.), in Y. Atsmon (ed.), *A Window on the Lives of Women in Jewish Societies* [Eshnav leḥayeihen shel nashim beḥevrot yehudiyot] (Jerusalem, 1995), 225–43.

MEYER, MICHAEL, *Between Tradition and Progress* [Bein masoret lekidmah] (Jerusalem, 1990).

MOSHE, YEHOSHUA, *End of the Days* [Kets hayamin] (Jerusalem, 1967).

AL-NAJJAR, JAMIL MUSA, *Ottoman Administration of the Province of Baghdad Syria from the Reign of the Wali Midhat Basha until the End of Ottoman Rule, 1869–1917* [Al-idara al-ʿuthmaniyya fi wilayat baghdad min ʿahd al-wali midhat basha ila nihayat al-hukm al-ʿuthmani, 1869–1917] (Cairo, 1991).

ORTAYLI, ILBER, 'Ottomanism and Zionism during the Second Constitutional Period, 1908–1915', in A. Levi (ed.), *The Jews of the Ottoman Empire* (Princeton, 1994), 527–37.

PHILIPP, THOMAS, 'The Farḥi Family and the Changing Position of the Jews in Syria, 1750–1860', *Middle Eastern Studies*, 20/4 (1984), 37–52.

—— 'French Merchants and Jews in the Ottoman Empire during the Eighteenth Century', in A. Levi (ed.), *The Jews of the Ottoman Empire* (Princeton, 1994), 315–25.

PICCIOTTO, EMILIO, *The Consular History of the Picciotto Family 1784–1895* (Milan, 1998).

POPPER, MICHA, *Charismatic Leadership and Loss of Self-Identity* [Manhigut kharismatit ve'ovdan hazehut ha'atsmit] (Tel Aviv, 1998).

RAFEQ (RAFIQ), ABDUL-KARIM, 'Manifestations of the Craft System in the Levant in the Ottoman Period' (Arab.), *Dirasat ta'rikhiyya*, 6 (1981), 30–62.

RAYYAN, MUHAMMAD RAJA'I, 'France's Economic Interests in Syria (1535–1920)' (Arab.), *Dirasat ta'rikhiyya*, 27–8 (1987), 33–65.

REGEV, SHAUL, 'The Attitude towards Enlightenment among the Rabbis of Babylonia: R. Joseph Hayim and R. Shimon Agassi' (Heb.), in Y. Avishur and Z. Yehudah (eds.), *Studies in the History of Iraqi Jewry and Their Culture* [Meḥkarim bekorot yehudei bavel uvetarbutam] (Or Yehudah, 2002), 97–118.

REGEV, SHAUL, 'Crisis of Leadership during R. Sadkah Houssin's Term in Baghdad' (Heb.), *Mimizraḥ umima'arav*, 8 (1988), 57–76.

—— 'The Homiletical and Ethical Literature of R. Joseph Hayim' (Heb.), *Yahadut bavel*, 1 (1996), 35–43.

RIVLIN, JOSEPH JOEL, 'Sir Shemaiah Angel, May His Merit Protect Us' (Heb.), *Hed hamizraḥ*, 19 (10 Mar. 1944), 4.

—— 'Joseph Aslan Farhi' (Heb.), *Hed hamizraḥ*, 3 (18 Nov. 1949), 11.

RODRIGUE, ARON, *De l'instruction à l'émancipation: Les Enseignants de l'Alliance Israélite Universelle et les Juifs d'Orient 1860–1939* (Paris, 1989).

—— *French Jews, Turkish Jews: The Alliance Israélite Universelle and the Politics of Jewish Schooling in Turkey, 1860–1925* (Bloomington, Ind., 1990).

—— *Images of Sephardi and Eastern Jewries in Transition: The Teachers of the Alliance Israélite Universelle, 1860–1939* (Seattle, 1993).

ROZEN, MINNA, 'The Archives of the Chamber of Commerce of Marseilles: On the History of the Jewish Community in the Levant and in North Africa' (Heb.), *Pe'amim*, 9 (1981), 112–24.

—— *In the Paths of the Mediterranean: The Jewish Spanish Diaspora from the Sixteenth to Eighteenth Centuries* [Bintivei hayam hatikhon: hapezurah hayehudit–sefaradit bame'ot ha 16–18] (Tel Aviv, 1993).

SAFWAT, NAJDA FATHI, *Iraq in the Memoirs of Foreign Diplomats* [Al-ʿiraq fi mudhakkarat al-diblumasiyyin al-ajanib] (Beirut, 1969).

SASSOON, DAVID SOLOMON, *A History of the Jews in Baghdad* (Letchworth, 1949).

AL-SAYYID, AHMAD LUTFI, *The Story of My Life* [Qissat hayati] (Cairo, 1962).

SCHLESINGER, AKIVA YOSEF, *Deeds of Fathers* [Ma'aseh avot] (Jerusalem, 1976).

SCHUR, WOLF (WILLIAM), *Pictures from Life* [Maḥazot haḥayim: shera'iti be'et halakhti lemasa'otai be'artsot hamizraḥ] (Vienna, 1884).

SCHWARZFUCHS, SIMON, 'La "Nazione Ebrea" au Levant', *Rassegna mensile di Israel*, 50 (1984), 707–24.

SEHAYIK, SHAUL, 'Chapters in the History of Hebrew Education in the Arab Middle East, 1900–1935' (Heb.), *Shorashim bamizraḥ*, 2 (1989), 11–64.

—— 'The Dreyfus Affair in the Arab Press' (Heb.), *Mikha'el*, 14 (1997), 187–214.

SHAMOSH, AMNON, *The Keter: The Story of the Aleppo Codex* [Haketer: sipuro shel keter aram tsovah] (Jerusalem, 1987).

SHILO, MARGALIT, *Princess or Captive?* [Nesikhah o shevuyah?] (Jerusalem, 2001).

—— 'The Promiscuity of the Women of Jerusalem after the First World War: A Male View and a Female View' (Heb.), *Yerushalayim ve'erets yisra'el*, 1 (2004), 173–96.

SHOCHETMAN, ELIAV, 'The Murder of "Sir" Hayim Farhi in Akko and the Incident of His Estate' (Heb.), *Asufot*, 6 (1992), 161–209.

—— 'New Sources on the Incident Involving the Estate of "Sir" Hayim Farhi' (Heb.), *Asufot*, 11 (1998), 281–308.

SHOHET, AZRIEL, *The Institution of the 'Official' Rabbinate in Russia* [Mosad 'harabanut mita'am' berusiyah] (Haifa, 1976).

SIMON, REEVA S., 'Education in the Baghdad Jewish Community through 1914' (Heb.), *Pe'amim*, 36 (1988), 52–63.

STERN, YEDIDYAH Z., *State, Law, and Halakhah*, vol. i: *Public Leadership as Halakhic Authority* [Medinah, mishpat vehalakhah. I. Manhigut tsiburit kesamkhut hilkhatit] (Jerusalem, 2000).

SUTTON, DAVID, *Aleppo: City of Scholars* (New York, 2005).

AL-TABBAKH, MUHAMMAD RAGHIB, *Eminent Nobles in the History of Aleppo* [Aʿlam al-nubala' bi-tarikh halab al-shahba'], vol. iii (Aleppo, 1924).

TAUBER, ELIEZER, *Secret Societies and Rebel Movements n the Fertile Crescent, 1875–1920* [Agudot ḥashayot utenuot mered besahar haporeh, 1875–1920] (Jerusalem, 1994).

TAWTAL AL-YASHUʿI, FARDINAN, *Historical Documents about Aleppo* [Watha'iq ta'rikihiyyaʿan halab], vol. i (Beirut, 1958).

TIBAWI, ABDUL LATIF, *A Modern History of Syria* (Edinburgh, 1969).

TIDHAR, D., *Encyclopedia of Pioneers of the Yishuv and Its Builders* [Entsiklopediyah leḥalutsei hayishuv uvonav] (Tel Aviv, 1947).

TOBI, YOSEF, 'Organization of Jewish Communities in the Near East in the Nineteenth and Twentieth Centuries' (Heb.), in Y. Bartal (ed.), *The Congregation of Israel: Jewish Self-Rule throughout History* [Kehal yisra'el: hashilton ha'atsmi hayehudi ledoratav], vol. iii (Jerusalem, 2004), 191–209.

TOLEDANO, YAAKOV MOSHE, 'On the History of the Jewish Settlement in Tiberias' (Heb.), *Shevet ve'am* (1959), 73–7.

TSIMHONI, DAPHNE, 'Babylonian Jewry—Modernization: Summary of the Beginnings' (Heb.), *Pe'amim*, 36 (1988), 7–34.

TSUR, YARON, 'France and the Jews of Tunisia: French Policy towards the Jews of the Country and the Activity of the Jewish Elites during the Transition from Independent Muslim Rule to Colonial Rule, 1873–1888' [Tsarfat viyehudei tunisiyah: hamediniyut hatsarfatit kelapei yehudei hamedinah ufe'ilut ha'elitot hayehudiyot bama'avar meshilton muslemi atsma'i leshilton kolone'ali 1873–1888], Ph.D. diss., Hebrew University (Jerusalem, 1988).

—— *Introduction to the History of the Jews in Muslim Countries in the Modern Period, 1750–1914* [Mavo letoledot hayehudim be'artsot ha'islam], 3 vols. (forthcoming).

AL-TUNJI, MUHAMMAD, 'Social Interaction between the Ottomans and the Arabs in the Province of Syria' (Arab.), in 'Abd al-Jalil al-Tamimi (ed.), *Social Life in the Arab Provinces in the Ottoman Period* [Al-hayat al-ijtimaʿiyya fi al-wilayat al-ʿarabiyya athna' al-ʿahd al-ʿuthmani], 2 vols. in 1 (Zaghwan, 1988), 213–27.

TWENA, AVRAHAM HAYYIM, *Exiled and Redeemed* [Golim uge'ulim], vol. vii (Ramleh, 1979).

WALZER, MICHAEL, MENAHEM LORBERBAUM, and NOAM J. ZOHAR (eds.), *The Jewish Political Tradition*, vol. i: *Authority* (New Haven, 2000).

WEBER, MAX, *Charisma and Institution Building* (Chicago, 1968).

WEIKER, WALTER F., *Ottomans, Turks and the Jewish Polity* (New York, 1992).

WEISS, SHRAGA, *Sages of the East* [Ḥakhmei hamizraḥ] (Jerusalem, 1982).

WEISS, SHRAGA, *Sephardi Sages in the Land of Israel* [Ḥakhmei hasefardim be'erets yisra'el] (Tel Aviv, 1975).

YA'ARI, ABRAHAM, *Emissaries from Israel* [Sheluḥei erets yisra'el] (Jerusalem, 1951).

—— 'Hebrew Printing in Aleppo' (Heb.), *Kiryat sefer*, 10 (1933), 100–18.

—— (ed.), *Travels of the Emissary from Safed to the Eastern Lands* [Masot sheliaḥ tsefat be'artsot hamizraḥ] (Jerusalem, 1942).

YEHEZKEL-SHAKED, EZRA, *Jews, Opium and the Kimono* [Hayehudim, ha'opiom vehakimono] (Jerusalem, 1996).

YEHUDAH, ZVI, 'Babylonian Jewry and Cultural Changes in the Educational Activity of the Alliance Israélite Universelle' (Heb.), *Yahadut bavel*, 1 (1996), 45–59.

—— 'Connections between Jews of Babylonia and Aleppo in the Eighteenth Century' (Heb.), *Neharde'a*, 21 (1999), 11–12.

—— (ed.), *Rabbi Joseph Hayim: Research and Studies Marking Ninety Years since His Death* [Harav yosef ḥayim: pirkei meḥkar ve'iyun bimlot tishim shanah liftirato] (Or Yehudah, 1999).

—— 'Transformations in the Jewish Settlement in Baghdad in the Twelfth to Eighteenth Centuries' (Heb.), in Y. Avishur and Z. Yehudah (eds.), *Studies in the History of Babylonian Jewry and Its Culture* [Meḥkarim bekorot yehudei bavel uvetarbutam] (Or Yehudah, 2002), 9–29.

ZE'EV, YA'AKOV, 'A Description of the Community of Aleppo and Its Environs at the Beginning of the 1840s' (Heb.), *Tsefunot*, 14/2 (1992), 82–8.

ZENNER, WALTER P., *A Global Community: The Jews from Aleppo, Syria* (Detroit, 2000).

ZIMMER, ERIC, *The Fiery Embers of the Scholars: The Trials and Tribulations of German Rabbis in the Sixteenth and Seventeenth Centuries* [Gaḥaltan shel ḥakhamim: perakim betoledot harabanut begermaniyah beme'ot hashesh-esreh vehasheva-esreh] (Jerusalem, 1999).

ZOHAR, ZVI, 'The Attitude of Rav Abdallah Somekh to the Transformations of the Nineteenth Century as Reflected in His Halakhic Work' (Heb.), *Pe'amim*, 36 (1988), 89–107.

—— *The Luminous Face of the East* [He'iru penei hamizraḥ] (Tel Aviv, 2001).

—— 'Militant Conservatism: On the Social-Religious Leadership of Aleppo Rabbis during the Modern Period' (Heb.), *Pe'amim*, 55 (1993), 57–78.

—— 'On the Influence of the Alliance Israélite Universelle on Jewish Communities in Muslim Countries and on Its Characteristics as a Missionary Movement' (Heb.), in S. Schwarzfuchs (ed.), *The Alliance in the Communities of the Mediterranean Basin at the End of the Nineteenth Century and Its Impact on the Social and Cultural Situation* (Heb.) (Jerusalem,1987), 31–5.

—— 'Orthodoxy Is Not the Only Authentic Halakhic Response to Modernity' (Heb.), *Akdamut*, 11 (2002), 139–51.

—— *Tradition and Change: The Confrontation of the Jewish Sages in Egypt and Syria with the Challenges of Modernization, 1880–1920* [Masoret utemurah: hitmodedut ḥakhmei yisra'el bemitsrayim uvesuryah im etgerei hamodernizatsiyah 1880–1920] (Jerusalem, 1993).

Index

Z